TELLING IT SLANT

Avant-Garde Poetics of the 1990s

TELLING IT SLANT

Edited by **MARK WALLACE** and **STEVEN MARKS**

THE UNIVERSITY OF ALABAMA PRESS

TUSCALOOSA AND LONDON

Copyright © 2002
The University of Alabama Press
Tuscaloosa, Alabama 35487-0380
All rights reserved
Manufactured in the United States of America

2 4 6 8 9 7 5 3 1
03 05 07 09 10 08 06 04 02

Cover and text design by Mary-Frances Burt, Burt & Burt Studio

∞

The paper on which this book is printed meets the minimum requirements
of American National Standard for Information Science-Permanence
of Paper for Printed Library Materials, ANSI Z39.48-1984.

Library of Congress Cataloging-in-Publication Data

Telling it slant : avant-garde poetics of the 1990s / edited by Mark
Wallace and Steven Marks.
        p. cm. — (Modern and contemporary poetics)
Includes bibliographical references and index.
    ISBN 0-8173-1096-7 (alk. paper) — ISBN 0-8173-1097-5 (pbk. : alk.
paper)
    1. American poetry—20th century—History and criticism. 2.
Experimental poetry, American—History and criticism. 3. Avant-garde
(Aesthetics)—United States. 4. Poetics. I. Wallace, Mark. II. Marks,
Steven, 1953–III. Series.
  PS325 .T45 2002
  811'.5409—dc21
                        2001001827

British Library Cataloguing-in-Publication Data available

Tell all the truth but tell it slant

Success in circuit lies

—Emily Dickinson

Contents

TELLING IT SLANT

Introduction |

Mark Wallace and Steven Marks

Perhaps the emergence of new poetries and poetics is always contested and uncertain. But at the same time it is always exciting, energetic, and engaged, the grassroots activity in which the possibilities of poetic innovation find their most intense refiguring.

It is clear that the number of practitioners of avant-garde poetries, in the United States and elsewhere, and the reading audience of such poetries have continued to grow. The audience has grown so much, in fact, that the sales of various types of non-"mainstream" poetries, if taken together, likely exceed the "mainstream" center whose shadow they supposedly occupy.[1] And individual books of poems by well-known nonmainstream poets published in alternative press editions often sell as much as half as many copies as books by mainstream poets who still win almost all major poetry prizes and have backing by major publishing houses.

Despite this increase in readership, the continued difficulty of publishing new avant-garde work should not be underestimated. Fortunately, in the face of such difficulty, many small presses and many magazines of various types and sizes continue to publish books and chapbooks, ranging in quality from professionally bound to Xerox sheets; and digital publications continue to find outlets on CD-ROMs and the Internet (particularly the World Wide Web). All of these media have helped to keep new avant-garde poetries alive. And if these poetries have not always been kept alive well in terms of their broader exposure to audiences unaware of these limited editions and alternative modes of publication, they have certainly been kept alive well in terms of the fervent interest of those devoted to reading and creating them.

Of course, it would be too easy to believe that the only resistance to new avant-garde poetries comes from those opposed to avant-garde practice in general. In the aftermath of the success of the poets associated with

L=A=N=G=U=A=G=E writing, and the success of essay collections by and about these writers, such as *The L=A=N=G=U=A=G=E Book* and *The Politics of Poetic Form*, at least two concerns have been voiced even by many people sympathetic to avant-garde practice. One is that no new and significant directions in avant-garde poetry have developed after those poets; the other is that part of the reason for this lack of development is that there has been no extensive or effective poetics by those writers who claim interest in developing such new directions.

The essays collected here answer both concerns. Much of the poetry discussed in the following pages has sought restlessly both new forms and the reorientation of older forms of poetry in order to embody its present moment and ongoing involvements. And much of the poetics developed in these pages, although certainly influenced by the powerful history of avant-garde theorization, shows how many new directions remain to be explored, as well as how avant-garde practice of the past continues to offer many possibilities. As a whole the collection shows exactly how large, and how open, the field of avant-garde poetries is at the present moment.

We have attempted to gather as many fine essays by critics and poet-critics as we could find on the subject of these new poetries. Because the form of criticism used to embody one's poetics becomes obviously a central question to writers so crucially interested in problems of literary form, many of the essays, although sophisticated and scholarly, do not conform to the linear argumentative style of academic criticism. Instead, they attempt, in various ways and to various degrees, to find a critical form more subtly related to poetic form than is usual in critical writing. They exemplify criticism not content to accept easy oppositions between critical and poetic activity; they are not simply criticism of poetry but also a poetics of criticism. We believe that, taken together, these essays constitute a primary work of literature valuable not just for today but for the future as well. Indeed we feel quite certain that many of the writers found in this book will become, if they are not already, significant names in the history of poetry.

Contributors were asked to focus on one or more of the following three issues: discussions of their own poetics, readings of other writers involved in new directions for avant-garde practice, and readings of precursors with an eye toward the specific value of those precursors for new avant-garde contexts. In practice, focus on these three issues evolved into four areas organized somewhat differently here: (1) Cultures: essays concerning the relation between poetics and contemporary cultural issues; (2) Forms and Approaches: essays on new directions for avant-garde practice; (3) Readings: in-depth explorations of current poets and predecessors; and (4) A Poetics of Criticism: essays that highlight innovative approaches to essay form or present various individual poetics. All four sections are loosely defined, which indicates precisely the difficulty of putting labels on the variability of avant-garde poetics. In fact many of the essays in this book challenge any kind of categorization and might easily have been placed in other sections.

Although the collection focuses primarily on the poetics of writers practicing in the United States, this geographic limitation should be seen as pragmatic rather than ideological; a truly international collection of essays by contemporary avant-gardists, as welcome as it may be, would constitute a far greater undertaking than is possible here.[2] This collection does, however, feature work by several Canadian writers and one European writer who have significantly interacted with avant-gardists in the United States; the inclusion of such writers tries to complicate, critique, and undermine any attempt to see the avant-garde through a narrowly nationalist lens.

The work collected here does not present some unified front on the question of what approach new avant-garde poetries should take. As editors, we do not want to remove what we believe to be one of the central values of avant-garde poetry—its powerful capacity to offer disagreement—by asserting that we have found group solutions to ongoing questions. Indeed, the notion that a pervasive group unity of poetics informs precursor collections such as *The L=A=N=G=U=A=G=E Book* may come more from the tendency of some critical commentators to impose unity on disparate poetic practices than from the actual writing contained in such collections. The actual specifics of poetry and poetics always develop not only from what is shared by writers but also from what is not shared, and both aspects should be kept in mind.

That said, the work here also does not offer a group take on avant-garde precursors, such as those associated with L=A=N=G=U=A=G=E writing. Some of the writers here see L=A=N=G=U=A=G=E writing as a positive influence, others as a negative one, and perhaps one or two as no influence at all. The absence of essays by the main writers associated with that movement should not be taken as an effort to exclude those writers or to deny the value of their work. Rather, it was simply the belief of the editors that many other publications already contain work by and about those writers, whereas it was our goal here to collect essays about possibilities in poetry that have not yet received attention outside the small but committed world of avant-garde poetries. In that sense the greater level of exposure for L=A=N=G=U=A=G=E writing, although undoubtedly insufficient, simply means that for the specific purposes of this collection such writing did not fit our admittedly narrow sense of "new" directions in avant-garde poetry.

Despite their differences, the essays in this collection often address a number of shared issues. Perhaps the most common of these issues is the subject of poetic form. A multiplicity of methods, techniques, lineages, and influences that bear on the production of present-day poetry make the interplay of form and content equally multiple. Juliana Spahr makes the case in her essay that working with often contradictory influences can be accomplished by joining what may appear as disparate poetics. She means "joining" in the sense that a carpenter joins two pieces of wood, and she thus consciously opposes the notion of joining as becoming a member of a group; she believes there can be a poetics of amalgamation that maintains no allegiance to any one school and remains in the interstices of various aesthetics. Spahr's poetics is close to what Jefferson Hansen describes in his essay as an anarchistic approach to poetry-making that allows for the exploration of new practices. How to remain in the interstices and not fall into the slots of production thus becomes the avant-garde's most difficult project. According to Hansen, this process of exploration is ideally continuous and must be so in order to avoid the creation of a calcified culture within the avant-garde itself.

Daniel Barbiero recognizes that despite the growing presence of a nonagonistic openness to a plurality of influences and lineages, various anxieties necessarily bear on avant-garde poets; one of those anxieties is the attempt to come to terms with previous generations of the avant-garde. Such coming to terms does not, however, require rejecting, supplanting, or overthrowing older movements.

Several essays explore the relation between poetry and the construction of meaning and the interplay between being and knowing. Kristin Prevallet has formulated a poetics based on the intersection between L=A=N=G=U=A=G=E poetries and what she calls investigative poetries. She contends that there is no reason why a poem cannot be both a reflection of the structures of language and a confrontational and emotional testimony of events. Such a view takes a stance against what mainstream critics say that contemporary avant-garde poetries cannot do. Jena Osman challenges the common belief that procedural poems written through overt language operations are essentially limited because they lack authorial intention and a transcendental meaning. She shows how meaning occurs in any use of language. It has to occur, she argues, because we seem unable not to put it there, although the disruption of meaning making has the often salutary effect of putting one both inside and outside the self. Some present-day avant-garde poets see the question of poetics as a metaphysical one. Leonard Schwartz investigates the underpinnings of perception that give rise to a poetic hybrid linked to the lyric. For Schwartz the transcendental becomes a condition in which there is both a synthesis and negation of the self. Andrew Levy, on the other hand, thinks that there is no transcending the contexts of experience. He describes what the *I* knows, how it interprets and represents, as a wondering and a wandering.

Many contributors here critique what they see as the limitations of contemporary avant-garde practices or suggest new directions for those practices. According to Jeff Derksen, only through an antisystemic writing that opposes the mutually enforcing normative subject/other dynamic can avant-garde practice attain a level of critical self-awareness that counteracts the deficiencies of multiculturalism as it becomes the official policy of Canada. Caroline

Bergvall attempts such a counteraction in a similar context by exploring textualities that operate across languages. Bergvall does not see the phenomenon of borderline writing as a battle over boundary lines but as "a localized carving out of these boundaries into zones of activity and experientiality that empty out the assumptions on which monolingual representation rests." Such a practice requires readers to question their own cultural location. Sherry Brennan critiques the value avant-garde work often places on a simplistic definition of the new, and she opts instead for a lively engagement with fellow practitioners past and present. She thus defines today's work as a poetry not about newness but about the present, not about the past but as responding to the past. Innovative poetry, she adds, is highly attuned to a number of cultural and temporal tensions that allow the poetry to shift, to build a demonstration of context and currency. Sianne Ngai questions the poetics of desire, which has informed much poetry and critical theory of the past several decades, and proposes instead a poetics of disgust that foregrounds the "raw matter" of language. This emphasis pointedly excludes what she sees as an insufficiently politicized multiculturalism in which language becomes merely an expression of the desire and experiences of culturally differing individuals. Mark Wallace, on the other hand, working with the issue of formal rather than cultural pluralism, argues against the notion of perceiving the avant-garde as a limited and recognizable set of forms that exist in contrast to the similarly identifiable forms of mainstream poetry. Rather, he proposes that to remain truly oppositional, the avant-garde might conceive of itself as existing in a constantly renewable formal openness that resists any attempt to stabilize notions of form. Avant-garde poetry might better be recognized in the desire to destabilize and refigure all forms of poetry than in a tradition of recognizable alternative forms.

The limitations and possibilities of the avant-garde are further discussed in those essays that directly consider the relation between avant-garde practice and issues of race, gender, and class. Harryette Mullen points out that practitioners of mainstream poetry have refused to consider that part of her poetry that does not create "speakerly" poems of easily identifiable "representative blackness" but that they have been willing to anthologize and praise those poems of hers that do present such an "emphatically ethnic" perspective. However, avant-gardists have often failed to recognize that such poems do make up part of her poetry and have preferred to concentrate only on her "formally innovative" prose poems. Many members of the avant-garde, she says, may still perceive "blackness as 'otherness,'" championing the formal innovation in her work while still considering "the innovative artist of minority background as an exceptional comrade." Brian Kim Stefans examines the history of avant-garde writing by Asian North Americans and looks at the complex and fruitful relation such writing has to postmodern aesthetics and issues of culture. He makes clear that no overarching descriptive rubric can account for the varied ways that Asian North American writers have negotiated the relation between culture, history, and poetic form. Lisa Robertson criticizes the pastoral tradition for its use of concepts such as femininity and nature as ways of coercing and controlling women's bodies and the environment. But she also argues that the pastoral, as a now "obsolete" genre, can help her enact her desire to "go phantom"; she wants to rewrite the pastoral in order to haunt the structures of contemporary capitalism and expose its violence. Bill Luoma's witty reading of poems, baseball, and related cultural and scientific phenomena looks for ways to particularize the different experiences of men and women without essentializing gender. He acknowledges the gendered nature of his own history as a writer and attempts to unsettle that history by critiquing masculinist assumptions and by looking at the sometimes odd ways that the false dialectic of masculinity/femininity plays out both in poetry and in relations between men and women.

Several essays discuss combinations of poetry with other art forms and new media. Christopher Funkhouser questions what the electronic future holds for poetry and shows ways "to use computers creatively and not destructively." He notes that as poetry continues to connect with other arts and to incorporate new media, answers to these and other questions will remain contested. Steven Marks takes advantage of some of the latest developments in computer technology to create a "visual essay" that contains elements of poetry and visual art and provides a reading, response, and refiguring of Joan Retallack's poem, "NOH S'EX."

Although we believe these essays explore most of the main issues that confronted the new avant-gardists of the 1990s, claims to complete representativeness are always troubling because they are never true. The field of new avant-garde poetics in the 1990s was much broader and more open than this collection can indicate, and many essays we would like to have included had to be dropped to reduce the collection to a manageable size. Far from summing up the critical practice of the new avant-gardists of the 1990s, then, this collection only suggests the wealth of that material. The project of avant-garde poetics is indeed continuous, already moving past what we have gathered here into new interests and new problems. Nonetheless, this collection represents the largest gathering of essays that exists on 1990s new avant-garde poetries and poetics. It is our intention, in collecting these essays, to put before a broad audience a significant sample of the finest writing on avant-garde poetry of the last decade of the twentieth century, writing that we believe will continue to have great value long after the environment that helped shape these essays becomes part of poetry's rich and enabling history.

Notes

1. See, e.g., Mallay Charters, "The Different Faces of Poetry," *Publishers Weekly*, March 3, 1997, 38–41, esp. the sales figures on p. 38.

2. In *99 Poets/1999: An International Poetics Symposium*, a special issue of the journal *boundary 2*, Charles Bernstein has gathered a series of short statements and works by an international group of avant-garde poets. The issue indicates how large a project of longer essays by and about such writers would be. And as Bernstein points out, even *99 Poets* "clearly emerges from the United States" because "many of the poets included here read or speak English and have some contact with those tendencies in American poetry to which I have been committed" (*99 Poets/1999: An International Poetics Symposium: boundary 2* 26.1 [spring 1999]: 1).

CULTURES

1 | Introduction to *Writing from the New Coast*

Steve Evans

The text that follows bears the unmistakable inflections of its initial occasion as an introduction to a collection of poetics statements by emergent writers that Juliana Spahr and Peter Gizzi edited in 1993 and published, together with an ample companion volume of poems edited by Gizzi and Connell McGrath, as *o•blēk 12: Writing from the New Coast.* That important collection, understandably but inaccurately received at the time as an "anthology," was by intention provisional and of necessity prospective: rather than documenting an accomplished fact, it projected a possible future on the basis of evidence perceptible but as yet inchoate in the present. As C. L. R. James once observed, "The future is not born all at once. It exists in the present. The thing is to know where to look."[1] The *New Coast* was, in 1993, such a place, and the subsequent publications of many of its contributors have since come to define the "contemporary" in American avant-garde poetry as it continues to endure and exceed the chronic limitations imposed upon it— and all significant culture—by an ever-intensifying, and increasingly unsurvivable, set of capitalist social relations.

The "hatred of Identity" I speak of at some length in the introduction has its genesis in social conditions, but the fierce resistance to all strategies of designation—whether conferred from within or imposed from without— that the writers I discuss carried with them into the poetic field has had important ramifications for American poetry after 1989. Not least, it has fostered a condition of irreducible multiplicity in poetic practice that, while making trouble for critics and scholars of the field, has drawn nearer to George Oppen's ideal of "being numerous" than any previous effort. The decision to dwell in a complex, intergenerational, and multicultural present is not without its difficulties, but the poets of the past decade have chosen so to dwell. As a reader, I for one am grateful.

You think maybe poetry is too important and you like that.

—Frank O'Hara

Generation is a verb. This is the first thing to keep in mind while reading and rereading, pondering over and arguing with, feeling dejected about and then again enthused by the statements that make up, and to my mind make so invaluable, the present document. If the experience weren't sometimes maddening, it would be evidence that generation had ceased. If it weren't maddening, it would mean that these acts of address, these partial articulations of desire and of allegiance, had entered a stable state. It would mean that they had lost their claim to our ever-restless impulse to *make something* of the conditions we are given, that something being of course *poetry*.

If even so brief and arguably incomplete a gathering as the one this spring in Buffalo, to which a number of the statements collected here were, in the first instance, addressed, could produce such a burst of discursive energies, could generate such a welter of concerned and concerted discussion, then the effects of this volume are certain to be substantial. It is not my hope, in these few words of preface, to predispose these effects. Rather, I want only to report some of the effects the volume has already had, to indicate some of the ways it has come to think in my head during the months prior to its publication, and to risk a response in the hope of generating further ones.

Back in 1907, under circumstances that in many ways differed starkly from those that currently confront us, Yeats noted that "the only movements on which literature can found itself . . . hate great and lasting things."[2] I take him to mean that, when it comes to cultural work, *negation* is inseparable from *generation* and, further, that in adverse and inhuman conditions (in his case, specifically, the conditions dictated by British imperialism) negation will precede generation, will be its precondition.

It is my contention that such a hatred as Yeats speaks of does animate the present generation, although it is a hatred so thoroughgoing, so pervasive, and so unremitting as to make the articulation of it seem gratuitous, even falsifying. It is the hatred of Identity. Mistake this hatred and I believe you mistake the entire constellation that is emergent in these pages. Mistake it and you are left with no more than incidental and furtive convergences, faint patterns, weak signals. But recognize it, recognize the multitude of forms it takes—from the most abstract to the most concrete—and you will see that few generations have chosen a greater or more lasting thing to oppose and in the process risked such consequences, such contradictions, as this one has in its opening move.

Admittedly, the resources for such a project seem at first glance, and given the magnitude of the struggle, rather unbefitting. Indeed, the most direct evidence concerning the existence of a "new coast" may be that so many have found themselves washed up upon it. Crevice-mongers, impercipients, mistakes, squatters, singular constellations of the minor and the miscellaneous, the oblique and the near obliterated: so this emergent collectivity appears, even to itself.

But it is in the nature of the defeated to appear so. With individuals, as with movements and communities, with material practices and entire epistemologies, and so also with that peculiar assemblage of all those things we call poetry, the defeated will appear eccentric, derisory, without consequence. This is how women appear to men under patriarchy; it is how the greater part of the globe, including Africa and Asia, appeared to Europe under colonialism; it is how writing, as Derrida and the L=A=N=G=U=A=G=E poets have shown us, appears under logocentrism; and so, I would argue, do *we all* appear to Capital as it now rushes, apparently unopposed, to close a deal long in negotiation, the deal whereby it at last achieves its dream of self-identity in the purge of its final, potentially fatal impurity—people.

Kwame Anthony Appiah has correctly interpreted Capital's dream to be that of gazing out over a world in which every element of the real has been turned into a sign, and all signs read "for sale." That it cannot be our dream, that this dream must be negated, woken up from, opens our acts of generation to a radical, a reconstituted, and virtually unrecognizable (to those accustomed to see in it only a long-exposed fakery) *humanism*, one that tears at the fabric of domination and offers, however intermittently, glimpses of a "new coast."

More than just a figure of thought, the "new coast" represents a human possibility lodged at the very heart of an inhuman world order. Like all possibilities, this one is fragile. The fact that much depends upon its preservation does not lessen the risk that it will be forfeited. To the contrary. The insistence that things could be different, and the demand that they be made so, entails rethinking the actual from the standpoint of the possible. And this project alone is enough to elicit horror and rage not only from those whose interests are served by the actual organization of society but also from those who, despite being dominated within that organization, have undertaken at considerable psychical and material cost the bitter task of adapting themselves to their domination.

But horror and rage are subjective responses that can, within certain limits, be altered. More intractable are the objective conditions that predispose individuals to these responses in the first place. Consider, for instance, the fate of a concept central to most progressive intellectuals and cultural workers since the end of the Second World War, the concept of "difference." If I have suggested that the writers in this volume are bound in their common opposition to identity, I have stopped short of asserting that they are therefore "for" difference. My reasoning has to do, precisely, with the conditions in which these writers are working.

Think of it this way: to the extent that capital's need to manufacture and mark "difference" (commodification) while preserving and intensifying domination (its own systemic identity) takes the form of a successfully managed crisis, difference is effectively abolished. As social space is forced to yield more and more of its autonomy to "the market"—where the mundane logic of the commodity dictates that nothing appear except under the aspect of identity—even progressive demands for the recognition of ethnic, linguistic, and sexual difference are converted into identity claims and sold back to the communities in which they originated at a markup. In other words, what has the potential to be, under other conditions, a complexly differentiated field of possibilities (the social) atrophies within capitalist relations until only one meaningful distinction remains—the distinction between identities-in-abeyance (markets awaiting "penetration") and Identity as such (penetrant capital).

This generation's hatred of Identity has been fed by the experience of the generations that immediately preceded them. It is the hatred of those who have learned that, given current conditions, there exists not a single socially recognized "difference" worth the having. Observation has taught them that the price of the ticket is as fixed as the fight to which one is admitted—and they are refusing to pay it. This does not mean that all traces of the abstract idiom of "otherness" and "difference" developed in the poststructuralist and multiculturalist discourses have been, at a single stroke, erased from this emergent discourse. As the following pages will attest, every available concept of nonidentity (the other, the alien, the amodal, the non- or extralinguistic, etc.) is employed—but with a sense of dissatisfaction, as though these concepts are not nonidentical enough.

And so it is that this "writing from the new coast"—aspiring to be a force in a world coasting with alarming speed to the new right, where xenophobic nativism thinks in more and more peoples' heads and determines the direction in which they will turn their more and more sophisticated weaponry—comes to propose poetry as a practice of nonidentity, a means of rescuing the kernel of *emergence* at the core of our emergency. The tenacious and cross-grained commitment to discernment, to telling a difference in order to make one, is perfectly captured by Sean Killian when he writes: "to figure out which threat is promising, and which promise threatening . . . this, too, is poetry."[3] And C. S. Giscombe captures it also when he calls poetry the work, "at once definitive and significantly destructive," of "coming to terms with the conditions, or bringing terms to them" (167). The "promise" of identity, discerned as a "threat" and rejected, this rejection opening a space in which transformation is finally possible: if I have been using the terms *negation* and *generation* to make the point, the sixth-grader whom C. S.

remembers first seeing enact them, first saw *making a poem*, did so no less deftly for his innocence of Hegel or Yeats.

As should be evident by now, poetry as technique here means far more than prosody pursued as an end in itself. Against such narrow aims these writers put at stake techniques of perception, techniques of cognition. With Emily Dickinson—and against the blackmail of demands for "politics now!"—these writers recognize that microscopes can be prudent in an emergency. They recognize that the labor of discerning the given, in order to negate and transform it, is painstaking and patience-trying *and* unforgoable. All the more impressive, then, if a number of them can also see to it that their analyses are, to wrench a Frank O'Hara line, at least as alive as those of the vulgar Marxists!

The techniques proposed, interrogated, and enacted in these pages, for all their diversity and splendid rejection of the already established, the consolidated, the self-identical, nevertheless *intend*—in their common commitment to negation and generation—the emergence of a "new coast." Techniques of specificity are no less crucial to the task than techniques of totality. Indeed, they must be employed simultaneously, for through what other means is it possible to grasp the "pure media enhanced pluralism of our age" (Liz Was 151) together with the fact that "very few people are free" (Andrew Levy 81)? How else to recognize, as Akua Lezli Hope does, that "while the sheer numbers of people with the keys to the kingdom increases, the probability that they'll unlock the doors, retreats" (174)? How else to pinpoint the contradiction Nick Lawrence identifies when he observes that "as the world approaches the condition of a closed / unified circuit of capital communications, issues of address / position / identity get raised all the more fiercely" (178)? And how else to arrive, as Myung Mi Kim does in a mere five words, at the crux of a global system: "From a bare fist relational" (175)?

It is this "bare fist relational" that strikes me as contemporary. The phrase suggests what is unprecedented about our conditions; it is the hieroglyph given us to decipher. But as I have already argued, a hatred such as this generation bears toward identity, and especially toward the type of identity conferred by the commodity form, cannot be made from scratch. It has long been under preparation, perhaps nowhere more concertedly than in poetry. This would be a consolation, one of the few involved in choosing to oppose a "great and lasting thing," if history could be counted on to preserve the knowledge and practices of the host of allies who engaged the struggle before you. Unfortunately, we know this not to be the case. The task of returning the traces of a "tradition" to collective memory and effective history demands a constantly renewed attention and a knowledge of the stakes involved. As Walter Benjamin wrote: "Only that historian will have the gift of fanning the spark of hope who is firmly convinced that *even the dead* will not be safe from the enemy if he wins. And this enemy has not ceased to be victorious."[4]

Two traditions, or two facets of a single tradition that is only slowly becoming recognizable as such, converge in the writings collected here. One is the consciously recognized and masterfully renewed tradition of radical linguistic practice that stretches back at least to the beginning of the twentieth century. Call it the "revolution of the word." The other is the tradition of radical social practice that took a decisive turn in the period of decolonization following the Second World War. Call this the "revolution of the world," as yet incomplete.

With the advent, in the 1920s, of the second wave of technological mass mediation (the printing press having occasioned the first), poetry underwent a transformation. It ceased to be in any important respect an elite discourse and became irremediably and unregrettably a queer one. Brecht and Shklovsky gave the transformation its conceptual expression (both the German and the Russian—*verfremdungen* and *ostranenie*—are aptly translated by the English transitive verbal *to queer*). And Stein had already written the slogan in 1914: "act so that there is no use in a centre."[5]

From that point forward the elective affinity between poetry and critical thought comes to produce an unbroken, if somewhat subterranean, tradition within American poetry. Against a backdrop of "total mobilization of all media for the defense of established reality,"[6] radical linguistic practice has worked to contest not only the way specific narratives participate in the reproduction of social reality; they have contested *narrative* itself. In refusing the attenuation of human sense-making that comes of equating it exclusively with "telling stories," such practices interrupt the norming of cognition. They reintroduce negativity into a life-world from which it has otherwise been expelled. And they expose the ideological commitment to narrative for what it is—a restriction of the horizons of the humanly thinkable.

The deliberate extension of this oppositional tradition is visible in these pages. Just tracking the names that occur here attests to that. An extremely abridged list, which is all that space allows, would include, alongside Stein (whose generativity seems inexhaustible), Robert Duncan, Laura Riding, Charles Bernstein, Paul Celan, Jack Spicer, Clark Coolidge, Robert Creeley, Sterling Brown, Keith and Rosmarie Waldrop, Louis Zukofsky, Garcia Lorca, Aimé Césaire, Ron Silliman, Michael Palmer, Barbara Guest, John Ashbery, Susan and Fanny Howe, Bernadette Mayer, John Cage, and Amiri Baraka—names by which are noted, not so much identities as inextinguishable flares of "the negative," openings through which thought can sometimes guide the possible into the real.

The other event informing these writings is, as I have said, less well understood. But if more than half a century after Stein's aesthetic injunction to "act so that there is no use in a centre," queer activist and poet Paul Goodman could echo it in the political injunction to "act that the society you live in is yours," it was not chiefly because of developments internal to oppositional poetry. Rather, it was the result of the real negation of colonialism on the part of peoples who had previously appeared to be "the wretched of the earth." It was their decisive appropriation of the human universal that irrevocably shattered the presumptive and hollow universalism of the Western bourgeoisie and opened a threshold through which subsequent liberation struggles would pass.

The effects of this collective act are everywhere evident in these pages. Theorizations of nonidentity owe their currency to it. The reconceptualization of history, now seen as a force all are subject to and none the privileged subjects of, would have been unthinkable without it. To it we owe the transformations of the terms by which access to literacy and "the literary" are secured, globally as well as nationally. And to it we owe the recognition of the foreignness of languages (Benjamin) as more than an abstraction. But most of all we owe to it the profound reorganization of imaginably human futures, of nondominant resolutions to the "brokenness of intersubjectivity"[7] and nonexploitative resolutions to the necessity of reproducing our existence.

It has become a commonplace to say that we have now witnessed the reification of liberation politics, that this politics has been reduced to yet another sign that reads "for sale" under the rubric of "identity" politics. Perhaps. But this does not discredit liberation as a project so much as it testifies to the formidable resources of those who oppose it. Perhaps Yeats's insight would be more accurate still if it were inverted: the only movements on which literature can found itself *are themselves* the "great and lasting things" that the ruling order must work ceaselessly to contain and negate.

The only thing less plausible than the sudden collapse of that ruling order is its indefinite extension into all imaginable futures. The crisis we present to it *will* become unmanageable, which is why the necessity of imagining alternatives now is such an urgent one. Pessimism and cynicism, the dominant cognitive moods of the past two decades, will no longer serve. As Adorno put it so memorably, "the world is systematized horror, but therefore it is to do the world too much honor to think of it entirely as a system."[8] I would add, as a corollary, Rod Smith's prediction that "optimism, about any social possibility" may be the form in which "radical negativity" next appears: "the next punks might believe things will get better" (188).

The "new coast" is only another name for the increasingly real possibility of overshooting the narrowly contracted band of relations—between bodies, between words, between objects and environments, between worlds—that Capital can annex in accordance with its interest. If the first imperative of politics is to seize control of potentiality, to impose discriminations between the actual, the really possible, and the merely wishful, the first impulse of poetry is to contest this imposition. The trick is, of course, to fan "small flares of hope" (Steven Farmer 29–31)[9] to the point where they burn, "taking up the incandescence which the civil systems shun" (Will

Alexander 16). It is not that the trick is necessarily hard to learn but rather that the wind that would have fed the fire has until now blown it out.

Notes

1. C. L. R. James, "Letters to Literary Critics," in *The C. L. R. James Reader*, ed. Anna Grimshaw (Oxford: Blackwell, 1992), 230.

2. William Butler Yeats, "Poetry and Tradition," in *Essays and Introductions* (New York: Collier, 1973), 250.

3. Sean Killian, *o•blēk 12: Writing from the New Coast*, 38. All subsequent citations of this special issue of *o•blēk* are cited parenthetically.

4. Walter Benjamin, "Theses on the Philosophy of History," in *Illuminations*, ed. Hannah Arendt, trans. Harry Zohn (New York: Schocken, 1968), 255.

5. Gertrude Stein, "Tender Buttons," in *Selected Writings of Gertrude Stein*, ed. Carl Van Vechten (New York: Vintage, 1990), 498.

6. Herbert Marcuse, *One-Dimensional Man* (Boston: Beacon, 1964), 68.

7. Jürgen Habermas, *The Hermeneutic Tradition: From Ast to Ricouer* (Albany: State University of New York Press, 1990), 219.

8. Theodor Adorno, *Minima Moralia*, trans. E. F. N. Jephcott (London: Verso, 1974), 113.

9. The phrase is taken from an early draft of Farmer's *New Coast* essay and did not appear in the published issue.

Lisa Robertson

I need a genre for the times that I go phantom. I need a genre to rampage Liberty, haunt the foul freedom of silence. I need to pry loose Liberty from an impacted marriage with the soil. I need a genre to gloss my ancestress's complicity with a socially expedient code, to invade my own illusions of historical innocence. The proud trees, the proud rocks, the proud sky, the proud fields, the proud poor have been held before my glazed face for centuries. I believed they were reflections. The trees leaned masochistically into my absence of satisfaction. They were trying to fulfill a space I thought of as my body. Through the bosco a fleecy blackness revealed the nation as its vapid twin. Yet nostalgia can locate those structured faults our embraces also seek. A surface parts. The nasty hours brim with the refinements of felicity. It's obvious now: Liberty was dressed up in the guise of an ambivalent expenditure.

My ancestress would not wait for me. I began to track her among the elegant tissue of echoes, quotations, shadows on the deepening green. Because she lacked a verifiable identity, I decided to construct her from kisses: puckers and fissures in use; and also from the flaking traces of her brittle dress. For I needed someone not useful to me but obnoxious, prosthetic, and irrelevant as my gender. Let's say Nature, like femininity, is obsolete. She's simply a phantom who indolently twists the melancholic mirror of sex. Far into the rural distance, the horizon splays beneath her florid grip. In deep sleep my ancestress tells me a story:

Ontology is the luxury of the landed. Let's pretend you "had" a land. Then you "lost" it. Now fondly describe it. That is pastoral. Consider your homeland, like all utopias, obsolete. Your rhetoric points to frightened obsolescence. The garden gate shut firmly. Yet Liberty must remain throned in her posh gazebo. What can the poor Lady do? Beauty, Pride, Envy, the Bounteous Land, the Romance of Citizenship: these mawkish paradigms flesh out the nation, fard its empty gaze. What if, for your new suit, you chose to parade obsolescence? Make a parallel nation, an anagram of the Land. Annex Liberty, absorb it, and recode it: infuse it with your nasty optics. The anagram will surpass and delete the first world yet, in all its elements, remain identical. Who can afford sincerity? It's an expensive monocle.

When I awake I find myself in a new world. The buildings, the clothes, the trees are no more or less coy than they were, yet I had been so intent on the dense, lush words that I had not realized a world could be subtracted from her fruiting skin. The old locutions could only lose themselves in that longed-for landscape, but now I pluck for myself "peace in our own time" and the desuetude of nostalgia. It's as if suddenly a pitcher of slim flowers needled that monumental absence of regret. So elegant, so precise, so evil, all the pleasures have become my own.

Commentary

Nature is not natural, and that is natural enough.

—Gertrude Stein, *Ida*

I wanted a form as obsolete yet necessary as the weather. I begin with the premise that pastoral, as a literary genre, is obsolete—originally obsolete. Once a hokey territory sussed by a hayseed diction, now the mawkish artificiality of the pastoral poem's constructed surface has settled down to a backyard expressivity. In the postpastoral poem (in evidence since the English romantics and their modernist successors) the evocation of "feeling" in poet or reader obeys a parallel planting of "nature" in the poem. Translate backyard utopia as political mythology. Appearing to serve a personally expressive function, the vocabulary of nature screens a symbolic appropriation of the Land. Her cut sublimity grafts to the Human. I'd call pastoral the nation-making genre: within a hothouse language we force the myth of the Land to act as both political resource and mystic origin. A perversely topical utopia has always been the duped by-product of the ideology that blindly describes, thus possesses, a landscape in which people are imagined to be at peace with the economics of production and consumption. The dream of Liberty poses itself within the specificity of this utopian landscape. Certainly on this five-hundredth anniversary of the so-called New World, we must acknowledge that the utopian practice of Liberty stands now as a looming representation of degrading and humiliating oppressions to the (pastoral) majority and that pastoral utopias have efficiently aestheticized and naturalized the political practices of genocide, misogyny, and class and race oppression. I consider that now pastoral's obvious obsolescence may offer a hybrid discursive potential to those who have been traditionally excluded from Utopia. To begin with, we must recognize Utopia as an accretion of nostalgias with no object other than the historiography of the imaginary. But do not assume the imaginary to be merely the fey playground of children and the doomed. Consider that the imaginary generates landscapes for political futures. To people these landscapes with our own desires and histories, we must implement pastoral as a seedy generic artifice and deny it the natural and hegemonic position of political ideology.

Historically, from Virgil to Spenser to Goldsmith, the pastoral poem narrated the exigencies of land tenure, labor's relation to the state and capital, and the establishment of a sense of place as a ground for philosophical and aesthetic being and discourse. The trajectory of the pastoral poem has prepared a self-congratulatory site for the reproduction of power. We can follow this trajectory from Virgil's gorgeously ambivalent justification of the Roman Empire to the Elizabethan articulation of imperial utopias, Augustan parallels between English and classical pleasures of enlightenment, and late-eighteenth-century evocations of nostalgia for agricultural capitalism. "Beauty" clinched pastoral's edifying function. The quaint archaisms of the language, the dainty evocations of springtime pleasures, the innocent characterization of the indolent shepherd: these niceties etched the pleasures of the genre as irrevocably sensual, masking imperialist ideology or at least couching it in the banalities of conquest and repose. Yet the irony of loss remained the pastoral's central trope. The difficulties and pleasures of maintaining a primary, legal, and productive entitlement to the land provided the pastoral subject since Virgil's first eclogue politicized the theocratic idyll: "You, Tityrus, lie under your spreading beech's covert, wooing the woodland Muse on slender reed, but we are leaving our country's bounds and sweet fields. We are outcasts from our country; you Tityrus, at ease beneath the shade, teach the woods to re-echo 'fair Amaryllis.'"[1]

Certainly, as a fin de siècle feminist, I cannot in good conscience perform even the simplest political identification with the pastoral genre. Within its scope women have been reduced to a cipher for the productively harnessed land within a legally sanctioned system of exchange. In pastoral the figure of woman appears as eroticized worker—the milkmaid or shepherdess swoons in an unproblematic ecstasy with the land. Moreover, she is pleased to give over her youthful presocial wildness to the domesticating and enclosed tenure of the marriage contract. This contract often gives occasion to the celebratory epithalamium, one of the many possible moments in the pastoral montage. Pastoral plants the agency of women's desire firmly within the patriarchal frame. And so it is with a masochistic embarrassment that I confess to having been seduced by the lure of archaic pleasures. Prime among these twist the convoluted interleavings of those beckoning and luscious tropes, femininity and nature. Yet I shall release them from their boredom.

By femininity and nature I mean the spurious concepts and purposeful misreadings that have served the specific use of supporting a singular structure of power and that therefore have been expediently maintained. I prefer to think of both the spuriousness of nature and the spuriousness of femininity as phantom. Once assigned a mythic base in biology, they function as ciphers that reproduce but don't enjoy the autonomy of the citizen. Femininity and nature float both as specters of the state imagination and as symbols for the nation. A defined locale or gendered body is cultivated to produce an image of benign power, discrete abundance, ontological anxiety, and enclosed exchange. Yet, recognized and deployed as ghosts, this pair certainly may haunt the polis, insinuate their horribly reproductive tentacles through its paved courts and closed chambers. It is in this sense that I wish to "go phantom." It is in this sense also that I wish to farm the notion of obsolescence.

A system is ecological when it consumes its own waste products. But within the capitalist narrative the utopia of the new asserts itself as the only productive teleology. Therefore I find it preferable to choose the dystopia of the obsolete. As a tactically uprooted use, deployment of the obsolete could cut short the feckless plot of productivity. When capital marks women as the abject and monstrous cyphers of both reproduction and consumption, our choice can only be to choke out the project of renovation. We must become history's dystopian ghosts, inserting our inconsistencies, demands, misinterpretations, and weedy appetites into the old bolstering narratives: We shall refuse to be useful.

Nostalgia, like hysteria, once commonly treated as a feminine pathology, must now be claimed as a method of reading or critiquing history—a pointer indicating a potential node of entry. Yet I'm referring to relations within language, looking at both nostalgia and history as functions within, or effects of, language systems. My own nostalgia reaches for an impossibly beautiful and abundant language. Rather than diagnosing this nostalgia as a symptom of loss (which would only buttress the capitalist fiction of possession), I deploy it as an almanac, planning a tentative landscape in which my inappropriate and disgraceful thought may circulate. Nostalgia will locate precisely those gaps or absences in a system we may now redefine as openings, freshly turned plots. Who is to circumscribe the geography in which thinking may take place? I deplore the enclosure staked out by a poetics of "place" in which the field of "man's" discrete ontological geography stands as a willful displacement, an emptying of a specifically peopled history. Descartes's new world, in which the "annoying" and unproductive contingencies of history are systematically forgotten, leaving the Western male thinker in a primary confrontation with his own thought, is emphatically not a world I wish to share. The only way I can begin to understand the potential of a poetics of historical responsibility is by shoring up the marks of history's excesses and elisions. The solipsist's position of singular innocence and sincerity erases all relations of historical difference and, with these, the tactical confrontations and crafty invasions language may deploy.

My intention is to slip into the narrative as a hybrid ghost and steal the solipsist's monocle as he sleeps and dreams of the rational future. What would the dreamland look like seen through at least two eyes simultaneously? What would the utopian land look like if it were not fenced by the violence of Liberty and the nation? How would my desire for a homeland read if I were to represent it with the moral promiscuity of any plant? These spores and seeds and bits of invasive root are the treasures I fling backward, over my shoulder, into the hokey loam of an old genre.

Note

1. Virgil, *Eclogues, Georgics, Aeneid*, trans. H. Ruston-Fairclough, vol. 1 (London: Loeb Classical Library, 1986), Eclogue 1:11:1–5.

Harryette Mullen

Some poems I wrote over a decade ago are only now earning a few bucks (and I do mean a few) as I am beginning to be included in anthologies of African American poets. Because of these recent nibbles (for which I am grateful), I have made an act of faith in the posterity of my work, legally naming my sister as my heir and executor of my literary estate. Anyone reading this knows that the living poet feels lucky to be paid in copies of the published work; but perhaps when I am dead, payments for future poetry permissions might help to sustain my sister, my nephews, or their children. My recent inclusion in these anthologies gives rise to this meditation on the various experiences of inclusion, exclusion, and marginality of a "formally innovative black poet."

It has been argued that if publication in anthologies from commercial presses, reviews and other coverage in mass media, space on bookstore shelves, adoption into course curricula, and library acquisitions are the measure, it would seem that representative "black" poets are currently more assimilable into the "mainstream" than "formally innovative" poets of any hue. Although both the "avant-garde poet" and the "minority poet" may be perceived as the other of the "mainstream" (regardless of the distance and the different concerns that might separate them from each other), it would seem that the mainstream has far more to gain by appropriating minority poets who work in recognizable and accessible forms and who can thus be marketed to the broadest possible audience of readers.

MTV notwithstanding, textbooks and anthologies—the most commercial and lucrative venues for poetry publication (profitable for the publishers if not for the poets)—continue to be the primary means of reaching the broadest audience of people who read poetry. Poets are anthologized as representatives of their era, nationality, region, race, ethnicity, gender, class, and/or aesthetic affiliation; and anthologies are driven by realities of marketing, as well as by critical activity and curricular needs. In the anthology and textbook markets poets "of color," given their automatic representational status, have a distinct advantage over "formally innovative" poets, who appeal to no large or easily identifiable demographic segment of the literary market.

"Avant-garde" poets—to the extent that they can be gathered together and made comprehensible (given sufficient critical energy and academic acceptance) as members of some distinctive and coherently articulated generation, school, or movement—can be packaged for mainly academic consumption in much the same manner that "poets of color" or "spoken word" practitioners have been labeled and gathered into anthologies aimed at both mainstream and academic audiences. It would seem, however, that the "avant-garde poet of color" threatens the cohesiveness of the accompanying narratives that allow the mainstream audience to recognize, comprehend, or imagine a collective identity, purpose, and aesthetics of a literary group or movement, whether it is a group "of color" or a movement defined by its commitment to "formal innovation."

"Formally innovative minority poets," when visible at all, are not likely to be perceived either as typical of a racial/ethnic group or as representative of an aesthetic movement. Their unaccountable existence therefore strains the seams of the critical narratives necessary to make them (individually and collectively) comprehensible and thus teachable and marketable. In each generation the erasure of the anomalous black writer abets the construction of a continuous, internally consistent tradition, and it deprives the idiosyncratic minority artist of a history, compelling her to struggle even harder to construct a cultural context out of her own radical individuality. She is unanticipated and often unacknowledged because of the imposed obscurity of her aesthetic antecedents.

Because my first book allowed me to be placed rather neatly within the category of "representative blackness" (as well as in the categories of "feminist" and "regional" poet), whereas my second and third books are more frequently described as "formally innovative" poetry rather than as "black poetry," I have had the sometimes unsettling experience of seeing my work divided into distinct taxonomies. Because I no longer write poems like the ones in *Tree Tall Woman* (Energy Earth, 1981), some readers perhaps perceive my world as "less black."

Evidently, publishers of African American anthologies are entirely uninterested in my more recent work, from *Trimmings* on. Only in the earlier poetry, represented by the work in *Tree Tall Woman*, or similarly "speakerly" poems, am I digestible as a black poet. My two prose poem books, *Trimmings* (Tender Buttons, 1991) and *S*PeRM**K*T* (Singing Horse, 1992), apparently go overlooked by those seeking to incorporate me into an African American poetic tradition, just as those who praise the prose poems generally do not connect them to the emphatically ethnic poetic "voice" of *Tree Tall Woman*, which seems markedly inflected by race, class, gender, culture, and region, compared to the more ambiguously located subjectivity of *Trimmings* and *S*PeRM**K*T*. The perceived gap that allows different parts of my work to be claimed or assimilated, ignored or rejected, by various readers is widened by the fact that not enough readers challenge or move beyond boundaries that continue to separate writing that appears in "black" or "minority" vs. "mainstream" vs. "avant-garde" books and journals.

Poet and critic Rachel Blau DuPlessis generously includes me in her essay on contemporary women's poetry in the recent *Oxford Companion to Women's Writing in the U.S.* A peculiar effect of the daunting constraints and demands of the encyclopedic essay, perhaps, is that I am not grouped with black women poets (of whom only Ntozake Shange is singled out as an exemplar of "experimental" writing). Instead, I am placed in a subcategory of formally innovative poets who are also women of color. Or rather (because "women of color" seems to occupy a separate category apart from innovative or experimental poets), I become an example of "innovative women poets of minority background," along with Mei-mei Berssenbrugge and Myung Mi Kim, as well as Erica Hunt (in fact, at different times I have read on the same program with the latter two).

Because I also work as a literary critic, I understand the desire to place each writer and her work in the proper critical cubbyhole: one constructs meaningful distinctions in order to articulate significant critical statements based on comparisons of different textual practices and traditions. As an African Americanist, I am aware that my scholarly discipline depends, in part, on defining what is distinct, particular, and continuous about our literary and cultural heritage; yet I have frequently been concerned to see how even editors and critics with the best intentions participate in draining the category "black" or "African American" of its complex internal diversity by removing from the category anything so eccentric or innovative that it seems unaccountable to a "traditional" or "canonical" notion of what properly belongs to a black or African American heritage. Excluding or ignoring the unconventional tends to homogenize the canon, marooning those divergent works that might be equally (or more) alien to the mainstream. Nor are such unanticipated works always likely to be embraced immediately by an "avant-garde" that might also view blackness as "otherness," even as, in making its own claim to diversity, it adopts the innovative artist of minority background as an exceptional comrade.

The assumption remains, however unexamined, that "avant-garde" poetry is not "black" and that "black" poetry, however singular its "voice," is not "formally innovative." It is my hope that *Muse & Drudge* (Singing Horse, 1995) might alter or challenge that assumption, bridging what apparently has been imagined as a gap (or chasm?) between my work as a "black" poet and my work as a "formally innovative" poet. I see this as a "Baraka vs. Jones" problem—although he has moved in the other direction. For me the dilemma is similar to the conflict Ron Silliman discusses, in *The New Sentence*, in terms of "codes of oppressed peoples" (a poetry with its own urgent aesthetics: hence the entire construction of Harlem Renaissance, Negritude, Black Arts/Black Aesthetics movements) vs. so-called purely aesthetic schools (whose aesthetic mode itself can be read as a social code and an ideological weapon).

I felt that my latest poetic experiment must be successful when selections from *Muse & Drudge* were chosen to appear in *Callaloo* and *Muleteeth*, as well as in mainstream publications seeking diversity and journals devoted to racially unspecified "avant-garde." It's also encouraging when my work is solicited for new literary magazines and student-edited publications by young African Americans, Asian Americans, Latinos, and other members of racially diverse editorial collectives. I would single out Nathaniel Mackey's *Hambone* as exemplary in the welcome it has offered to challenging and idiosyncratic work from a diverse spectrum of writers. Mackey, in *Hambone*, and Ishmael Reed, in *Quilt*, were two African American poet-editors (each with his own eccentric relation to black traditions) who published transitional poems that I wrote in the period between *Tree Tall Woman* and *Trimmings*. Is it a coincidence that both reside in California, where I myself was living when I began to write "differently" as I interrogated my previously unexamined black identity? Yet my most immediate and influential model of a black poet engaged in formal innovation was Lorenzo Thomas, a poet born in Panama, reared in New York, and transplanted to Houston, Texas.

My marginality as a black artist teaches me important lessons for my survival and integrity as an aesthetic innovator; and certainly my experience crossing boundaries as a participant-observer in the "mysterious" avant-garde has provided me with additional models, resources, alliances, and readers in my development as an African American artist whose work struggles to overcome aesthetic apartheid.

Feeling no nostalgia for segregation nor any need or desire to divest myself of my black identity and connections to black communities nor any particular stake in defending traditional "humanism," I hope that my work continues to challenge that deadly distinction between "blackness" and "humanity"—or "universality"—that is still imposed on black human beings.

4 | Anarchism and Culture

Jefferson Hansen

If *culture* is taken to refer to accepted standards of taste in the arts, where conventional notions of beauty flit across the stage and poets ask questions about the meaning (or meaninglessness) of war and the necessity of seizing the day, then *anarchism* refers to that edge of the so-called cultural world where the questions and standards are unsettled. The unruly questions and sulfurous motions and shocking techniques of anarchism are form finding itself rather than replicating itself.

It is not quite that simple. Assume that culture and anarchism are two poles on a continuum. No poetic act of any value is wholly anarchistic or wholly cultural. Every poetic act embodies elements of both culture and anarchism.

There is no one, underlying continuum. Every poem is produced within a poetic network (or as it is more commonly known, "community") with its own calcified culture opening onto various anarchistic possibilities.

The anarchistic end of the pole is never pure. It reaches into a body of possibility partially hemmed in by cultural networks yet with openings to wider anarchistic vistas, like a bay off a large lake.

At the moment of composition a poem is at the nexus of four forces: the writer, the assumed audience, potential publishing venues, and potential performance venues. Each of these forces contains elements of anarchism and culture.

Because the audience and publishing and performance venues precede the writer, both temporally and logically, I will discuss them first.

The "audience" is the segment of the reading public that purchases, discusses, and reads the type of poetry being written. (The audience may, in turn, be further subdivided into general readers, critics, and other poets, but such subdivisions are beyond the scope of this essay.) This audience has a general preference for certain poetic forms, for certain techniques, for the expression of certain sensibilities, and for certain ways of reading. I leave these preferences ill-defined because they must be. For the poem to be written they must not be strictures but guideposts, not definitive but provisional and flexible. These preferences are the cultural element of the work; the anarchistic element is their lack of definitiveness. On the one hand, a poem that invokes no preferences currently at play among a network is to create poetry unable to be read because it is *outside* an audience's practices of reading. On the other hand, if these preferences have become too well-defined among the audience, or if the writing is too sensitive to some of the audience's demands, then the writing veers sharply toward the cultural end of the continuum and becomes calcified. The anarchistic impulse is lost. While the artistic value of the work diminishes, its possibilities for use as an emblem of culture are sometimes heightened.

Any act of writing, if it has value, will be met with disdain by a portion of the audience because it is either too "cultural" or too "anarchistic." If the dissenting voices are few, yet strident and clear, it may be a sign that the work is too safely cultural.

Performance and publishing venues are similar to the audience in that they exhibit certain preferences, but they differ from audience in that only a few people, namely editors or curators of reading series, decide on these preferences. The exact "taste" of these editors and curators can be more easily established than that of an audience. They then become lightning rods not only for hostile poets from other networks but for those within their network who feel that they have been personally rejected or have had their particular ideology ignored.

Every network is replete with tensions, backbiting, disagreements, and contradictions. There is no center to culture, just a loose cohesion.

The audience and the potential public venues for the poem being written usually act on the writing moment as mulch, as subconscious assumptions about poetry and its possibilities that the poet has developed through his or her participation in a network of publishing, performing, writing, and reading. The study of and general exposure to the poetic assumptions and characteristic techniques of this network have a cumulative effect on the poet, who now puts them into play as the poem is written. *The good poet has learned the assumptions and techniques so thoroughly that they seem to naturally flow through the poet's fingertips to the computer screen.* The poet may agonize over words and combinations, but in general these words and combinations are a logical possibility opened by the network. The more this poem can locate and use previously unexplored possibilities of this network (i.e., push the network toward anarchism), the more original the poem seems. Such a poem subtly deforms (anarchism) one of the many ways of forming poetry established within a network (culture).

The writer is the final, and most unpredictable, force that impinges on the writing of a poem. Whereas the general outlines of audience and, to a lesser degree, publishing can be discerned, the writer's very individuality makes this force impossible to precisely pinpoint. Every writer has a unique relationship to the general poetic tradition and to the specific emphases of his or her particular network. There is no such thing as a writer "mastering" the poetic tradition in the same way as a literary critic is sometimes said to do so.

Influence is nebulous and unequal, flowing as much from minor writers as from major. Indeed, a writer may be as influenced by extrapoetic material—pop culture, politics, domestic relations—as by strictly poetic sources. Granted, these materials will be refracted and reflected by the writer's favorite techniques (provided by one or more networks), but the source is outside poetry proper. The writer is a wild card.

A writer must balance the demands of culture and the demands of anarchism. Poor grounding in a network dooms a poet. (The criteria for good grounding, like everything having anything to do with the peculiarities of an individual poet, are nebulous. Some writers may gain an intuitive feel for the basics of a network after reading only a small selection of poets and poems. Others may need years of study. The key, it seems to me, is the ability to apply and transform the network's techniques and assumptions.) Similarly, a stifling grounding dooms a poet creatively, although it may prove helpful for short-term career moves.

Charles Bernstein's "Virtual Reality," from his collection *Dark City*, offers a wonderful example of a poem probing the limits of its own method of creation. It is dedicated to "Susan," presumably Bernstein's wife, Susan Bee, and has a tender, personable quality not often associated with Language poems and their frequent structuralist critiques:

> For I've
> learned that relations
> are a small
> twig in the blizzard
> of projections
> & expectations.[1]

The rhyme and metaphor, devices unusual for a Language poet to use, are obviously associated with networks that preceded Bernstein. Although much of the poem contains the wordplays and jokes common in Bernstein's work, this sentence shows him stretching away from some of the techniques and habits of his network. He is probing the edges of an anarchistic realm and moving toward poetic techniques that preceded him: metaphor, imagery, rhyme. In the end, however, the rhyme is isolated and offbeat, and it is the title, "Virtual Reality," that jostles everything in the poem, making it seem a bit unreal, like we are stuck in the "blizzard / of projections / & expectations."

When poets find themselves coming upon assumptions and techniques expressly forbidden by a network, they may respond by pushing ahead and ignoring the strictures—thereby alienating some of the audience and perhaps dooming the poem's publication or performance prospects—or they may bow to the network's strictures by altering or abandoning the poem. I recently heard of a poet working within a network highly skeptical of traditional narrative techniques. When he found these techniques creeping into his poetry, he quit writing. In this case the culture of his network overwhelmed the anarchistic impulse. Perhaps if he had allowed himself to move into narrative he would have discovered possibilities *between* his former network and traditional notions of narrative still operative in other places. Or he may have written himself into obscurity, been in at the founding of a new network, or switched into a more "traditional" network. But at least he would be writing and exploring rather than letting the audience and publishing vectors overwhelm his writing.

This example shows that even "avant-garde" artists can be overwhelmed by culture. The main difference between "avant-garde" culture and traditional or mainstream culture is that the techniques informing and assumptions underlying the mainstream are generally taken more seriously by local literary centers and the university system. Nothing is out in front anymore.

There is no longer an edge with which to cut.

There is no such thing as the arts community. Art is factions.

Presently in the United States poetry happens within a number of highly specific networks. Various networks, therefore, compete for attention and funding. This seems obvious: if four poets deeply committed to confessionalism manage to get seated on a committee deciding on an award, you can be sure that a confessional poet will win.

The more visible networks are those whose cultural pole is found congenial by the universities and other institutions, such as literary centers and presses, that fund poetry.

For most people in the general public, poetry, if they pay any attention to it at all, is a single network, not a number of competing ones. If, therefore, a poet manages to interest someone in any poetry whatsoever, it is to every poet's advantage, regardless of his or her network. The more people browsing the poetry shelves of libraries and bookstores, the better. It might rankle some poets in less visible networks that their work is less likely to be available to this poetry browser, but at a later date their poetry might become available if things are shaken up.

Poetry's best chance for attracting more readers is to offer a diversified product.

Although the frustration expressed by poets in less publicized networks is understandable, I believe that the wholesale dismissal of networks by other poets is counterproductive to poetry as a whole. Such dismissal tends to harden the cultural ends of all networks involved, both those being attacked and those doing the attacking, by forcing poets to proclaim or defend fundamental allegiances. Although such explicitness is valuable because it opens poetic assumptions and techniques to scrutiny, it ultimately hurts because poetry, as such, is not an explanation of itself nor a justification of itself. And if a poet spends a lot of effort defining, in explanatory prose, a poetics, then deviations from that poetics will be problematic. The gap between the poet's "theory" and "practice" will unsettle and even turn off some readers and perhaps confuse the poet. Unless a poet has the courage to change in midstream and alienate readers, he or she will likely become more and more programmatic as time passes. In the end the poems may become a monument to their cultural base.

If forced to defend some of my own poems, I would hope to first point out that all my poems are not like the specimens being attacked; then I would hope to explain the value of the attacked poems; finally I would hope to emphasize that in the future I may be writing very different kinds of poems.

Commitment to the assumptions and techniques of a single network often entails a reification of the cultural end of its continuum—a belief that this way of reading and writing is one of the few ways or, more extremely, the only valuable way to read and write.

Nonetheless, if I ever find myself on a panel judging poetry, it is likely that I would fight hard for so-called avant-garde work because poetry in general loses so much by the marginalization of one of its most innovative and surprising factions. I am committed to giving this poetry more exposure. Poetry politics, though, will not dictate my own poetics.

Restricting the repertoire of poetic assumptions and techniques impoverishes poetry. What we need are more connections, not fewer. We need surprising and eclectic connections, texture, and humor. I do not like attempts to banish figures of speech, techniques, forms, sensibilities from poetry. How do I know that these tools are wholly outdated? Nonetheless, we poets will always be fighting among ourselves, and this may be good.

A certain limitation of the "avant-garde" notion of artistic progress is the reification of the "heretofore undiscovered by the mainstream." I do not believe that there is any "in front of": there is "next to," "around," "about," "with." Poetry networks exist in the wider field termed *poetry*. This field is not linear but spatial. Various networks take up various positions, each with its own culture-anarchism continuum. There is some overlap. There are some open spaces in between networks. Some networks hearken back to centuries-old techniques. Some use techniques first developed only a decade or two ago. None are out in front.

I like to think I write in the anarchistic tension opened by the techniques and assumptions of a variety of networks. The act of writing magnetically pulls together particles from various networks.

What distinguishes my point of view in this essay from Charles Olson's "Projective Verse" is my insistence that form, as it interpenetrates with content, always occurs within a poetic field littered with various forms, techniques, and assumptions. Olson implies that poetry can burst beyond this poetic field into a form entirely specific to the moment of composition. For Olson poetic history, ideally, does not mediate between the poet and the poem. For me poetic history always mediates. Poetry cannot simply present perception; it must poetically present perception. The important distinction for me is not between closed form, which is mediated by history, and open form, which is not, but between excitement and calcification, between rigidity and the thrill of creation.

The Olson I feel closest to is the one who writes, "Limits / are what any of us / are inside of."[2]

Poetic tools such as rhyme, meter, dialect, collage, obfuscation, syntactical displacement—to name a few—are not in themselves ideological. Only their implementation is ideological. How a poet chooses to use rhyme is the question, not the nature of rhyme. Rhyme has no more of a nature than does a wrench.

But doesn't rhyme have a history that overloads it with meaning in a way that a wrench does not? Or is the history of a device itself a tool, to be used in an infinite number of ideological directions? I am only certain that this history cannot be discarded.

A poetry network often becomes creatively moribund when it begins to establish publishing and conferencing institutions, retrospective anthologies, and awards. Yet I applaud such entities. Rather than letting the techniques and assumptions used by a network disappear along with its most creative moment, they put forth and codify its ways, ways now more available to the rest of us because of this codification—as distinguished from calcification. People most upset by such institutionalization are poets in the network left out of the official representations and poets in other networks who feel their established territory is being impinged upon.

Almost every network has at least one window of opportunity through which to establish itself as a cultural product dispersed into the wider reading public. Such opportunities usually occur after the most interesting work has been written. Codification necessarily reduces the complexity and diversity of the network's production.

Interaction between networks provides the mulch for the writing moment. I write in order to be surprised at what I find language can do, to untangle an emotional knot, to find out what others may perceive and feel, to learn, perhaps about consciousness in general. Procedural limits on this searching only weaken it.

I write in order to be surprised.

Notes

1. Charles Bernstein, "Virtual Reality," in *Dark City* (Los Angeles: Sun and Moon, 1994), 80.

2. Charles Olson, *The Maximus Poems*, ed. George F. Butterick (Berkeley: University of California Press, 1983), 21.

Gary Sullivan

      An Alternative Grammar of Asian North American Poetry

Brian Kim Stefans

. . . descended on all sides from the Idiosyncrasy, the kid disdained grammar class, refused to parse, opted to be remote parsee.

—Jam Ismail, "from the Diction Air"

There's certainly no comprehensive way to account for the wide range of what is here being called "alternative" poetry written by people of Asian descent on the North American continent. In general, the more radical theories of Asian American poetry—whether deduced from readings of Theresa Hak Kyung Cha's *Dictee* or from the cogent, overtly activist valorizing of "deterritorialization" by Canadian poet Roy Miki—would not suggest that such a suturing, politically mollifying project be pursued. Issues of "community," for example, which have served mainstream theories of Asian American literature well in attempts to circumscribe a visible "movement," are rendered problematic by the presence of writers like John Yau, who has only recently been considered part of the historical phenomenon of minority literature as a result of more sophisticated critical paradigms. Such new paradigms acknowledge, for example, that a language that doubles its meanings contains a content that relates to central themes of ethnic literature, such as the imposition of Orientalist codes on the perceived outsider and the consequential interiorization of these codes, an interiorization that finds its expression, in Yau's work, through often opaque languages that spit back, in defiantly infantile yet damnably material forms, the range of racially motivated languages from the ethnic slur to the exoticizing compliment. Indeed, as will become clear in the following essay, such tactics have been on the table for Asian American poets for quite some time but have simply not been embraced in a large way, a testament, perhaps, to their efficacy. Ronald Tanaka, for example, in his 1978 essay for the *Journal of Ethnic Studies* (*JES*), "Towards a Systems Analysis of Ethnic Minority Literature," writes that "ethnic literature can be seen as the attempt by a majority culture to deal with the hermeneutic problems created by the necessity of cross-cultural communication," an open window that he perceives as only strengthening power relations. He continues:

> This interpretation is opposed to the more popular view that the various ethnic literatures are the independent products of their respective subcultures. Our claim is that ethnic systems have a very specific function to perform within the majority literary system and the result is a constrained and distorted output. This means that ultimately ethnic groups do not "have a literature" in the same way that majority societies "have a literature" in spite of what appears to be empirical evidence to the contrary.[1]

This theme of "empirical evidence to the contrary," of eyeing the crux of identity only to find it is a plant by enemy spies, will show up in many different guises throughout the following essay. Tanaka goes on to consider the concept of "communication stress," which he says can be created via the tactics of the "anomaly" and the "opaque," viable means of resistance for him from the days when Language poetics was not widely disseminated. What becomes clear in reading this nonlinear history of Asian American poetics is that many of the writers appear to have reached this element of their poetics without having had much communication with each other, at least not in the manner that many poetry movements—from imagism to the Umbra poets—have in the past. In fact, it was not until the publication of Walter Lew's anthology *Premonitions* in 1995 that poets like Cha, Tanaka, Yau, Lew, Myung Mi Kim, Tan Lin, Miki, and his fellow Canadians Roy Kiyooka, Fred Wah, and Gerry Shikatani could even be considered a constellation of experimental ethnic poets. Although an anthology hardly constitutes community, at least as a lived and malleable social space, it does give face to a series of disparate tendencies in a way that, finally, could create the atmosphere of exploration into literary difference that Asian American "ethnic" literature—at least in the way Tanaka proposes—could be said to have been lacking.

A chronological history of Asian American poetry is out of the question for reasons stated above but also because certain works, like Tanaka's writing for *JES* in the late seventies and early eighties and Cha's writings and films of the eighties, have suffered from an obscurity that places them outside of any cause-effect nomenclature necessary to comfortable narrative. How, for example, to account for the "role" of the first Asian American poet, Sadakichi Hartmann (1867–1944), who didn't in fact write good poems but who, through his art theory and the example of his creative writing—the shameless Orientalism of his symbolist aesthetics, for example, or the hybrid nature of his three plays *Buddha*, *Confucius*, and *Christ*, or even the clownish, partially Zen-inspired bohemian bon mots of his late years, which contain something of the tone of a writer like Yuki Hartman (no relation)— somehow anticipated what was to come? Indeed, Hartmann's long and varied life—which Pound famously admired in the *Guide to Kulchur*— spanned the time of the West's first integration of Asian mores into its aesthetics (he was a friend of Whitman and Stuart Merrill and the young Kenneth Rexroth) right up to the time of World War II, during which he was hounded by FBI agents while he was living in a shack on the border of an Indian reservation. Although grouping tendencies is probably not the best method—we've been wary of clasping divisive titles to the inchoate wilds of American poetry since the first edition of Allen's *New American Poetry*—it might serve to use temporary frameworks here, at least as a way to organize the paragraphs.

The two most visible writers of Asian descent in the States are probably John Yau and Mei-mei Berssenbrugge, and they each made noticeable shifts at some point in their writing careers. Yau moved from the early somewhat "magical realist" quasi-narrative lyrics of his first major book, *Corpse and*

Mirror, to his recent explorations of literary doubling, whether in the pun or the procedural subversions of the literary *I*. Berssenbrugge moved from the unobscured spirituality of her early poems written with short lines —

> When the Indian stops
> across old rock
> and his spirit sheds form
> and cleaves the earth
> an instant
> and he settles his dry hand
> across our valley
> his terror is decayed with age[2] —

to the long lines and the nouveau roman–like absent spectator, based partially on a collage poetics, for which she is best known. A third writer, Tan Lin, only seven years younger than Yau but whose first collection, *Lotion Bullwhip Giraffe*, was published in 1996, seems to fit into this group for his innovative attention to high postmodern aesthetics. Coincidentally, all three writers have engaged in collaborations with visual artists in several works over the past years, and their writing is probably the most purely "aesthetic" of the writers discussed later. They each opt to focus on effects of tone and color in their writing over political and expressionistic concerns, and the never-ending conundrum of the I/eye provides their central field of play.

In Yau the shift may be seen as a move away from self-decimating Orientalism, in which all emotion and expression is understood as consumable artifice and rarefied effect, to the lumpy presence of finger painting. As Oscar Wilde has written, "[T]he Japanese people are, as I have said, simply a mode of style, an exquisite fancy of art. And so, if you desire to see a Japanese effect, you will not behave like a tourist and go to Tokio. On the contrary, you will stay at home, and steep yourself in the work of certain Japanese artists."[3] The early Yau—too mischievous not to notice how Wilde's paradigm could be used to great fun—plays this up at times, as in the short "Shanghai Shenanigans": "The moon empties its cigarette over a row of clouds / whose windows tremble in the breeze / The breeze pushed my boat through a series / of telephone conversations started by perfume."[4] However, most of the poems in *Corpse and Mirror* inhabit a surrealist range of images and techniques, such as "Persons in the Presence of a Meta-morphosis":

> The porcelain bayonet of noon scrapes the face
> of a man who has forgotten why he started
> to spit. A uniformed girl,
>
> tiny and tireless, memorizes words
> she believes make accurate mirrors.
> A nun felt damp and gray,
>
> like the windows of a plumber.[5]

High aestheticism creates the author figure in the shape of a tour guide, of sorts, exhibiting the presence of, at most, the possessor of fine sentiments, however sadistic he or she may be in intentions under the surface. "Persons" shows, however, that Yau was already working on his later style, in which each enjambment provides something like the space between a film's edit, a portal through which narrative proceeds to an unexpected end. The suggestion of Johnson's remark on the metaphysical poets, who "violently yoked" their imagery together to create shock, is not lost on Yau, who is more a folk metaphysician of language, even in his later stages, than a student of post-Marxist semiotics. The first poem of the "Genghis Chan: Private Eye" series demonstrates most of the qualities of his later style:

> I was floating through a cross section
> with my dusty wine glass, when she entered,
> a shivering bundle of shredded starlight.
> You don't need words to tell a story,
> a gesture will do. These days,

we're all parasites looking for a body
to cling to. I'm nothing more
than riffraff splendor drifting past the runway.
I always keep a supply of lamprey lipstick around,
just in case.[6]

The sound qualities are heightened in this excerpt, and, indeed, some of the images, such as the "shredded starlight," are made more vivid yet concealed by the tempered awkwardness of the aural quality. Most important, the *I* and *you* enter as well, bringing the absent narrator of *Corpse and Mirror* out into the open as a libidinous, and often androgynous, stalker of the imagination. As Yau writes at the end of his essay on Wilfredo Lam: "Lam's hybrid figures—their combinations of male and female anatomy—can be seen as a sign of his belief that the self had to give birth to the self, that the self is not a privileged place given to him by society, but something made up and discovered in the world."[7] By his use of often uncomplicated syntax—a unique tone of sounding like a child stating the obvious, although in a room of mirrors—jarring imagery and sound qualities, obscured yet revealed narrative instincts, and a lyric *I* and *you*, Yau creates a singular presence for the author-figure while emphasizing the Steinian "everybody" quality of its singular absence.

Unlike Yau, Mei-mei Berssenbrugge has worked frequently with individuals and organizations in the ethnic community. Her early books were published by the Greenfield Review Press and I. Reed Books, and an early play of hers was produced by playwright Frank Chin. She has lived in New Mexico for most of her literary career, and as the excerpt above suggests, her early poetry, like that of another poet living in that state, Arthur Sze, was very much informed by the landscape and the Native American history and mythology that inhabits it. Like Yau's, though, some of her early poetry exhibits a taste for the macabre and the surreal, often achieving its effects via a quasi-cosmic or mythological sense of the interrelation of all things, accepting the pedestrian chores of narrative as a task of sensing the possibility. However, whereas Yau's settings are suburban basements where late-night

TV provides the only solace, Berssenbrugge's, in *The Heat Bird*, are exteriors, and more geographically specific:

> A dog is amenable to dust under a different house
> though he tells me by phone she still sniffs
> the mud on tires from El Rito. The old lady
> is mother of the boy who chopped up his friend
> and scattered parts all on the road to Dripping Springs
> That's why he thinks I shouldn't go there, because
> they haven't found all the pieces, but
> pretty soon they'll begin to smell and I won't get surprised
> Then I won't get surprised[8]

Surprise, however, is very much her instinct in many of these poems: "I demeaned myself in front of a / blind man, because I'm afraid of myself at night. If / he lights my cigarette when I complain how it goes out, the / flame goes out."[9] The *I* in Berssenbrugge soon becomes the site of all her narrative negotiations, however, as the lines grow to those monumental lengths for which she is known: "Attention was commanded through a simple, unadorned, unexplained, often decentered presence, / up to now, a margin of empty space like water, its surface contracting, then melting / along buried pipelines, where gulls gather in euphoric buoyancy."[10] The presence of New Mexico is still apparent in such lines, but the previous mythologies and narrative determinacies are replaced by the perceiving mind. As Robbe-Grillet has written in "A Future for the Novel," "Even the least conditioned observer is unable to see the world around him through entirely unprejudiced eyes." He suggests, however, that literary narrative can be attained through a filmic use of objects such that the eye, like the camera, is nothing more than a constant: "In this future universe of the novel, gestures and objects will be there before being something; and they will still be there afterwards, hard, unalterable, eternally present, mocking their own 'meaning,' that meaning which vainly tries to reduce them to the role of precarious tools."[11] Berssenbrugge's protagonist in much of *Empathy* is one such eye/*I*, though one both gendered and—as if defiantly not sacrificing agency for the objects that challenge it—acknowledging yet concealing psychological content from the gaze:

> She considers these the unconscious lessons of a dominant force
> that is being born, and as it becomes, its being is received structure.
> First ice crystals, then heavier glass obscures the light,
> so she walks back and forth talking to herself in a white soundless
> sphere past the trash of the village.[12]

That *so*, coming after the line break, defiantly conceals all the decision making (or lack thereof) that is normally the sinews of narrative. "My process is so cerebral that I try to get things in front of me that hold an emotional element—that's where the family pictures come in," Berssenbrugge says in her interview for *Black Lightning*.[13] She is explaining the detailed construction of her poem "Four Year Old Girl," which involves a painstaking assembling and editing of "found" texts, and it is clear that, at least in her new poems, Berssenbrugge is as observant of language as an "othered" entity as she is of the light, further reducing her author role to that of a spectator.

Tan Lin's long essay "Language Poetry, Language Technology, and the Fractal Dimension: Michael Palmer Prints Out a Kingdom" is a manifesto of sorts disguised as an analysis of the poetry of Michael Palmer, by whom he is undoubtedly influenced. It contains, for example, a fake interview with the poet in which he is asked, "What is the relation between a joke, a lie, and a poem?" "Palmer" purportedly offers the answer: "They constitute systems of self-deceptions (i.e., they can be read two ways or in both directions). Although all have an endpoint, all would like to continue indefinitely. All reverse themselves as conclusion. All are essentially non-linear, as they approach their opposite, truth. They resemble clouds and empty gas tanks. A lie and a poem lack a punchline. A joke is a metrical delusion. Gussied fragments fly? Mope thaw."[14]

Later, in an analysis of Palmer's poem "Sun," Lin writes "a straightforward march into linearity . . . is abandoned for circularity, perpetual return,

non-linearity, iteration, re-writing, and repetition with minute variations";
and on the final page of the essay, in the context of fractal geometry, he
writes that "a Palmer poem creates the illusion that it is the most complex
orderly object." All of these statements aptly describe what Lin is doing in
much of *Lotion Bullwhip Giraffe*, although unlike Palmer he approaches his
tasks with the hyperkinetic mind-set of a coked-up speed skater, slinging
words as if he is too impatient to bear out their often microsecond-long
duration, as in this excerpt, in which words like *ambiance*, *Echos*, and *dis-
tance* suggest that he is approaching some sort of poetic or narrative
topography, a topography that is not even truly approached:

> Ruckus stone, ambiance undone and cramped echos.
> To rock like mahogany Nazis, exempt
> from a late date. The starling flattens hah hah.
> All vices are distant and strung pastel rejection.
>
> Cramped Echos: seven lined leaflets trouble
> the clay pots. I guess a blessed hairy amplifier. Come and expend
> a loud distance, my floral beckoning. A sound
> ticks out like a fire. Here a spree
> of fragments. Solid predictions like a sweating bat.[15]

Many of the poems of *Lotion Bullwhip Giraffe* challenge the idea of poetic
content not just on the level of the word or sentence but on the level of scale,
as many of the longer prose poems never even threaten to descend into nar-
rative, lyrical subjectivity, or "humanistic" political content but rumble on
in a sort of intoxicated way through a variety of postmodern gestures, tweak-
ing the voids of meaning with a trickster-like facility. This scale suggests Lin's
primary concern, which is an almost clinical interest in the fractal possibili-
ties of a self-determining language, such that language is left to operate
almost as if a computer were producing it, but always with an attention that
highlights its fetishistic nature, such that the poetry resembles a pornogra-
phy of the word, or an attempt to render *material* the digital presence of

words, more than anything else. Although Lin is clearly attentive to the project of Yau, especially in his use of language in a way that suggests the metaslur ("Ship carp do doped pressure bag go famous pure fuck your shrag / lozenge movie geisha whittle drip drop," begins "Talc Bull Dogface,"[16] a poem that continues to run the gamut of sounds in a way that suggests a spastic temper tantrum conveyed with pseudo-Chinese phonemes), his surrealism, and his questioning of narrative conventions, Lin's poetics are clearly more unhinged—"liberated" in the futurist sense—consequently free to roam at will in a countereschatological eternity.

Another grouping of writers centers around the work of Theresa Hak Kyung Cha, a video artist, performer, and writer who died in 1982. Cha's work had gotten only limited exposure in Asian American literary communities because of its deconstructionist and hybrid formal characteristics, which seemed to make it unassimilable to the social-realist paradigms then ascendant. It wasn't until the early nineties, when many young Korean American artists began to take an interest in her work, that she began to exert an influence, and thenceforth her work began to appear in anthologies and critical essays. Indeed, judging by the change of face that the most stalwart of social-realist literary critics have made in the past five years, including many for a previous emphasis on totalizing and reductive views of what it means to be "Korean American," one would almost think that Cha's work, especially the book *Dictee* and the attention afforded to it, was the most instrumental force in critiquing the dominant sociological paradigms so that they could accept writers like Yau as "Asian American." This is not to say that Cha was the only writer conscious of the limitations of these paradigms (Tanaka, for example, went to great lengths to outline the inadequacies of the "movement" approach, only to throw up his hands at the linear, limning approach of the critical project). Two very different writers, Walter K. Lew and Myung Mi Kim, by no accident Korean American, have each in their different ways partially taken up Cha's project, in Lew's case, utilizing the techniques of *Dictee* in his critical collage *Excerpts from Δikth/* 딕테/딕티 /*DIKTE for DICTEE* (1982) also instrumental in reviving interest in Cha.

Dictee has been written about quite frequently since its rediscovery, both by critics working within the Asian American tradition and not. A recent essay by Juliana Spahr, "Postmodernism, Readers, and Theresa Hak Kyung Cha's *Dictee*," uses Cha's work for the basis of a far-ranging critique of postmodern reading practices, especially Jameson's contention that postmodernism signaled "the emergence of a new kind of flatness or depthlessness, a new kind of superficiality in the most literal sense."[17] *Dictee* seems to play a similar role as the final excerpt (prior to the three "Postludes" poems) in the *Poems for the Millennium* anthology edited by Jerome Rothenberg and Pierre Joris, an anthology that, in general, is critical of the constructivist modes of much twentieth-century poetry and seeks to reify the lyric epic traditions inaugurated by Pound. Why Cha's work stands at this unique position in so many different late-twentieth-century discourses—both as the prescient "avant-garde" work in Asian American discourses (and, one might argue, feminist discourses, although feminism has a richer tradition of experimental writing), but consequently as a window onto a more humanist conception of art in the central European traditions of experimental writing—has ultimately to do with the incredible freedoms that Cha exploited in its construction. As Shelley Sun Wong writes in her exceptional essay "Unnaming the Same: Theresa Hak Kyung Cha's *Dictee*": "In *Dictee*, the different genres, or modes of literary (and I might add, cinematic) production, do not coexist harmoniously but, rather, undermine each other through a process of reciprocal critique. Cha works with the representation that genres are not innocent or neutral aesthetic conventions or idea types but are, instead, formal constructs which are implicated in the very processes of ideological production."[18] Although the second sentence from Wong might suggest Cha as something of a player in the tradition of the Language poets—indeed, Steve McCaffery's *Panopticon* may resemble *Dictee* more than any other work—Cha was not approaching literature from the angle of one invested in its various subversions of tradition but rather as a filmmaker, and hence she takes a more anthropological view of writing genres, remaining free of the literary ideological battles. Flipping the pages of *Dictee*[19] takes one from photographs of a Korean martyr to Mallarméan writings in both French and English by Cha, from diagrams of the inner workings of the throat (linked to intense passages describing the both demeaning and empowering effects of having to learn English) to images of the scribbled-over earlier versions of passages from *Dictee*. The "Petition from the Koreans of Hawaii to President Roosevelt," a failed attempt by Korean exiles including Syngman Rhee to have the United States intercede in the Japanese occupation of Korea (still historically shadowed), is included in its entirety, which links not just with the autobiographical passages about Cha's brother participating in anticolonial marches but with the map of Korea, exaggerating its national entity, and the face of Renée Falconetti playing the martyr St. Joan in Dryer's film. A passage addressing her mother and her plight under the Japanese occupation, in which she wasn't permitted to speak English ("They have sheltered you from life. Still, you speak the tongue of the mandatory language like the others. It is not your own. Even if it is not you know you must. You are Bi-lingual. You are Tri-lingual. The tongue that is forbidden is your own mother tongue. You speak in the dark."),[20] runs up against passages describing the ethical and emotional challenges of historical witness, not inconsequentially cinematic witness, as in the important "Memory" passages of the "Thalia / Comedy" section. The following sentence contains something of a specifically filmic—it seems peculiarly about the edit and the blank white screen—mourning over lost time:

> It had been snowing. During the while.
> Interval. Recess. Pause.
> It snowed. The name. The term. The noun.
> It had snowed. The verb. The predicate. The act of.
> Fell.
> Luminescent substance more so in black night.
> Inwardly luscent. More. So much so that its entry
> closes the eyes.
> Interim. Briefly.
> In the enclosed darkness memory is fugitive.

Of white. Mist offers to snow self
In the weightless slow all the time it takes long
ages precedes time pronounces it alone on its own
while. In the whiteness
no distinction between her body invariable no dissonance
synonymous her body all the time de composes
eclipses to be come yours.[21]

Cha edited a unique anthology of film criticism in 1980 called *Apparatus*, and indeed many of the included writings seem to relate almost directly to the formal qualities of her book, published two years later. As Vertov writes, "The movie camera is present at the supreme battle between the world of capitalists, speculators, factory owners, and landlords and the world of workers, peasants and colonial slaves."[22] The passage seems obviously relevant, considering the collage aspects of *Dictee;* on the literary front Cha's writing resembles the "objects being what they are" aspect of the nouveau roman, perhaps escalating the maxim so that languages themselves—French as both the colonial language of Vietnam, for example, and the arbiter of Western knowledge—are a type of content.

Undoubtedly the most important figure in bringing attention to the formally radical possibilities of Asian American writing has been Walter K. Lew, who recognized early the fecundity of Cha's techniques in *Dictee*, as his dedication of his brief selection of poetry for the journal *Bridge* in 1983, "A New Decade of Singular Poetry," to her suggests. This selection includes writing by a wide range of people such as Eric Chock, Marilyn Chin, the "movement" poet Nellie Wong, John Yau, Mei-mei Berssenbrugge, Arthur Sze, and Ho Hon Leung,[23] suggesting the hybrid ethos that an editor in Asian American studies must possess. In his introduction to the selection he describes a form of poetry that he believes would be of particular use to Asian American writing, the "matrix," which "employs a wide range of rapidly juxtaposed languages, media, historical frameworks, motifs and rhetorical moods. It is almost demanded by the normally multicultural situation of Asian Americans and the accelerated information flow and collisions of contemporary society in general."[24] This statement, which contains something of a nod to the art of Nam Jun Paik, also anticipates the recent vogue among critical circles for hypertext poetics, and Lew's own work since that introduction—which ranges from film and video, poetry, performance, and editing—fulfills this call for intermedia. His critical book on *Dictee*, for example, *Excerpts from Dikte/for* Dictee *(1982)*, directly adopts many of Cha's formal methods, creating a sort of stabilizing double for the former work and at the same time destabilizing politically encoded reductive readings. The series of Korean cartoons that depict images of a colonized Korea—cartoons that have been recaptioned with French tags—for example, provides a diagrammatic parallel to the many strands of narrative existing in Cha's work, pointing to its reassessed meanings—to the space between edits—and to the nationally specific contexts. Cha's emphasis on female martyrdom—from the revolutionary Yu Guan Soon to Joan of Arc—finds a source in Korean mythology, as Lew includes a section from a book on shamanistic rituals that tells the story of a daughter shut up in a coffin by her father and cast into a pond. The girl was rescued by the Dragon King, and after discovering her mother was ill, she "went great distances to the Western sky and brought back healing water that saved her from death."[25] The split significance of the "Western sky" points to what many see as the rift in Cha's work between a turn toward high modernist (some critics just call it "white") poetics to uncover the allusive truths of colonialism. Lew's hybrid poetics comes into play in the important anthology he edited, *Premonitions*, which was the first anthology to embrace the entire spectrum of writing in both the United States and Canada by writers of Asian descent. Again, it seems to allude to Cha's work in its form—with its contrasting black-and-white pages, it mimics the structure of Cha's "Commentaire," which she included in *Apparatus*—not to mention its rejection of overly stabilized binaries in the literary world—"experimental" vs. "mainstream," "Language" vs. "New American," or "movement" vs. "white avant-gardist"— in a sense adopting Cha's stance as a cinematographer to collide, with a sort of "kino-eye" aesthetic, with the disparate range of Asian American writing being done today. This aesthetic clearly comes into play with his inclusion of Buddhist work and poetry by Asians about atrocities such as the Vietnam and Korean Wars. Lew has also translated the work of the primary Korean avant-garde figure, Yi Sang, who died young under the Occupation but who was, perhaps alone, attempting to transform the constructivist end of modernist poetics into a Korean idiom. He has also published important poems such as "The Movieteller,"[26] based on his own performances of the text along with reedited Korean film footage. The piece concerns the phenomenon of the *pyonsa*—an individual who would speak an often politically encoded monologue over silent or untranslated Western film imports—in Asian cinema, and, indeed, the ethos of the pyonsa may give insight into the cumulative content of Lew's various works, which is that he redirects and unencodes stable meanings in previously monolithic cultural products or formations. Lew's reputation as a poet has yet to catch up to his reputation as a critic and editor, a situation that is the product of his intense, singular attention to a variety of writers—from Cha to Francis Chung—who were or are in danger of disappearing from the Asian American canon, even though Lew's work would suggest that such a canon is anathema to the particular contours of the Asian American literary situation. Consequently, Lew has taken the genre-crossing implications of the "matrix" to the extreme, rendering the standard text-based lyric—which he has widely explored, mastered, but grown dissatisfied with as his primary art, as his unpublished collection of poetry, "Brine," demonstrates—perhaps a little too stable for his collage-activated mature poetics.

Like Tan Lin, Myung Mi Kim belongs to a group of slightly younger poets who have already begun to reap the benefits of their radical predecessors in the experimental Asian American tradition, in Kim's case the predecessor being Theresa Cha. Even in her first book, *Under Flag*, published in 1991 around the time of Cha's "rediscovery," echoes of *Dictee* can be heard in the idiom—spare, notational, but often circling a refrain or variation of a phrase—and in the emphatic synthesis of personal and public concerns, as in issues of nationhood and language acquisition. However, Kim's writing is more politically pointed, as her quest for witness is not tied to a haunted conversation with the "homeland" but is involved in the urgency of contemporary life, even if that, in the end, is elusive. As she states in an interview for *Tripwire*:

> How long can one sit and be attentive when the world is blowing up? These are questions to be answered as they come up; there is no a priori answer because then it would in effect be a summation rather than an answer. Those uncertain and undecidable spaces of— am I making a difference?—will this contribute?—how can I know?—those undecidable locations are part of the work. It doesn't feel great, it's not an exhilarated state, or at least not for very extended periods of time, but it is a lived state, and a true one.[27]

As this excerpt suggests, Kim's poetics involves an ontological questioning of political or "movement" poetry, a quality that keeps her writing far from that of the ritualistic Cha and another big influence, Susan Howe, mostly because her attitude toward reality is pointillist (accumulative) at first and narrative (paradigmatic) only afterward. Her book *Dura* opens with three sections of mostly fragmented text, none of which, however, boldly challenges the felt linkages of the sign with the signified so much as offers the particulars of experience prior to any totalizing structure (she resembles, curiously, Larry Eigner in this way). She writes in "Chart":

> Swag drum
> Inland filth
> Surmise commodity
> Anemic shed
> Corollary held
> Second stock
> Force lack
> Acute lily[28]

This list poem alludes to the various discourses Kim is involved in but never abstracts truths from its particulars (even if the particulars arrive through a process of deduction). A later section, "Thirty and Five Books," contains many of the themes of the earlier sections in brief prose paragraphs but grants them more of a cinematic presence:

Heat the gaping sound constrains. Remind the herders and poison growth. Cover distances deemed impossible to cover.

Great highways indicated by means of stones.

Invention where the tomatoes dangling from one end are not the tomatoes hanging from the other end.

And the unremarkable become the stuff of dust.

Where is the start. Dress of blue chiffon and a white straw hat in its own hat box.

Heat the gaping ground constrains. Turbulence. Ridicule.

The desktops tilt up and you may place inside them several books and a lunch.

Various kinds of rice in the manner of living in that country.[29]

As *Dura* suggests, the march of technological innovation, especially in transport—the work abounds with allusions to ships bearing commerce and cultural domination—but also in such scientific exercises as making the tomatoes at one end different from those at the other, is such that the "unremarkable"—in a vision of the final solution—"become the stuff of dust." But even with this global perspective, she asks "Where to start," and finds the answer somewhere in a "dress of blue chiffon," which, like the "acute lily" from the earlier passage, is an image that resonates less with symbolic meanings—although the "lily" could be the "lily of the fields," its "acute" state suggests that it is punching through such parables—than with epistemological ones. Despite its opaque nature, Kim's poetry manages to synthesize some of the fruits of a linguistically radical poetics with the emotive, emphatic gestures and tones of an activist poetics attentive to the particulars of group, place, and time.[30]

Two writers who are not obviously part of the experimental strand of Asian American poetry are Ronald Tanaka and Lawson Fusao Inada. However, their outsider status—neither is particularly comfortable in mainstream contexts such as those shaped by *American Poetry Review, Paris Review,* or *Grand Street,* yet both are highly critical of the social realist expectations of the Asian American literary community—along with their radical synthesis of Japanese poetics and "New American" poetry forms suggests they deserve an important place in this lineage. As the excerpt from Tanaka's essay quoted earlier, the forfeiting of information on the terms of the dominant class plays an insidious role in confirming existent power relations, contrary to the oft-cited maxim that minority writers are obliged to "tell their stories" first in order to achieve the basic plateaus of legitimacy as artists.

In a series of genre-eluding writings—they are neither essays nor strictly poems but masquerade as anthropology—titled *On the Metaphysical Foundations of a Sansei Poetics: Ethnicity and Social Science,* Tanaka considers the issue of Sansei—third-generation Japanese—"personhood" amid the paradigms that social science has created. "Being by definition an 'ethnic group,' we have from the very beginning been 'given over to' social scientists, as opposed to, say, philosophers, artists, or theologians. In turn, social science has affected our own thinking far more than any other academic thinking,"[31] he writes, sketching in broad strokes the critical arenas in which Asian American writers—whether conscious of it or not—are forced to work. The clinical tenor of Tanaka's approach replicates the overdetermination of the very sciences he critiques, motivated primarily by an analysis of Milton Gordon's 1964 study, *Assimilation in American Life,* which reaches such conclusions as this: "In virtually all instances of inter-ethnic conflict, no matter how great the initial differences between the groups, people sooner or later become integrated into a single unit and convinced of their descent from common ancestors."[32] Tanaka's stated responses are too detailed to reproduce here; in general, he discovers that assimilation involves the preserving of only those characteristics of ethnic culture that can be linguistically substantiated in the dominant society but that conceptualization in "white" terms is not adequate for a range of Sansei emotions that are not replaced or replaceable. This leads the "essays" themselves into a retreat from straightforward logical critiques of terms and propositions into genres like the Wittgensteinian philosophical maxim, the short lyric, and the parable into what one might consider a Buddhist distrust of knowledge. Stylistically, parts of the essay seem to enter the territory of the "New Sentence":

5.0 I take what's given to me and try to make do.
5.1 I dress as best I can. And smile a lot. Perhaps excessively concerned with appearances. Manners.
5.2 (I got shoes! You got shoes!)
6.0 I'm not as worried about Sansei as I am about *life*.
6.1 Do you understand me when I say this?
6.2 When I go to Pt. Peyes, I have to remind myself that it is not a part of my own body.
6.3 So I call the rain different kinds of names.
6.4 I am immersed in the world. All that is and was and will be. Rocky Road.
7.0 My preoccupation with ethnicity is strictly logical.
7.1 It's a product of my class interests.[33]

Tanaka explains in the introduction to the fourth and last of the essays, titled "Shido, or the Way of Poetry," that he has lost his funding from the Heike Society and that his "work has been labeled 'solipsistic,' and 'unprofessional,' and I have been branded an 'academic quack.'" Although he published a few more "essays" in *JES* over the next two years, he has since devoted his attentions entirely to poetry and visual work, such as the photo/poetry sequence "The Mount Eden Poems," each of which is dedicated to a different vintage wine from the Mount Eden Vineyards and accompanied by a strange, faux fashion shot of Melanie A. Slootweg dressed, not very obviously, as "the kindergarten teacher, Madeline Giboin." This sequence runs the gamut from absurdity to romance, from ritual to nihilism, and can be tied in somewhat with his notions of Sansei personhood in terms of interethnic relations, yet its deceptively calm surfaces eventually lead to damning voids of meaning, suggesting the struggling logician concealed beneath them.

Lawson Fusao Inada, often cited as the first Asian American poet to have a complete book of poems published (*Before the War*, 1971), is equally distrustful yet mindful of the social realist paradigms proffered as the most suitable for portraying history and the Asian American experience. He is probably the most accomplished lyricist in the Asian American tradition. "Since When As Ever More," a process poem, stands out in *Breaking Silence*, an early anthology of Asian American poetry, for its suggestion of discursive relevance despite its meandering around determinate meanings. His early jazz-inspired poems, such as "The Great Bassist," dedicated to Charles Mingus, convey an anger suggestive of Amiri Baraka in his Black Nationalist phase, yet their easy flow suggests a countering weight of Buddhist peace and include a somewhat narcissistic irreverence not entirely alien to Tanaka, as when in "The Great Bassist" he observes, "I'm in Levi's now— / that doesn't matter." *Legends from Camp*, his second book (published twenty-two years after the first one), centers on his youth in the detention camps during World War II and is almost as much a hybrid work as Cha's, not just formally but in terms of its openness to themes and manifestations of cultural synthesis. "Listening Images,"[34] for example, is a series of haiku (that they don't conform to syllabic convention doesn't disqualify them), each of which is dedicated to a jazz musician, and the poems, in their accessing of American cultural experiences rather than some exoticized "Asian" experience, are probably truer to the spirit of haiku than the many tepid attempts at minimal nature poetry that characterize the genre in America. The one titled "Ben Webster," for instance, runs in its entirety "Such fragile moss / In a massive tree." The one to Billie Holiday is simpler: "Hold a microphone / Close to the moon." The poems of the title sequence are reminiscent of Langston Hughes in their poignant simplicity and in their attempt to eulogize a passing moment, although each of these fabled moments is underscored by the determinations of the society at large, as in "Legend of the Humane Society":

> This is as
> simple
> as it gets:
> In a pinch,
> dispose
> of your pets.[35]

Inada is also a noted educator, and the primary motivation of *Legends* may be seen as didactic, but not to the world at large so much as to future generations of Japanese Americans who will need to know what happened in the camps—not through statistics, cloying declarations of "identity," or liberal apologia but through the eyes of an artistically inclined, hyperinterested young boy. It is so unpretentious that it might be said to slip beneath the radar of one looking for grand theoretical gestures and displays of knowledge, blinding imagery and revelatory rhetoric, but its tone, formal variety, and accomplishment—not unlike that of another writer on the fringes of the avant-garde, Ron Padgett—is convincing in portraying the mind of one who has found a sense of measure in a life of extremes.

The publication of Lew's *Premonitions* brought to the attention of Americans the radically investigative writing of a number of Canadian writers, notably Roy Kiyooka and Fred Wah.[36] Kiyooka was known as one of the most important painters in Vancouver until he published his first book of poems, *Kyoto Airs*, in his late thirties. Like Cha in the United States he is the most generative writer of Asian descent in his country's tradition and like her also sought to utilize visual elements in no secondary way in his work. *Pacific Windows*, his collection of poems published posthumously in 1997 and edited by Roy Miki, traces a compelling yet mostly hidden literary career (he self-published most of his later sequences in editions of less than fifty) from the relatively understated *Kyoto Airs*, through several literary-visual projects such as "StoneDGloves" and "The Fontainebleau Dream Machine" and on to his dynamic later poems, which collaged an extremely wide range of writing styles to create nexuses of meanings both boldly stated and void of determinates. With an ego comparable to Whitman's in its breadth, generosity, and libidinous capacity to incorporate and innovate new forms, he drew from a wide range of influences. At times he seems a footloose, rather Shakespearian Basho (most notably in parts of "Wheels: A Trip thru Honshu's Backcountry"); at other times he is the grand magistrate of ontological play in the manner of Stevens ("The Pear Tree Pomes," which starts with an address to "Credences of Summer"). In "Fontainebleau"—which includes several Ernst-like collages by Kiyooka along with stanza-length captions—he is a writer/artist with all the agonic countersystemic thrust of Blake but with an analytic and reifying view of the dream/death longings of the surrealist project. Christian Bök likens the effect of this last work to the phenomenon of picnolepsy, "in which a perceptual discontinuity requires a response of conceptual continuity, since the special effects of kinesic realism rely upon periodic lapses of attention at a constant speed of movement."[37] Eva-Marie Kröller, in a compelling interpretation of the visual historical overlays of the sequence, writes in an aside that it contributes to an "exploring of the surrealist and dadaist intertexts in English-Canadian literature, an area which has, unlike its Québec counterpart, remained largely unexplored so far,"[38] suggesting that Kiyooka had, in his plunge into the depths of consciousness, hit upon certain aspects of Canadian nationhood that may have, for political reasons, remained largely hidden. The following excerpt, which, like each poem, rests atop one of the collages as a sort of explanation, is replete with poignant, suggestive, quick edits:

sifting the Rune/s for

the Behemoth of Speech: the absolute truth of

those huge white tusks curving in the moon-light marsh
a million years ago, today. searching the Sahara
for the Algebra-of-Awe Rimbaud wept when he stumbled
on them in front of the pygmy king's palace. the impossible
death of Chairman Mao on late night television. nuclear
frisson. Hermann Goring & Separatism. on the
tusk of a dream i beheld the Elephant on the promenade:
his inflamed ear thrums the mammalian silences

the 8th frame hides

the real pigeon shit spattered on the back of a bronze Napoleon.[39]

Language is a ruin/rune, a rebus of sorts, that resonates with the ecstasy
of an all-encompassing truth, an "Algebra-of-Awe," perhaps the hermetic
vision of eternal interrelations, but that, in the end, points even in its encap-
sulated and emasculated present—"Chairman Mao on late night
television"—toward "a million years ago, today." This excerpt aptly demon-
strates the syntactic quality of Kiyooka's writing—singular capitalization of
certain nouns, never-capitalized *i*'s and first words of sentences, for exam-
ple—that, as Miki writes in his afterword to the collected edition, has both
a transformative yet generative content. "It was in the intimacy of the bond
between mother and child that RK would also come to inhabit the imagi-
nation of his 'mother tongue' which would shape the parameters of poetic
language—the 'inglish' with the lower-case 'i' which he distinguished from
'English,' the dominant language of what was for him an anglocentric
norm," Miki writes. Kiyooka's life was completely uprooted during the
Canadian internment of the Japanese in 1941: "Overnight, the transparent
signs of childhood became the opaque space of state control, a machinery
that homogenized his 'Kiyooka' name in a system of codes in which the 'i'
of his consciousness became a body 'of the Japanese race'—the nomenclature
used to register, finger-print, and revoke the rights of innocent people."[40] In
a sense Kiyooka's paranoiac, individualistic method in his "Dream

Machine"—whose major motif is the hot-air balloon, which paradoxically signifies dream perspective and panoptic state observation, as Kröller notes—can be seen as an attempt to force the fissures in the monolith of government power, meeting the opacities of control with those of ellipsis. Important for Miki, and Canadian Asian poetics in general, Kiyooka assembled out of the myriad arenas of language, a sort of hybrid idiom—more "Zen" and more "surreal" than O'Hara's, to parse Ashbery's famous comment—that on the one hand was "mastered" by a constraining, implacable ego ("that irresistible / raga-of-longing that droned through me / riddling my psyche . . . / had to be lanced before i could begin to sing")[41] but that, nonetheless, never gave ground to what he considered empty in the historical context of the millennia, the "dung hill mind."[42] Kiyooka's work, not unlike Blake's, bedevils the editorializing mind that would want to conform its syntax to stable norms.

One quality of the generation of Asian Canadian poets who follow Kiyooka is that they have found ways to theorize issues of agency in minority discourses without sacrificing the technically innovative, resistant qualities of postmodern praxis. Fred Wah, whose early poetry stemmed from a deep engagement with the New American poetics of Olson and Creeley, with whom he studied in Buffalo in the sixties, incorporates in his essay "Speak My Language: Racing the Lyric Poetic" issues of linguistic variance or "othering" with those of the racialized subject. Commenting on statements by Nicaraguan poet Margaret Randall and Québecois poet Nicole Brossard, he writes:

> Randall [says] that the revolution will succeed on the common tongue of the people and Brossard [says] there will be no revolution until that (male-based) common tongue is troubled into change. Since then the range of political possibility in poetic language has pretty much dwelled between those two poles. I know which one I opt for but I'm always a little bothered by those race writers who go for the other, that seemingly solid lyric subject ground I can't trust. I can't trust it since, for my generation, racing the lyric entails rac-

ing against it; erasing it in order to subvert the restrictions of a dom-
inating and centralising aesthetic.[43]

Although times are changing, in the past Asian American poets have not led
the discussion concerning linguistic innovation in poetry among or for eth-
nic writers, for reasons too deep to go into here but that probably have to do
with the institutionalization of Asian American writing through the mecha-
nisms of the oppositional "movement" literatures that took place in the
States. These mechanisms occluded formal concerns and left those on the
periphery with no real audience to address. As Wah writes later in his essay,
"Social and cultural production has, in recent years, appropriated the figure
of the racialized writer as a measure of containment and control," and he
advocates a Janus-like looking-both-ways in his attitude toward the lyric,
such that "a racialized lyric, caught in the hinges of inherited poetic forms,
might adopt an ambiguous regard to both lyric interference and lyric con-
vention in order to recuperate, even, the agency of linguistic choice."[44] For
Wah all forms of excess and incorporation have political content, and his
statements on the exercising of linguistic "choice" are borne out in his wide-
ranging work. The poems of *Mountain* (1967) spill down the page as they
mimetically place the self amid the flux of nature as much as the lyric amid
language ("Hey our ice your ice / it hides / moves and slides [. . .]/ flower
out in the lakes of my eyes shimmering Kootenai waters green [. . .]").[45]
More formally varied poems like "Cruise" and *Pictograms from the Interior of
B.C.* speed through forms reminiscent of everything from Italian futurism to
Snyder-esque nature poetry, the latter sequence incorporating reproductions
of actual prehistoric pictograms. Later ongoing sequences such as "Music at
the Heart of Thinking" (whose "method of composition is the practice of
negative capability and estrangement I've recognized for many years,
through playing jazz trumpet, looking at art, and writing poetry");[46] the
"ArtKnots" (short lyric poems inspired by art exhibits); and the series of
"Utaniki" (in which he combines lyric, dated prose entries, and page spa-
tialization to create fields of paratactic meaning) convey, or rather trace, the
thematically nomadic, unbounded *I* as it moves among the cultures and

geographies of Canada. For Wah meaning is "something that is strangely familiar, not quite what we expect, but familiar. . . . That quick little gasp in the daydream, a sudden sigh of recognition, a little sock of baby breath. Writing into meaning starts at the white page, nothing but intention."[47] His poem "Scree-Sure Dancing," one of his most formally challenging works, is almost a manifesto for this poetics:

> thoughts different
> sky's all animals, all
> paper, all chalk. Our

> writing as   the tableaus
> anamorphous   =   of voyage
> river cliffs   forgetting

> She danced the strict linguistic sense.
> babbled bavardage   finger-painted thick
> memo-clouds in the darkening sky

> $h_{om}{}^{om}e$

> That's the secret
> ticket
> to silence
> na (frame) na's notation.[48]

Not unlike Kiyooka (and influential Canadian poet bpNichol), Wah's poetry suggests the nexus where a Mallarméan poetics of the mind-as-sign meets the proprioceptive poetics of an Olson, in which language is a medium whose message is mostly the self. Because of his awareness of these myriad strands and his dedication to a "negative capability," Wah's work has grown and transformed such that his later poetry, collected in *So Far*, even approaches the status of "Language-centered" writing but meets head-on transparent, formally fluid "Utaniki." In this way Wah's statements on the lyric expand to include the different degrees of opacity that language could be said to possess, traversing not just a vertical axis of the lyric-then and the lyric-now but the vertical axis of the borderless language-centered lyric and the transparently subjective lyric.

A third "Canadian" poet who has yet to attain the attention she deserves is Jam Ismail, who is rumored to spend half of each year in Hong Kong and half in Vancouver. Excerpts from her sequence "Scared Texts" (or, alternately, "Sacred Texts") were a standout in terms of literary exploration in the 1991 anthology of Canadian Chinese writing *Many-Mouthed Birds*—indeed, in a development of Joycean stream-of-consciousness narrative, it is a many-mouthed plethora of dialogue and narrative moments: "hibiscus mentioned that mushrooms are good for cholesterol / jaggery scoffed: what d'you mean, good for! / chestnut dehisced: she means good against, good against cholesterol. / flame-o'-the-forest said to jaggery: we know you speak better english & that you know what we mean."[49] A later sequence, "from the Diction Air," takes accumulation of a diasporic experience deep into the language game to produce a multivalent, part-narrational and part-lyrical autobiographical riff:

:"didi" meant big sister (bengali), little brother (cantonese), DDT (english). to begin with, inglish had been at home, with cantonese & hindustani. one of the indian languages, the kid felt in bombay, which british hongkong tried to colonize. descended on all sides from the Idiosyncrasy, the kid disdained grammar class, refused to parse, opted to be remote parsee.

:at school wrote her first poem, *DAMON NOMAD*, (damon nomad). & what mean while was writing her, what *nom de womb*? reverb with '47 (indian, pakistan), '48 (koreas), '49 (chinas, germanies), '54 (vietnams).

:"hey," he bellowed, pants down in quebec, "bring in some english mags, i can't shit in french!" claude nearly kicked him in the anglo. macauley's minute & roosevelt's second unearthed in canadian library digs, chattel feared english had him in its grip, spooken for, pun-ish.[50]

As Fred Wah writes in "Speak My Language," "the proximity of the autobiographical realism is still only deflected momentarily by a reading of syntactic and punctuative gestures"[51] such that this text is a negotiation of lyric subjectivity and disruptive grammar. Ismail, Kiyooka, and Cha are true "interstitial" poets of the "English" language—perhaps the heirs of the world citizenry attributed to Coleridge and implicit in the later Joyce—as they are privy to a great deal of firsthand cultural knowledge, sitting in on the Senates of linguistic negotiation, aware yet wary of the call of academic discourse (perversely leveling while attempting to be inclusive) and the Western poetic tradition, its scales of value and its hunger for conformity.[52]

As Allen Ginsberg may have been wont to ask: "Does a tomato have an angel?" In postcolonial terms *angel* might be exchanged for *nation* or *genealogy* and *tomato* with "the externally racialized body." As Kim suggests, even a "tomato" is open for interpretation, and the scientific paradigms determine its final content perhaps more than its singular features. As the variety of writing considered in this essay demonstrates, there is no longer a single thread of discourse that an Asian American writer feels obliged to confirm or argue, as there may have been in the early seventies when Tanaka was writing his "Metaphysics" series, but rather a system of discourses that only becomes abhorrent to the racialized writer once the progressive liberalism of its purported content reduces to abstraction (or distraction) the singularity of the writing itself—a curious position, indeed. In this sense it is probably not surprising that a recent controversial critique of the politics of desire, titled "Raw Matter: A Poetics of Disgust," which doesn't consider ethnic discourse in any way directly, was written by an Asian American writer, Sianne Ngai. She writes early in the essay that "postmodernity . . . and pluralism are virtually synonymous" and moves on to offer another critical and reading model that, she concludes, is only destined to self-destruct:

> What makes disgust a viable theoretical approach to innovative writing is thus its negative potentiality as a figure of exclusion, the radical externalization it enacts in facilitating the subject's turn away from the object. In this manner, the possibility of disgust as a poetics resides in its resistance to pluralism and its ideology of all-inclusiveness which allows it to recuperate and neutralize any critical discourse emphasizing conflict, dissent, or discontinuity. What makes disgust particularly strategic in organizing and informing a critical approach to contemporary writing is that *disgust thwarts seductive reasoning*. I will also argue that *disgust thwarts close reading*, the generally unquestioned, seemingly irrefutable practice criticism can't seem to do without. Lastly, as an operation of exclusion or externalization, always turning away from its object, *disgust thwarts its own use as a critical paradigm*.[53]

This line of reasoning echoes Canadian poet Jeff Derksen's essay on Fred Wah's "alienethnic" poetics called "Making Race Opaque," a critique of Canadian state-sanctioned multiculturalism in which he observes: "Writing that focuses on a polyvalent sign, that utilizes this sign strategically, is *non-representational*—but not culturally meaningless as it is sometimes characterized as—because it doesn't represent hybrid subjectivities in a manner that is assimilable by multicultural discourse."[54] The range of Asian American writing, which also includes an oppositional strand—feminist, lesbian, working class, ethnocentric—most strongly represented in the 1982 anthology *Breaking Silence* (but that wasn't nearly as formally exploratory as the writers discussed here), is full of instances in which the "subjective I" is site of negotiations that rely on no stable paradigm for its enactment but that, on the other hand, must engage in a state of covert action because of the panoptic gaze of discourse that utilizes its terms for alternative ends. This isn't to say that Mei-mei Berssenbrugge had reached her particular poetics via a process of eluding "presence" and hence assimilation, nor that nonethnic writers do not also feel the brunt of mollifying interpretation. Ngai's essay, after all, was founded on a reading of writers as wide ranging as Deanna Ferguson, Bruce Andrews, Kevin Davies, and Dorothy Trujillo Lusk. However, Asian American writers, probably more often than not—whether they are "up" on postmodern theory or are fully convinced, as Lin might be said to be, that humanist discourse has run its course—are forced into a consideration of the Western literary tradition, especially the "avant-garde," in a peculiar way because of a vague sense of membership in a racially defined community that often is not loyal to the various binaries mentioned earlier in this essay, especially that one that sees no negotiation between subjectivity and objectivity. In this sense "neutralization" of the past through the freeing of the sign is a vexed operation for many Asian American poets, even one like Tan Lin, who writes in a recent essay, "Forgetting a word is among the most beautiful things that can happen to the human brain. The dumb poem is the most beautiful poem."[55] However, as these writers show, this loosening of the grip of the sign created an open space for dialogic cultural negotiation that wasn't a clear option for, say, Paul Lawrence Dunbar. In this sense both the monistic romantic tradition and the totally desubjectifying strands of the postmodern tradition find a sort of dissenting tomato in the Asian American arena.

Notes

1. Ronald Tanaka, "Towards a Systems Analysis of Ethnic Minority Literature," *Journal of Ethnic Studies* [hereafter *JES*] 6.1 (1978): 49.

2. Mei-mei Berssenbrugge, "Ghosts," in *Summits Move with the Tide* (New York: Greenfield Review Press, 1974), 21.

3. See Jeff Nunokawa, "Oscar Wilde in Japan: Aestheticism, Orientalism, and the Derealization of the Homosexual," in *Privileging Positions: The Sites of Asian American Studies* (Pullman, Wash.: Washington State University Press, 1995), 289.

4. John Yau, *Corpse and Mirror* (New York: Alfred A. Knopf, 1983), 57.

5. Ibid., 119.

6. John Yau, *Radiant Silhouette* (Santa Rosa, Calif.: Black Sparrow Press, 1989), 189.

7. John Yau, "Who Was Wilfredo Lam?" reprinted in *Talisman* 5 (fall 1990): 146.

8. Mei-mei Berssenbrugge, *The Heat Bird* (Providence: Burning Deck, 1983), 29.

9. Ibid., 38.

10. Mei-mei Berssenbrugge, *Empathy* (New York: Station Hill Press, 1989), 33.

11. Alain Robbe-Grillet, "A Future for the Novel," in *For a New Novel* (New York: Grove Press, 1965), 21.

12. Berssenbrugge, *Empathy*, 21.

13. Mei-mei Berssenbrugge, interview by Eileen Tabios, *Black Lightning* (New York: Asian American Writer's Workshop, 1998), 135.

14. Tan Lin, "Michael Palmer Prints Out a Kingdom," in *A Poetics of Criticism*, ed. Juliana Spahr, Mark Wallace, Kristin Prevallet, and Pam Rehm (New York: Leave Books, 1994), 237–48.

15. Tan Lin, *Lotion Bullwhip Giraffe* (Los Angeles: Sun and Moon, 1996), 116.

16. Ibid., 89.

17. Fredric Jameson, quoted in Juliana Spahr, "Postmodernism, Readers, and Theresa Hak Kyung Cha's *Dictee*," *College Literature* (1997): 24.

18. Shelley Sun Wong, "Unnaming the Same: Theresa Hak Kyung Cha's *Dictee*," in *Writing Self Writing Nation* (Berkeley: Third Woman Press, 1994), 106.

19. Theresa Hak Kyung Cha, *Dictee* (New York: Tanam Press, 1982).

20. Ibid., 45.

21. Ibid., 118.

22. Dziga Vertov, "The Vertov Papers," in *Apparatus* (New York: Tanam, 1981), 9.

23. Two notable poems by Leung, "After the 'Three Characters'" and "A Symphonic Poem 'Unfinished,'" are reprinted in *Premonitions*. He seems to have vanished after the publication of his poems in *Bridge*.

24. Walter K. Lew, introduction to *Bridge* (winter 1983): 11.

25. Walter K. Lew, *Excerpts from ∆ikth/ 딕테 / 딕티 / DIKTE for DICTEE* (1982) (Seoul: Yeul Eum Press, 1992), 14. See also my analysis of this book, "A Search for Lost Time: A Review of Walter K. Lew's *Excerpts from ∆ikth/ 딕테 / 딕티 / DIKTE for DICTEE* (1982)," *Korean Culture* 15.1 (spring 1994): 18–25 (a publication of the Korean Cultural Center in Los Angeles).

26. Walter K. Lew, "The Movieteller," *Chain* 3.2 (fall 1996): 90–97.

27. Myung Mi Kim, interview in *Tripwire* 1.1 (spring 1998): 79.

28. Myung Mi Kim, *Dura* (Los Angeles: Sun and Moon, 1998), 43.

29. Ibid., 55.

30. A more detailed consideration of Cha, Lew, and Kim, along with Cathy Song, appears in "Korean American Poetry," *Korean Culture* 18.4 (winter 1997): 4–16.

31. *JES* 7.2 (1979): 1.

32. *JES* 7.2 (1979): 7.

33. *JES* 8.4 (1980): 56.

34. Lawson Fusao Inada, "Listening Images," in *Legends from Camp* (Minneapolis: Coffee House Books, 1992), 69.

35. Lawson Fusao Inada, "Legend of the Humane Society," in *Legends from Camp* (Minneapolis: Coffee House Books, 1992), 9.

36. For reasons of space I have had to exclude discussion on Roy Miki and Gerry Shikitani.

37. Christian Bök, "Oneiromechanics: Notes on the Dream Machine of Roy Kiyooka," *West Coast Line* (1995): 25.

38. Eva-Marie Kröller, "Roy Kiyooka's 'The Fountainebleu Dream Machine': A Reading," in *Canadian Literature*, no. 113–14 (summer 1987): 48.

39. Roy Kiyooka, *Pacific Windows* (Vancouver: Talonbooks, 1997), 117.

40. Ibid., 304.

41. From "Gotenyama," in Kiyooka, *Pacific Windows* (Vancouver: Talonbooks, 1997), 229.

42. From "Struck from the Heat of a Cold December Sun," in Kiyooka, *Pacific Windows* (Vancouver: Talonbooks, 1997), 179.

43. Fred Wah, "Speak My Language: Racing the Lyric Poetic," ms. copy, n.d, n.p. (Although I quote from an unpaginated manuscript copy, Wah's essay appears in the 1995 volume of *West Coast Line*.)

44. Ibid.

45. Fred Wah, *Selected Poems* (Vancouver: Talonbooks, 1980), 28.

46. Fred Wah, *Music at the Heart of Thinking* (Alberta: Red Deer College Press, 1987), preface.

47. Fred Wah, *Alley Alley Home Free* (Alberta: Red Deer College Press, 1992), 5.

48. Fred Wah, *So Far* (Vancouver: Talonbooks, 1991), 10.

49. Jam Ismail, *Many-Mouthed Birds* (Vancouver: Douglas and McIntyre, 1991), 124.

50. From Jam Ismail's "from the Diction Air," as cited in Fred Wah's "Speak My Language." The original text, like most of Ismail's work, is self-published.

51. Wah, "Speak My Language," unpaginated manuscript.

52. Several short paragraphs on younger writers such as Barry Masuda and Hoa Nguyen have been cut because of space limitations.

53. Sianne Ngai, "Raw Matter: A Poetics of Disgust," *Open Letter* 10.1 (winter 1998): 102 (Ngai's italics).

54. Jeff Derksen, "Making Race Opaque: Fred Wah's Poetics of Opposition and Differentiation," *West Coast Line* (1996): 76.

55. Tan Lin, "Interview for an Ambient Stylistics," *Tripwire* 1.1 (spring 1998): 40.

FORMS AND APPROACHES

7 | Avant-Garde without Agonism?

Daniel Barbiero

One of the remarkable things about the currently emerging poetics is the manner in which it is undertaking its own self-definition. A number of statements have been circulating recently—statements on poetics by promising writers such as Mark Wallace, John Noto, Lew Daly, Susan Smith Nash, and Jefferson Hansen. Although each statement reflects the particular concerns of its writer, all seem to share one underlying question: in what does (can) an avant-garde poetry now consist? The answers suggested to this question are, again, as varied as the writers offering them and cover a number of overlapping fields, for example, the role within poetry of theory and social criticism, the poetic influences of subjectivity and identity, the relationship between lived experience and language, and other concerns. Of particular interest, though, are the ways in which (some) emerging writers define themselves in relation to current and past formal structures and possibilities, both avant-garde and other.

In and of itself, there is nothing remarkable about up-and-coming or newly established experimentalists attempting to define themselves—one might even suggest that such self-definition is something of an obligation. What is remarkable, though, is the appearance of an attitude that has been articulated in varying—sometimes radically varying—ways in such programmatic statements as Wallace's "On the Lyric as Experimental Possibility"[1] and Noto's outline of a poetic "New Synthesis"[2] among others. That attitude is one of synthesis or syncretism concerning the formal relation between emerging work and the work of the current avant-garde and others. Within the emerging new writing there seems to be, in short, an avant-garde without agonism—although, as we will see, agonism has hardly disappeared.

Agonism

In his important work *Theory of the Avant-Garde*,[3] Renato Poggioli has suggested that agonism is an essential feature of avant-garde movements. Poggioli's definition of *agonism* is of struggle and sacrifice—the self-sacrifice of the artist in the interests of the future. In short, "agonism means tension" (66). Although I would agree that agonism historically has been an important element in avant-gardism, I would modify the definition to eliminate the element of sacrifice and indeed, of fatalism, that Poggioli puts at its center. (Poggioli's definition, it must be remarked, is heavily indebted to his reading of Italian futurism and his corresponding tendency to take futurism as exemplary of avant-gardism in general.) I would instead suggest that agonism is the attitude of tension between an emerging experimentalist or group of experimentalists and those tendencies, whether or not they are (or were) avant-garde, that are taken to define the situation in which those emerging experimentalists find themselves. Agonism, in other words, is differentiation that defines itself in struggle.

I would add that agonistic opposition frequently is animated by a moral, or quasi-moral, urgency. The target of agonistic struggle is rejected not only on technical or methodological grounds but on aesthetic, political, or even religious grounds that are if not morally derived at least morally couched. The tendency that is to be rejected is not simply inappropriate or irrelevant but rather is in fundamental error; it is corrupt or corrupting.

A good, and as far as new poetics is concerned, particularly relevant, example of agonistic definition-through-opposition can be found in Charles Olson's manifesto of projective verse. Olson opens with an immediate delineation of sides: "PROJECTIVE VERSE vs. the NON-Projective."[4] From the outset Olson makes clear that his breath-based "projectile percussive prospective" poetics should be distinguished from the closed, print-bound, English and American "verse now, 1950." What is striking is not so much Olson's target—who, really, would want to declare in favor of "closed verse"?—but that his poetics is framed right at the outset in terms of the relation signified by the preposition *versus* and carries an urgency conveyed by Olson's use of typography and syntax.[5]

When I defined *agonism* as consisting in the tension between an emerging avant-garde and the tendencies "that are taken to define" the existing situation, I used a deliberately vague, passive construction. My reason for doing so is that agonism is a plural phenomenon arising from the perceptions of the emerging avant-garde and others. A new avant-garde erupts at the point of convergence of a multiplicity of social and cultural formations, the features of which some, more than others, will appear—to the emerging avant-garde or to its interested and disinterested observers—salient and thus worthy of adversarial engagement. Agonism, in other words, need not be directed exclusively (or even at all) toward an entrenched avant-garde. On the contrary, what is at issue is the definition of one's art (or one's group) over and against the given, and the given may consist as much in the products and processes of the larger culture(s) as in those of the current or most recent avant-gardes. The futurists, for instance, issued manifestos denouncing the corrupting influence of the "passéism" they saw not only in D'Annunzio's novels and poems but in what they held to be Italy's encompassing culture.[6] The early surrealists, as spoken for by Breton's *First Manifesto of Surrealism*, defined themselves against the realist attitude that manifested itself in the multiple domains of science, art, and literature—particularly, as far as the latter was concerned, in the novel, against which Breton displayed a special moral vehemence.[7] More recently the Beats defined themselves in opposition not only to the academic and literary establishments centered on, among other journals, the *Partisan Review* and the *Kenyon Review* but to the larger society's postwar habits of consumption and conformity as well. An analogous opposition to the surrounding culture, frequently (although by no means always) articulated in terms of the normatively derived political categories of Marxism, has, of course, been a conspicuous aspect of the work of a number of the writers grouped, for whatever reason, into the "language" school.

But the adversarial stance of much language-centered writing was directed as much against then-current poetics as it was against larger social formations. In fact the language-centeredness of "language" poetry can be understood as a manifestation of agonism directed toward, in Charles

Bernstein's words, "Realist & mimetic ideas about poetry."[8] By designating language as the site of poetic struggle, a number of language-centered writers effectively questioned the conditions underlying the possibility of poetics and, by extension, the legitimacy of those poetics. This comes out very clearly in Bernstein's early writings on semantics and the representational capacity of language[9] and in Silliman's essays in *The New Sentence*—particularly the title essay—which develop the idea of a poetics based on a reworking of syntactic structures and the corresponding reconfiguration of the relation between sound and sense.[10] Interesting in this context is Silliman's acknowledgment that the criteria he used for selecting the poets to appear in the *American Tree* anthology imbued that work with an "air of militancy"[11]—a militancy that, in its de facto self-definition in terms of opposition, was consummately agonistic. No less agonistic is Silliman's assertion, offered in the essay "Of Theory to Practice," that "a poetics is articulated only to be broken" (*NS* 60). (Interestingly, this statement hints at the self-sacrifice integral to Poggioli's definition of agonism.)[12]

Contrast Silliman's aphorism with this statement by Mark Wallace: "For many emerging writers, the previous . . . avant-garde poets—language writers and others—are . . . not figures to reject."[13] Quite the contrary, for as Wallace emphasizes in an essay on "language" poetry bashing,[14] many of the possibilities open to the new writing have been afforded by the intellectual infrastructure, as it were, that the "language" poets put in place. This infrastructure consists in both accumulated formal devices as well as a practical domain structured by the interactions of, and examples set by, its practitioners. Jefferson Hansen reinforces this point when he declares that *"The creative act is preceded by a community formed by shared assumptions or beliefs about what constitutes valuable artistic products."*[15] If a number of emerging experimental writers (tentatively) can be identified as an avant-garde without agonism, it is because they understand that certain (contingent) aspects of their emergence depend on a field already constituted both synchronically (in terms of the community already in place) and diachronically (in terms of the evolution of poetic forms available for appropriation and reconfiguration). Again, as Hansen puts it, *"Truly new writing carries the aesthetic* assumptions and beliefs of [a group of writers] into new territory. . . . Such writing challenges or even attacks a few of the assumptions of this group, but remains within it because it accepts those most deeply held" ("Mainstream" 206). It is in this context that Susan Smith Nash's recent defense of "language" poetry[16] can be understood—as an apologia for precisely those assumptions that in many respects continue to be most deeply held.

If agonism is about the (often selective) exclusion of influences or practices that, for whatever reason, are considered worthy of rejection, John Noto's poetics of the "New Synthesis" is explicitly about inclusion. In a piece defining the New Synthesis Noto declares his wish to draw from the "streets, malls and video screens of mid-90s America" ("Synthesis" 16) and from there to respond to the plurality of domains he inhabits. These include "alternative music, third world cultures, cybernetics, day hikes in the redwoods, the city streets, overheard fragments of conversation, data trash and contemporary cutting-edge visual/multimedia arts" ("Synthesis" 17). If Noto rejects the exclusive use of the compositional habits associated with language-centered and "Broken Lyric" poetics, it is not because they are held to be deficient or erroneous in and of themselves but because they don't "blow enough light" ("Synthesis" 19). Such rejection, it seems to me, is not qualitative (that is to say, agonistic) but rather quantitative: Noto's objection seems to be directed largely at the formal and thematic exclusiveness implicit in "pure" language-centered writing. If we are to take the New Synthesis at its word and through its examples, we can attribute to it a pluralist nonagonism vis-à-vis the encompassing cultures—and one that would seem neatly to reverse the multiple agonisms of the historical avant-gardes mentioned above.

Verwindung

If a noticeable portion of the new avant-garde can be characterized negatively as not holding an attitude of agonism toward the given—whether that given is understood in terms of established avant-garde practices or the cultural artifacts of the non-avant-garde—how can it be characterized positively? To answer this question I look to Heidegger's concept of

Verwindung, as interpreted by Gianni Vattimo.[17] As Vattimo points out in "Verwindung: Nihilism and the Postmodern in Philosophy,"[18] the basic meaning of the noun *Verwindung* is "distortion," and the verb from which it derives—*verwinden*—means "twist" or "to get over." What these meanings have in common is the notion of a change of state, which Vattimo paraphrases as "transformation." What interests Vattimo most about this transformation is its implicit sense of surpassing and/or recovery.[19] Although Vattimo likes to emphasize *Verwindung* as a convalescent recovery, his use carries the force of recovery as a gathering in or salvaging of a thing that is attenuated or broken. Thus if *Verwindung* is a transformation, it is one that gathers in as it transforms, while nonetheless managing to distort that which it transforms. The kind of transformation implied in *Verwindung* is not based on a necessarily antithetical—and thus agonistic—relation.

Although Vattimo emphasizes the aspect of convalescence embedded in *Verwindung*, I would like to emphasize a different aspect of the term, one that Vattimo does not mention. This aspect derives from a colloquial meaning of *verwinden*, which is "to get the better of," which I would like to twist (distort?) into the related "to use to advantage." (There is a certain irony here that does not escape me: a secondhand term has now become thirdhand—and is applied to a field for which it was not originally intended—which in itself represents a kind of *Verwindung*.) I emphasize this meaning because I believe it underlies the point at which Vattimo and the nonagonistic avant-garde diverge. For Vattimo the acceptance implicit in *Verwindung* brings with it a certain resignation or sense of belatedness. Far from expressing a sense of resignation, though, Wallace, for example, has stated the desire to seek "ways of incorporating, without being subservient to, the insights of [previous] generations" ("Emerging" 8). This statement implies acknowledgment that previous generations' having had insight does not create necessary and sufficient conditions for forcing a resigned subservience on those who, through no fault of their own, come afterward.

If resignation does not allow a subsequent generation to use to advantage the insights of an established or past generation, neither does outright dismissal. In fact, a number of emerging writers do not see the choices facing them as consisting in the either/or of resignation versus dismissal, and it is this attitude that characterizes not only these emerging writers but the outlook of *Verwindung* generally. In this regard the fact that Hansen has written a piece almost entirely devoted to the dismissal of dismissal is telling.[20] For at least some of the emerging avant-garde, the contingency of their own position within an already constituted field—and not the dismissal of that contingency—is precisely what allows them to get the better of, by using to advantage, the forms and structures of the past(s). The past may be felt as a constraint, but it is felt as an enabling constraint—and one to be transvalued, when appropriate.

In borrowing Vattimo's reading of *Verwindung,* then, I mean to characterize (among other things) a transvaluation of the past in terms of which the new is understood not as logically entailing a rejection of the past but rather as necessitating a deepening engagement with precedent. The category of "the new" is almost always a normative category and rarely one providing purely descriptive criteria simply for locating a point along a temporal continuum. And in fact the most striking way in which the emerging avant-garde manifests its antiagonism is in its revision of the avant-garde attitude toward the new. Wallace again: "The new is made by borrowing from, changing, refiguring, perhaps demolishing the past" ("Lyric" 2). As this statement implies, the value of "the new" is no longer seen to consist only or primarily in novelty but in the capacity to open art out to an increased complexity and a renewed possibility ("Lyric" 2).

The transvaluation of "the new" as a normative category has its roots in the emerging avant-garde's reconceptualization of the notion of time. Time is no longer thought of as tracing a single line of development toward a given and perhaps predestined end (which, it must be remembered, can only be grasped as such after the fact); instead, the diachronic aspect of history generally, and any given field specifically—including and especially poetics—is seen as consisting in a multiplicity of purposes and techniques, some currently in use and some not. Epitomizing this view is Hansen's blunt admonition to "give up on the notion of 'avant garde' linear progression" ("LPBII" 3). In short, the model of a unitary history embodying progress no longer commands belief. This is a recognizably, if not emblematically, post-modern position. But one might well ask how one can dislodge the notion of progress and retain the notion of an avant-garde at the same time. For the definition of *avant-garde* would have to be based on some criterion of progress—an advance guard has to advance toward something, it would seem. It is beyond the scope of this essay to argue for or against the appropriateness of "avant-garde" as a description for the emerging poetics under discussion; it should be noted, however, that the abandonment of the "myth of progress" ("LPBII" 3) does render the term *avant-garde* problematic.[21]

Be that as it may, the emerging poetics' transvaluation of the past finds expression in what I would call the rhetoric of *Verwindung.* This rhetoric consists not only in a certain vocabulary but in the rehabilitation of terms that have, for whatever reason, taken on negative overtones. The vocabulary of *Verwindung* can be found in Wallace's call to explore "refigurings" of the lyric ("Lyric" 3), in Noto's call for a "return" to poetic lyricism,[22] in the claim by the editors of *Art of Practice* that their anthology represents, to some extent, poetry's past "rediscovered" (*AP* xiv), and again, in Hansen's assertion that new writing "remains within" certain conceptual and pragmatic constraints ("Mainstream" 206). It seems to me that all these terms—*refigure, return, rediscover, remain*—have in common the sense put across by the morpheme *re-*, which, when prefixed to a verb, carries the force of "to do anew."[23] The message seems to be that Pound's famous dictum, "Make it new," should be rewritten as "Make it anew." The difference is subtle but substantial.

Perhaps the most striking of terms to be rehabilitated are *derivative* and *imitation.* These terms appear in Wallace's "Lyric"—not as terms of opprobrium but as words describing, respectively, a quality and an activity, both of which, far from representing a failure of imagination or method, are in fact "unavoidable" ("Lyric" 2). As hinted in Wallace's article, derivation in poetics would appear to be analogous to derivation in logic or mathematics—it is a process of extracting a consequence from previous accepted assumptions or methods. Similarly, imitation seems to be understood as a method of acquiring and developing competence.

To be sure, the rehabilitation of terms such as *derivative* and *imitation* has resulted from the deeper assumption, mentioned above, that progress, as a normative category, is not appropriate to art and literature. But I think the reevaluation of the place of derivation and imitation in artistic formation reflects a more realistic view of how a discipline or method or artistic community develops and asserts influence on, and is influenced by, its practitioners. This is a view more realistic than the myth, rightly or wrongly associated with high modernism, of absolute originality. To acknowledge the role of imitation and derivation is to acknowledge, even if implicitly, the often overlooked roles played by apprenticeship, the authorial function as a guarantee of competence,[24] and sheer historical accident as crucial factors in literary domains.

To anyone who has followed the visual arts during the last two decades or so, or academic music in the decade prior to that, the notion of an avant-garde without agonism will not seem wholly strange. The willingness of contemporary poets to use a spectrum of devices without undue prejudice recalls German and Italian painting of the late 1970s and early 1980s, which saw painters self-consciously working within, for example, older traditions of figurative painting. In this art there was little of the irony (and even sarcasm) that marked the roughly contemporary American excursions into past art forms—for whereas American appropriation art seemed to (re)take old forms (and indeed even entire works), the message was that these forms were no longer possible. By contrast, Italian Anacronismo, German neoexpressionism, and related efforts showed that there was still a possibility of producing valid work using old forms.

In a sense it would appear that poetry (and poetics as well) is lagging behind the visual arts and music, but I think that this is the wrong way to look at it. The dominance throughout the 1980s and early 1990s of language-centered writing among a significant sector of the avant-garde may have postponed the kinds of reckoning that preoccupied visual art and music during that decade, but such dominance seems to have been the result of the coming to maturity of a path of inquiry that was still fruitful and still opening up technical possibilities.

I do not want to suggest that all of the emerging avant-garde has abandoned agonism altogether. On the contrary, the desire to define oneself implies at least a measure of setting oneself apart in that one by necessity defines oneself in terms of, and in contrast to, one's immediate predecessors. This is apparent even in the most pragmatic of the emerging poets, who reserve the right to a certain selectivity in their formal (and other) appropriations from the previous avant-garde and elsewhere. Yet what Poggioli would recognize as an exemplary manifestation of agonism is by no means absent from emergent poetics, as can be seen in Lew Daly's *Swallowing the Scroll*.[25] This self-consciously visionary document is remarkable in a number of ways—not least because of its deliberately archaic style of presentation, which recalls something of the seventeenth-century controversialists.

Swallowing the Scroll is a book-length interpretive essay that offers theologically inspired readings of two poems: Susan Howe's "The Nonconformist's Memorial" and John Taggart's "Rothko Chapel Poem." Beyond this, though, it is an agonistic attack on the current avant-garde—indeed, it proclaims its "resistance to current trends in the literary avant-garde" (*Swallowing* 84), hints at a generational struggle within that avant-garde (*Swallowing* 8, 47, 48), and has as its stated goal the promotion of an "irreconcilable but revitalizing rift" within the avant-garde, which would result in its "categorical . . . uprooting" (*Swallowing* 8). Consequently, attacks on the established avant-garde of language-centered writing are frequent, especially in the first and last sections of the essay. The most basic charge is that this avant-garde's "moment of discovery has passed" and that the result has been a stale "one-dimensionality at the level of practice" (*Swallowing* 84), on account of which the poetics of the "'play' of signifiers" has degenerated into a "dogma" (*Swallowing* 25). Further, Daly calls "preposterous" the influence on an English-language avant-garde of models taken from Russian formalism and European structuralism (*Swallowing* 22) and declares that "[l]anguage is not constitutive, nor is what it operates within circumscribed by it" (*Swallowing* 91). With this last statement Daly has, of course, cut right to one of the deeper assumptions of the language-centered avant-garde.

In addition to its critical program *Swallowing the Scroll* puts forward a constructive program advocating a new orientation for poetics. But even this constructive program is presented in a series of countermoves aimed against the established avant-garde. Thus the normative conception of language that Daly develops over the course of the essay is introduced in terms of a deliberate rejection of the current avant-garde's "textualized" language. Against this textualized language Daly advocates a prophetic language that would embody an "auditory breakthrough . . . [transmitting] both the face and revelation of a God in history" (*Swallowing* 63). Against language-centered writing's structuralism Daly calls for a poetic language that would be "experienced as a redistributive tribunal, rather than as a shifting code" (*Swallowing* 48); against language-centered writing's emphasis on the materiality of language, Daly insists on a "radically transparent language" to be used for an "address to the other" (*Swallowing* 91). The either/or choice Daly thus offers is between what he considers the current avant-garde's "reflective mimesis of the virtuality and atomization of language in an information age" and a "theological idea of language as influx" of the non-(or pre-)linguistic (*Swallowing* 23).

As even a cursory reading of *Swallowing the Scroll* will show, the essay's agonism is highly developed and forcefully articulated. What is most striking, though, is the extent to which this agonism contains a moral urgency that is manifested in an uncompromising, religiously derived rhetoric of judgment and guilt. This rhetoric, perhaps most dramatically voiced in the call for a "vast expiation" on the part of the avant-garde for its "betrayal" of the sacred tradition (*Swallowing* 84), derives from Daly's commitment to a "heterodox, largely Protestant religious tradition"—a tradition that, he emphasizes, has been "rejected by the dominant mainstream *and* oppositional poetry worlds alike" (*Swallowing* 55). Such marginality—and here I think this overused word truly applies—breeds nothing so much as combat, and thus Daly describes his position as "[b]urdened on all sides by compromise and nominalism" (*Swallowing* 9) and speaks, presumably approvingly, of the "terrorism" of the prophetic tradition he wishes to invoke (*Swallowing* 56).

Interestingly, Daly's essay is permeated with the call to self-sacrifice, which, recall, is an essential element of Poggioli's original concept of agonism. For Daly, self-sacrifice is a function of the openness to alterity, and consequently poetry is imagined as consisting in self-sacrifice on the altar of the other person (*Swallowing* 86)—an other person who "may only be glimpsed in masochism" (*Swallowing* 92). Daly goes even further and suggests that Masada would provide the proper model for the coming community of theologically inspired poets (*Swallowing* 16). To drive this point home, he closes the essay with the statement "*we will be gathered for a martyrdom*" (*Swallowing* 96, Daly's emphasis).

Despite his declared rejection of much, if not all, that is crucial to language-centered writing, Daly does seem to share at least some of language-centered writing's most deeply held assumptions (to borrow Hansen's expression). For Daly declares the necessity of a poetry that would reverse the slide into anonymity and "the effacement of meaning within the regime of capital" (*Swallowing* 21). This last formula sounds remarkably like a restatement of Silliman's basic assumption regarding the effacement of meaning as a consequence of commodity fetishism. Further, Daly's claim that language is "in the first instance always piped-in from the superstructure" (*Swallowing* 22) seems to assume the same kind of social constructivism that animated much language-centered writing. And like a number of the "language" poets, Daly accepts a radical antisubjectivism, proclaiming at one point that "a primary source of . . . violence may lie in the very instance of having a view" (*Swallowing* 48), that is, in subjective consciousness.

Just as interesting as Daly's sharing of assumptions with language-centered writing is his sharing of other assumptions with other emerging writers. Both Daly, on the one hand, and Wallace, Hansen, and others, on the other, would seem to agree on the fundamental value of preserving alterity and on the central importance of avant-garde communities for the development of new writing. The centrality of alterity to Daly's poetics has already been shown; comparably, Wallace has expressed his discomfort with the objectification that may follow from lyric address ("Lyric" 2). All of these writers' attitudes toward community are complex and often ambivalent, but it is an issue that has been addressed in virtually all of the statements I have been drawing upon over the course of this discussion.

Coda

I have been concerned here to show a trait that I think is shared by a number of emerging avant-garde writers. I do not mean to imply that there is profound agreement among these writers about all the issues important to avant-garde poetics. In restricting my scope to programmatic statements, I have, regrettably, not mentioned emerging writers who have not issued such statements. Nor have I attempted to examine these programmatic statements in light of the poetry actually being produced by these and other emerging writers.

In the end it is important to acknowledge the extent to which the emerging avant-garde is motivated by a genuine desire for a breakthrough. The nonagonistic openness to the past and to a plurality of influences is, if anything, an attempt to forestall epigonism—and, paradoxically, is no less an attempt than that associated with the agonistic struggle against those same influences.

Notes

1. Mark Wallace, "On the Lyric as Experimental Possibility," *Witz: A Journal of Contemporary Poetics* 3.2 (spring 1995): 1–3, 10. Subsequent internal cites will be to "Lyric," followed by page number.

2. John Noto, "Synthesis: Nova—The Thermodynamics of Broken Lifestyles Collapsed into Timeless Gene-Pool Mandalas Bifurcate into Smart Grooves [The Ambient Muse—Live!]," *Juxta*, no. 2 (1995): 16–20. Subsequent internal cites will be to "Synthesis" followed by page number.

3. Renato Poggioli, *The Theory of the Avant-Garde*, trans. Gerald Fitzgerald (Cambridge: Harvard University Press, 1968).

4. Charles Olson, *Selected Writings* (New York: New Directions, 1966), 15. All subsequent quotes are from the same page.

5. For examples of agonism in the visual arts see the various manifestos collected in Herschel B. Chipp's *Theories of Modern Art* (Berkeley: University of California Press, 1968). Nor is agonism restricted to art and poetics: Randy Allen Harris's *The Linguistics Wars* (New York: Oxford University Press, 1993) recounts the agonistic relationship of generative semantics to the Chomskyan linguistics that spawned it.

6. See, for example, "Contro Venezia passatista"; "La 'Divina Commedia' è un verminaio di glossatori"; "Contro Roma passatista"; "Trieste, la nostra bella polveria"; and others, in F. T. Marinetti, *Teoria e Invenzione Futurista* (Milan: Mondodori, 1983).

7. André Breton, *Manifestes du surréalisme* (Paris: Gallimard, 1966), 14–18. Interestingly, Proust is one of the authors singled out for denunciation.

8. Charles Bernstein, *The Artifice of Absorption* (Philadelphia: Singing Horse Press, 1987), 30.

9. See, for example, Charles Bernstein, "The Objects of Meaning: Reading Cavell Reading Wittgenstein," in *Content's Dream: Essays 1974–1984* (Los Angeles: Sun and Moon, 1986), 165–83.

10. Ron Silliman, *The New Sentence* (New York: Roof, 1987). Subsequent internal cites will be to "*NS*," followed by page number.

11. As he points out in his afterword to *The Art of Practice: 45 Contemporary Poets* (Potes & Poets Press, 1995), 372. Subsequent internal cites will be to *AP*, followed by page number.

12. But it is important to acknowledge the extent to which some "language" poets' agonism was tempered by a sympathetic understanding of their precursors. Silliman, in "Z-Sited Path," offers a nuanced and not unsympathetic reading of the lines of influence running from Pound and Williams and the vicissitudes that influence underwent as it was refracted through the New American poetry and later work of the Objectivists. And even Bernstein's quarrel with "official verse culture" does not prevent him from granting that there are some "remarkable works" to be found even there. See Bernstein, *Artifice*, 30, 68 n. 25.

13. Mark Wallace, "Emerging Avant-Garde Poetries and the 'Post-Language Crisis,'" *Poetic Briefs* 19, suppl. (August 1995). Subsequent internal cites will be to "Emerging," followed by page number.

14. Mark Wallace, *Poetic Briefs*, no. 13 (October/November 1993): unpaginated.

15. Jefferson Hansen and Mark Wallace, "Is This a Mainstream Dialogue?" *Central Park* no. 24 (spring 1995): 205–11, esp. p. 206 (emphasis in the original). Subsequent internal cites will be to "Mainstream," followed by page number.

16. Susan Smith Nash, "Language Poetry: Not Fit for Human Consumption?" *Juxta*, no. 1 (1994): 63–71.

17. Martin Heidegger, "Der Spruch des Anaximanders," in *Holzwege* (Frankfurt a.M.: Vittorio Klostermann, 1980); *Identität und Differenz* (Pfulligen: Neske, 1957). The English translators of "Der Spruch des Anaximanders" render the two appearances of *Verwindung* as "surmounting" and "transformation," respectively, whereas the translation of *verwinden* in *Identität und Differenz* is "turn." See "The Anaximander Fragment," in Martin Heidegger, *Early Greek Thinking*, trans. David Farrell Krell and Frank A. Capuzzi (San Francisco: Harper and Row, 1984), 47; and *Identity and Difference*, trans. Joan Stambaugh (New York: Harper and Row, 1969), 37.

18. In *SubStance* 16.2 (1987): 7–17. An earlier version of this article appears as chapter 10 of Vattimo's *The End of Modernity: Nihilism and Hermeneutics in Postmodern Culture*, trans. Jon R. Snyder (Baltimore: Johns Hopkins University Press, 1988).

19. Vattimo, "Verwindung," 11–12.

20. See Jefferson Hansen, "Language Poetry Bashing Part II," *Poetic Briefs*, no. 17 (August/September 1994): unpaginated. Subsequent internal cites will be to "LPBII," followed by page number.

21. There has in fact been some recent debate on this issue. See, for example, "Forum on the Avant-Garde (In Honor of David Antin)," *Poetic Briefs*, no. 14 (December 93/January 94): unpaginated.

22. John Noto, "Response to the Postmoderns (and Post-Punkers!)," *Talisman*, no. 11 (fall 1993): 188.

23. This is not to say that all of these terms mean the same thing or carry the same implications for a poetics.

24. For an examination of this topic see my "What Guarantees a Text? Authorship, Competence, and Imitation," in *SubStance* 75 (1994): 100–116. It should be noted that "competence" is not meant as the "right way of doing things" or as rule-following but rather as an outcome of becoming conversant with—and in the process converting—salient examples in a given domain.

25. Lew Daly, *Swallowing the Scroll: Late in a Prophetic Tradition with the Poetry of Susan Howe and John Taggart*, special issue of *apex of the M*, supp. no. 1 (1994). Subsequent internal cites will be to *Swallowing*, followed by page number.

8 | A Flicker at the Edge of Things: Some Thoughts on Lyric Poetry

Leonard Schwartz

A Poverty of Awareness

Experience teaches us that any state of awareness we manage to achieve is pretty soon after going to be buffeted by all sorts of waves intent on submerging it. Therefore, we are obliged to perpetually strive to keep our heads from vanishing underseas, at least if we want to maintain any modicum of self-consciousness, any cognitive hold over the world that presses in all around us. Unfortunately, we are not usually aware of this obligation to struggle or, if we are, never at the right moments; how could we be when it is precisely the forces of unawareness that these waves represent? So they bowl us over every time, and we are flung downward from the rocks without even offering the slightest resistance, without ever even knowing what hit us. A certain mood in this room, a saucer on a table hit by sun, a feeling of clarity or a turn in the conversation that yields up a revitalizing insight, perhaps even the flutterings of an imminent awakening . . . such fragile entities as these are easily dispersed, and you would think we would do all in our power to safeguard them. But as I say, we are caught unaware. The flood emanates from a point too near our vision for us to have guessed its presence. That is because the flood *is* us, or at least that aspect of a being that tends toward oblivion, that point at which a personality founders in its own oblivion. Ripples of a Nothingness at our very core, a Nothingness that cannot be conceived of without immediately being falsified as it is turned into something determinate by that conception, and that must therefore by definition remain outside our grasp even as all along it remains our own projection, this flood should not be understood in terms of the traditional concept of the unconscious, which is always active, but as a sort of sublime inertia we experience metaphorically as "waves," as activity, only to the extent we remain conscious that we are falling at all. To complain of this fall becomes a sort of mock imperative: if we were to lose hold of the consciousness of falling as well, we would pass over into Nothingness with an uncomplaining shiver and be shut up in the inert forever.

Of course, that possibility exists too. Indeed, because consciousness must always work to sustain itself, whereas its opponent, by definition inert, never must worry about running out of energy, in the long run one suspects oblivion must always win out and that even in the short run consciousness will not muster the necessary force to remain standing. And if it is true that clarity is so rare, then it follows that we are more essentially this oblivion than we are any clarity, that, therefore, we are most truly ourselves when we are emptied of everything, when we have been reduced to a husk, to a zero, to a mental condition distinguishable from stone only to the extent that an indefinable anxiety continues to make itself felt, an anxiety provoked by our failure to become stone, no matter how deep our stupor. Not able to remain lucid, not cut out to make it as rock, we do achieve a state of inertia that all the same apes stone to the highest degree of similitude. Almost any other state would have been preferable.

In this way we come to understand the phenomena of our stupors, of our speechlessness, of the bewilderment and the numbing of thought; they are the product of our inability to overcome our own projections of the void. But the source of our failure to form a unity with this failure, the source of this damning anxiety that maintains our humanity and costs us our escape? The enfeebled thought that we are not trying hard enough, that however murky the water, still, a little light ought to be able to get through, a little filtering ought to be possible, and therefore, that our enfeebled state of being can be overcome. A quavering voice that tells us to fix the bottom with a glance, to comb the seabeds with thoughts and words, especially with words, to negate negation, and to be happy with what we find. . . . It is as if our very cells have acquired the instinct to act on the presumption that words come equipped with these capacities, as if our very cells agitate against us when we begin to allow ourselves to drift, to recede, to wallow. . . . The word, revealing to the mind a vast plenitude, not the undersea Nothingness with which we are flooded; the word, lighting up the interior of things; the word, instrument of illumination, spark synonymous with the delirium of lucidity . . . such thoughts, in one watered-down form or another, perpetually torment us, nagging at the brain, creasing the forehead, preventing us from simply letting go, bottoming out. We attach such importance to the word, and always end up swamped—ultimately, of course, a much more traumatic experience than that of bottoming out. But giving up on the word—that would be even worse.

> I do not speak here of that river (Lethe)
>   you read to be an allusion
>   to ancient myth and poetry,
> though it too belongs to a story,
> but of a rushing underground in the very life-flow,
>   a sinking back,
>   a loss of the essential in the
> shadows and undertow—
>
> from which I come up into the daytime.[1]

Some Definitions

I have the impression sometimes that we are left with only one wealth: the wealth of the language, celebrated from all sides, in all manners of quality, quantity, and style. In spite of all complaint, language *is* rich, of which the richness of contemporary complaint is only a further proof. Indeed, the language has never been richer. Not with things—what language has to do with things is of course a very touchy subject: not with currencies—as is already clear I want to argue in large part that language is more than a commodity—but rich with possibilities, potentials, swirls of notion and image. I thought here to examine some of the current possibilities of *poetry*, that art most identical with language, and specifically to discuss the possibility for what I have referred to in several other essays and locales as *transcendental lyric*, a kind of poem that would reclaim, in as contemporary a way as possible, much of the ground that it is presumed poetry has lost to sophistication and to social science—a kind of lyric in the mode of Stevens's tune beyond us yet ourselves.

Transcendental lyric "involves an art in which language is used in such a way as to produce at least the illusion of the presence of regions of being outside personal experience, an art in which subjectivity is again given access to visions—and vision happens when image and idea are no longer separable, the contents of thought and the objects of the eye attaining a kind of synesthesia."[2] This recent comment of mine has elicited, among other things, a great deal of skepticism, the grounds of which are obvious and fair. By and large, the possibility of lyric in this mode is said to be "exhausted." (One thing I hope to show is that the notion of history on the basis of which the "exhaustion" comment is possible already implies the existence of a transcendental imagination: how could one make such judgments about the development and demise of a thing or an idea without the capacity to detach from the thing directly at hand, in order to see in it the entirety of its historical arc?) The dominant currents in American poetry today insist either on the exclusivity of the personal self, the empirical ego, or what I will call here the "the immediacy of the self" or simply "the immediate"; or else, and in direct opposition, the other dominant current, with another name and with other players, insists on the exclusivity of the material, social, and linguistic nexus from which the poem arises, a material and social nexus the poem sees itself as the subversion of, in a mode of composition I will therefore here refer to as "the negation of the immediate." To state the matter more simply: on the one hand, the daily self, posited in a routine and unproblematic manner, achieving its occasional epiphanies in a routine and unproblematic manner, glancing out the window at a bird or at a worm and seeing itself; on the other hand, those poetries influenced by very specific moments in the history of French structuralism and poststructuralism, in which a system of interlocking parts operates without an atomized self at its center or even at its edge taking notes, a system of socially grounded language that is analyzed into its constituent parts the better to be understood, subverted, or distorted, a kind of writing now referred to generically as Language poetry. Two epistemologies of the poem—the self at the window, finding its words in the need to express: or else the materiality of found and unfound (but equally immediate) language organized through an impersonal science or magic:—aspects of the same imperative of immediacy.

Of course the term *transcendental*—which I will posit as the successful synthesis of the self and the negation of the self, the immediate and the negation of the immediate—itself needs further explication. Stated baldly, it could mean anything, from Thoreau to TM, or could easily be confused with the term *transcendent*, meaning the object or being always outside or beyond the thinking self. By way of clarification let me say a few things about this term in Kant, in whom it originates; in Husserl, in whom it is turned into a tool of phenomenology; and in Hegel, in whom it becomes the possibility of understanding history; since it is mainly the technical usage made of the term in this continental tradition that interests me.

In *The Critique of Pure Reason* Kant states, "I entitle *transcendental* all knowledge which is occupied not so much with objects as with the mode of our knowledge of objects insofar as this mode of knowledge is to be possible a priori"; and again, "transcendental philosophy is therefore a philosophy of pure and merely speculative reason."[3] Explicating Kant: in order for us to be in a position to make observations of objects, let us say of that bird eating that worm on the other side of the pane of glass, certain conditions must pertain without which I could not perceive the bird or the worm, in this case the prior existence of space and time, conditions that themselves *are not objects*. What cannot be seen, touched, or heard, at least under any immediately recognizable definition of what it means to see, touch, or hear, but what must all the same be at work behind the scenes in order for us to carry on any of these ordinary activities of experience: these are in Kant the necessary and universal grounds that make observation possible, conceived of as a set of categories or principles. Philosophically, then, a transcendental investigation involves an investigation into the underpinnings of perception, into those preconditions that themselves cannot be perceived but without which there can be no perception. For Kant this investigation, although necessary, is in large part a "merely speculative" one, that is to say, a formal necessity that in many cases does not yield apodictic or certain results. Depending on whether we are reading *Transcendental Deductions A or B*, for example, it is unclear if apperception, or self-consciousness, plays any role or, if it does, on the basis of what faculty. But it is an investigation whose formal necessity cannot be denied, lest ordinary perception merely be taken for granted in all its ungrounded naivete. No doubt Kant's caution remains reasonable. On the other hand, in poetry we are less preoccupied with apodicticity, with universality, with the existence or nonexistence of categories, or even with knowledge, and it would suffice to employ techniques of the word that would produce enough of a rustle in perception to make us aware of that invisible set or sets of laws freely created from our own imaginations, our own rustlings, to use Kantian vocabulary. This region of consciousness—my thought as it passes over into a thought over and beyond myself, the impersonal imagination that is all the same my own—cannot be addressed by either the time-and-sense-bound self of the poem of observation and of personality or by the pure Language poem, if it be stripped of subjectivity altogether.

Edmund Husserl, founder of phenomenology, employs the term *transcendental* quite a bit in the late stages of his writing. Often this usage indicates his increasing sympathy for Kant, although there are some significant differences in the way he uses the word, as well as in Husserl's appraisal of what can be known, which is in general less cautious, and in which apperception is the foundation on which all other knowledge is necessarily based. In Husserl's *Cartesian Meditations* it is clear that what is transcendental about phenomenology is that it allows us to "suspend all claims about reality," that is to say, to "bracket experience." To bracket experience means that we are able to suspend belief in the existence or nonexistence of the objects around us and in the experiences overtaking us, the better to concentrate on what is apparently happening, regardless of whether the object or mental representation that we confront actually exists. For Husserl, to bracket experience in such a manner implies as its precondition a capacity of the mind to detach from the world of experience in order to examine it from a contemplative distance that in turn guarantees us freedom from the tyranny of appearances, from the representations that the natural and social world casts up in such rapid procession. What for poetry is often couched in the language of ecstasy, of standing outside oneself, in phenomenology is spoken of more soberly as a negating of the natural standpoint, a new lucidity. What does it feel like to experience the mind in detachment from immediate experience, in effect, to experience the freedom of one's own mind, and what would one hear and see in the process? Even if all detachment is actually a fiction, even if all clarity is actually a form of delirium, perhaps from the perspective of this fiction, of this delirium, consciousness once again becomes possible, and thinking can survive the various forces that flood it.

In the case of Hegel the concept of the transcendental is not only a tool of epistemology but also the active principle that makes both self-consciousness and history possible. For Hegel the True is the Whole, and the meaning of any position or stance toward oneself or other beings and things is intelligible only in relation to all other possible positions and stances. The fantastic system of Hegel's logic presents itself, then, as containing a transcendental deduction of all the attitudes that the human mind is capable of striking up toward nature, God, and itself. This Totality only becomes visible from the high wire of Hegelian dialectic, and the fact that every philosophical position coined since Hegel can seemingly be found discussed and sublated in a few pages of his work makes reading Hegel especially breathtaking. As the Idea weaves its way through *The Phenomenology Of Spirit*, for example, from *Sense-Certainty* to *Perception*, from *Lordship and Bondage* to the *Freedom of Self-Consciousness*, transcendental logic is revealed as the ground of an evolving subjectivity, and the spaces between opposing viewpoints are broken down. As is generally understood, Hegel's notion of the transcendental is actually a radical critique of Kantian modesty concerning the limits of apperception and of knowledge. For Hegel there is no limit that cannot be thought through because, as in Parmenides, being and thinking are identical. To be is to be thought, and by a principle of self-consciousness that is not itself a limited being in the simple subjective or objective sense. "Rather, being gives, shows, or uncovers itself in human discourse (we might say, in language), and Hegel's philosophy becomes both an account of this discourse and of the humans who speak it."[4] Reading Hegel today, one is still struck by a logic as undeniable, ambiguous, and arresting as that contained in the most powerful mythologies.

One might fairly ask, however, what any of this ancient intellectual history has to do with *the postmodern* and with contemporary American poetics. After all, in the postmodern condition, we are told, all are simulacra, all illusion. I can only assume that this must apply to programmatic skepticism as well, as part of the totalized set of repudiated beliefs. Even so, who can categorically reject the point of view that claims all content is flawed? It is true that all the grand systems have failed, but Hegel's failure may feel like our truth. Poetry, though, is other than system, other than belief. My argument here, then, is that poetry remains better equipped to carry the transcendental signifier than does philosophy because poetry remains closer to the living body and because it is perhaps precisely a matter of breathing life into illusions not hardened into beliefs just yet, and of breathing out what is poisonous to the imagination, until the illusion is as central as breath, until we can draw in the next one and then the next. The qualities of necessity, of "standing outside" oneself, of attempting to grasp the historical picture: all these figures of philosophical thought accrue to the contemporary lyric, just as all these qualities are considered "over." Everything is dead, no question. But when by definition everything is dead, by that same logic, nothing is dead. Above all, it is a question of overcoming our own projections of the void.

In the Dark

Robert Duncan's final book, *Ground Work II*, published in 1987, is an extraordinary work, and the last piece in that work is an extraordinary poem. Just as Duncan's first book, *The Opening of the Field*, opened things up to a range of new poetic utterances at a moment in the history of American poetry when such an opening in formal possibility was very badly needed, so too *In the Dark* has replenished the sense of lyric I have just been discussing, and the last poem, "After a Long Illness," has made that lyric actual, as if American poetry too were arising after a long illness. In conversation this January the poet Michael Palmer mentioned to me that Duncan had shown him "After a Long Illness" at a point after which Duncan himself had felt the writing had to have come to an end, at a point after which there could be no more writing—and that suddenly the poem had come to him, as if a coda, as if a final gift, as if after a long illness. Here are some key sections:

No faculty not   ill at ease
        lets us
        begin where I must

from the failure of systems   breath
        less,   heart
        and lungs water-logd.

. . . .

-I didn't have a prayer-   your care
        alone kept my love clear.

I will be there again the ways
        must become crosst and again
        dark passages,   dangerous straits.
My Death attended me and I knew
        I was not going to die,
nursed me thru.   Life took hold.

. . . .

In the real I have always known myself
        in this realm where no Wind   stirs
        no Night
turns in turn to Day,   the Pool of the motionless water.
        the absolute Stillness.   In the World, death after death.
In this realm,   no last thrall of Life stirs.

The imagination alone knows this condition.
As if this were before the War,   before
    What Is,   in the dark this state
that knows nor sleep nor waking, nor dream
    -an eternal arrest.[5]

There are many extraordinary things about this poem, of course, but the
most extraordinary is that it was written—extraordinary not only from the
point of view of the fragility of a life but also from the point of view of the
power of a language that is revealed as containing anew the field of possibil-
ities in which such a poem could be made and the wealth to make it stand.
Starting from the sickbed and the viscerally disintegrating body, the poem
ends by appealing to a form of reality prior to experience: and when there is
something prior to experience, what is of experience becomes that much
more terrible and amazing. In "After a Long Illness" there is an extraordinary
contiguity between the personal self and its impersonal ground, an oscillat-
ing border between the self and the limits of the self. Overlying this is an
extraordinary imaginative landscape in which the religious is specifically
rejected ("I didn't have a prayer") and the only solace comes from the human
other ("your care alone / kept my love clear")—right next to a motion of
thought that concludes with "the Pool of motionless water / the absolute
Stillness." Given this rejection of obvious religious hope, how does Duncan
come by this absolute, except by and through the composition of poetry
itself, in and through the imaginative activity of the word?

Certainly it is not enough for me to simply ride out the high emotion
of the poem, to replace argument with pathos. But for the moment I am at
a loss for any other means by which to make the case for the possibility of
the poem as Vision. *The imagination alone knows this condition.* If such writ-
ing as this does not provoke the contemplative distance that brings us
freedom from the tyranny of appearances, if such writing is not seen as
involving an investigation into the underpinnings of perception, if such
writing does not awaken a sense of what it means to be a historical being
aware of its own history only by reference to an absolute that it both is and

is not—"A tune beyond us, yet ourselves"—then the language is poorer than I had originally hoped. This of course is a possibility to which I am not oblivious. Above all it is a question of overcoming our own projections of the void.

A Hidden Mimetic?

The poet Charles Borkhuis provides me with three quotations with which to begin further reflections, each of which I find stimulating in its own way. The first of these quotes is from a recent poem of his entitled "Inside Language":

> a silent wind
> settles in
> behind the motion of naming
> collecting loose words
> at the corner of our lips
> where they masquerade
> as things
> a miniature world
> talks itself into being. . . .

This miniature world that talks its way into being—that is very strong, I think, and the general direction of Borkhuis's writing, that of a poetry that achieves Vision in and through language, "by talking itself into being," is one that I find quite sympathetic.

Second, Borkhuis begins a recent article in the literary journal *ONTHE-BUS* by stating, "It has become increasingly clear in recent years that most ground-breaking avant-garde work originated during the earlier part of this century, and that what avant-garde artists are drawing on today is a panoply of hybrids, a plurality of appearing and disappearing echoes and ghosts to whom they still remain deeply indebted."[6] This position is to my mind irrefutable.

The major thrust of his essay, however, lies in making a comparison between surrealism and Language Poetry. Although surrealism "postulates an ideal of absolute reality," whereas "Language poetry insists on a horizontal axis of multiple meanings and multiple I's," Borkhuis argues that "some curious parallels persist," that "[b]oth Surrealism and Language poetry are attempts to decenter the idea of the self as creator."[7] Writing specifically about a book of Bruce Andrews's titled *I Don't Have Any Paper so Shut Up (On Social Romanticism)*,[8] Borkhuis claims:

> Andrews' manic pulse redesigns the reader's body out of a giant switchboard, into which the author plugs and unplugs his disparate connections. Torn speech and constant interruptions dominate. . . . [Andrews's writing does not involve] the spark from Surreal juxtapositions that tends to turn us dreamward; it's more like the spark from a slap in the face that suddenly turns us public. . . . Andrews has invented a collage machine for writing that reflects the intricately coded, constantly interruptive nature of our high-tech communications with both ourselves and the world."[9]

What is of interest here is the last claim: that *Shut Up* is a poetry that *reflects* the intricately coded, constantly interruptive nature of high-tech communications and that such a poem may therefore well represent the technological veil it critiques—of interest, of course, because if this poem reflects anything, it forces us to conclude that in the final analysis it is as mimetic an art as the poetry of the immediate its author might claim to leave behind. What is being reflected in the mirror of art may differ in the two instances—in the conventional lyric, a pastoral scene perhaps, or more precisely a suburban one, while in the Andrews language poem, the experience of high-tech communication, a life of constant interruption—but both remain reflections or representations all the same.

I am not so sure the mimetic rationale for his poems offered up in the Borkhuis essay would be embraced by Bruce Andrews himself: but I do find it interesting that a clearly sympathetic reader like Borkhuis can arrive at such a conclusion in his article.

In some ways the Borkhuis reading of Andrews echoes Norman

Finkelstein's reading of a Charles Bernstein poem in Finkelstein's article "The Problem of the Self in Recent American Poetry." Finkelstein quotes from a Bernstein poem[10] and writes that what makes this poem more than a display of postmodern techniques is the way that the lyric "'I' reasserts itself about halfway through the text. Language poets admire Jack Spicer for the ghostly voices which disturb personal utterance in many of his books. In Bernstein's poem, just the opposite occurs, as out of the cacophony a relatively stable voice begins to speak, and quite movingly at that."[11] Again, my only insertion here is that it is quite interesting that such a reading is possible, a reading that claims not only reference takes place in the language poem, which is obvious and unavoidable, but also that stability, representation, a mirror-like reflection of the self are parts of this linguistic practice. Perhaps the achievement of Language poetry is to have created a new reproductive lingo, a new realism.

Is such an argument tenable, and what are its consequences? Certainly, any conclusions here are fragile and tentative, based as they are on other people's readings. All the same, the claim that "[t]orn speech and constant interruption dominate" in the poems of Andrews, and perhaps Bernstein, is defensible. Torn speech and constant interruption certainly characterize the way we live. Yet if language poetry intentionally or unintentionally turns out to be a reflection of this fragmentary state of modern urban affairs, then it also is another form of positivism; that is to say, it assumes a given reality prior to the work of language or composition itself, high-tech as that given reality may be conceived. This given forces the poem back to the plane of the immediate, even as the poem seeks to negate the immediate by the abstraction of its particular choice of a given. The impersonality of the poem is thus shipwrecked on the reef of a very particular experience of the everyday world—its interruptive quality. To be sure, this is an important quality of city life to reflect on, in whatever mode one feels able: and in no way do I even wish to argue against the desire to represent per se. All that would follow from this line of reasoning is that Language poetry cannot be considered *subversive*, as it claims itself, just as mimetic art in general cannot be considered subversive because it depends on the object it reflects, which comes first, because, that is, representation is always reactive, never active. A poem like Duncan's, on the other hand, striking out into the imaginative acts that make material experiences possible, stands a chance of being more subversive than the Andrews poem. Although at points in its development Duncan's lyric certainly employs representation, although his poems are not categorically committed to syntactic dishevelment, although the poem I quoted does not position itself in a self-consciously ideological manner, it does construct for itself a set of possibilities that can never be mimetically represented in their entirety because the absolute, even the simulacra of the absolute, can never be represented or reflected or reproduced, only translated into poetic language with which it is synonymous in the act of reference or talked into being by the process of composition or intimated as language, presented in thought, heard in the form of a rustling. And what cannot be represented, however obscure its form, is always dangerous because it cannot be made either to hold still or to go away.

One final point on Language Poetry. If it is true that this movement contains within itself the residue of the conventions it hopes to negate, it is also true that in some of its political as well as aesthetic proclamations, it contains an unacknowledged shadow of the notion of the transcendental I have attempted to invoke. The poet Ron Silliman, many of whose encyclopedic-like poems of perception are quite significant works, writes in *The L=A=N=G=U=A=G=E Book*: "But the words are never our own. Rather, they are our own usages of a determinate coding passed down to us like all other products of civilization, organized into a single, capitalist, world economy. Questions of national language and those of genre parallel one another in that they primarily reflect positionality within the total, historical, social fact."[12] In this passage Silliman, like Borkhuis and Finkelstein, insists that literature is a reflection of other forces. Of course Silliman's comment is more materialist in rhetoric and style. But anywhere we see the notions of totality and historicity invoked, we know we remain in the presence of the shadow of the Hegelian project: that there exists a point of view from which the totality is visible, from which the historical development of things, however convoluted that development, remains intelligible. How could the totality ever be invoked unless we were able to detach from the immediacy of the fragmentary material instant in order to grasp the whole? How glimpse the development of a thing or event except by standing far enough outside its swirl of particles to make out their arrangement? It hardly matters that detachment or even lucidity may themselves be only fantasies of the intellect, deliriums of the word. Positionality is only intelligible on the basis of a revelation of totality—and totality can never be grasped by a merely finite perception or from the natural standpoint. To be able to grasp the totality . . . it is up to us to make the words our own, to fill them with new meaning. To be able to say that everything is exhausted means at the same time that nothing is exhausted.

Rapture as Act

Speaking of something that is our own, or that is at least contemporaneous with us, I thought I might conclude by looking at a poem of a former instructor here at Stevens, the poet Joseph Donahue. To my mind his recent book, *Before Creation*, is a very important one. Indeed, the last piece in that book, a long poem entitled "Desire," achieves precisely the kind of visionary poetic called for here. Only Duncan's *In the Dark* and Ashbery's *The New Spirit* and *The Wave* stand ahead of it in terms of recent accomplishment in the region of metaphysical vision. Beginning with a cell in which one's thoughts circle back to Juan De La Cruz and his grimy dungeon, "Desire" seeks a liberty from the immediate and ends up in a place where sensation and feeling from time to time reveal their own inner logic. From a middle section:

> Desire a city across the water which the attrition of leaves
> makes visible or a time when place was simply the notation
> of silence as through smoke and rain millennia exfoliate.
>
> It's someone else's dream
> this bewildered amusement left on your tape
> this surprise party the world has arranged for you

and your life passes and you wait for the secret call
when the guests have arrived, you wait for
the one who will intimately mislead you through the rain.

Yes things seem to be happening
but far off and illegible like the bottom line of an eye chart.
You are frustrated in your search for some collapse of clarity

or deletion sufficient to break your
ritualized gestures of defeat, the way a sudden turn
toward intimacy in a conversation can resemble

a cycle of fire purifying your past.
But can you say what presses for entrance at the stern gate?
Now and then there is a flicker at the edge of things

canceling all disappointment
lifting you in the wave of others en route to work
as the world opens into amplitude and rushes into stillness.

You have lived in the expectation
of some startling recompense, like some secret
Spanish Jew enduring the Reformation you have tended

this law in silence, amid adversity.
Meaninglessness was simply a mood which bothered you
but now you appear to shiver in this chaste defilement,

this voluptuous schism revitalizing all thought.[13]

Let us take the poem seriously in terms of what it names. What is "this voluptuous schism revitalizing all thought"? On one level, no doubt, it is human desire, the defile from which we extend toward either ecstasy or despair, the basis of self-consciousness, a nothingness in and of itself, without which we are nothing in an even more profound sense. Human desire, then, is directed toward a city not beyond this earth but just across the water—the city we knew to be there all along but were too much a part of to notice. It is the attrition of leaves that now makes it visible: things die, to reveal the even greater presence of a more complex world behind them: negations of the immediate yield more than absence, they yield the possibility of distance itself. But when place ends up identical to "a notation of silence," we know too that we are at a remove from the ordinarily visible, that we are here dealing with vision on another level. Nor are we located in the dream, or at most in "someone else's dream," where the rag-tag amplitude of the world catches one by surprise: or is there any amplitude, anything or anyone at all to be found moving about in these distant but emotive regions? In "Desire" the mind fluctuates between inflation and depression, depression and inflation, from "ritualized gestures of defeat" to "a cycle of fire purifying your past." "Now and then there is a flicker at the edge of things / cancelling all disappointment"—this flicker at the edge of things must be the poetic line itself, an encapsulation of distance and memory flickering in the reaches of a language put to work, composition itself canceling all disappointment, a release most anyone who has ever written a poem is already aware of, an experience one indeed tends to in silence, amid adversity. This "voluptuous schism revitalizing all thought" is where one seeks to locate oneself, again and again, in order to shuck off the contingent, to find more than oneself, to be more than the hold the world has on that self as object.

Toward the conclusion of "Desire" Donahue writes:

> facts bespeak an altered emptiness
> and you sense a desire behind desire
> and to taste that

would be to know
the beauty God knew
the moment before Creation

when meanings mirrored
the need which evinced them.[14]

Again, to question the poem seriously: how is "emptiness altered"? Let me submit that this poem demonstrates that emptiness is altered by way of a rapture that does not recognize the limits imposed by knowledge (because knowledge always implies limits). Just as stupor is the relation to the world in which the desire to know has become most deeply frustrated, the world so far beyond comprehension that the subject is left at a loss, rapture too is a release from knowledge, accompanied however, by a sense of inflation: it is the moment in which we give up on ever knowing the hovering mystery even as we apprehend it on the verge of its rising before us. Rapture begins with the annihilation of the immediate in favor of the imaginary and is synonymous with this apprehension. To the extent that rapture is an act, it thrusts what is imagined into the field of vision. Nothingness fills with chimeras, with images without location. Yearning finds no place here; here it is a question of the mind having briefly overcome its nihilating projections. Our constructions vanish; the eye shines in meditation. Transcendental lyric is the poem written in the moment before the world of representations is created, before the trap of projection ensnares us, before the world we project upon gets its chance to fix us in place as bodies, objects, commodities. The imagination alone *alters* our condition.

Notes

1. Robert Duncan, "The Quotidian," *Ground Work II: In the Dark* (New York: New Directions, 1987), 11.

2. "Transcendental Lyric," in *Poetry Flash* (August 1991).

3. Immanuel Kant, *Critique of Pure Reason*, trans. Norman Kemp Smith (New York: St. Martin's Press, 1965), 59.

4. Stanley Rosen, *G. W. F. Hegel* (New Haven, Conn.: Yale University Press, 1974), 264.

5. Duncan, *Ground Work II*, 89–90.

6. Charles Borkhuis, "Writing from Inside Language: Late Surrealism and Textual Poetry in France and the U.S.," *ONTHEBUS* 8/9 (winter 1991): 268.

7. Ibid.

8. The quoted passage from the Andrews book reads in part: "The skull beneath the skin: wacs in slacks / tan shark sausages, don't live in Arkansas. The lynch mob and geriatric lynch / sponsors—one reason I like music so much is I can listen to it while I read, / baby wants / the slogan (says white woman) manage stress while you bathe."

9. Charles Borkhuis, "Writing from Inside Language," 269.

10. The quoted passage from the Bernstein poem reads in part:

> This darkness, how richer than a moat it lies. And
> my love, who takes my hand, now, to watch all this
> pass by, has only care, she and I. We deceive
> ourselves in this matter because we are in
> the habit of thinking the leaves will fall or
> that there are few ways of breaking the circuit.
> How much the stronger we would have been had
> not—but it is something when one is lonely
> and miserable to imagine history on your side. On
> the stoop, by the door ledge, we stand here, coffee
> in hand.

11. Norman Finkelstein, "The Problem of the Self in Recent American Poetry," *Poetics Journal* 9 (June 1991): 7.

12. Ron Silliman, "If by Writing We Mean Literature," in *The L=A=N=G=U=A=G=E Book*, ed. Bruce Andrews and Charles Bernstein (Carbondale: Southern Illinois University Press, 1984), 167.

13. Joseph Donahue, *Before Creation* (New York: Central Park Editions, 1989), 74.

14. Ibid., 77.

Kristin Prevallet

In 1976 a series of events-in-poetry occurred that catalyzed an ideological spill still felt in thought and in action twenty years later by practitioners of antiofficial verse. These events directed poetry away from a quest for transparent meaning and toward the revelation of source texts, procedures, and language experiments within the body of the poem itself. Poets refer to these events using a variety of terms, all of which can be contextualized within specific literary moments occurring before and after 1976. Because these terms were used to specify a particular movement in poetry—projective verse, Language poetry, investigative poetics, open-field poetics—they have been defined as oppositional and not at all reflective of one another. It will take the creation of an entirely new event-in-poetry to reinvestigate this and to bring the various terms into a useful poetic practice based not on opposition but mutual re-formulation.

1976: First Instance

In 1976 City Lights published Edward Sanders's book *Investigative Poetry*, which had been presented as a lecture at the Visiting Spontaneous Poetics Academy of the Naropa Institute in Boulder, Colorado, in the summer of 1975. Just before the table of contents, Sanders inscribes the unique purpose of investigative poetry: "that poetry should again assume responsibility for the description of history." Sanders designs new forms for poetic presentation based on Charles Olson's manifesto of projective verse. Sanders calls these forms "High Energy Verse Grids" or "Data Clusters" (*IP* 8). Through these grids or clusters the poet can be a historical scholar, embarking on a voyage through the world, with the facts, theories, statistics, and raw information transformed through the "bard's" singular voice into a "description of historical reality" (*IP* 7). The poet is a researcher, investigator, interpreter, singer, and prophet who engages in an active relationship with the political, social, and cultural forces around him or her. The poet is a manifesto-creating, opinionated, ranting, perpetual surveyor and tireless investigator of history. The poet is busy creating verse grids out of whatever materials are present before him or her at the time; the poet is an appropriator of sources, a thief of facts, a collage-creating scoundrel in a hyper state of awareness and inspiration. Flowcharts, newspaper articles, photographs, etymology, and ethnography become the raw materials for the poet's unique assemblage.

As with all great manifestos, Sanders's poetical goals are lofty and ambitious, outrageous and impossible:

> Investigative poetry is freed from capitalism, churchism, and other totalitarianisms; free from racisms, free from allegiance to napalm-dropping military police states—a poetry adequate to discharge from its verse-grids the undefiled high energy purely-distilled verse-frags, using *every* bardic skill and meter and method of the last 5 or 6 generations, in order to describe *every* aspect (no more secret governments!) of the historical present, while aiding the future, even placing bard-babble once again into a role as shaper of the future. (*IP* 11)

Although times and poets have changed, the impulse for poets to create an intellectual life for themselves that resists totalitarianisms has not. Sanders's theory, which in "Creativity and the Fully Developed Bard" he called "the multi-decade research project" (238), outlines a strategy for staying intellectually afloat for those who have chosen poetry as a means of living a life of the mind. The procedure is cumulative: pick a project that will take the next sixty years to research. Immediately begin by creating files for the project. As you read through the sources, begin taking notes in verse to be cut up and arranged as "fact strips" (244) on the page. Move them around until the fact strips become a sequence, a shape, a "data cluster" (244). Through this arrangement of data clusters you will slowly develop your own unique system for organizing information. As Sanders writes:

The look & feel
& the way you array
your information systems
in your Creativity Zone
has meaning
for your work. (248)

Once you get into the zone, you are able to create sequences of data and poetry anytime, anywhere, whether inspired or not, sick or healthy, stuck or in transit. The creative zone is not just a notebook filled with data clusters—it is an intellectual pursuit, a way of approaching life and being perpetually in tune with the world mix.

Sanders continues:

IT SHOULD BE THERE IN YOUR LIFE
so that
      in your best
            creative moments
you can spiffle
         through it
            for materials
        useful to your writing. ("Creativity" 256)

• RAPID EXPERIMENT #1: A ONE-DAY DATA CLUSTER RESEARCH PROJECT FOR THE YEAR 1976. SUBJECT: KRISTIN PREVALLET EXPERIMENTS WITH SANDERS'S PROCEDURE TO MINE HER MEMORY OF PERSONAL AND CULTURAL EVENTS.
I was ten years old
and knew nothing about
what it meant to be alive
in the year 1976:
    Highest rate of bank
    failures since 1933 and the economy

plummets to its deepest
recession since the Great
Depression when the federal deficit hits
a record $60 billion also President Ford is mocked
for his "Whip Inflation Now"
buttons while 10,000 Cuban
troops are airlifted to Angola
with USSR backing and back home
Cocaine becomes noticeably fashionable . . .
What I did know was that
July 4, 1976
was a bicentennial
celebration: 1776–1976
and since July 2 was my mother's birthday
there was no real difference
between the two.
My mother was not shy
nor was she particularly
patriotic. She was a
    beer-guzzling trout fisher
    tax evading "stop the arms race" marcher
    feminist angry letters-to-the-editor writer
    "sit on the tracks" to stop
    trainloads of plutonium
    en route to Rocky Flats
    a John Denver fan
    guitar strumming soloist
    maker of gigantic felt banners
    with cut-out "peace doves" and bumper-stickers
    proclaiming her religion:
    "Trust in God, She Provides"
    and "Adam was a Rough Draft."
There was plenty to be mad about

in 1976: I was forbidden
from watching *Charlie's
Angels* and could only
watch *Wonder Woman*
once a month.

    I was not aware of Leonard Peltier's
    arrest nor that the Stock Market topped
    1,000 while Steve Jobs was starting Apple
    Computer in his basement I didn't know
    that the FBI had burglarized
    the Socialist Party 92 times between 1960
    and 1966 or that Phil Ochs hung himself
    and an Earthquake destroyed
    the city of T'ang-shan nor did I know about
    10,000 students demonstrating in Soweto which left
    128 dead and 1,112 injured.

I did know that on July 4, 1976
America's bi-centennial birthday
my mother wore
    a red-white-and-blue American flag Oxford shirt
    a red bandanna around her neck
    knee-length cut-off jean shorts
    red-white-and-blue tube socks
    and blue tennis shoes
and I refused to be seen
with her in public.

1976: Second Instance

In May of 1976 Ron Silliman, Charles Bernstein, and Steve McCaffery
began a concentrated correspondence, which McCaffery later described as
revealing "many of the differences felt in the early struggles of post-referen-
tial conceptualization outside of academic discourse" (72–73). Although also

forging an intellectual space where poetry and theory converge to create a life of the mind, this group's procedures were antithetical to Sanders's ideas of "investigative poetics." In a 1977 letter to Steve McCaffery, Charles Bernstein wrote:

> What seems exciting abt our diad, to me, is that it doesnt simply use "cut-up" language or neologisms to create a unified field of meaning on one plane, but actually calls into play notions of variant simultaneously existing realms of discourse constantly criss-crossing, intersecting, creating new gells, new forms—very much the description that Wittgenstein uses to describe language—as a city with some streets straight & narrow, other windy &&&.
>
>   . . . the simple display of alternative forms of making meaning is alone not enuf—wrk that really attracts me has an impermeability that this open field is really counter to—while this stuff is an opening up that gives the mind plenty of room to move around, associate, pass over—what I mean by impermeable wrtng is its opacity, charged with an electric density you cant get through. (*Line* 73)

Wittgenstein, Derrida, Saussure, and Stein come together to forge the language poets' initial articulation of their "cipheral" poetics, with sharp ideological differences separating them from the projects of the New American poets, the Black Mountain poets, the ethnopoetics poets, and the investigative poets. The distinction between the l=a=n=g=u=a=g=e poets' concern with impermeability, opacity, and method over the investigative poet's concern with generating meaning and writing history is here noted. Also noted, however, is the crossover of interests in data, collage, appropriation, and cutups among both the l=a=n=g=u=a=g=e and the investigative poets. Both see the concept of witness as key to their process, although they define it quite differently:

> [*Bernstein*:] A friend recently sd that one of the strongest characteristics of my wrtng was a sense of *witness* . . . looking at yr life

go by while at the same time being in it is the way i've expressed it at times—wch actually is the attitude twrd language itself, the thing thru wch we experience, see things as one thing or another, as meanings. . . . "The record of observation" is not the "world" at least in the sense of the naive concept of the physical world . . . but an observing, a looking out onto, language. (*Line* 71)

[*Sanders:*] Nor shall we forget how the Chilean poet-singer Victor Jara was leading a group of singers while imprisoned in the soccer stadium following the 1973 CIA-coup in Chile, and the killers chopped off his fingers to silence his guitar, and still he lead the singing—til they killed him, another bard butchered because of the U.S. secret police. (*IP* 12)

These differing points of witness center primarily on how language is used to navigate through the "world." In 1976 the differences between how these two approaches were manifest in poetry was radical; in experimental poetry today the two approaches are combined to generate texts. A reflection of the structures of language, and the importance of a confrontational and emotional testimony of events, can now happen at the same time. Language used to witness is simultaneously a witness of language. In the antiofficial verse tradition the moving forward of thought and writing should not be in the prioritizing of one kind of thinking over another but in the process of absorbing multiple influences simultaneously.

Reading the Procedure

Providing a relevant analysis of this point are two poetic accounts of the year 1968: Tina Darragh's *adv. fans—the 1968 series* and Ed Sanders's *1968: A History in Verse*. Both texts are generated from the raw data of the year 1968, and both can be discussed as procedural poems. According to poet Jena Osman in a paper called "Can you tell me how to reduce 'long' simultaneously with 'fine'?: The Procedural Poetry of Tina Darragh and Joan Retallack," Darragh has collected words whose first usage occurred in 1968.

She made photocopies of pages from the dictionary, randomly tore and pasted one dictionary page over another, folded the pages into a fan, and finally, transcribed a section and then placed it "between two definitions attributed to having first been said in 1968" (qtd. in Osman 7). What is revealed by this procedural poem, writes Osman, is "a truly provocative insight into an era of American history. Most of the words first coined in 1968 are from the field of communications, science fiction, and sports: 'shot line,' 'tele-player,' 'teletransport,' 'shopper,' 'sidefoot,' 'tie-off,' 'washerette,' etc." (Osman 7). The dictionary sources of Darragh's investigation are revealed as a part of the poem, and what is exposed, according to Osman, is "a side of language that has previously been hidden/suppressed" (Osman 3). Osman wrote that Joan Retallack called Darragh's work "investigative poetry," saying that "there is the ability to identify with the playful inquirer setting out on an investigation and leaving markers along the way" (Retallack qtd. in Osman 6). These markers are the poet's tracks of investigation through newspapers, history books, dictionaries, or encyclopedias that appear ripped from their sources and worked into the body of the poem. Such use of source texts demystifies them as omnipotent, authorial, master texts. The investigative poet is tuned in to this fact and removes these sources from their referential status in order to challenge the manipulative language structures that reinforce the status quo.

• RAPID EXPERIMENT #2: A ONE-DAY LYRICAL FAN STRIP— RE. 1976. KRISTIN PREVALLET EXPERIMENTS WITH DARRAGHS'S PROCEDURE TO REVEAL A MULTIPLE FUNCTIONING OF LANGUAGE IN THE YEAR 1976.

The Procedure
1. Xerox "fake book" lyrics to songs from *Saturday Night Fever* and tear them into different shapes.
2. Xerox two articles from the first issue of *Mother Jones* (published Feb. 1976).
3. Paste the lyric strips randomly onto the *Mother Jones* articles.

4. Fold into a fan with varying pleat sizes.

5. Cut around the most interesting pleated clusters.

6. Transcribe, and place as answers to questions from the "TV QUIZ" found on page 49 of the first issue of *Mother Jones*. (Correct answers on page 86 of *Mother Jones*, Feb. Mar. 1976)

Q. What are the first two lines to the theme song of "Car 54, Where Are You?"

```
what wa
    th-er you're a
x women
d rapist
before he
son, twen
  -ev nos-
ated for wounds
    shoulder and arms
    detective
live,– Stay-in' Alive.–
```

Q. What was Jim Anderson's occupation on "Father Knows Best"?

```
-y break-in' and        women who do
justice. Yet I am     On July 18, 1975
ies of women who      at the time as "si
   anecdotes of the    knifed an accuse


                  Beach, Florida, b
   is frightening to      rested. John Dot
              I use - my wai-     ized and trea
-low and I - get high.- omach,
                  ng to
         Fe
           A-
```

Q. Who played Sgt. Garcia on "Zorro"?

```
At the heart of
fight lie two
assignments
let me live a-gain
```
Gibb B.V.

Stigwood Music, Inc. Unichappell Music,

  ghts RESERVED

1968: The Politics of the Page

The obvious critique of this kind of procedure is that it denies the reader's desire for meaning or analysis, and simultaneously demands a sophisticated, privileged reader who knows beforehand that process and procedure in themselves are ways of reading. The writing is nonreferential: its content is not explicit but rather is buried in the procedure and masked by the language. In anticipation of this critique Osman writes that in fact Darragh's text is implicitly referential and political because it points to the "real" language of 1968 that is suppressed. "Whereas cultural 'revolution' may have been the key-word that most think of when the year 1968 is evoked, it was particularly non-revolutionary vocabulary that was being generated at the time. The real revolution of the time had more to do with fantasy and consumerism than anything else. Language was the true indicator of what the future held" (Osman 7).

Sanders, of course, would disagree. But instead of expecting Darragh's text to be politically accountable, it might be better to value procedural writing in terms of what poet Alan Gilbert has referred to as the "politics of the page": to appreciate the games and experimentation of such processes as a pushing forward of form and a necessary shattering of the expectations of what a poem, or poetry, is or should be. If the vocabulary of the cultural revolution is missing from Darragh's text, then her procedure is not about revolution and does not need to be valued as contributing to a political critique of 1968. On the other hand, Ed Sanders's *1968: A History in Verse* does use the vocabulary of both the cultural and the consumer revolution. He uses chunks of information from his files of anarchist magazines, FBI files, letters, and photographs. His poem is procedural, but the end result is very different.

In *1968* Sanders displays his skills as an investigative poet, using his own theories of data clusters, information flows, fact strips, etc. to organize a narrative history about 1968. The series of data clusters that make up *1968* flows with lucidity, emotion, precision, and information. This book reveals the social implications of investigative poets who reveal sources in their work as a way of articulating concrete facts to create an alternative narrative history. This is procedural writing in which an alternative form for the articulation of history gestures toward depicting a countercultural past. Evidence drives the poem forward and creates its context. Through sampling, the poem becomes a project that is continually changing along with the social and political forces that shape it. Unlike collage, which decontextualizes and removes the reference from the object by forcing a cohesion with other objects, sampling preserves the reference by presenting it as a chunk of information, rather than as a fragmented cutup. Both recontextualize the original reference—but whereas collage consumes the reference, sampling allows the seams, and the points of convergence with other references, to show.

The point here is not to choose which poet—the "fan" poet or the "data-strip" poet—is better. Nor is it to determine which poet is more or less at the cutting edge of social change. In each is the depiction of a year, 1968. In each is an assembly of information that confronts readers, asking them to evaluate their position within time and history. In each is the document, the source, and the reference foregrounded and opened for readers to discover their own perceptions. In each are the shortcomings of experimental texts: both revelation and alienation are predictable; the dramatics of lyric are as tiresome as the babble of language; both the impulse toward documentary and the impulse toward nonreferentiality are manipulative. But how exciting is the possibility of putting it all together and creating a form that can handle the urge to articulate an explosive content.

1997: Language-Based/Content-Driven (vice versa)

From 1968 to 2000 the speed, variety, and flow of information has been facilitated by electronic communication capabilities; movies and TV have adapted the quick edit that came originally from avant-garde film techniques, and it has trained a new generation of viewers to perceive narrative structures as not demanding fixed sequences of beginnings, middles, and ends; the Gulf War was perceived as having no casualties because every shot of it was taken from the video-game perception of fighter pilots firing missiles on distant targets; ordinary people with video cameras have the power to be surveillance sources for FOX-TV snuff programs depicting car crashes, sports accidents, and aviation tragedies; anarchist politics, traditionally associated with leftist ideology, have been reformulated to right-wing militia groups; Interpol, the international police organization, is operating a global spy network that allows the United States to spy on its own citizens; the World Bank generated $28 billion in loans to "developing" countries in 1999 under the condition that they destabilize their governments and embrace democracy.

1. *Response* by Juliana Spahr is a book through which the poet works as an inquisitor and questioner of the problematic power structures inherent in poetic language. What constitutes "poetry" is overturned—for the tone of this book is flat, assured, blasé, mechanic. Her sources are drawn from disturbing Oprah shows, Hollywood movies, and alien-abductee stories. *Response* is a response to a surge of sources to which Spahr is the deciphering witness. Through revealing them she challenges us to think through both what sources mean and what language means. The testimonies that we seek to give emotive power to our world are a misrevelation, a nonsensical space, an expanding diatribe with no center from which truth, accuracy, or singular interpretation is possible. The matrix of language as assumed authority is questioned but not to illustrate the impossibility of meaning. The reader's position—I or he, she or we and you—is constantly shifting. One is not privileged over the other in her critique, and we move through the book as an ever-shifting pronoun, never grasping identity or trusting our appearance.

2. In Alan Gilbert's *Eve of Jubilee* rigorous documentary research into, for example, the Union Carbide chemical spill at Bhopal, the Hormel meat-packers' strike, and the random sterilization of Native American women is presented alongside a series of poetic explorations from a tangled lyrical landscape. The contrast between the two voices is startling, and the transitions from reading one into the other are rough along the edges. But the edges are there, present in the intent to challenge poetic language. Gilbert's poetry tests the capability of the lyrical voice, with its power over meaning and language, to relay hard-hitting information and documentary evidence. The confrontation of lyric and documentary on facing sides of the page questions the way we place value either on a historical source or on a poem. In the space between poetry and document is the breaking down of the definitions of both.

3. Sherry Brennan is also working from within the limitations of the lyric and does not trust its claim to heal the wounds of history by masking them in poetic language. In *Taken* she utilizes the lyric not to patch meaning over the holes of a violent history (in this case the pillage of the Native Americans) nor to intersect with the lost or silent voices of the past. History is not portrayed as a series of patches but as a series of reported occurrences, a sampling of representations, each coming from within the poetic language that attempts to articulate it.

4. Lisa Jarnot, by facing her poems in *Some Other Kind of Mission* with collages of her manuscripts, crossed out and reshaped, provides a constant reminder of the labor and material circumstances that go into the production of a poem. Her work points to an outside that is within the bounds of the book itself, with the text constantly referring back to itself and its modes of production. The sources that are revealed in Jarnot's book are generated through her own process, but this does not preclude the gesture of the text as reaching for an ever-unreachable exterior. There is no single plane in which the poetic address is situated, no precise or definable reference from which the poet's voice is inspired. As is the world, so is the text both confused and illuminated within a plethora of possible mergings.

Of course, numerous other poets are investigating the possibilities of poetry. Rob Fitterman, in his magazine *Object #9*, assembled twenty-seven poets who use what he calls "Inventory: sampling, cut-n-paste, summary, assemblage, synthesis, appropriation." Fitterman writes, "As we negotiate or document or influence the end of the century, it seems to me that an *inventory* poetics more closely reflects today's cultural phenomena of *summary* or *repetition*, rather than a 'make it new' poetics of invention" (n.p.). In the projects of these poets there is a noticeable merging of techniques of referential, nonreferential, and hyperreferential investigative poetics. Implicit in many of them is the attention and constant questioning of the position of the writer to both the language and the sources by which he or she is both surrounded and limited. The space of writing is not a manageable space; the laboratory of writing is a vast sampling of information combined with experience. It is a mix of thought that is never static. The fast edit of the documentary, which presents an attempt at a contextual whole out of the various fragments of its editing, is one place where experimental practitioners of poetry are forging mindful spaces.

Poetry will not raise mass consciousness, although it will articulate new systems in which sources, language, lyric, document, collage, and process come together as presentations of an alternative logic. Contemporary research projects do not claim an intersection with the world as a way of assimilating all of its various parts in order to build them up anew. These are projects that take on several guises, which will inevitably expand with time as new forms and approaches to language emerge to confront the content of our times.

References

Brennan, Sherry. *Taken*. Washington, D.C.: Primitive Publications, 1997.

Darragh, Tina. *adv. fans—the 1968 series*. Buffalo: Leave Books, 1995.

Fitterman, Rob, ed. *Object 9-Inventory* (1999).

Gilbert, Alan. *Eve of Jubilee*. Sections of this manuscript were published in *apex of the M* 4 (winter 1996) and in *First Intensity* 10 (winter 1998).

Jarnot, Lisa. *Some Other Kind of Mission*. Providence: Burning Deck, 1997.

McCaffery, Steve, ed. "Steve McCaffery, Ron Silliman & Charles Bernstein, Correspondence May 1976–December 1977." *Line* (1985): 59–89.

Osman, Jena. "Can you tell me how to reduce 'long' simultaneously with 'fine'?: The Procedural Poetry of Tina Darragh and Joan Retallack." Paper presented at the Twentieth Century Literature Conference, University of Louisville, February 1996.

Sanders, Ed. "Creativity and the Fully Developed Bard." In *Disembodied Poetics, Annals of the Jack Kerouac School*, ed. Anne Waldman and Andrew Schelling. Albuquerque: University of New Mexico Press, 1994.

———. *Investigative Poetry*. San Francisco: City Lights, 1976.

———. *1968: A History in Verse*. Santa Rosa: Black Sparrow Press, 1997.

Spahr, Juliana. *Response*. Los Angeles: Sun and Moon, 1996.

"TV Quiz for Video Freaks Only." *Mother Jones*, February/March 1976, 49.

"What Are the Farmworkers Voting For?" *Mother Jones*, February/March 1976, 5.

"The Women Are Talking about Anger." *Mother Jones*, February/March 1976, 67.

Christopher Funkhouser

Literary journals and new poetic authorship have begun to inject technology with human sensitivities and sensibilities. As writing mixes with digital media, cyberspace becomes something other than an information-exchange mechanism. Poets and poetry publications working with electronic formats continue to ride a tradition of writing that merges poetry and image presentation like William Blake's plates and other historical texts that use pigment, language, cultural observation, and expressive symbols in creative ways. Cyberpoetry embraces all modes between hieroglyph and laser: being in the present, thinking of the future and the past. With digitally encoded letters and colored images, sometimes rendered by hand, a reembodiment of Blake's "The Tyger" is engaged. Symbols for the human/creative imagination reverberate from his etchings and lyric: "In what furnace was thy brain?" (99). Today's "furnace" is partially preoccupied with, and enabled by, the creative heat generated by the advent of a new tool: the computer.

Until the last years of the twentieth century the majority of "experimental" writers, with few exceptions, held tightly to the landscape of a printed page as the tried-and-true platform on which to build and extend expression. This seemingly automatic default to a tradition-bound textual space presented a puzzle in terms of studying "avant-garde"/"postatomic"/ contemporary/innovative writing. One might posit that it was a function of the "nature" of "poets" to define themselves by virtue of their words printed on paper. A defining shift has since occurred. Methods have evolved, and many poets around the globe have begun to conceive and present their work in a paperless space via computer. Since 1995 a rapid proliferation of cyberpoetry has occurred as a result of the advent of the World Wide Web. The World Wide Web allows poets to make direct links to core and associated texts, as well as to external texts. It also allows links to radiant graphical texts and soundtracks. A small body of offline work predates this moment, but the appearance of this large network absolutely ignited a wider-scale movement in cyberpoetry.

Several creative and cultural elements contribute to the onset of cyber-textuality. Computer software, for print or online editors and writers, alters the functional dynamics of text. Publishers and commercial printers, mainly for practical reasons (i.e., ease and speed of transmission and reproduction), make widespread use of computers because such use makes their work easier to conduct. Writers open to working in hypertext forms are able to take advantage of added and inclusive layering dimensions that are impossible to enact on a printed page, such as sonic, visual, and layering/linking capabilities. Transforming material contained in poems for computer presentation is a different process from simply writing words down, but a similar type of translation, of (or from) world to literary content, occurs in both cases. Cyberpoetry reflects and takes advantage of the "expansive," if mechanical, aspects of the cultural moment we live in; it challenges us to find ways to use computers creatively. A new look and vision for writing, desired by some but certainly not all writers, is becoming more widely practiced.

Being able to connect our forms of historical expression is at present a considerable endeavor. However possible, bringing eternal pulsation of poetic concern to forms available to us in the present is also important. Emerging from an oral tradition, writing and the printed page were the popular mode for the transmission of poetry for centuries strictly out of necessity. A printing press was all writers had to rely on besides their voice (perhaps accompanied by acoustic music) and the soapbox. Electronic poetry shares with archetypal poetry at least two matters of primary importance: word selection and placement of words on the "page," now expanded to include sonic and visual effects. The additional layer of computer coding allows multiple layers of textuality for the viewer/reader.

Writers today are in no way required to forsake whatever expressive potency is allowed by typewriters, ink and quill, chisels, ballpoints, graphite, or Xerox machines exclusively in favor of computers. All are valid vehicles for communication. No mandate insists that poets use multimedia workstations. Quite possibly, though, work of writers in the next century will be handled using tools developed after the word processor. Books and other printed forms will likely continue to thrive. Electronically based work poses no threat of destruction to writing in other mediums. However, as far as the transmission of language and art go, it is a reality that, with the advent of the television and computer era, our species' former incarnation as a print-oriented culture has seriously embraced electronically based textuality. New understandings of poetry united with technology may extend and elevate writing in computerized formulations. Cyberpoetry in which all of the old orders are included will most powerfully engage the minds and imaginations of viewers eager for sophisticated content.

Many arguments are made against a poetry that relies on technology; others may be made in its favor. When computer-based literary publications began to appear on the Internet in the early to mid-1990s, many writers resisted using the medium because of its limited accessibility to readers. Some viewed technology as reducing poetry, which is breath and bone, to dehumanized bits of data. Others saw digital media as too impermanent a form: the world is not yet in an era where a computer is found in every home. An ominous elitism threatens any sense of cyberpoetry. Each of these criticisms holds some merit: writers, artists, and publishers working with high technology must consider issues of hegemony related to computer technology. For some these issues may become complications.

Digital technology, for better or worse, has made a great impact on industrialized nations in the present era, and one can protest this by refusal to engage with it. Others will, and do, see issues of access and form as a function or condition of time and space in such a way as to react by using the media for ends that challenge, question, take advantage of, and perhaps subvert its initial intent. Undoubtedly, hardware and software are used for destructive and exploitative purposes, but they have not exerted an overwhelming takeover of literature or poetry, and it is doubtful that this will happen to any extreme degree. Using computers creatively, altering the way the machines and programs are generally used, is not in itself a large step toward balancing cultural inequalities related to digital media. Nonetheless, how can providing legitimate humanist content to networks be seen as a harmful act, especially if it seeks to transform the way people see themselves and the world around them?

The age of the book as a popular medium in minds of creative young adults is undergoing some transformation. Many children in our culture undergo heavy exposure to the moving-picture monitor from an early age; reading is often secondary. Somebody who resists the book-to-TV continuum will argue, accordingly, that video-screen space is not the space that poetry should presently consider. Dangers held by the digital world, of its perhaps fragmented and exclusive agency, are still unknown. How accessible a medium is this? It is not a global democratic network, as producers of *Wired* magazine would lead people to think it is. Truly, digital art does not exist in the world as books do; it is site specific.

Gerrit Lansing's poem "Working in the Lower Red Field," addresses the making of poetry. The poem's opening line—"But handle the stone . . ." (*Heavenly Tree* 103)—quickly reminds one of the impossibility of touching binary codes. Neither can language actually be touched. New (programming) languages are learned in order to make the machine work to creative ends. From an open perspective it can just as easily be stated that writing is, in its own way, language and sound as "bits of data." If current trends continue, fiber-optic cables will be running in and out of billions of homes in North America and other technologized countries. These cables will transport digitized information in addition to television; in certain regions, such as most colleges and corporations, they already do. Is it more "poetic" not to work with computers beyond word processing? Ultimately, the answer is up to the individual. It is important to focus on what direct effects on humans come as a result of our relationship with digital machinery. For now, despite hesitation and resistance, computers have unquestionably begun to impact the presentation of writing in books and on terminal screens.

Is the process of translating being, vision, experience, and/or other poetic elements into language much different from translating the same using software? The same forces are at work; the former today can precede and extend the latter. Electronic writing and publications merge with traditional modes of language use, creating additional layers—linking, graphical, sonic, and animated possibilities—and use the combination of these attributes for poetic effect. Poets tend to develop a complex relationship with language in a society where language tends to be oversimplified in the popular media. It will be interesting to see the impact, if any, of a more televisual poetry on the culture at large (especially highly animated, visceral "Shockwave" or "Flash" "poems" and hypertext works in general on the World Wide Web). Projective technology, video, and multimedia are currently being used in projects unrelated to the objectives of economic profit or the manipulation of people and information.

Artistically, poetry presented via new media most closely reinvents previous twentieth-century forms. Direct connections can be discerned especially between cyberpoetry and the interdisciplinary Black Mountain School, visually based concrete poetry, and the animated qualities of performance poetry. Computer hardware and software are used to amplify and generate writing; they present visual and/or oral and/or alphabetic dimensions of text. Although the terminology and focus of discourse in this new area of textuality differ from that of most traditional modes of literary criticism, similar criteria can be used to critique these developing texts, even though perplexities have grown in the age of the computer. In the film *Poetry in Motion* (later transferred to CD-ROM by Voyager Company), in an interview with director Ron Mann, Ed Sanders heralds a new muse for the electronic era, "Retentia." In the literary field of Retentia, it is possible to preserve the voice and the literal or figurative image. The alphabetic is retained, expanded by electricity and electronic "space." Digital media allow the manifestation of a generative form, reaching future factions of writers with whom a historical perspective and electronic connection is shared.

One recurring motif in the early stages of cyberpoetry is a self-reflexive critique of technologically driven work. Betalab, and other works, adopt the icons, metaphors, and terminology of computers and networks to subvert them and to critique the medium itself. This process is achieved by disorienting viewers with excessive graphics and animations, using ambiguous navigational principles, drawing links that reach dead ends, and other easy programming foibles. Relatively few authors practice these methods, however. Numerous works earnestly attempt to use new media to advance poetry into the electronic realm, and multiple interpretations of cyberpoetry have been produced. Presumably, many more will be. Given that cyberpoetry is still in its infancy, it is likely that new abilities, developments, and trends will continue to transform it.

Types of cyberpoetry to emerge thus far may be roughly outlined as follows (combinations of these also occur):

- Graphical poetry, driven by visual aspects of the interface or images that are mapped/linked to connected materials
- Animated or kinetic poetry, usually also highly graphical, where several static screens are programmed to create a sense of movement in, or through, the text (videographic poetry relying in part or whole on digitized video also falls into this category)
- Collaborative poetry; potentially images and text, linear and nonlinear
- Computer-aided or generated compositions
- Text-based link-node poetry
- Shockwave audio poetry
- Java poetry (could also be considered animated or kinetic)
- Poems distributed as HTML code

Diana Slattery's Alphaweb and Christy Sheffield Sanford's work—which include more than a dozen varied cyberpoems on the World Wide Web—are remarkable for their graphical appearance and utility. These poets have discovered ways to connect disparate forms of text by using graphical communication. Alphaweb combines the use of visual and alphabetic cues to guide the reader through the text. Accordingly, at the end of each passage the viewer has the option to navigate texts subjectively by choosing from images or an alphabetic table. Sanford's work is consistently exciting because of its high-quality imagery, inventive technical application, and breadth of subject matter. She has produced high-quality and inventive work continuously for half a decade. Two pieces, "Boucher En Vogue" and "Spring," use the World

Wide Web's capabilities to great effect by linking to external sites elsewhere on the World Wide Web. She fortifies and expands her own writing by combining alphabetic texts, radiant imagery, and links to guide the viewer from one section of text to another. Sanford's visual imagery is dynamic: images are not used to illustrate the narrative or as decoration but to layer meaning and as navigational levers. Initially, Sanford's poems were static, but gradually they have become driven by moving imagery related to the theme of the poem. One multifaceted work that particularly stands out is "Safara in the Beginning (With Bible Verses, Motion Pictures and Field Guides)." In this presentation Sanford uses animated images (such as insects), virtual collages, and texts with an antioppression theme. A parallel story employing biblical passages exists simultaneously in the left margin of the frames in each screen the viewer encounters.

Laura Jordan (programmer) and Yolanda Astuy (writer) collaborate to present poetry that combines Shockwave and Java (sound and visual animation) effects. Jordan and Astuy create several types of poems in this electronic collection. In "Haiku" the poem unfolds as the viewer clicks on the word *haiku*. Thunder begins to sound and a poem is read in Spanish, with a stormy background soundtrack. In "Eating Apples" words of a poem about anorexia slowly fade onto and off the screen. The soundtrack of the poem is spoken in Spanish, accompanied by a sample of someone loudly eating an apple. The words pulsate across a shimmering background.

A commentary on the eye and photography, "fleshthresholdnarrative," by Eugene Thacker, appears in the electronic journal *The New River*. Thacker's piece starts with a blank screen, words hidden against the background of a page. Using the mouse, a viewer finds areas to click and the words of a full text become exposed. The links are invisible but obvious: the reader must learn how to "read" (or unveil) this recombinant piece. An invisible text (mainly prose, although there are scattered words on the map page) with links embedded is programmed so that the map is a poem that ultimately covers most of the screen.

The "Garden of Forklike Paths," by Marzenna and Julius Donajski, uses JavaScript to create an unusual combination of symbols and linking structure to orient the viewer. At first this piece presents itself as a puzzle. Because its concept and interface are unique, it takes more than a few moments for viewers to orient themselves within it. The creators of this text write in a prefatory note, "Inspired by Jorge Luis Borges, this peaceful garden will bear fruit to those with patience." Links and different areas of text unveil themselves and their connections to different areas of text, including graphical text, via the position of the mouse. Passing the icons over certain areas of the screen activates embedded images and textual passages, which appear in boxes that emerge on the screen.

A wider recognition emerges in just these few examples: cyberpoetry is a nonparticular, hybrid form, a form that is not yet whole, comprising many parts, authorial energies, and nascent technological capabilities. Visually kinetic texts, and to a lesser degree software programs that automatically generate work, have characterized cyberpoetry. These approaches have yielded some interesting work, yet as computers evolve it is likely that cyberprosody will change dramatically. In a decade it is conceivable that computers themselves will not resemble today's machines. Elements currently under development, such as vocal-response mechanisms and iris-tracking mechanisms, in which a viewer's voice and eye-movement activate paths and dimensions to the text, will alter demonstrably the ways texts are produced and absorbed.

Limitations in software and in other aspects of technology have diminished in the past decade. Unfortunately, nonstandardized operating systems (e.g., Windows/Macintosh), browser differences (e.g., Netscape and Explorer), and the need for specialized software extensions (e.g., "plug-in" devices) do, at times, create lack of fluidity in computer networks. Interference from the interface may prevent the medium from infusing the form with depth. Aesthetically, the predominant condition of formal linearity in cyberpoetry seems like a contradiction; even cyberpoetry that makes use of "randomized" "animation" "loops" consists of relatively self-confined, linear segments. Within a much larger domain of potential images, the teleologies and terminal points at which a reader may go no farther are no less invisible in today's networked practices than they are in the writing in most books. The work is overtly mechanical, and although it is image driven, only some of it is remarkably "hand crafted," as were Blake's etchings. Viewers may perceive one-dimensionalities or lack in sophistication in much of the cyberpoetry produced thus far; it may be true that relatively few pieces exist that inspire repeated viewing.

As platforms and equipment become standardized, perhaps writers will be more willing to explore the possibilities of "writing" in these areas, where words become images and words are voices. With "digital multimedia design" the prefix on the final word of the phrase should be used with intent, as in *de*sign: "from the sign." In themselves digital imaging and multimedia do not provide any solution to various educational, ideological, and post-structural dilemmas. Computers do, however, evidently allow a type of expansive communication through electronic networks and connect readers who have become accustomed to a screen rather than a page.

Digital multimedia and other forms of hypertext are both performance and translation. As "performance" cyberpoetry may not match a living theater, a stage on which voices are amplified to an audience. Although digital performances might be classified as "interactive," this interaction is not the same as a room where breathing bodies share a space. Perhaps, then, it is best to view digitized poetry as creative interdisciplinary exhibition or "screening," where language and computers serve as mediators, as futuristic interpretations of writing. For certain, a completely different language—the language of computer "programming," an incorporated language—intervenes and re-creates sense and vision within electronic poetry. Code is language that handles writing, the work of writers; it can be amazingly simple on one end and fearfully complicated and precise on another.

Cyberpoetry is historically in line with multiple traditions, including this century's wide-ranging "New American poetry." From an odd slant, cyberpoetry particularly relates to the "doubling" aspects in Jack Spicer's work (Blaser 290). Spicer viewed his work as a "compound of the invisible and visible" (Blaser 276). Spicer not only allowed for but insisted on one's openness to outside forces, something beyond one's self, as a key element in the process of writing contemporaneously. This openness comes into the text and is left open. The work of cyberpoets and editors, with its intervening computer language, furthers this compound. By definition, it is a visible poetry whereby the act of viewing the magazine is overdetermined by its medium. What is visible in the poem—or the translation of the poem—be it language, imagery, or a link, is now before us on the screen. At the same time, the igniting, invisible computer language, and authorial/editorial mode of presentation is hyperpresent below the surface of the text. Creative activity is altered by the machine's presence; the code itself can then also be seen as a type of poetry.

To illustrate briefly this formulation, a basic script used in one CD-ROM poetry magazine (*The Little Magazine*, vol. 21) is shown below. In this piece, a collaboration between Meg Arthurs and Stefan Said, a musical soundtrack accompanies a sequence of hand-rendered static images. As digital multimedia it operates using a language known as OpenScript, through a software program called Asymetrix Multimedia ToolBook. Beginning where the first button apparent on the screen is clicked, the source code reads:

```
                    to handle buttonUp
            set sysCursor to 4
            if mmIsOpen of clip "said" is false then
                    mmOpen clip "said" wait
                    mmPlay clip "said" autoclose
            else
                    mmStop clip "said" wait
            end if
            transition "dissolve" to next page
            set sysCursor to default
    end
```

Sound clips and image files are engaged as such throughout this particular magazine. Similar "languages" are used to manifest every cyberpoem: complicated presentations make use of complicated techniques. The language is precision based and unforgiving. If any letter or other character of the code is out of place, the program/presentation will not operate correctly. Other digital editing software will automatically write the code for the author, as do most World Wide Web editing programs. As in any language, the alphabetic and numeric symbols in code can be used imaginatively to conceptualize and realize poetic ideas.

Cyberpoetry on the World Wide Web is programmed in Hypertext Markup Language (HTML), a comparatively uncomplicated type of coding that allows a synthesis of graphical (color), animated, and sound elements in addition to what might be the "written" text itself. What this means for poetry in terms of form is relatively straightforward. Language—its principle vehicle—is no longer lodged on a fixed, silent page, as it is in print (even if readers "sound" poems as they read). As a result of this other—computerized—language, poetry inhabits a flexible, dynamic, and transmittable circuitry that allows built-in links, intricate graphical components, soundtracks, and other capabilities, such as various forms of animation. The vividness of poetry as it extends to the present is charged with additional elements. A listing of selected thoughtful cyberpoetry available on the Internet is appended to this essay.

Editors of creative literary publications and World Wide Web sites are making obvious efforts to use computers creatively. These efforts may be viewed as an attempt to build community with technology rather than to assist in its degradation as so much "technological innovation" does. To use computers creatively is to make a conscious effort to prove computers can be used for things other than data processing, storage, informational "control," and the domination and oppression of people. Poetry, broadly defined as open writing, is not merely information, the transference of which is the predominant function of the computer; it is far from it. Living poetry can be a device—an expression—that is capable of severing the customary space occupied by computers. Computers are ripe to be taken up for the poet's purposes: machines are used more and more as a platform for poetry. On this platform are the concerns of the writer; they are now a part of our compound.

In the introduction to *Poems for the Millennium: A University of California Book of Modern Poetry* (1995), Jerome Rothenberg and Pierre Joris write: "With regard to twentieth century poetry, a new look has been long overdue" (11). Writers now using digital media to combine their vision and language skills with visual and auditory communication have created a new moment of form. We are challenged to find ways to bring a tactile sense of language and expression alive through computerized multimedia. Much of the work, moved from page to screen, has been able to make use of the possibilities held by the alphabet and other symbols/images in electronic space. Eternal and intrinsic ties exist among the sonic, visual, and alphabetic connections in writing. Forward-looking producers of the art believe that digital technology offers something quite valuable for writers and the preservation and promotion of writing in a species of literature that combines essential senses of "the word" with imagery, linking, digital layering, and thought.

References

Blake, William. *Songs of Innocence and Experience*. Oxford: Oxford University Press, 1986.

Blaser, Robin. "The Practice of Outside." In *The Collected Poems of Jack Spicer*. Santa Rosa: Black Sparrow Press, 1989.

Funkhouser, Christopher, Belle Gironda, and Ben Henry, eds. *The Little Magazine*. Vol. 21. Albany: State University of New York Press, 1995. CD-ROM.

Lansing, Gerrit. *The Heavenly Tree Grows Downward*. Jersey City: Talisman House, 1995.

Mann, Ron. *Poetry in Motion*. Vol. 1. New York: Voyager, 1985 (video), 1994 (CD-ROM).

Rothenberg, Jerome, and Pierre Joris. *Poems for the Millennium: A University of California Book of Modern Poetry*. Vol. 1. Berkeley: University of California Press, 1995.

Selected Webography of Cyberpoetry

Amerika, Mark. *GRAMMATRON*. <http://www.grammatron.com/index2.html>.
Anderson, Lori. *Slices*. <http://www.rpi.edu/~anderl2/>.

Andrews, Jim. *Online Writings*. <http://vispo.com/writings/index.htm#poems>.

The Astrophysicist's Tango Partner Speaks. <http://www.heelstone.com/>.

Baczewska, Christine. *Vocabulary*. <http://www.turbulence.org/Works/Xtine/index.html>.

Betalab. <http://www.jodi.org/>.

Campbell, Ian. "Glimpses of an Afternoon." *Enterzone* 10 (1997). <http://ezone.org/ez/e10/articles/ianc/1.html>.

Campbell, Meredith. "Driving." <http://www.curtin.edu.au/org/telepoetics/drive1.html>.

Carroli, Linda, and Josephine Wilson. "a woman stands on a street corner . . ." <http://ensemble.va.com.au/water/>.

Cayley, John. *Eastfield Shadoof*. <http://www.shadoof.net/>.

da Rimini, Francesca, Ricardo Dominguez, Michael Grimm. *dollspace . . . hauntologies*. <http://www.thing.net/~dollyoko/title.htm>.

Di Ball, Bound & Gagged. <http://smople.thehub.com.au/dibbles/writing/menu.htm>.

Doctorovich, Fabio. ABYSSMO. <http://www.postypographika.com/menu-en1/genres/hyperpo/abyss/menu-en.htm>.

Donajski, Marzenna, and Julius Donajski. "Garden of Forklike Paths." <http://www.ddg.com.pl/galeria/exhibits/maga/ogrod/index.html>.

Felberbaum, Alicia. holes – linings – threads. <http://www.felber.dircon.co.uk/holeslin-ingsthreads/info.htm>.

Glazier, Loss Pequeño. <http://wings.buffalo.edu/epc/authors/glazier/>.

Györi, Ladislao Pablo. VIRTUAL POETRY. <http://www.postypographika.com/menu-en1/genres/vpoetry/menu-en.htm>.

Harbison, Sally. Video Wall. <http://206.251.6.116/geekgirl/009dogs/videow.html>.

Hartman, Charles. MacProse. <http://www.conncoll.edu/ccother/cohar/programs/>.

Jordan, Laura (programmer), and Yolanda Astuy (writer). menstrual pudding. <http://206.251.6.116/geekgirl/008fruit/menstrua.html>.

Kac, Eduardo. <http://www.ekac.org/>.

Knoebel, David. *Click Poetry*. 1996. <http://home.ptd.net/~clkpoet/maincont.html>.

Ley, Jennifer. The Body Politic. <http://www.heelstone.com/subtext/driftwood.html>.

Lialina, Olia. *My boyfriend came back from the war.* . . . <http://www.teleportacia.org/war/>.

Malloy, Judy. The Roar of Destiny Emanated from the Refrigerator. <http://www.well.com/user/jmalloy/control.html>.

mez, mo[ve.men]tion does . . . <http://www.wollongong.starway.net.au/~mezandwalt/>.

Platt, Janan. *Janan Platt's Birdhouse Visit*. <http://www.birdhouse.org/words/janan/>.

Rosenberg, Jim. <http://www.well.com/user/jer/>.

Rothenberg, David. *The Zone. Newark Review* 2.2 (1998–99). <http://www-ec.njit.edu/~newrev/v2s2/>.

Sanford, Christy Sheffield. <http://gnv.fdt.net/~christys/index.html>.

Slattery, Diana. *Alphaweb.* <http://raven.ubalt.edu/guests/alphaweb/>.

Strickland, Stephanie. *The Ballad of Sand and Harry Soot.* 1999. <http://wordcircuits.com/gallery/sandsoot/>.

Waber, Dan. *Strings.* <http://vispo.com/guests/DanWaber/index.html>.

Warnell, Ted. *Poem by Nari.* <http://vispo.com/guests/TedWarnell/ted1.htm>.

Zervos, Komninos. *Surrealist Poem Generator.* <http://www.birdhouse.org/words/komninos/generator.html>.

Publications/Resources

Cyberpoetry <http://student.uq.edu.au/~s271502/>

Java Poetry <http://www.prominence.com/java/poetry/>

The Little Magazine <http://www.albany.edu/~litmag>

New River <http://www.cddc.vt.edu/journals/newriver/>

NWHQ <http://www.knosso.com/NWHQ/>

Parallel <http://www.va.com.au/parallel/x2/index.html>

POSTYPOGRAPHIKA <http://www.postypographika.com/>

Riding the Meridian <http://www.heelstone.com/meridian/>

ubuweb <http://www.ubu.com/>

Jeff Derksen

Narratives and nations love an originary moment. On October 8, 1971, Pierre Elliott Trudeau, Canada's intellectual playboy prime minister and leader of the Liberal party addressed Parliament with a speech that moved multiculturalism into governmental policy. Seventeen years later, in 1988, and under a very different government, Canadian multiculturalism passed into law: Canada—in another originary moment—was the first country to pass a national multiculturalism law. But prior to these documented moments, multiculturalism in Canada arose out of a framework of biculturalism and bilingualism between the so-called charter groups, the English and the French. Merging his philosophical liberalism with an opportunity to counter Quebec nationalism—articulated during the Quiet Revolution of the sixties—Trudeau's vision of a "Just Society" made an individual's rights paramount over group rights. Trudeau, through his "pure" liberalism, sought to block the Quebec government's attempt to identify a linguistic collectivity under the sign of Quebec; that is, language (and cultural) rights were attached, by Trudeau, to the individual, not a group, and this set Quebec's quest for group identity and group rights in tension with the Canadian Charter. This tension between universal rights and group rights, or between the politics of equal recognition and the politics of difference, is likewise embedded in official multicultural policy itself.

Within the national bilingual and bicultural framework, the Multiculturalism Act was designed to maintain the cultural heritage of all groups within a pluralist population and to recognize the rights of members of "minority" groups as equal to those of the two "charter" groups. Out of this, official multiculturalism seeks a "unity in diversity" stance that allows "ethnics" to celebrate their cultures while still remaining full participants within Canadian culture. Conscious of the need to construct and manage a national identity through a balance of the universal and particular, multiculturalism tries then to accommodate demographic diversity by recognizing such diversity as a founding principle of a national identity: out of this formation the metaphor of cultural mosaic, the favored official metaphor, arises. Within the discourse of multiculturalism the acceptance of "our" cultural pluralism is the key to Canadian national cultural and social unity.

Multiculturalism is perceived to have developed in three stages: the demographic stage, the symbolic stage, and the structural stage (Kobayashi). However, it is best to approach the various formations of multiculturalism in Canada not as stages that lead progressively to one another but as a set of relations that contains within it, at any point, all of the stages that I will outline. That is, official multiculturalism in Canada is subject to an uneven development, having both retrograde and progressive aspects in circulation in any of its many institutions and effects at any point. The first conceptual stage is the demographic stage, which existed prior to official multiculturalism as an articulation of "ethnic" groups who emerged as a "third force" in Canadian politics. Driven by demographics, from the Second World War to the intensely nationalistic sixties, the place and function of Canada's "ethnics" in a national identity led to the consideration of multicultural policies. The second stage, the symbolic stage, was initiated by Trudeau's government in 1971 and led to the appointment of a minister of state for multiculturalism and funding for the celebration of ethnic cultures, cultures that were imagined as folklore; the emphasis in this stage was on the preservation of cultural heritage. The symbolic stage reveals multiculturalism policy's inability to transform Canadian politics in a material way; recognition and symbolic equality did not lead to social change, and this emergent "third force" was relegated to an advisory role. The act may speak of guaranteeing equal rights, but it does not set up systemic means to equalize rights. At this point the discourse of race was strategically subsumed within the term *ethnic*, in Roxanna Ng's analysis, to "diffuse the antagonistic relations between Quebec and English Canada, and between the native people, other minority groups, and the Canadian state" (297). The third stage, structural multiculturalism, lobbies for more proactive legislation to enact multiculturalism and enhance the equality of opportunity. Antiracist policy remains largely symbolic, addressing racism as an "attitude," not a systemic problem, and continues to figure race as a natural category. As Ng also notes, this emphasis on race relations is a "reverse movement" from the totalizing effect of an undifferentiated discourse of ethnicity.[1]

Other criticisms of multiculturalism argue that it remains merely symbolic, reducing ethnic and racialized cultures to folklore and sponsoring celebrations of "red boot" ethnicity but never actually alleviating the real inequities within Canadian society. This criticism of multiculturalism charges that it cannot forcefully address racism (and sexism as a link in the system of labor) precisely because, as a policy and a law, multiculturalism fails to recognize race and ethnicity as socially constructed and rather deals with them as natural. The result is that multiculturalism does not seek systematic changes that challenge the categories (and the use of these categories) of race and ethnicity. As well, attention has been focused on the "assimilationist" tendency of early multiculturalism and the later "integrationist" stance, pointing out that the act recognizes "ethnicity" at the same time that it seeks to control it through cultural absorption. In fact this tension between an integrationist and a particularist position is written into the act itself.

Multiculturalism as a conceptual guarantor of equity and "full access" to Canadian society could be read as a strong oppositional potential within the nation—exercising as it does a particularization against a national universal. Yet analyzed as a discourse or a technology (see Kamboureli), official multiculturalism is not a liberating articulatory practice. For official multiculturalism cannot address its role in the social construction and categorization of race and ethnicity because it is itself one of the articulatory sites of that construction and in Canada is literally the law that articulates these positions and moments. In my analysis, then, multiculturalism in Canada has two main functions and effects. One function is the particularizing function that both designates a subject as ethnic or racialized and recognizes them as such: this designation, or particularizing, brings with it the rights guaranteed to citizens. The second function is as an articulatory practice that is necessary in the construction of the nation to complete the sign of Canada by subsuming the ethnic and racialized subject (with class-defined subjects subsumed into these designations) into a national citizen. In this sense this national citizen symbolizes a missing fullness that seeks to suture particularized identities into its own fullness, or completion. This universalizing effect obfuscates the relations among *race*, *ethnicity*, and *class* and their relationship to gender in its rush to completion. These italicized nouns, so often and necessarily conjoined in analysis of identity formation, are materialized and performed within a shifting field of social relations; yet emphasis can be moved from the multiplicity and contingency of identity formation to the shifting and multiple social relations that these identities are situated in. This would involve a movement from multiplicity to situatedness in the analysis of identity formations.

Yet there is a tension between the official intention and the discursive act and its social effects in Canadian multiculturalism. Racialized and gendered subjects and their subordination are necessary to continue the economic union of a nation—and to support its role within the world system—and an official act will not undermine this. Yet the Multiculturalism Act is designed to alleviate this subordination under the auspices of "full access." In the emphasis toward "full participation" in the economic and political life of Canada, an ethnic or racialized subject is interpellated by the act more properly as a commodity within the race-labor system of Canada. Splicing the emphasis of social biology in Canadian immigration policies (see Porter) with Etienne Balibar and Immanuel Wallerstein's analysis of the interrelatedness of ethnicity, race, and gender in terms of class and occupational position (literally the construction of racialized and ethnic, as well as gendered, cheap labor), "full participation" comes to mean the ability to create surplus value in Canadian society. In keeping with the *use* of immigrants, multiculturalism constructs racialized and ethnic subjects as labor commodities through which surplus value is created, whether it is via low-paying and commonly dangerous jobs, such as the building of the railway (which was given to male Chinese immigrants); more benign functions, such as using lower-class Eastern European immigrants (itself a shifting category) to "populate" and, in a sense, enclose the prairies. More recently, Canadian immigration policies have been designed to attract immigrants who bring investment capital into the country.[2] Multiculturalism, then, functions as the ideological and economic management of diversity and is best analyzed within a matrix of race, class, ethnicity, and gender and their relations to the means of production and reproduction. As Jon Cruz suggests, in an American context, multiculturalism can be looked at "as part of a *social logic* of late capitalism and as a cultural feature at the intersection of economic globalization and the fiscal-domestic crisis of the state" (19). Canadian governments, with their social management skills, recognized this early and put in place a multicultural policy for both the domestic and global needs of its own social/cultural logic.

Yet both national and ethnic and racialized subjects exist in excess of the sign of nationalism and the social logic of multiculturalism—that is, interpellation does not cancel agency, and multiculturalism is not a seamless hegemony but rather an uneasy totality. Canadian multiculturalism is involved in a sort of "rearguard damage control" (Cruz) of the domestic national unity crisis and a more global economic crisis and is itself historically embedded in a long tradition of Enlightenment ideals of equality that are not being fulfilled because of a social "deinvestment" prompted by the domestic fiscal crisis (the debt hysteria).[3] In this moment, within these relations, the contradictions and overdeterminations within the Multiculturalism Act and its discursive and social employment are more readily seen; the stitching of the suture is showing and is perhaps a bit frayed. Yet the possibilities for equalization of rights through a rearticulation of multiculturalism also arises within this moment and set of relations; for multiculturalism does provide the discourse for "diversity"—a site that can be entered—and (unwittingly) creates liminal space, and even supplies resources, where effective rearticulatory practices take place.

The text, itself a matrix of social relations in its production and circulation, is one such liminal space. The writing of "multicultural" subjects—and texts read as multicultural (for reception is a production as well)—are produced from a variety of positions, ranging from assertions of a politics of recognition, the disarticulatory practice of resistance, to an antisystemic rearticulation of the sites and effects of multiculturalism itself. This uneven development represents, at any time, differential positions, or moments and communities, and is constantly being refigured, recalculated. In recent multicultural writing, in acknowledgment of the articulatory power of language, language itself has arisen as the site of resistance. Roy Kiyooka provides a clear analysis of his own tactics in this regard: "I did have a sense, when I was quite young, that to survive in this culture was essentially a quest for language as the modality of power about which you could be present in the world" (48).

This turn to language as a material ideological site can be seen in some writers as a move away from the politics of recognition that Charles Taylor promotes. For Taylor recognition leads to identity, which enables a politics of difference in which "we [by *we* I assume he means the dominant culture] are asked to recognize the unique identity of this individual or group" (38). This recognition could lead in turn to provisions for particular rights, such as linguistic or self-government rights. Recognition has become necessary, according to Taylor, as societal hierarchies have broken down and become more complicated because of the emergence of individual identity. In this representational mode of rights Taylor holds steadfastly to the articulatory practice of the dominant culture: "But the further demand [of multiculturalism] we are looking at here is that we all *recognize* the equal value of different cultures; that we not only let them survive, but acknowledge their *worth*" (64). How does acknowledgment and recognition within a cultural relativist frame where a dominant culture maintains its absolute powers of definition and whose gaze grants worth to the spectated subject address systemic oppression within a race-labor system? And, given the analysis of Canadian multiculturalism as a discursive exterior that interpellates a subject who is then absorbed under the sign of a national universal, recognition within such a discourse is not without risk. And as Judith Butler points out, the moment of address and recognition in Althusser is also the moment of an ideological hailing (Butler 106–31). What occurs, then, when a writer turns away from the politics of recognition through a tactical refusal to be recognized or interpellated under and through a discursive exterior that, in making the subject recognizable, regulates it? What happens when a writer produces a text that resists or shuns recognition by such articulatory forces. I don't mean how can an ethnic or racialized writer pass or write an unmarked text; rather, how can a text counter the system of official multiculturalism? How can a text move from being oppositional—from a position of refusal—to being an agent of rearticulation?

To borrow a term from Immanuel Wallerstein, a text that is situated not in an exterior position of opposition but as an articulatory agent within a site could be designated *antisystemic*: writing that consciously counters a system that seeks to interpellate a subject within a particular field of relations. This does not mean that antisystemic writing is trying to do away with multiculturalism and the particularized rights it could potentially bring but rather that the more subordinating aspects of the Multiculturalism Act are themselves situated within a larger set of cultural relations. By foregrounding the relations that multicultural policy is within and linking these to the effects of the Multiculturalism Act, a sort of ideological laying bare of relations is set in motion. This linking could show the contradictions contained within the act and how they are played out in the tension between particularism and universalism, as well as situate multiculturalism within the gendered race-labor system of the nation and its place within the world system. Once situated, antisystemic writing, in this instance, becomes a rearticulation of multiculturalism: the moments, effects, and implementation of multiculturalism are countered, and another system is proposed. This situated writing goes past a modernist imagining of relations *exterior* to a dominant social formation.

Differently situated communities and writers take varying tactics of rearticulation: from George Ryga's grit-in-the-teeth realist novels that represent a Ukrainian "rock farmer's" life in northern Alberta and bring social relations rather than literary thematics to the landscape; to Di Brandt's prose poems that counter the multicultural view of united communities functioning as ideal immigrants and contest the role of the church in Mennonite culture; to Tom Wayman's Wobblie-influenced social democracy narratives that refuse to forget the social justices that are overridden by the right's budgetary gospel of facts; to Ian Iqbal Rashid's queering of race relations and multiculturalism that brings the banished queer body to counter the reproductive body of the gendered race-labor system. In terms of a cultural poetics this move to a situated rather than a multiple subject moves beyond the reductive homology of poetic form and subject position where the text is a register of a subjective reflexivity rather than the social reflexivity of a situated subject.[4] As Barrett Watten so concisely argues, what is needed at this moment "is a cultural poetics that rejects a universalist distinction between 'normative' and 'nonstandard' modes of writing and that thus requires, as a form of politics, a specific history of difference" (7). In this way a cultural poetics would approach the kind of antisystemic counterings that I have catalogued above, as well as avant-garde or "nonstandard"[5] counterings as situated moments within an antisystemic movement rather than different formal approaches to identity formation. Rearticulations and resistances are acted out variously in sites that call for tactical decisions on formal strategies; a formally politicized text is not identical in every site. The texts that I have chosen to briefly focus on below move language as an embodiment of ideology into a problematic with multiculturalism.

A well-recognized text that moves into this problematic is Dionne Brand's "No Language Is Neutral." Countering the positive immigrant experience where "full participation" is achieved, Brand enacts language as the mark that links race and class in an economic system that relies on such marked subjects for a source of cheap labor, a labor that is gendered as well: ". . . calling Spadina *Spadeena* until I listen good for what the white people call it, saying I coming just to holiday to the immigration officer when me and the son-of a bitch know I have labourer mark all over my face" (29). Whereas Brand tends to play her antisystemic gestures on the semantic level, Ashok Mathur foregrounds the breakdown of language's semantic effect as it passes between differently class- and race-defined subjects. His poetic novel or prose poem *Loveruage* disrupts syntax and individual words to illustrate that communication is altered by the relationship of class and race. Tellingly, it is the speech of the dominant culture that fragments into clipped vowelless phrases and unintelligibility. Both of these texts reinsert class into the discourse of racialization, contaminating a view of multiculturalism as "heritage" outside of social relations. A rearticulation occurs by the forceful insistence on the role that class plays not only in identity formation (an element that too often is rendered transparent or set in false contradiction to other elements) but in how racialized or ethnic identities take place within a set of social relations of which class is a part. For class to be left out of this formation, or to have it merely tacked onto the string of nouns that currently constitute the elements of identity formation, is to mimic, in some senses, capitalism's historic dampening of the relationship of race and class within the race-labor system—a dampening that creates antagonisms rather than coalitions.

Roy Miki invades the archive of the Japanese Canadian internment in *Random Access File* to reveal the systemic racism that enabled this act. Stripping official discourse of its context with formal syntactic and authorial interventions, Miki shows how the "japanese problem" was lifted out of history and social relations and placed into a discourse of assimilation. Official discourse is overturned not in a moment of carnivalization but in a recognition of the ideology saturating that discourse. The government memo that is transculturated in Miki's "Membrane Translate" tells Japanese Canadians that "by your own words & / actions you can do more / to solve 'the japanese / problem' in canada / than any other group" (60) and urges that Japanese Canadians be "their own best 'salesmen'" by moving to assimilation. Intruding into this appropriated memo are Miki's more oblique, more multivalent comments, bracketed off by Olsonian open parenthesis: "(engineer the values / in the wine-cellars / of deepest taste"; "(the ethnic is / yearned for": "(the by-product of waste / management you say." Miki ups the ante on the criticism of multiculturalism as the management of diversity to "waste management" of which the "ethnic" is the by-product. The constitutive and subordinating effects of multiculturalism as an articulatory practice in which subordinated subjects are created and managed is laid bare as Miki moves the memo into a dialogic position—a position that authoritative speech is usually imagined outside of. This dialogic opening of language is extended to the dialogic opening of a racist historical archive.

As I have outlined, the discourse of multiculturalism enacts race and ethnicity as a naturalized category and reduces the characteristics of these categories to heritage or folklore; these categories are not seen as social or constructed, nor are they imagined as interdiscursive. In *Diamond Grill* Fred Wah complicates these categories and shows them not to be natural or even categorizable but rather socially and contextually constituted at every moment: "Better watch out for the craw, better watch out for the goat. That's the mix, the breed, the half-breed, metis, quarter-breed, trace-of-a-breed, true demi-semi-ethnic polluted rootless living technicolour snarl to complicate the underbelly panavision of racism and bigotry across this country. I know, you're going to say, that's just being Canadian. The only people who call themselves Canadian live in Ontario and have national sea-to-sea twenty-twenty CPR vision" (53). The happy multiculti vision of a Canada united by its shared differences and tolerance hits the discursive skids here, ending up in a hyphenated space outside of assimilable categories and outside of liberal recognition. Being "Canadian" in this angry rearticulation is engaging in an identity construct in which the universal is a particular—a "minority"—that has become dominant. *Diamond Grill*, despite its oblique narrative structure, narrativizes the economic and cultural forces that initiate the migration of peoples in order to supply a world system with the type of laborers it needs and approaches the identity formations that "mix" within this uprootedness.

This complicating of identity categories and of the technology of multiculturalism is presented as a deferral of both meaning and identity by Mark Nakada in his "Dreaming Okinawa." Moving through a differentiated subject's possible identity combinations, Nakada brackets off identity by refusing formal closure:

> open parenthesis uh comma Japanese close parenthesis
> open parenthesis but Okinawan close parenthesis
> open parenthesis and Danish close parenthesis
> open parenthesis and American close parenthesis
> open parenthesis but Canadian close parenthesis

open parenthesis but white close parenthesis
open parenthesis guilty close parenthesis
open parenthesis but not close parenthesis
open parenthesis both close parenthesis. . . .

This poem terminates with a single word line: *open*. This is not the homology of textual form and subject position in which the text stands in for subject position but is the refusal of closure on identity. Identity and position remain in process by moving through sets of relations, yet these relations are situated in the geographical names (not unlike a reversal of Olson's ideas on place and names). Nakada posits that identity is relational, and the relations he chooses to juxtapose are antagonistic. The "and American" followed by the "but Canadian" sets in motion a binary not assimilable within the national imaginary: Canadian identity can subsume "ethnic" identity, but it cannot be grafted onto its own negative discursive exterior, "American."[6] Nakada floods the discourse of multiculturalism to set an identity in motion that is too excessive to be recognizable. This is an anti-systemic gesture that refuses to be interpellated by a system of multiculturalism. But, crucially, "Dreaming Okinawa" does not privilege an ahistorical multiplicity or openness but insists on the economic and cultural relations that identity formation is within.

In some ways all of the texts I have touched on here demonstrate that the tropes of play and opposition within poetics could more effectively be rethought of in terms of rearticulation and situatedness. Without predictably invoking Jameson as closure, this situatedness is similar to his "aesthetic of cognitive mapping—a pedagogical political culture which seeks to endow the individual with some new heightened sense of its place in the global system"(54). But where Jameson claims that "the new political art (if it is possible at all) will have to hold to the truth of postmodernism, that is to say, to its fundamental object—the world space of multinational capital—at the same time it achieves a breakthrough to some as yet unimaginable new mode of representing this last," Jameson returns to a mimetic (and truth) function and asks for a new realism that can enlighten subjects who are "at present neutralized by our spatial as well as our social confusion" (54). A poetics of situatedness and rearticulation would not again try to make the stone stony in an attempt to have a return of our (multinational) senses, or to imagine new senses outside of a cognitive mapping, but would articulate links that are currently deflected within social relations and disarticulate other links that give the appearance of an immobile social totality. The move from the politics of recognition and representation to an antisystemic rearticulation is the move from award-winning voter apathy to agency within sites.

Notes

1. Criticism of official multiculturalism as a discourse and a discursive exterior charges that, through law, it names but does not particularize ethnicity: hence the ethnic subject is lifted out of history and "instead becomes a commonality: what all Canadians have in common is ethnic difference" (Kamboureli 209).

2. Jon Cruz asserts a similar positioning of social identities: "Under capitalism and commodity production, the social identities of individuals are increasingly mediated by commodity production and regulated, too, as if they were *things*, reified along with commodities" (23). Once having made this link of social identity and commodity status, Cruz fine-tunes his argument by adding that this comparison is not strict and that identity formations "come into being as political, social, moral—and classed, raced, and gendered—currencies; they draw their value not in and from themselves as isolated entities, but from within a socially and historically embedded grid of meanings and multiple powers of investment, brokerage, and exchange" (25).

3. One might also argue that the debt crisis is itself heterosexist given that the pleas of "saving" something to give to one's children or grandchildren always seem to buttress the argument for the stripping away of the state's social responsibilities.

4. Watten calls for a rereading of "modernism for its moments of *social* reflexivity" (12). Countering Charles Altieri's view in "What Is Living and What Is Dead in American Postmodernism: Establishing the Contemporaneity of Some American Poetry" (*Social Text* 22.4 [summer 1996]: 764–90), Watten proposes: "Rather than being the site of a critique of representation presumed 'to exemplify ways of feeling, thinking, and imaginatively projecting investments *not bound to dominant social structures*,' in Altieri's view (767, my italics), modernism is best imagined not retro-

spectively, as a politics of form, but prospectively, as the site of an emerging cultural order that structures ways of feeling, thinking, and imagining difference within modernity" (12). Watten's move is to situate modernism within social relations, not to sever it from modernity and modernization. Altieri's position would perpetually relegate a poetics to an oppositional role in that it is to imagine ways of being outside of social relations, as if it is the aesthetic role of poetry to imagine a site outside of ideology. A situated antisystem poetics, as I propose, seeks to rearticulate ideological sites, not to vacation outside of a false consciousness.

5. I am carrying over Watten's usage of Charles Bernstein's designation of "standard" and "nonstandard" poetries from his essay "Poetics of the Americas" (*Modernism/Modernity* 3.3 [1996]: 1–23 <http://128.220.50.88/journals/modernism-modernity/v003/3.3bernstein.html>). Watten charges Bernstein with a universalizing or ironically standardizing tendency to read "standard" poetries as necessarily reactionary and to create an emergent "new set of norms" of nonstandard poetry (4). Watten accuses Bernstein of an assimilationist policy for racialized writers in which, in order to be understood as oppositional, their work must take on the same formal tactics as language poetry; that is, they must refute normative forms of representation. This universalizing tendency, Watten argues further, does not allow for the social reflexivity of the material text and the situatedness of its production and, ultimately, "neglects . . . the status of the subject in relation to the reflexivity of form" (11). However, Bernstein's "universalizing" is not based on liberal humanist notions of a universal self but on the relation of the ideology and effects of globalization both as a discursive exterior and as a process that gives rise to similar forms of resistance in varied sites. Watten is right to point out that the actual sites, flows, and engines of globalization are not sufficiently defined by Bernstein, but this is also a characteristic flaw in discussions of globalism and culture. Bernstein's emphasis is on a transnationalism that is coalitional: "I am convinced, however, that nonstandard writing practices share a technical commonality that overrides the necessary differences in interpretation and motivation, and this commonality may be the vortical prosodic force that gives us footing with one another" (6). In this sense Bernstein addresses the deficit of universalism that theorists such as Ernesto Laclau believe is necessary for effective coalitional politics.

Another tension in this debate, however, lies not in the status of the subject but in the status of the nation. Bernstein risks a universalizing force for the potentials of a transnational oppositional force that is based on a centrifugal or noncentralizing force. Watten's distrust of this transnationalism (in that it overrides specific contexts) tends to reinforce the centrality of the nation.

6. I've yet to hear of the category, or identity formation, "American-Canadian."

References

Balibar, Etienne, and Immanuel Wallerstein. *Race, Nation, Class: Ambiguous Identities*. London: Verso, 1991.

Brand, Dionne. *No Language Is Neutral*. Toronto: Coach House, 1990.

Butler, Judith. *The Psychic Life of Power: Theories in Subjection*. Stanford: Stanford University Press, 1997.

Cruz, John. "From Farce to Tragedy: Reflections on the Reification of Race at Century's End," in *Mapping Multiculturalism*, ed. Avery F. Gordon and Christopher Newfield. Minneapolis: University of Minnesota Press, 1996.

Department of Multiculturalism and Citizenship Act. *Statutes of Canada*. Vol. 8, Chap. M-12.6. Ottawa: Queen's Printer, 1993.

Jameson, Fredric. *Postmodernism, or, The Cultural Logic of Late Capitalism*. Durham: Duke University Press, 1991.

Kamboureli, Smaro. "The Technology of Ethnicity: Law and Discourse." *Open Letter* 8.5/6 (1993): 202–17.

Kiyooka, Roy, and Roy Miki. "Inter-Face: Roy Kiyooka's Writing. A Commentary/Interview." Roy Kiyooka catalogue. Vancouver: Or/Artspeak Galleries, 1991.

Kobayashi, Audrey. "Multiculturalism: Representing a Canadian Institution." In *Place/Culture/Representation*, ed. James Duncan and David Ley, 205–31. London and New York: Routledge, 1993.

Mathur, Ashok. *Loveruage*. Toronto: Wolsak and Wynn, *1994*.

Miki, Roy. *Random Access File*. Writing West Series. Edmonton: NeWest Press, 1995.

Nakada, Mark. "Dreaming Okinawa: A Poetic and Critical Investigation of Mixed-Race Subjectivity." Master's thesis, University of Calgary, 1997.

Ng, Roxanna. "Sexism, Racism, Canadian Nationalism." In *Returning the Gaze: Essays on Racism, Feminism, and Politics*, ed. Himani Bannerji, 223–41. Toronto: Sister Vision, 1993.

Taylor, Charles. *Multiculturalism and the "Politics of Recognition."* Princeton: Princeton University Press, 1992.

Wah, Fred. *Diamond Grill*. Edmonton: NeWest Press, 1996.

Wallerstein, Immanuel. *Geopolitics and Geoculture.* Cambridge: Cambridge University Press, 1991.

Watten, Barrett. *The Bride of the Assembly Line: From Material Text to Cultural Poetics.* Impercipient Lecture Series. Vol. 1, no. 8 (October 1997).

Sianne Ngai

Shit has to be encountered in another way. It is now necessary to think of the usefulness of the unuseful, the productivity of the unproductive, philosophically speaking: to unlock the positivity of the negative and to recognize our responsibility also for what is intended. Kynical philosophers are those who do not get nauseated. In this they are related to children, who do not yet know anything about the negativity of their excrement.

—Peter Sloterdijk, *Critique of Cynical Reason*

•

How else could I refer to that horrible, brute raw matter and dry plasma that was simply there while I shrank back within myself in dry nausea, I sinking centuries and centuries deep in mud—it as mud, and not even dried mud but mud still wet, still alive, it was an ooze in which the roots of my identity were twisting about with an intolerable slowness.

Take, take all that for yourself, I don't want to be a living person! I disgust myself, I marvel at myself, thick ooze coming slowly forth. [. . .]

I had reached nothingness, and the nothingness was live and moist.

—Clarice Lispector, *The Passion According to G. H.*

•

A dictionary begins when it no longer gives the meaning of words but their tasks. Thus *formless* is not only an adjective having a given meaning, but a term that serves to bring things down in the world, generally requiring that each thing have its form. What it designates has no rights in any sense and gets itself squashed everywhere, like a spider or an earthworm. In fact, for academic men to be happy, the universe would have to take shape. All of philosophy has no other goal: it is a matter of giving a frock coat to what is, a mathematical frock coat. On the other hand, affirming that the universe resembled nothing and is only *formless* amounts to saying that the universe is something like a spider or spit.

—Georges Bataille, *Visions of Excess*

•

Your civilization has big teeth, o fathers, so big that it ended by gobbling itself. Now, we must pick over the pile of shit and each seek his piece of the tongue/language. No history, everything's putrified!

—Bernard Nöel, *The L=A=N=G=U=A=G=E Book*

•

The point is Gee Whiz is excrement
and if you think you are going to drag all that mess into the moment "you" are another thing coming.

—Deanna Ferguson, *Rough Bush*

•

I'm happy to have a little waste.

—Bruce Andrews, *I Don't Have Any Paper so Shut Up*

Theories, poetics, and hermeneutics of "desire" abound, but there seems to be something about disgust that resists similar discursive formations.[1] In contrast to the striking number of critical abstractions produced around the category of "desire" that have strategically informed theoretical writing for the past twenty years (for example, jouissance, polysemia, and libidinal economy), disgust has no well-known paradigms associated with it and has largely remained outside the range of any theoretical zone. This is surprising given that this affect often plays a prominent role in structuring our responses to capitalism and patriarchy. Its primacy in characterizing how we experience these symbolic and political systems raises the question of why our understanding of repulsion has been taken less seriously than that of attractions, specifically as a linguistic or literary concern. Even though disgust obviously impacts on questions of desire and vice versa, there has been less motivation to examine how the former experience might inform the work of reading and producing texts. The goal of this essay is to investigate possible reasons for this critical skittishness, or squeamishness, and to imagine what a "poetics of disgust" would look like were it to exist.

In the social and material world we inhabit today it is arguable that potential objects of disgust (corporate ideology, bigotry, brute assertions of power and military force, all forms of institutionalized inequality) continue to balance if not outweigh those of desire. A poetics of disgust would begin with this basic position: that there are at least as many things to turn away from as things to be drawn to and that this repulsion is worth thinking about seriously. That issues of repulsion remain theoretically undervalued or subordinate to issues of desire, then, is also surprising because the former tends to be a highly specific, identifiable phenomenon, whereas the parameters of attraction are notoriously difficult to locate and define. The problem of certainty is simply less relevant in cases of disgust, as an experience less open to epistemological questioning and doubt. This may be because the spectrum of what we call desires in our language is much broader than that of disgusts or because the criteria for "being disgusted," as a particular mode of responding to an object, are limited in a way that the criteria for "desiring" that object are not. The language of consumer culture simply offers more ostensible definitions for desire because it must accommodate so many permutations of this relation to persons and things. At the same time, middle-class morality imposes a limit on ways of expressing outrage against the dominant power structure that *has the effect of deliberately curbing our poten-*

tial to articulate our abhorrence to it, and thus the additional effect of curbing our potential to fully comprehend or theorize our response. This may explain why "desire" is commonly spoken of in pluralized forms (as polysemic, eclectic, or polymorphous), whereas disgust remains indissociably singular.

The fact that there are fewer ways of "being disgusted" than ways of "desiring," which is to say fewer ways of *articulating* disgust, fewer terms available in the language of consumer culture to give it agency or voice, should foreground the question of the role it might play in a contemporary poetics committed to ideology critique. All the more so because the power of this affective response still manages to undermine attempts made to curtail its expression. In its specificity, certainty, and force, the expression of disgust maintains a negative insistence that cannot be recuperated by the "seductive reasoning"[2] of global capitalism and its pluralist dynamics, in spite of all efforts to neutralize such utterances. In resistance to all-inclusive strategies, a poetics of disgust would thus take the form of a poetics of both exclusion and radical externality, based on outwardness and excess.

By describing poststructuralist "desire" as polysemic, polymorphous, eclectic, and all-inclusive, I am deliberately drawing an analogy between its elevated status as a critical and aesthetic paradigm and the logic of pluralism as a contemporary cultural norm. As many social commentators have noted, postmodernity and pluralism are virtually synonymous; Andreas Huyssen describes the former, for example, as "cultural eclecticism or pluralism" (130) and Alex Callinicos as a situation in which "cultural life becomes more fragmented or pluralistic" (134). More than any other theory currently in circulation, political pluralism shapes our ideas of liberal democracy; and as Hal Foster notes, pluralism or eclecticism in art has also been de rigueur for the last two decades: "No style or even mode of art is dominant and no critical position is orthodox. Yet this state is also a position, and this position is also an alibi . . . for in a pluralist state art and criticism tend to be dispersed and so rendered impotent. Minor deviation is allowed only in order to resist radical change, and it is this subtle conformism that one must challenge" (13). If aesthetic eclecticism and other all-inclusive strategies have the effect of "absorb[ing] argument" (Foster) and neutralizing critique, then the privileged role played by "desire" in both experimental poetry and literary theory needs to be reexamined. For the last twenty years in both cultural arenas, the libidinal as theoretical paradigm has been of unquestionable service by *generating* critique; but in the pluralistic form assumed by it today, it would seem to shut critique down—particularly because of the romanticization or false profundity that so frequently accompanies its use. I place my examination of disgust against "desire" for this reason, not just because of the latter's ubiquity in critical discourse but also because the disproportional roles assigned to these affective structures masks the fact that the two are often concomitant. Yet disgust seems most often at odds or in conflict with desire, functioning as its obverse or negation.

Moving Outside "Desire" as a Theoretical Model for Writing

Has seduction placated me so well? It is, if I wish to know, quiet need of extraordinary aim framed by tiny voices.

—Dorothy Trujillo Lusk, "First"

What operates on the other side of the libidinal? The ready answer, as supplied by Kant, has been the law; but as Lacan shows in his readings of Kant, Sade, and Sophocles,[3] desire similarly posits obligations to be complied with and followed, to the extent that it becomes coterminous with the ultimate imperative: "The moral law, looked at more closely, is simply desire in its pure state."[4]

To say that "desire" has its own system of discipline and thus its own set of legal parameters, including above all the injunction that the subject meet his or her demands for satisfaction, is to *continue* raising the question of what happens when such an imperative (or any imperative within a dominant system) goes unanswered. Or is answered by the subject's *refusal* to answer.

Clearly, "desire" by itself is not automatically resistance to censorship or the law. The libidinal threatens aspects of the symbolic order at times, it is true; but we can see that the law has a way of prescribing if not instating these very desires, particularly if we follow Judith Butler in considering them inextricably intertwined with prohibitions. If desire and prohibition come into existence in tandem, then the "subversiveness" that tends to be automatically attributed to the libidinal and its discursive models (jouissances, etc.), based on the assumption that it fundamentally opposes the dictates of the symbolic order, needs to be reconsidered—particularly because the libidinal is so frequently relied on as a convenient catchall in poststructural theories of language and selfhood for explaining all that transgresses the norm. With its privileged and generally unquestioned status as a theoretical paradigm, it currently exists as a ubiquitous frame of reference in postmodern criticism and theory, especially in the reading of contemporary texts.

What seems to lie outside the realms of both desire and the law is disgust: repugnance, abhorrence, revulsion, repulsion. Not a moving *toward* the object, either to possess it or to be possessed by it, to engulf it or to be engulfed by it (as in desire's familiar trajectory), but a turning *away*. If disgust cannot be fully assimilated or internalized by either the libidinal or the law, it becomes available to us as a crucial third term—one that is itself a term *of* exclusion and thus irreducible to the current pluralism of "desire" or to pluralist conceptions of the democratic state. To say that desire and democracy are typically configured as pluralisms is to point out that both have been privileged as all-inclusive economies that, as Ellen Rooney notes, *paradoxically exclude forms of exclusion*—namely, Marxisms and other materialist discourses that "challenge the theoretical possibility of general [consensus and] take the process of exclusion to be *necessary* to the production of meaning or community" (Rooney 5). Throughout *Seductive Reasonings* Rooney argues that pluralism manipulates the rhetoric of "consensus" and "understanding" in order to reduce oppositional politics to "monolithic totalitarianism[s]" (27), avoiding the problem of Marxist theory and "the urgent question it asks, the question of exclusion" (26). Using various sources from newspapers and magazines that depict socialist movements as betrayals of pluralism, Rooney shows how "political pluralism, 'American-style,' is nothing but the exclusion of marxisms, both in domestic politics and abroad" (27).

What makes disgust an important force in contemporary experimental writing engaged with ideological concerns, as well as in our methods of reading this work, is thus its negative potentiality as a figure of exclusion, the radical externalization it enacts in facilitating the subject's turn away from the object. In this manner the possibility of disgust as a political poetics resides in its resistance to pluralism and its ideology of all-inclusiveness enabling it to "recuperate and neutralize any critical discourse emphasizing conflict, dissent, or discontinuity" (Rooney 5).

A Parable of Repulsion

Buying a newspaper at a local deli: I'm at the front counter when I hear a loud though muffled noise, something between a groan and a cry, from a man standing half inside, half outside the open door. It's an exclamation but not of any recognizable words with recognizable meanings. My head automatically swivels to follow the direction of his gaze, but I can't make out what he's looking at. He's got his hand to his mouth, covering it. I say, "What is it?" Wordlessly again, he points. I walk closer to him and see he is looking at a piece of shit on the sidewalk. There's a roach on this turd, and the roach is eating it. We look at this for a while together. As if we were compelled to, fascinated in spite of ourselves. Then he makes that inarticulate sound again, hand still over the mouth, and turns his head away. As do I. After he has vanished around the corner, I realize that I am still standing in the place he just left, with my hand also positioned over my mouth, head turned away. As if I had followed or copied his exact gestures in order to take his place, continue a series in which the experience gets passed on to another stranger. Who might say: Buying a newspaper at a local deli, I heard this woman make a noise . . . and so on. But eventually the shit dwindles into a stain, the roach crawls away and finds something else to eat or doo; the story expires. Objects of disgust have no shelf life.

There are elements of this encounter I want to isolate, which requires that I strip down the narrative and shuffle its elements around:

> That inarticulate sound.
> Head automatically swivels to follow the direction of gaze.
> Wordlessly points.
> Fascinated in spite of ourselves.
> Turns away.
> In the place he just left.
> Copied his exact gestures in order to take his place.

Of the above the following points should be stressed in schematizing a possible grammar of disgust:

(1) *The negative utterance.* An "inarticulate sound" made in response to the object. No words are used in the expression of disgust and thus the question of what words "mean" is simply irrelevant to this particular type of utterance. Yet an affect is clearly conveyed;

(2) *The gesture of pointing.* With emphasis on its role in prompting (3) and instigating (4);

(3) *A negative fascination with the object.* Not wanting to look at it but staring nonetheless—for a limited duration;

(4) *The figure of the turn or moment of exclusion.* The movement *away* from the object as if to shun it. This turn is mobilized by (2) and (3);

(5) *The inclusion of the other in that act of excluding the object.* The participation of the other in following the subject's previous gestures, both (2) and (3). A form of sociability or mutual attunement facilitated by the turn away. Paradoxically, the other is included in the subject's response of disgust via his act of exclusion, his shunning of the object;

(6) *The absence, void, or hole created by the turn away from the object.* A negative space is created, or opened up, by the evacuation of the subject following his negative interaction with the object. The "place he just left," a [ ] into which the other steps;

(7) *The repetition that takes place in this void.* Inside the [ ], the other copies the gestures made by the subject in excluding the object.

The rhetoric of disgust conveys an insistence or affective force mobilized by the sequence of events in its entirety: the inarticulate or "formless" utterance, the gesture of pointing, the subject's negative fascination with the object, his exclusion of or turning away from the object, and the other's assumption of the empty place defined by the subject's withdrawal. In the next section of this essay I discuss the relevance of these elements independently, including the way each bears on aspects of contemporary postmodern writing, in order to show that there is a discursive logic to emotional response, that expressions of disgust have their own particular grammar.

(1) Negative Utterances

Formless is not only an adjective having a given meaning but a term that serves to bring things down in the world, generally requiring that each thing have its form. What it designates has no rights in any sense and gets itself squashed everywhere, like a spider or an earthworm.

—Georges Bataille

Clarice Lispector's *The Passion According to G. H.*, a hybrid of philosophy and fantasy that is also the narrative of a woman smashing and eating a cockroach, ends with the narrator's ecstatic depersonalization. This culminating event is brought about through her encounter with the cockroach and the "brute raw matter" of its guts oozing forth, a confrontation that in turn leads to the discovery of a new form of language: a means of paradoxically expressing her own inexpressiveness.[5] What the narrator calls her "condition of inexpressiveness" is a nonsymbolic state of being that manifests itself only in response to the soft and formless matter gushing from the roach's body; a relation to the world that can be articulated only through a specific kind of hyperbolic utterance. Inexpressiveness is also, G. H. suggests, a social condition that can be expressed through certain kinds of innovative artistic production, including poetry:

> At times—at times we manifest inexpressiveness ourselves—in art that is done . . . to manifest the inexpressive is to create. At bottom we are so, so happy! for there is not just one way to enter in contact with life, there are also the negative ways! also the painful ways, even the all-impossible ones. . . . And there is also at times the exasperation of the atonal, which is a profound happiness: *exasperated atonality* is flight rising—nature is exasperated atonality, thus it was that worlds were formed: atonality became exasperated. (Lispector, 135, my italics)

A text may thus bear witness to its creator's articulate expression of his or her own inarticulateness or to his or her potential to not-express or to not-articulate. This negative potentiality exists only for the work of a poet who knows that the laws of the symbolic order will always determine certain things in advance of what any individual means to say. Acknowledging this and confronting it directly, the writer takes her text *beyond* the traditional goal of poetic expression or representational thinking (thought that has form) in order to realize what Lispector calls the "happiness" of an inexpressiveness inspired by formless matter. This is the negative potentiality of representations of representational impotence. As Giorgio Agamben might say, the agency of these utterances resides in their syncretism of an ability to express *as well as* not-express: "Only a power that is capable of both power and impotence, then, is the supreme power. . . . The perfect act of writing comes not from a power to write but from an impotence that turns back on itself and in this way comes to itself as a pure act [of unfathomable potentiality]" (37).

Only the poet who recognizes the negative agency of exasperated utterances, their ability to not-express or to not-articulate, is able to paradoxically express her own inexpressiveness and give form to what is formless. Lispector: "When art is good it is because it has touched inexpressiveness, the worst art is expressive art, the kind that transgresses the piece of iron and the piece of glass, and smiles, and the shouts" (136). In committing such transgressions the poet strains the limits of even modernist atonality, the logic that radically transformed musical theory. Applicable to language, as well as music, the atonal is a system in which there is no central key or referent, only a series of relations or differences between terms. A semiotician might describe this impartial chromaticism as metonymic: signifiers endlessly referring and deferring to other signifiers rather than designating unitary signifieds. Yet metonymy, which Lyotard describes as "the avant-garde of capital," is also a systemic logic effecting the same dematerialization of the sign done by systems of centralized reference or metaphorical substitution.[6] Although atonality enables us to go beyond the referent privileged in tonal music, as a system of slippages between terms it similarly delivers a "message" or fulfills a representative function; that is, the import of the operation lies in something other than the terms in their material embodiments: "See what you have done, the material is immediately annihilated. Where there is a message, there is no material. Adorno said this admirably of Schoenberg: the material, he explained, in serialism *does not count as such*, but only as a relation between terms. And in Boulez there will be nothing but relations, not only between pitches, but also between intensities, timbres, durations. Dematerialization" (Lyotard 44).

The paradoxical expression of one's own inexpressiveness takes the form of what Lispector calls "exasperated atonality," an atonality that, strained to the limit, gets fed up with itself. "Fed up" in the sense of the once-radical system eating or turning on itself but also suggesting strained limits or surplus: the rhetorical excess paradoxically produced by the poet's foregrounding of his or her lack. It's the articulation of this negative potentiality in language that most strongly informs the politicized writing of poets Bruce

Andrews, Kevin Davies, Jeff Derksen, Deanna Ferguson, and Dorothy Trujillo Lusk. Disgust with capitalism and its subject-centered reason compels these writers to take the impartial chromaticism of language to the extreme: "Help defeat your country—power faults keep cranium free of lint wrench to choose from a mind as free as Republicanism: late as silk, backstabbers, drop your mental candy bars, the ascension of the cookies womb, swank accommodation for that coathanger: train your friends to shit on newsprint."[7]

The exasperated atonality of these utterances suggests that negative potentiality itself (manifest in paradoxical expressions of inexpressiveness) is not just an abstract signifying operation but an agency realized through a particular affect: utter repugnance. This affect is amplified in Ferguson's work; consider this moment of disgust from "Still Life, with the law" (*Rough Bush* 1995), which seems to offer an implicit commentary on techniques used to articulate the experience: "Rebellion hallowed, hollered. These magic games aren't fun anymore, aren't [dead] addicted—only want to make a buy. Used words and phrases that apply part of an esoteric jargon of grunting and straining—woo, braah, phonographic recall retched sounds from bathroom splashes, formal off the road" (no page number).

In expressions of disgust language becomes *formless*, the "esoteric jargon of grunting and straining," "retched sounds from bathroom splashes." As with the inarticulate sound made by the subject in our parable, the poet's expression of inexpressiveness thrusts the base materiality of language into the foreground: "woo, braah." Here the question of what a word means (the form it gives to a preexistent thought) *as well as* the question of how it relates abstractly to another word in the system (form deferring to form) becomes secondary to its simply "being there," in all its insistence and affective force.

Even when comprising articulate sounds, the expression of disgust counteracts both referential language and purely relational language, relying instead on more stolid formations that continue to trouble certain conceptions of language but are nonetheless part of it: "brute raw matter that [is] simply there" (Lispector, 35), flows and outpourings, noise. This is where

Saussure's anxiety about onomatopoeia and interjections comes in. For disgust's utterances are not propositions, or assertion-like in structure, but more like *sounds and exclamations*. They are, in this sense, "empty": [ ]. The "inarticulate sounds" of disgust are expletives and obscenities: like onomatopoeia, these are units of language that seem less to "mean" than to simply "be." At the same time, however, these exorbitant forms are "indissociably singular" and do not refer or defer themselves to other signs. Nothing may be contained within the brackets, but the brackets themselves cannot be budged. In their insistence or intensity, expletives and onomatopoeia resist *both* the potentially endless movement from one signifier to another *and* the fixation of signifier to signified.

Discursive raw matter is what is simply and irreducibly there; it neither instigates a horizontal voyage from term to term (which is a dynamic Lacan attributes to "desire" in "Agency of the Letter"), nor does it bring forth a vertical fixation. In this manner the discursive materials that make up a grammar of disgust resemble what Lyotard calls tensors, referring to the tension in a sign that exceeds this semiotic dialectic of condensation and displacement: both the metaphorical fixation of word to concept (the drive toward a unitary, preestablished designation or meaning) *and* the "interminable metonymy" of slippage from word to word (desire's polysemia), in which "we never get anything but cross-references, signification is always deferred, and meaning is never present in flesh and blood" (41).

As forms of the tensor, expletives and onomatopoeia counteract the dematerialization of language that occurs in *both* cases, a dematerialization that is very possibly "equivalent to the work of capital in the affairs of sensibility and affect." For although the later instance, that of metonymic slippage or polysemia ("avant-garde of capital") is frequently privileged by innovative writers over the substitutive or representational logic of metaphor (in Stein's work, for example), it belongs to the same semiotic value system that annihilates the materiality of the sign. Unlike Lacan, who imputes that there is a freedom in the postponement and displacement of signifiers ("what does man find in metonymy if not the power to circumvent the obstacles of social censure?" ["Agency of the Letter" 167]), Lyotard argues that even metonymic slippage produces the same dematerializing effects in language as metaphor, that it is equally intent on turning matter into abstract relation, if not direct reference.

Since the Objectivists, metaphor has been somewhat out of fashion in experimental poetry, attacked for affirming the values of official verse culture or the representational status quo. But for Lyotard metonymy is similarly circumscribed by the institutionalized logics of capital. Although one term seems to freely lead to another, one will "always need to work to determine the terms to which, in a given *corpus*, the term under examination can and must lead" (45). According to this claim, even polysemia ("signification constituted by signs alone") cannot accommodate the intensities of affect informing and exceeding the sign: here, it is true, "there are only divergences, and if there is any meaning, it's because there is a divergence"; yet this proliferation of divergences is itself systemic: "there is . . . not any old divergence of course, we don't move from one element to the other in any old way, on the contrary it is a journey organized from one term to another, and involves the extreme precision of a system or structure" (44).

Woo, braah. In their insistence, exclamatory and onomatopoeic words and phrases manifest the tension in the sign that prevents this annihilation. There's an irreducible materiality to them that cannot be found in language that refers vertically (metaphorically) or horizontally (metonymically). If exclamations and onomatopoeia just "are," rather than substituting or deferring, it's no surprise that Saussure singles them out as potential threats to his theory of the arbitrary sign.[8] It's important to note the possibility that these marginalized formations pose the greatest threat to structuralist theories of signification *because they cannot be divorced from their insistence*—the affects they convey or the noises they make. "Get thee outta the ball park, onto the marsh—freeze over morass! Hell yes we will talk. World enough & unbearable though detextable. Picky Picky" (Lusk, "Oral Tragedy"). It could be said that onomatopoeia and exclamations are the most "passionate" forms of linguistic expression, written or spoken, and thus the problem they pose to traditional semioticians makes sense: the question of affect (and its effects) has been generally avoided by those concerned primarily with language as a set of neutral, objective, or purely mechanical functions unrelated to social or cultural factors. Here affect is viewed as remaining "outside" the text's "internal" signifying machinery, its system of tropological operations, its metaphors and metonymies.

Lispector: "And then, the cockroach: what is the only sense the cockroach has? attentiveness to living, *inseparable from its body.*" A poetics of disgust would therefore rely on the use of such raw matter: words with insistence or "attentiveness to living," inseparable from their material embodiments, as letters on the page. Language's raw matter (flow, gush, outpouring; inarticulate sound; "something between a groan and a cry"; ow, help, no; woo, braah; smiles and shouts) does not seek to be evaluated epistemologically or symbolically as one might evaluate a proposition, for the truth value or representational value of the assertion it makes. Its rhetorical force comes from elsewhere and is perceived differently: as that which solicits a *response* from the other in the form of pure affect or noise.[9]

(2) The Insistence of Pointing

This: a flaw that I talk like: This

—Dorothy Trujillo Lusk, "The Worst"

•

All members of society contain [ ].

—Kevin Davies, *Pause Button*

According to the parable above, a gesture is made concomitantly with the subject's utterance of disgust, one that dramatizes the inadequacy of conventionally expressive or representational language in sudden confrontation with raw matter (feces on the sidewalk, Lispector's cockroach entrails, Bataille's spider or spit, etc.). The grammatical correlate of this gesture is the deictic: "the use of words which have no content or independent reference at all, only a deictic or pointing function."[10] Figuring prominently in the work of the poets discussed above, this stylistic device also dominates the later writings of Henry James, to which the preceding quotation by Seymour Chatman refers. In his rigorous study of James's technical difficulty, Chatman describes the deictic nouns so excessively utilized in the typical sentence as "almost empty words" (54). The emptiness thus attributed to deixis recalls the role played by expletives and onomatopoeia in the rhetoric of disgust, as discursive formations in which a similar representational lack is articulated. Again, to say that utterances of disgust are nonrepresentational or formless is really to say that they are paradoxical representations of their nonrepresentationality, formations of the formlessness within language that threatens the stability of semantic fixation as well as word-to-word slippage. The gesture of pointing also constitutes part of disgust's rhetoric for similar reasons, particularly when *the object implicated by deixis is excluded or negated.* In other words, when grammatical pointers are dutifully pointing, presumably to an object, but the identity of this object is deliberately obscured or withdrawn; when the object is purposely made difficult to find, paradoxically, by the very condition of its being pointed at; or when it can't be found at all.

This paradoxical situation (of pointers pointing but to no readily discernible or identifiable object or to an object already in the process of being lost) is what makes late James so difficult to follow. Consider this moment cited by Chatman in *The Wings of the Dove*: "Whatever it was it had showed in this brief interval as better than the alternative; and it now presented itself altogether in the image and in the place in which she had left it . . . that depended more or less of course on the idea of the thing—into which at the present, however, she wouldn't go." As Chatman notes, "No mercy for the poor reader who cannot remember what 'it' is" (55); i.e., the object of reference. As in our initial parable of disgust, where the subject's gesture of pointing becomes exaggerated or even melodramatic in his attempt to express his inexpressiveness, the use of deixis in the work of James is deliberately overdetermined. In sentences crowded with adjectival pointers (*this, that, these, those*) and deictic nouns (*it, thing, matter*), the gesture of pointing becomes so insistent, repeated over and over again and always aiming at more than one direction, that it actually robs the object it implicitly designates of identity. In this manner the gesture of pointing when overdetermined becomes a way of dramatizing negation and lack. In order to articulate his experience of having been rendered *inarticulate* by disgust, the subject points to the object as an exaggerated gesture of *refusal.* This insistent action (hand to mouth, arm dramatically flung outward, index finger stretched as far as possible from the rest of the hand) immediately precedes his final action of turning away. In this manner the very act of pointing at the object paradoxically becomes a means of repudiating it—a potentially political gesture of exclusion.[11]

Although pointing at an object would seem to create a pathway toward it, or provide means of drawing nearer, in disgust it actually produces a movement in the opposite direction: a withdrawal or deliberate turning away. Consider, for example, Heidegger's account of how pointing establishes the trajectory of an exclusion, calling attention to the radical exteriority of any sign from itself:

> What withdraws from us, draws us along by its very withdrawal, whether or not we become aware of it immediately, or at all. Once we are drawn into the withdrawal, we are drawing toward what draws, attracts us by its withdrawal. And once we, being so attracted, are drawing toward what draws us, our essential nature already bears the stamp of "drawing toward." As we are drawing toward what withdraws, we ourselves are pointers pointing toward it. We are who we are by pointing in that direction—not like an incidental adjunct but as follows: this "drawing toward" is in itself an essential and therefore constant pointing toward what withdraws. To say "drawing toward" is to say "pointing toward what withdraws."
>
> To the extent that man *is* drawing that way, he *points* toward what withdraws. *As* he is pointing that way, man *is* the pointer. Man here is not first of all man, and then also occasionally someone who

points. No: drawn into what withdraws, drawing toward it and thus pointing into the withdrawal, man first *is* man. His essential nature lies in being such a pointer. Something which in itself, by its essential nature, is pointing, we call a sign. As he draws toward what withdraws, man is a sign. But since this sign points toward what *draws away*, it points, not so much at what draws away as into the withdrawal. The sign stays without interpretation. (9–10)

"Since this sign points toward what *draws away*, it points, not so much at *what* draws away as into the withdrawal" (second italics are mine). This is exactly how the deictic functions in our parable: what the man outside the deli points at is less the object than his own turning away from it. There is an insistence in the gesture of pointing, but where this insistence is placed is not on the identity of the object pointed at but on its loss or exclusion. And on the outwardness of the gesture itself, with its emphasis on what is external to any subject or object's self-identity.

It may seem strange to bring up grammatical concerns endemic to James's highbrow fiction in relation to the poetry of Andrews, Ferguson, or Lusk. But perhaps it will seem less so if we consider the possibility, with Chatman, that what's at stake for James in his excessive deixis is his preoccupation with relations. The writer's awareness that "behind every petty individual circumstance there ramifies an endless network of general, moral, social, and historical relations" is what motivates his effort to "relate *every* event and *every* moment of life to the full complexity of circumambient conditions" (Chatman 78).[12] This overwhelming task is none other than that of describing what informs the subject's individual consciousness and is simultaneously radically beyond it. The dilemma becomes that of being a small subject inscribed by a big System, say "capitalism," a subject who tries to pit herself against the System yet being fully aware of how it defines her. One is easily threatened by terror and paralysis in the face of this vast interconnectedness of relations, a network so complex it seems ungraspable in its entirety. But then one runs the risk of approaching capitalism as sublime, when its effects are all too unsublime in daily life. The writer's strategy in interrogating this network of relations, without being subsumed by them in their enormity, is to refuse them as abstraction. In order to foreground the social and political spaces *between* subjects in a discursive network, the writer finds herself relying on rhetorical devices that materialize these "intangibles" without simply objectifying them. Discursive matter with the ability to designate the particular form of formlessness: as [ ], a constitutive lack or structural void. Here I am thinking of Kevin Davies' *Pause Button*, where the insistence of *this/that/it* constructions makes abstract relations under capitalism lived and concrete. These constructions are also used, at different moments, to relentlessly stage the disappearance or exclusion of the referential objects they point at. In such cases the exclusion of the referent itself is what gets materialized: "—The trembles.// A bank on every corner & a [ ] in every pot" (22). In Davies' incorporation of these brackets containing nothing, the insistence is on the place of the object, or its surroundings, rather than the object itself:

> — experimental pigeon between two towers.

> That's what happens
> when you give a [ ] a [ ] & tell it to start shooting.

> Flash of light along
> suburban horizon. (28)

If the grammatical gesture of pointing has the ability to both materialize that which is formless as well as make the referential object pointed at disappear, to paradoxically exclude or refuse it, it seems to perform the function of other linguistic raw matter in the grammar of disgust. As in the case of expletives and onomatopoeia: formations that are simultaneously presence ("being") and absence ("not-meaning"), positivity (material embodiments) and negativity (nonrepresentational). In breaking down these oppositional dualisms the deictic [ ] again performs the function of the tensor, that "intensity" counteracting the dematerialization of language occurring in both unitary designations of meaning and in the pluralist economy of poly-semia. The intense gesture accompanying expressions of disgust, in its paradoxical materiality and affective insistence, thus remains exterior to a semiotic value system stuck between two poles, the metaphorical fixa-tion/metonymic slippage, meaningful/meaningless dichotomy.

(3) Mutilated Utterances
(4) Excluding and Externalizing
(5) The Space Opens Up for the Other

OUT OF ORDER signs won't work
Someone will piss in it anyway

—Kevin Davies, *Pause Button*

A poetics of disgust, one that accommodates the subject's negative potentiality in impotence or lack, can only emerge from poetry built from linguistic raw matter. In focusing on disgust's characteristic expressions of inexpressiveness, it becomes apparent that the terms of this affective gram-mar share the common attribute of always pointing beyond themselves. And, paradoxically, this outwardness (the exteriority of a sign to itself) *is pre-cisely where the materiality of the sign is preserved and resides.* The deictic, the expletive or onomatopoeic phrase, @#$%!!?!s, brackets containing nothing: these forms of formlessness are strategically utilized by the writer against the dematerialization of language occurring daily in the communicative circuits of capital. Above, I mentioned Heidegger's interpretation of the gesture of pointing as an example of how its outward or externalizing function reveals the subject's own radical exteriority from himself—and how that subjective exteriority becomes *the basis for a new definition of the sign.* Man is a sign without interpretation *insofar as he points.* But significantly: insofar as he points not at an object but at the process of its becoming lost. What the deictic "insists" on is this very operation of withdrawal or exclusion, not the identity of the object excluded. What is "simply there" (as material) is simply there only insofar as it remains always exterior to itself.

If the real "object" of a deictic is thus not the identity or ontological consistency of any object but its withdrawal or exclusion, then the materiality of deictic utterances is one based on nonidentity. In other words, the deictic materializes or gives form *to that which is formless*, as evinced in Davies' use of [ ] along with the more conventional forms of deixis (*this, that,* and *its*) in *Pause Button*. Another example of unusual deictic construction is Jeff Derksen's use of the maimed statistic in the poem "Interface":

Anxiety punctuated by time.

West Germany 5.4%

"I'm a man—spell it I apostrophe M."

Patience dispersed through the legs leads me to "I become my job" now I'm pulling together like white blood cells. (10)

Like @%$#!! and [ ], other negative utterances or expressions of outrage, the brute number ("West Germany 5.4%") functions as semiotic raw matter, insisting on the disappearance of its referent and at the same time refusing to defer to other terms. It won't coagulate into a unitary meaning, and it also won't move; it can't be displaced. This statistic only covers a space; the reader cannot fix it metaphorically, assign a concept to it, or send it on a metonymic voyage along a chain of other terms. There's no substantive meaning, yet there's also no possibility of polysemia: West Germany 5.4% doesn't budge. It only sits there, in its material embodiment, its stolidity. The reader can act on it only by not acting on it, by turning away—just as the maimed statistic itself turns away from its implicit referent, excluding it. This unit of information is OUT OF ORDER: raw matter is sitting in the poet's lines—a deliberate obstruction of the semiotic system's machinery yet a part of it.

The effect of the mutilated statistic in Derksen's work recalls a moment from Sterne's *Tristram Shandy*, where the most commonly relied-on expression of disgust, the expletive, is itself mutilated or chopped in two because of bourgeois censorship of its articulation. Two nuns, a novice and an abbess, are trying to make their mules go up a hill. When these modes of transportation stubbornly refuse to move, the nuns find themselves forced to rely on the material productivity of crass utterances:

> My dear mother, quoth the novice . . . ——there are two certain words which I have been told will force any horse, or ass, or mule to go up a hill whether he will or no; be he never so obstinate or ill-willed, the moment he hears them he obeys. They are words magic! cried the abbess, in the utmost horror——No, replied Margarita calmly——but they are words sinful——What are they? quoth the abbess, interrupting her: They are sinful in the first degree, answered Margarita, ——they are mortal——and if we die unabsolved of them, we shall both——but you may pronounce them to me, quoth the Abbess of Andoüillets——They cannot, my dear mother, said the novice, be pronounced at all; they will make all the blood from one's body fly up into one's face——But you may whisper them to me, quoth the abbess.

Yet the horrid words are *not* pronounced in their entirety in the text. Instead, they are maimed: halved in the nuns' attempt to get to their destination without violating a prohibition laid down by the symbolic order:

> Now I see no sin in saying, *bou, bou, bou, bou, bou,* a hundred times together; nor is there any turpitude in pronouncing the syllable *ger, ger, ger, ger, ger,* were it from our matins to our vespers: Therefore, my dear daughter, continued the Abbess of Andoüillets——I will say *bou,* and thou shalt say *ger;* and then

alternately, as there is more sin in *fou* than in *bou*——Thou shalt say *fou*——and I will come in (like fa, sol, la, re, mi, ut, at our complines) with *ter*. And accordingly the abbess, giving the pitch, set off thus:

Abbess,	Bou — bou — bou
Margarita,	——ger, — ger, — ger
Margarita,	Fou — fou — fou
Abbess,	——ter, — ter, — ter.

The two mules acknowledged the notes by a mutual lash of their tails; but it went no further.——'Twill answer by an' by, said the novice.

Abbess,	Bou- bou- bou- bou- bou- bou-
Margarita,	——ger, ger, ger, ger, ger, ger.

Quicker still, cried Margarita.

Fou, fou, fou, fou, fou, fou, fou, fou, fou.

Quicker still, cried Margarita.

Bou, bou, bou, bou, bou, bou, bou, bou.

Quicker still——God preserve me! said the abbess——They do not understand us, cried Margarita——But the devil does, said the Abbess of Andoüillets. (411–12)

Even when mutilated by censorship, deformed or rendered "out of order" by bourgeois social or religious prohibitions, the expletive (Fuck!) continues to serve its externalizing/exclusionary function as linguistic raw matter. Like a worm that seems to become two worms when chopped in two, both pieces wriggling away, the formless form @#$!%!!?! achieves the same grammatical effects when halved: "@#$!" "%!!?!" Yet these effects are achieved only for a certain kind of reader, one who inhabits the diabolical subject position constituted or made available by the very use of the expletive. In Sterne's parable the broken expletive remains "understood" only insofar as *a third receiver is posited*, one who is neither nunish nor mulish. The very articulation of the expletive, even in mutilated form, introduces this other into the discursive scenario: the other who, unlike the donkey, has the capacity to understand. Lispector: "The unexpressive is diabolical" (92). In other words, the expletive (expression of outrage, expression of inexpressiveness) has the potential to clear a space for an other who might not otherwise be present.

The expletive *externalizes* in making room for this other who is devilishly other; it does so by *excluding* the donkeys. Similarly, in our parable we witnessed *the inclusion of the other* (the narrator who witnesses) *in the disgusted speaker's act of excluding the object*. This act of exclusion, of turning away from the object, creates an absence or void *that becomes the space for the other to step in*. The outwardness of the subject's gestures of exclusion, in other words, enables the mutual attunement between him and this other—this other who plays the role of the devil in Sterne's story. To be attuned to the work of Andrews, for instance, requires that one occupy the subject position the work itself creates; paradoxically, one is included by the very act of shunning or exclusion performed by the writing. If, as Sterne's parable suggests, as readers or users of language in the economy of disgust we are all either nuns, donkeys, or devils, who wouldn't want to be a devil?

Disgust Obstructs the "Seductive Reasoning" of Pluralism

We have also seen how the grammar of disgust "insists" on exclusions through its strategic deployment of linguistic raw matter (onomatopoeia, expletive, deixis, proper names, [ ], @$%!!?!), as well as how the psychosomatics of disgust, or its corporeal grammar, does so through the bodily equivalents of such discursive figures (cry or groan, gesture of pointing, the turn away from the object, the creation of an exteriorized space for the other to step in, her attunement with him in doing so). *The dominant mode of disgust is thus one of exclusion.* As such, disgust deliberately interferes with a reading practice based on the principle that what is at stake in every textual encounter is a hidden object, one that can be discovered by the reader only if he or she reads deeply enough. But in persistently and insistently reenacting the turn *away* from this object, whether it be a signified/referent or another signifier/term to which the present terms might defer, the grammar of disgust poses an obstruction to these normative modes of reading. By relying on linguistic elements that interfere with both metaphorical fixation (assignment of concept to word) and interminable metonymic slippage (word referring to other words in a horizontal, linear chain), actively counteracting the dematerialization of language occurring in both cases, disgust as externalizing exclusion suggests a form of textual engagement other than what is ordinarily described as "close" reading. Because the force of its utterances is aimed outward rather than inward, the social attunement between subjects disgust *does* achieve is paradoxically effected by a distancing. One ordinarily thinks of the "face-to-face encounter" as achieved through a process of drawing closer. But in disgust the opposite trajectory makes this ethically important moment happen. Pulling away from the object in revulsion, you're suddenly in front of the other, who, unlike the others, is attuned to you, who stands in the space you've prepared for him though that act of withdrawal. Paradoxically, in the economy of disgust, it is by means of an originary exclusion that the textual encounter is made intersubjective.

The grammar of desire is essentially, as Lacan suggests in relating it to the potentially endless movement from signifier to signifier, eclectic, polysemic, and plural, all-inclusive of the differences it produces. Thus desire is not merely pluralistic but a figure for pluralism. "Desire" includes everything—all forms belong, everyone participates; what desire *is* is precisely this all-inclusiveness. On the other hand, because the primary mechanism of disgust is exclusionary, because it insists on exclusion as the very *means* for enabling inclusion, disgust is *not* pluralistic and *cannot be a pluralism*. Although the language of consumer culture permits us to conceive of desire as polymorphous or even "polymorphously perverse," it simultaneously limits and inhibits both our common concept of disgust (the criteria by which this affective response is identified and defined) and our means of expressing it. Thus whereas the category of desire is plural, polysemic, eclectic, etc., the category of disgust can only accommodate a highly specific, rigidly defined type of experience. Desire is a *trope* of inclusion because it depends on a drawing-nearer to objects, to engulf or to be engulfed by them, whereas disgust, as a mode of withdrawal and exclusion, is logically excluded from all-inclusive systems.

Despite capitalism's curtailment of potential ways of articulating abhorrence without moralizing it, disgust in its irreducible singularity, in its specificity, certainty, and insistent force, continues to undermine attempts to neutralize its negative potentiality. Like Marxisms, a poetics of disgust "theorizes the necessity as well as inevitability of exclusions" (Rooney 63); that a community may be defined by members who refuse to engage in "open dialogue" with a universal anyone, regardless of their political stance or affiliation (Rooney 5). Both discourses assert that "the process of exclusion [is in fact] *necessary* to the production of meaning and community . . . that it is the definition of a field which, by 'excluding what it is not, makes it what it is'" (Rooney, citing Althusser and Balibar, 4–5). Because pluralism in its all-inclusive ideology excludes exclusions, as Rooney argues, the exclusion of Marxisms becomes theoretically essential to a pluralist conception of liberal democracy. This exclusion of Marxisms bears directly on the relationship between disgust and desire; there's no coincidence that among other political theories, Marxism stands out as the one in which disgust is most explicitly and forcefully articulated. Disgust is intrinsically exclusionary; in its function of articulating a profound disgust with capitalism, the rhetoric of Marxism is also exclusionary, and thus neither Marxism or the disgust it expresses can be recuperated by pluralism.

Thus the poetry of disgust, I would argue, again making an analogy with Marxist theory, *deliberately excludes* "the general reader" in order to make the space for the devil, or a reader *willing* to occupy the externalized place of radically other. Which makes the disgusted poet inevitably unpopular as well as antipopulist, easily labeled or morally dismissed as an elitist, dogmatist, or preacher to the diabolically converted. But: implying that the diabolically converted should not be addressed?[13] What lies behind the fantasy of all-inclusive readership, and the condemnation of "prescriptiveness" it supports, particularly when the demand that none be excluded is itself a prescription? This is exactly the way political pluralism in Western liberal democracies treats Marxism, as Rooney points out, harnessing the rhetoric of "consensus" and "understanding" in order to reduce socialist movements to *betrayals* of pluralism (27). As Hal Foster notes, "In a pluralist state art and criticism tend to be dispersed and so rendered impotent. . . . Here pluralism becomes an overtly political issue, for the idea of pluralism in art is often conflated with the idea of pluralism in society. Somehow, to be an advocate of pluralism is to be democratic—is to resist the dominance of any one faction (nation, class or style). But this is no more true than the converse: that to be a critic of pluralism is to be authoritarian" (30).

Foster goes on to suggest that pluralism in postmodern art and criticism replicates the logic of multinational capitalism as a mode of "false resistance" to its hegemonic structures. Like Rooney, Foster points out how pluralism resists theory, as it exists "without criteria of its own" and "seems to dismiss the need of a critical art" (17). The "lack of cogent discourse" in postmodern art and criticism, he suggests, is perhaps "*the* signal of the concession to pluralism" (15). Moreover, "the problem of critical methods (like demystification) rendered conventional, emptied of meaning, is fundamental to the problem of pluralism, for pluralism is a condition that tends to remove art, culture, and society in general from the claims of criticism and change" (26). A similar critique of this social logic is provided by Rosemary Hennessy in *Materialist Feminism and the Politics of Discourse*, in which she identifies the postmodern intellectual sphere as a site where "the dominant mode of reading is eclecticism": "Eclecticism uncritically links explanatory frames without making visible the contesting assumptions on which they are often premised. Underlying this easy mingling of contesting problematics is a pluralist social logic in which the production of knowledge is seen as consensual. Such a social logic underlies many 'new,' 'postmodernized' narratives which use terms like 'discourse,' 'subject,' and 'positionality' but without engaging the assumptions upon which these concepts are founded" (15).

It's not true to say that "desire," as one such "postmodernized" narrative, *resists* theory; in fact, achievements in critical thought from the last two decades prove the very opposite. But *as a form of pluralism*, as an eclectic, all-inclusive critical discourse or signifying economy, "desire" falls short as a materialism. What disgust may have to offer us as a poetics is precisely this capacity to function as such, as evinced in innovative work by writers who remain committed to the dirty work (as Ferguson might say, "the good doo-doo") of ideology critique.

Notes

1. Jonathan Dollimore made this observation in his lecture "Sexual Disgust" (Harvard University, March 1995). This essay was largely inspired by the implications of Dollimore's remark, as well as by his immediately following comment that he did not intend to propose a "theory of disgust." It should be clear that in contrast to Dollimore, when speaking of "desire" throughout this essay, I am not referring to sexuality or sexual practices but rather to forms of textual production and critique that depend on libidinal models. What I am interested in, in other words, is a theoretical engagement with language's negative affectivity, or those aspects of poetic language that fall outside the domains of both textual bliss and pleasure.

2. Ellen Rooney equates "seductive reasoning" with the "practice of pluralism" (57) in her rigorous critique of the ideology of general persuasion.

3. See "Kant Avec Sade," in Jacques Lacan, *The Seminar of Jacques Lacan*.

4. Jacques Lacan, *The Four Fundamental Concepts of Psycho-Analysis* (275), cited by Slavoj Zizek in *The Metastases of Enjoyment* (69). As Zizek notes, "Desire and Kantian ethical rigor coincide here in their disregard for 'the demands of reality'; neither of them acknowledges the excuse of circumstances or unfavourable consequences, which is why Lacan ultimately identifies them" (68–69).

5. In striking contrast to the expression of inexpressiveness, a recent full-page advertisement on the back cover of the *New York Times Magazine* (March 7, 1999) announces, "For Every Expression There's a Toyota." The backdrop of this text is an image frequently deployed by corporate advertising in the age of global capitalism: a mosaic of smiling, expressive faces suggesting multicultural all-inclusiveness. In its flattening-out of multiculturalism as site of political conflict and struggle, this ad offers a perspicuous example of how easily pluralist expressivism can be yoked to making money for multinational corporations.

6. Jean-François Lyotard, *Libidinal Economy*, trans. Iain Hamilton Grant (Bloomington: Indiana University Press, 1993).

7. Bruce Andrews, "Help Defeat Your Country," in *I Don't Have Any Paper so Shut Up*, 102.

8. See *Course in General Linguistics*, ed. Charles Bally and Albert Sechehaye, trans. Wade Baskin (New York: McGraw-Hill, 1966).

9. I am indebted to Stanley Cavell for this observation.

10. Seymour Chatman, *The Later Style of Henry James* (Oxford: Basil Blackwell, 1972), 54.

11. As evinced in the use of pointing in political demonstrations: the activist aims her index finger at the homophobe while yelling, "Shame!"

12. Chatman quotes from Ian Watt, "The First Paragraph of *The Ambassadors*: An Explication," *Essays in Criticism* 10 (1960): 475.

13. "Even if a [critical or aesthetic position] has public implications, must it conform to the rhetoric of a common reader?" I am rephrasing questions asked by Barbara Johnson in "The Alchemy of Style and Law" (176), in which she examines a reviewer's criticism of Patricia Williams for addressing academics rather than a general public in *The Alchemy of Race and Rights*.

References

Primary Texts

Andrews, Bruce. *I Don't Have Any Paper so Shut Up*. Los Angeles: Sun and Moon, 1992.

Derksen, Jeff. *Dwell*. Toronto: Talonbooks, 1993.

Davies, Kevin. *Pause Button*. Vancouver: Tsunami Editions, 1992.

Ferguson, Deanna. *Rough Bush*. Buffalo: Meow Press, 1996.

Lusk, Dorothy Trujillo. *Redactive*. Toronto: Talonbooks, 1990.

Secondary Texts

Agamben, Giorgio. *The Coming Community*. Minneapolis: University of Minnesota Press, 1993.

Althusser, Louis, and Etienne Balibar. *Reading Capital*. Trans. Ben Brewster. London: New Left Books, 1979.

Andrews, Bruce. *Paradise and Method: Poetics and Praxis*. Evanston: Northwestern University Press, 1996.

Bataille, Georges. "Formless." In *Visions of Excess: Selected Writings, 1927–1939*, ed. Allan Stoekel. Minneapolis: University of Minnesota Press, 1985.

Chatman, Seymour. *The Later Style of Henry James*. Oxford: Basil Blackwell, 1972.

Deleuze, Gilles, and Felix Guattari, *Anti-Oedipus: Capitalism and Schizophrenia.* Minneapolis: University of Minnesota Press, 1992.

Callinicos, Alex. *Against Postmodernism: A Marxist Critique.* New York: St. Martin's Press, 1989.

Farrell, Dan. *Thimking [sic] of You.* Vancouver: Tsunami Editions, 1994.

Foster, Hal. "Against Pluralism." In *Recodings,* by Hal Foster. Seattle: Bay Press, 1985.

Heidegger, Martin. *What Is Called Thinking?* New York: Harper and Row, 1968.

Hennessy, Rosemary. *Materialist Feminism and the Politics of Discourse.* New York: Routledge, 1993.

Huyssen, Andreas. "Mapping the Postmodern." In *A Postmodern Reader,* ed. Andreas Huyssen. New York: State University of New York Press, 1990.

Jameson, Fredric. *Postmodernism, or, The Cultural Logic of Late Capitalism.* Durham: Duke University Press, 1991.

Johnson, Barbara. *The Feminist Difference.* Cambridge: Harvard University Press, 1996.

Lacan, Jacques. *The Four Fundamental Concepts of Psycho-Analysis.* Trans. Alan Sheridan. New York: Norton, 1981.

———. *The Seminar of Jacques Lacan: Book VII, The Ethics of Psychoanalysis.* Trans. Dennis Porter. New York: Norton, 1992.

Lispector, Clarice. *The Passion According to G. H.* Trans. Ronald W. Sousa. Minneapolis: University of Minnesota Press, 1994.

Lyotard, Jean-François. *Libidinal Economy.* Trans. Iain Hamilton Grant. Bloomington: Indiana University Press, 1993.

Nöel, Bernard. "The Outrage against Words." In *The L=A=N=G=U=A=G=E Book,* ed. Bruce Andrews and Charles Bernstein. Carbondale: Southern Illinois University Press, 1984.

Rooney, Ellen. *Seductive Reasoning: Pluralism as the Problematic of Contemporary Literary Theory.* Ithaca: Cornell University Press, 1989.

Saussure, Ferdinand de. *Course in General Linguistics.* Ed. Charles Bally and Albert Sechehaye. Trans. Wade Baskin. New York: McGraw-Hill, 1966.

Sloterdijk, Peter. *Critique of Cynical Reason.* Minneapolis: University of Minnesota Press, 1987.

Sterne, Laurence. *Tristram Shandy.* New York: Signet, 1962.

Wittgenstein, Ludwig. *Philosophical Investigations.* Trans. G. E. M. Anscombe. Oxford: Basil Blackwell, 1958.

Zizek, Slavoj. *The Metastases of Enjoyment: Six Essays on Woman and Causality.* London: Verso, 1994.

Mark Wallace

1. The crisis of art in the twentieth century, which has been essentially a crisis of form, has been consistently related to the crises of cultural and political life that have marked this century. In the twentieth century the idea that a particular set of artistic forms can constitute not only the best way to create art but also the best way to live is responsible for the form of writing known as the manifesto.

Modernist and postmodernist theorists of poetics have consistently found it essential to equate the forms of poetry that they are promoting to a form of cultural and political life that they are also promoting. For instance, whatever contradictions there may have been in his project, for Ezra Pound the poetics of *The Cantos* were inextricably linked with his cultural politics. The same holds true for T. S. Eliot, Langston Hughes, Allen Tate, Charles Olson, Allen Ginsberg, Adrienne Rich, Charles Bernstein, June Jordan, Joan Retallack, Frederick Turner, and Nicole Brossard, to name just a few. Because the manifesto, of all literary forms, makes the most direct link between literary forms and cultural life, it can be considered (with only a little irony) the paradigmatic form of modernist and postmodernist literature.

Consistently, from whatever source, the poetic manifesto has three characteristics: (1) it asserts the value of its poetic practices; (2) it relates the value of its poetics to the value of a group of life practices, which it also promotes; and (3) it denounces those forms of poetry and living that exist in contradiction to it. The surrealist manifestos of Breton, Pound's essays, William Carlos Williams's commentaries in *Spring and All,* Charles Olson's essay "Projective Verse," Ron Silliman's *The New Sentence,* and Nicole Brossard's essay "Poetic Politics" are just a few examples of works displaying the key characteristics of the poetic manifesto.

2. One factor leading to the explosive expansion of poetic forms during modernism was the increasing availability of poetic and cultural alternatives

to the dominant notions of any single culture. The increased availability of information regarding other cultures, including non-Western cultures, as well as of information produced in the West that was critical of Western culture, helped poets in the twentieth century invent a growing array of formal possibilities. Many of these forms were created as direct responses to the social upheaval of the early twentieth century.

For writers at the end of the twentieth century this ever-expanding information gives poets an increasingly wide variety of poetic forms and traditions in which to explore their concerns. Having so many possibilities available is leading many contemporary poets to work in multiple and intersecting forms, mixing and reshaping forms from a variety of traditions to fit the needs of their poetry at a given moment. Whereas many poets of earlier parts of the twentieth century are identified with one particular tradition or form, even when those forms involve radical changes from earlier poetic forms, contemporary poets are increasingly likely to be identified as working with a multiplicity of forms and traditions.

3. It would be a mistake to say that in Western civilization, interest in innovative poetic forms begins only with the twentieth century. However much the nostalgia of various poetics might wish it was otherwise, poetic form has never been a stable entity and has always been related to problems of cultural life. Villon's rough and colloquial energy, satirizing the forms of high European culture, Milton's use of blank verse, Wordsworth's promotion of a natural rural language as an antidote to what he saw as the urban, artificial and deadly excess of European political life are only a few examples of revolutions in poetic form conceived of as having cultural and even immediately political pertinence. The explosion of poetic forms occurring during modernism is not a break from past concerns regarding poetic form but rather an intensification of energies that have always been present in Western culture.

4. Although the pre–twentieth century notion that forms of writing can directly establish transcendent truth has been for the most part dismantled, the notion that forms of writing still establish proper modes of cultural life has not only not been dismantled but remains an unquestioned mode of

activity among almost all schools of contemporary poetry, despite the increasing availability of forms from a variety of traditions. Social groups, publishing enterprises, production networks, poetry awards, reading series, and academic programs are often organized around the notion that a particular group of poetic forms constitutes the best way to write and live. The often semiconscious religious motivations behind this behavior are the subject of my essay "Genre as Conversion Experience" (*Talisman* 17 186–91).

5. At this time I take the major networks of poetry production in the United States to be the following: (1) the proponents of "traditional" formalism, with central strongholds in the South, New England, and New York; (2) the proponents of confessionalism, sometimes related to the first group but more specifically associated with university MFA programs across the nation; (3) the proponents of identity-based poetries, also associated with MFA confessionalism but tending to be more directly political in their concern with poetry by differing races, classes, cultures, and gender orientations and increasingly involved with spoken-word, performance "slam" poetry; (4) the proponents of the New American poetry speech-based poetics, often associated with Beat generation, ethnopoetics, or New York school writing; (5) the avant-garde, with current central power bases on the East and West Coasts but with pockets of activity in some other states, and among whom the L=A=N=G=U=A=G=E network has been a vital force (one now beginning to gain some small access to universities).

These groups vary greatly in terms of their access to finances and institutional power. At this time groups 1 and 2 have almost total control of such resources—poetry prizes, institutional programming, media exposure, etc.— and are only beginning to experience some small competition for those resources from group 3 and to a lesser extent from groups 4 and 5. However, each of these groups, on their own, has sufficient power to produce a broad array of poetry publications.

By no means are these groups absolutely distinct; a significant level of contact does occur across groups. Particular mingling occurs between groups 1 and 2, groups 2 and 3, groups 3 and 4, and groups 4 and 5 (which are so intermingled as to be indistinguishable in many cases). There are also very definite subgroups within each group. New formations are always possible; for instance, the recent development of a large group of "poets of witness" has developed out of a variety of conjunctions between groups 2 and 3. Avant-garde poetry in particular is marked by a huge variation in localized networks and formal concerns.

It is essential to understand, that is, that these production networks are by no means clearly and singularly defined. They are complex—loosely organized in some places, tightly bound in others. They often consist of many subnetworks and exist in complex relation to the activity of individual poets, who may or may not be aware that they are operating inside a production network. Some poets are very active power brokers within production networks; other poets tend toward a lower profile in network activities. Some poets directly identify themselves with one network, but many poets like to think of themselves as free agents, whether or not their particular poetic productions match the professed concerns of a given production network. However, whether or not given poets think of themselves as members of a production network, it is almost uniformly true that poets without strong ties to one production network or another will have great trouble getting their poetry known beyond local environments.

6. The desire to issue manifestos is more pronounced among some poets and more intense in some networks. Groups 1 and 5 tend at this time to be particularly strident in issuing manifestos, at least partly because those groups are the most interested in issues of poetic form that U.S. literary culture, on the whole, tends at the current moment to repress. Group 4, once a highly vocal producer of manifestos, has tended to become less so as the more polemical edges of its concerns have been co-opted by group 5 or group 3. Group 3 is also given to manifesto production, but its manifestos tend to repress issues of poetic form and highlight issues of direct political action. Group 2, because of its financial and promotional power and its current popularity (it is far more popular than the previously dominant group 1, with whom it still shares finances and resources), at this time is the most likely of these five groups to think of its own poetic practices as natural and therefore as not needing defense. Thus group 2, at this time, seems to feel

less need to issue manifestos, although should its popularity and institutional position be threatened, that feeling will certainly change.

7. Poets grouped around a particular poetry production network not only share many aesthetic values, but they tend to share certain political and social values as well. Nonetheless, it does not logically follow that use of the forms promoted by a given production network lead necessarily to a form of cultural life that is in general promoted by that network. Whatever claims of ownership and value a given network makes about poetic forms, poetic forms remain free-floating in terms of their possible cultural implications.

The current avant-garde tends as a group (although this is not uniformly so) to be socially radical in its political and cultural concerns. But some key modernist writers responsible for the invention of many literary forms associated with the avant-garde were conservative, reactionary, sometimes even fascist in their political and cultural concerns—Pound, Eliot, Wyndham Lewis, and Stevens being examples of various degrees. Although later uses of the formal possibilities suggested by these writers have been more consistently socially radical, the uses of those forms made by high modernist writers prove that the forms themselves, as forms, are not by definition radical or liberating in their implications.

As an example of the limitations of thinking of certain forms as inevitably liberating, it is argued frequently that parataxis (a technique in which various pieces of writing, sentences or poetic lines usually, stand on their own as pieces and are not structured into a grammatical hierarchy) offers a direct critique of the *social* hierarchies of Western capitalist countries. Yet it is possible that a social hierarchy of writers could be based on the use of parataxis, with writers receiving resources and opportunities on the basis of their ability to be expert in parataxis. Some would say—I don't agree with them, for reasons unnecessary to go into here—that a similar hierarchy actually exists in the contemporary avant-garde. Whether or not such a hierarchy exists, the fact remains that it could exist and that nothing in the nature of parataxis prevents its existence. Whatever metaphors about social life parataxis may suggest, they remain metaphors, and they exist in complex relation to the other social activities of the writers who use parataxis.

The struggles over form of the current poetry production networks are essentially struggles for the control of metaphors about form.

Furthermore, the implications of parataxis, or any other formal structure, depend hugely on what the pieces of that structure actually mean. It is possible that a poem with a paratactic structure could contain ethnic, racial, or gender slurs; desires for violence; and so forth. Indeed, one could argue that the logic of certain extreme hate groups is also paratactic in the sense that the logic of such groups is random and disconnected—although such parataxis is unconscious rather than conscious. In any case, without going too deeply into the unresolvable dilemmas of form and content, it seems clear that what one does with a form is the key ethical component of writing and not the form as it exists as a possibility, whatever historical use has been made of that form. The historical implications of any form are always subject to revision. I would go so far as to say that there might be a need sometimes to refigure forms that have historically been used to promote repressive cultural activity, as a way of proving that those who have engaged in that repressive activity have no right to the ownership of poetic forms.

8. I mean by "a free multiplicity of form" a cultural circumstance in which knowledge about issues of poetic form is not repressed and controlled by poetry production networks competing for ownership of forms. In a free multiplicity of form the issue of form in poetry becomes always an explicit problem that writers of poetry are allowed to explore in all its variance and that they must encounter. In such a circumstance it would no longer be possible either to ignore issues of form or to assume that the significance of any form can be known outside the specific uses that are made of it and can continue to be made of it. Writers would be aware of the need to question their own choices of form and would understand that the value of form can be discovered only by a conscious exploration of form in particular instances. A free multiplicity of form posits a level of critical self-awareness, regarding uses of form, in the recognition that choices of poetic form have all sorts of specific effects on language and other cultural practices.

In a free multiplicity of form all forms of writing are possibilities that may or may not lead to any particular kind of cultural life. In such a circumstance use of a poetic form does not become the equivalent of a mani-festo-like assertion of one's values but instead becomes a matter of exploration. Within a culture open to a free multiplicity of form, any form of poetry is a legitimate possibility. Furthermore, use of a form would no longer be considered necessarily an attack, or even a critique, of other possi-ble forms. Within a culture open to a free multiplicity of form, a wide variety of forms can be used by any writer and can exist side by side with other forms.

9. A free multiplicity of form does not make all partisan activity on the part of certain forms of writing irrelevant. Clearly, poets will always have an interest in promoting the forms of writing that they find most engaging. It is simply that the promotion of forms of poetry will be adjusted to another level, promoted as an intriguing possibility rather than as a mark of group allegiance or of one's position in a capitalist struggle for ownership. And although, on the level of poetic form, a free multiplicity asserts, in William Burroughs's phrase, "nothing is true, everything is permitted," it does not follow from that assertion that all actual uses of a poetic form are equally sig-nificant. Rather, it means simply that all forms are possibilities that can be engaged by a writer attempting to become aware of the implications of form. Clearly, poets will continue to be read, and evaluated, on the results of their writing, and the form that they use to achieve those results will continue to be a central aspect of the way they are read.

Second, a free multiplicity of form does not suggest that the aesthetic tensions between various forms of writing will be resolved into harmony. Rather, in a free multiplicity of form even extreme disjunctions of form could be understood as a fruitful ground of poetic possibility, not as some-thing that calls into suspicion one's production allegiances.

Third, it is also not true that a free multiplicity of form eliminates the relation between writing and cultural life. A free multiplicity of form is not the same as a multiplicity of individuals speaking in their own individual "voices" without awareness of form or any possibility of cultural impact, each equally unable to have any ground other than their own subjectivity from which to speak. A free multiplicity of form calls for a conscious exploration of the relation between poetic form and cultural meaning, in the recognition that the value of a specific form of writing can be understood only through the uses that can be made of it. Clearly, within a culture open to a free multiplicity of form, writers will continue to promote their ideas about cultural life through their writing and to critique, perhaps ferociously, those with whom they do not agree.

10. Any promotion of a free multiplicity of form cannot be restrained to a discussion of boundary crossings, permutations, and multiplicities solely in literature. Rather, a free multiplicity of form extends past and opens the boundaries between various art forms, exploring the relations between the visual arts and literature, music and literature, any form of art with any other form of art. Indeed, opening up such possibilities is one of the most fruitful areas of current artistic practice (see, for instance, as only one of countless examples, the book *Core: A Symposium on Contemporary Visual Poetry*), with a huge range of artists exploring a vast array of formal and genre hybrids. Yet it is important to remember that even inside that vast array a free multiplicity of form can be achieved only by attempting to dislodge currently existing relations of artistic production, in which given kinds of artistic forms are taken to be exclusively proper by specific production networks, and to be the exclusive property of those networks.

11. Because in the contemporary United States the avant-garde is the one production network that comes closest to regarding issues of poetic form as not only a necessary but also an open question, I have found individuals related to that network to be the most open to possibilities of a free multiplicity of form. Members of group 1 tend to insist that poetic form is a predetermined given, although there are exceptions, like the traditional formalist Henry Taylor, who has also written an essay promoting the value of the open form and chance-based texts of avant-garde poet Jackson Mac Low. Members of group 3 (identity poetries), although insisting on the value of cultural multiplicity, have nonetheless tended to embody that insistence in overly homogenous uses of form. Thus, although a collection such as *An Ear to the Ground: An Anthology of Contemporary American Poetry* presents a huge range of voices from many different cultures within the United States, the

form of the poems in that volume are astonishingly similar—as if all these people from different backgrounds are accidentally expressing themselves in the same form. Members of group 2, like many members of group 3, often remain unaware that form is an issue at all, and thus they remain blind to the forms of their own writing.

However, it would be easy to exaggerate the openness of the avant-garde network to a free multiplicity of form. Although it is not uniformly true, the avant-garde has tended to vehemently reject those poetic forms associated with other production networks. In many ways this rejection is understandable; members of those other networks have often denied the value of avant-garde work and have attempted to prevent it from gaining readers or any sort of institutional foothold. But the mistake that the avant-garde often makes is to confuse certain poetic forms with the production network that promotes them. The possibilities of lyric poetry, for instance, are by no means necessarily limited to what the main proponents of lyric poetry (group 2) say about its value. But many members of the avant-garde have tended to accept the idea that the forms being promoted by other groups, because they *are* promoted by them, are dangerous in their implications and limited in their possibilities.

Furthermore, it can be argued that many members of the avant-garde network may not be able to accept these other formal possibilities because they believe in the cultural correctness of the poetic forms that the avant-garde network promotes. I say correctness rather than value because although those forms claimed by the avant-garde clearly have value, it does not necessarily follow that those forms lead to the establishment of a better form of cultural life, although it's certainly true that increased information about them could only be beneficial.

12. Whether a free multiplicity of form is possible, given the emotional, intellectual, ideological, institutional, and financial investments of the currently existing poetry production networks, seems at best an open question. Among writers and publishers of my own generation there has been a variety of attempts to open some of the boundaries determined by the estab-

lished poetry production networks. Probably I am familiar only with some of the attempts that deserve mention.

The review newspaper *Taproot Reviews*, for instance, reviews small-press books in an astonishing range of forms not limited to the productions of one network. The poetics newsletter *Poetic Briefs*, considered by many people too theoretical and L=A=N=G=U=A=G=E-poetry oriented and by others as too directionless in its concerns, has offered many essays that challenge the boundaries of poetry production networks, avant-garde and otherwise. In some of its incarnations the small-press publishing cooperative Leave Books reached outside the avant-garde production network in the direction of a free multiplicity of form. My own small magazine, *Situation*, was defined initially by the issue of questioning and redefining the relation between poetic form and cultural life and has attempted to present work addressing that issue in a variety of poetic forms. Writers and editors such as Jefferson Hansen, Elizabeth Burns, Luigi Bob-Drake, Hank Lazer, Jackson Mac Low, Charles Borkhuis, Chris Reiner, Rod Smith, Joe Ross, Susan Smith Nash, Juliana Spahr, Jena Osman, Ed Foster, Ira Lightman, A. L. Nielsen, Gale Nelson, Nick Piombino, Buck Downs, Jordan Davis, Heather Fuller, Susan Schultz, and myself, among others, have at some point given support to the notion of a free multiplicity of form, whether in their own poetry, critical writing, or editorial activity.

However, it would be easy to exaggerate the influence of these activities. The above publications do not reach a large audience and are not well funded. Furthermore, it is not clear that a free multiplicity of form is a significant concern even for avant-garde writers of my own generation. For instance, early issues of one of the most commonly mentioned recent avant-garde publications, *Apex of the M*, were committed to a program of ideological uniformity and an editorial policy that was theoretically and formally exclusionary.[1]

Nonetheless, I have been heartened to note, in my conversations with other writers and in the emergence of truly eclectic reading series and publications, some broad sympathy for the notion of a free multiplicity of form among emerging and even established writers both inside and outside the avant-garde. Of course, whether that sympathy will have any lasting effects on established production networks remains to be seen.

13. It might be argued that a free multiplicity, of poetic forms or anything else, is a deluded goal. Such an argument might say that in any social framework some ideas (and people) are always central, others marginalized or silent. Extended specifically to poetic forms, this argument would suggest that there will never come a day when all forms of poetry seem equally available for exploration.

But whether or not freedom of any kind is illusory (and I would suggest that one should not be too quick to believe that one knows what can or cannot happen), and whether or not some forms of poetry will always be more central than others, the basic principle of a free multiplicity of form—that the potential value of any form is always open to change and refiguring—will at the very least make clear that any attempt to state definitively the value of poetic forms, and to make any form or set of forms seem dominantly correct, will always be based on faulty reasoning.

In that sense attacks on any form of poetry, as a form, can only damage the potential cultural significance of poetry, whatever the misguided uses to which that form is put by any specific group of practitioners. Certainly such attacks prohibit individuals from having access to the range of poetic possibilities currently available. I would go so far as to suggest that attacking other forms of poetry would even prove damaging, in the long run, to a production network that succeeded in achieving cultural hegemony over poetic production. From whatever quarter it comes, fixing the value of poetic forms, and determining in advance the forms that poets may use, will only shut down, like a case of severely enforced biological in-breeding, the potential of those forms and make many poets more committed to finding other forms in which to embody their perceptions.

14. As I pointed out in my dialogue with Jefferson Hansen, "Direction," it could be argued that my promotion of a free multiplicity of form contains some of the manifesto characteristics that I am also critiquing and ironizing in this essay (*Shadows* 12). Such an argument has value but only if one recognizes that my "manifesto" here is *not* a manifesto promoting a literary

form or genre. In that sense my promotion of a free multiplicity of form does not exhibit the characteristics of the twentieth-century manifesto. That is, as I also point out in that dialogue, if my argument here is to a certain extent a manifesto, it is one that points out that the quickest road to Rome may be to go someplace else entirely.

15. In a recent series of articles on "the end of art," the philosopher and art critic Arthur Danto has argued that when forms of art are no longer directly equated to forms of cultural life, and all forms of art therefore become equally possible (that is, when a free multiplicity of artistic forms finally exists), art has reached what he calls a "posthistorical" phase, a time when "art makers are freed from the task of finding the essence of art" and thus "have been liberated from history and have entered the era of freedom"(344). He diagnoses that moment, in the visual arts, to be now. When it comes to applying Danto's ideas to issues regarding poetry (and, by implication, other arts, although their circumstances of production differ), his conclusions are troubling for two reasons but also visionary for reasons he does not quite diagnose correctly.

One reason his conclusions are troubling is that no free multiplicity of form exists within the poetry world today; repression of poetic forms remains rampant. The other reason is perhaps more subtle: a free multiplicity of form does not imply freedom from history and from problems of form. If anything, in a free multiplicity of form poets will need continually to question the relation between history, culture, and forms of poetry and to come to critical decisions about how best to enact their relations to these questions through their choices of poetic form. There is no historical necessity for future poetry to take some form rather than another. But that doesn't mean that the problem of form is over—if anything, a free multiplicity of form will help poets become more aware of their choices of form and more conscious of the implications of those choices.

However, in directly equating a free multiplicity of form with "the end of art," Danto wants to move past the limits and assumptions of modernism, which argued that art has value only as long as its forms are considered directly equivalent to forms of cultural life. That is, what he refers to as "the end of art" is really the end of the key modernist assumption about art. The history of art, and the importance of history for art, will not end with such a change any more than will the necessity for critical choices about forms of art. Rather, all these problems will enter a new historical phase whose outcomes remain to be seen. In prophesying that the end of equating forms of art with forms of cultural life is at hand, what Danto is revealing is that a free multiplicity of form, should it occur, means the end of modernism as we have known it.

Notes

1. Later issues of this magazine broadened the early rhetorical gestures of the editors, and, to be fair, even the early issues of the magazine published much worthwhile poetry.

References

Danto, Arthur C. *Encounters and Reflections*. New York: Farrar, Straus, and Giroux, 1990.
Wallace, Mark, and Jefferson Hansen. *Shadows: New and Selected Dialogues on Poetics. Poetic Briefs* 22 and 23 (1997).

READINGS

Caroline Bergvall

How does one read a text constructed out of several languages? What kind of cultural text might emerge from such a jigsaw environment? By placing itself at odds with the traffic of monolingual identity, the Same speaking off the accent of any Other, can such writing be seen to be breaking out of some of the regulatory conditions that national identity and monolingual environments apply to issues of linguistic belonging and of cultural translatability? Using pieces by Joan Retallack, Rosmarie Waldrop, and Theresa Hak Kyung Cha as my leading texts, I will be reflecting on some of the details of these plurilingual poetics, and I will be asking what kind of implications they may have on the performativity of textual identity.

At entry it should be noted that in the work I'll be reading the concerted cross-fertilization of linguistic environments does not subscribe to modernist assumptions of a pancultural scholarly availability, nor does it subscribe to the assumptions of translatability that the recent banners of "global culture" and "multiculturalism" have come to signify. Rather, it is used to articulate and revalorize sites of tension and untranslatability. As Nikos Papastergiadis usefully suggests, "[I]nteraction between two cultures proceeds with the illusion of transferable forms and transparent knowledge but leads increasingly into resistant, opaque and dissonant exchanges."[1] Issues of displacement, dislocation, and plurilingualism will be here positively envisaged as an investigation of the particularities of cultural localization and linguistic exchanges. Sometimes subterraneanly, sometimes overtly, it is therefore also the question of origins, the myth of Home(coming), that this work critiques and responds to.

Unmastery

Discussing the poetics of Gertrude Stein in relation to her non-English-speaking background, the poet Charles Bernstein argues that "unmastering language is not a position of inadequacy; on the contrary, mastery requires repression and is the mark of an almost unrecoverable lack."[2] Language acquisition is here perceived as a continuous process of language-making and handled as such, "not something to be translated away but something to enter into, to inhabit without losing the wildness." Starting from an initial and reiterated position of "unmastery," the writer can utilize traces of first-language acquisition, or second- or third-, to ground themselves in language, to explicate, rather than edit out, the process of language use.

Of course one can find in this a reevaluation of the modernist myth of the inherent exile in language, which, according to Mallarmé and a proto-modernist messianism, the motivation of writing would seek to master and transcend.[3] It is not by way of sublimating language (*langue*) into the per-fected *parole* of writing but rather by developing writing strategies through a sense of "unmastery" and that of a language not "possessed" that situations of linguistic excess and cultural displacement (not replacement) can perhaps best be forwarded. Displacement is not here envisaged as exile but as the very condition for a positive understanding of relocation across and against the unifying, mythicized, and frequently exclusionary principles of national lan-guage and of monolingual culture. This also frees up writing from the constraints that the utopian longing for the one unalterable Language, hid-den behind the imperfections of all languages, sets irremediably into place. It is in this respect telling that the nostalgia for Babel has frequently guaran-teed the deployment of exclusionary and nationalistic approaches to mysticisms of writing.[4]

Deleuze and Guattari's notion, developed in *Kafka: Toward a Minor Literature*, that the native language is always both deterritorialized by use and recontextualized by the value systems of ambient referentiality also seeks to minimize the unifying stronghold of origination and belonging. Their view of language is that of a changing and dynamic assemblage, rooted in the con-ceptualizing machines of the speaker's sociophysiological body.

There is never one language to speak of, and hybrid textualities and their palpable locatability of difference can, by operating against the grain of a totalizing project, forward dialogues based on an appraisal of the positive nature of differentiality and of differences. Deleuze and Guattari read "unmastery" as an act of stuttering that valorizes and enables the manifestation of the inherent plurilingualism contained within any live language. This act of stuttering reveals the "assemblage" that is language and inscribes the complex vitality of linguistic affect: "The assemblage's only unity is that of co-functioning: it is a symbiosis, a 'sympathy.' It is never filiations which are important but alliances, alloys; these are not successions, lines of descent, but contagions, epidemics, the wind."[5] For Deleuze and Guattari the point would be to write "like a dog digging a hole" in order to find the language's "own point of under-development."[6]

The poetic and cultural significance of thinking about language in this Deleuzean-Guattarian "minor" scale, as a pooling of culturally buried, blind-spotted, or underdeveloped fields, is that it seeks to establish the activity of writing as an ongoing composite that must open itself to the particulars of space and place, while remaining forever suspect of any kind of standardizing national literature. "Only the possibility of setting up a minor practice of major language from within allows one to define popular literature, marginal literature and so on. Only in this way can literature really become a collective machine of expression and really be able to develop its contents."[7]

Deleuze and Guattari's insistence on a positive "stuttering in one's own language" inscribes a relation to language that hystericizes any claim to homogeneity and recontextualizes the particulars of their multifarious histories. This also has major consequences on the way one might come to view the operations of translation and the notion of translatability.

A Thing Das Ding a Ling

Joan Retallack's work as a whole, and her latest pieces even more pointedly, provides a challenging reflection on the demands of translation as seen from the point of view of writerly practice. In fact, one of her latest pieces, "Scenes of Translation," subtitled ironically "(from the Translation)," uses the translative activity as its explicit motif and motivation. The text is also, perhaps inevitably, one of Retallack's most plurilingual so far.

"Scenes of Translation"[8] presents itself as written in three languages (American English, Cuban, and German) that are organized across three distinct columns, each respectively headed: LOCAL TRAVELLING; EXCURSIONS; SIGHT-SEEING. Hence, at entry, and with an eye on the heritage of translated literature, Retallack makes a point of assimilating the activities of the poet-translator as that of a tourist who absorbs and appropriates by snapshotting his or her way in and out of languages and literatures. Allusions to the writing of postcards, to being photographed, to carrying a (misleading) phrase book, to deciphering phonetic transcriptions of some of the Cuban segments are scattered across the text and act as reminders that no amount of factual and associative investigations into the landscape or environment of the text can ever piece together a complete, settled and settling, picture of what is taking place. No package tour to "the woodland." If the poet as tourist had intended to translate, to superimpose, from German to American the work of Georg Trakl ("Trakl, I don't speak" being the very first words of the text in the left column and excerpts of his poems being dispersed throughout the text), the setting into play, in the second line, of Cuban poet Jorge Guitart's own text entitled *Trakl, Yo No Se Aleman* immediately disturbs the dual traffic of conventional translation by introducing a third term (Spanish) into it. Translation becomes explored, teased out as an operation of dispersion and collation of a range of visual, phonic, linguistic, and translinguistic games. Here "all der Fall ist / inflatable, growing" from the strains of Retallack's prosthetic reading and writing of Trakl. And if the writer is, at one point, sarcastically tempted to call up the "untransvest" of writing and translating, it is unswayingly that she sets up "a sort of / unc conditional hypothermal / of accident untransflatable."

Retallack's "untransflatability," which one could take to mean both conflation and dispersion, points here to a network of fielded navigations among German, Spanish, and English, among sonic games that extort lost familiarities out of crosslingual rapprochements "a thing das Ding a ling / pebbles fall-ing l'ink Kiesel-stein," and among sections of syllabic splittings ". . . LOSS / NINOS MO URNING BECAUSE EL ECTRICK CIT YO AS PERGES NACHT AS PERITE(Y) / LOSSNINOS MOURN IN GBE

CAUSEEL LECT RICK CITY O. . . ." Through its insisting syllabic variations this section inevitably reminds that to leave blanks between words has always been used to minimize, voire disable, ambiguities and to control the dissemination of sense. It is telling that Retallack should choose to close her text by opening it up to a beyond of our present literacy and translative awareness: "[the rest of this poem is (also) (too) in tatters]."

In many ways one could see in this piece a writerly and highly problematized application of Walter Benjamin's claim that translation should be envisaged as a process that addresses the foreignness of languages and that needs to take place at the site of the language text being translated, not to take its place by appropriating it into the language and culture of arrival. By turning translation into an unpacking of various sources, and allowing for these sources to be relayed to the reader without being churned into an intelligibly smooth, "translated," ultimately ideologically obscuring, text mass, Retallack attempts to broaden that site. Here translation is made to function as a reflection on writing. As such no unique original text leads it on. The Trakl sections act as prompts, only one motif amongst others. "There is no unity to be recovered, no task of thinking of the origin as such, since the origin, now the anorigin, is already that on which rests the move to a synthetic unity. Any unity will be an after-effect."[9] Or as the critic Rosie Braidotti succinctly puts it in her essay on the polyglot: "[T]here cannot be fragments where there is no whole."[10]

Perhaps one could therefore talk of Retallack's work as an approach to cultural and linguistic material that provides a cybernetic understanding of writing, one that constructs interpretative, located, and reconstructed environments for reading. Indeed, the practice of translation as a writerly form can strain readers' understanding of the relations they might entertain with their own and with other linguistic cultures. By "unmastering" the principles of translation and "stuttering" through its utilization of materials, such a practice problematizes the viability of monolingualism and critiques the colonialist and nationalistic strands that still underlie more conventional views on translation. It also sets up a bridge between process-based procedural work (which much of Retallack's work rests on) and the issues of social and personal relocation that much plurilingual and experimental translation work comes out of.

Make Notice Me

For second- or third-language writers such as Theresa Hak Kyung Cha, Rosmary Waldrop, Anne Tardos, Guillermo Gomez-Pena, and others, translation procedures and the stylization of multiple languages are used very directly to enhance an awareness of dis/locatedness. Structural and thematic concerns will often be that of finding ways of grappling textually with the dictates of personal relocation and of added-on linguistic identities. These concerns form part and parcel of the conceptualizations and un/readabilities of their writing. From the onset it is the unmastering, rather than the unmastery, of language that is embedded in the textual project. From the onset the plurilingual activity of writing cannot but articulate itself at a cultural and linguistic slant from the dominant, and often officially monolingual, linguistic cultures it is writing itself into. This underlying "unmastering" may in turn choose to apply itself to master, to resorb, to neutralize this gap, as in the oft-cited case of Joseph Conrad's more English than the English English.[11] It may also be explored to politicize rhetorics of unmastery within the second language, as was the case for Beckett or Stein.

One could now ask what kind of articulacies arise from projects that forever navigate between the givens of the writer's own cultural language and the acquired familiarities of the adopted tongue and what kind of formal and ideological strategies, what kind of cultural placing, it does enable (and disable). Given that writers cannot mirror themselves into or, for that matter, divorce themselves from the larger agencies of the language they write themselves into, one could speculate that the parallelism between the construction of identity and the coming to language is here reactivated by this move into another sociolinguistic environment.

"You have the feeling that the new language is a resurrection: new skin, new sex," writes Kristeva in her book *Strangers to Ourselves*.[12] Beckett's well-known explanation of his switching to French as a means "pour faire remarquer moi" (literally and in "estranged" French: to make notice me)[13] is in this respect telling of the potential for diverting and rethinking the performance of identity that writing in the second (and third) language may provoke.

For Beckett, whose French textuality never fails to call into question the making and unmaking of language, as much as for Joyce, who did intralingually "invent a new language within English" (Bernstein), it is furthermore difficult to ignore that their work was one way or another articulated in response to the British attempts at eradicating Irish culture and language. Writing oneself out of one's language while recirculating it textually could hence be seen not as a way of mourning the language left behind but as a way of unmasking the role any aggressively dominant linguistic culture plays to guarantee the authentication of its memory and the univocality of its identity.

Simulated Belonging

For the Korean American writer Theresa Hak Kyung Cha, writing constructs its own particularized environment by problematizing the lessons of history and language. More specifically, writing will seek to deconstruct her status of naturalized exile by refusing to allow her to master a social identity through it. In her book *Dictee* the issue is one that announces "a second coming" out of the "simulated pasts resurrected in memoriam."[14] The emphasis is on the artificiality of memory, the construction of the past.

The title of her cross-genre, plurilingual book, first published in 1982 in the United States and recently reprinted, is in itself immediately indicative of her textual strategies. Indeed, the title means "dictation" in French, but, tellingly, it has lost its required French accent (dictée). Losing the conventional accent announces another kind of accentuation. Recollecting the accented past is only feasible as a montage among cultures and languages. It is by losing one accent at entry that Cha signals the multiple accents of her polyglot identity and the activities of translation it implicitly demands.

The first few pages provide Cha with the opportunity to set the wider scene for the tellings of the book—"Tell me the story / Of all these things /

Beginning wherever you wish, tell even us"—in the languages that make her up:

> From A Far
> What nationality
> or what kindred and relation
> . . . .
> Tertium Quid neither one thing nor the other
> Tombe des nues de naturalized
> what transplant to dispel upon. (20)

The accompanying theme of school dictation is telling of the more deep-rooted cultural and historical dictations that form the main motifs and questions of her book: how does one manage one's languages in relation to history, memory, identity, gender. What barbarisms assist language's and identity's foundational plots.

The textual work of *Dictee* consists of an amalgamate of stylistic devices and of fact-finding props, such as photographic "evidence," hand-written "documents," official administrative letters, Western and Eastern anatomical maps, French-English translations, dual-language poems, Chinese calligraphic texts. The narratives are full of loosely attributed *I*s and mutable *she*s and *we*s embedded in incomplete stories that crisscross between the "personal" and the "historical." All of this draws a tenuous line between activating and creating memory. The violence of the political situations described throughout is also set up elliptically, never approaching the explicitness of witness reports. Cha seems to be questioning the tenability of taking refuge in exile narratives when constructing her naturalized Asian American identity. Her dotted accounts of her family history set against the backdrop of horrific political events are carefully disabling the seduction of the often nostalgic and reconciliatory project of much postcolonial writing. The inscription of loss is not here integrated to the promises held by redemptive and/or confessional narratives. Indeed, this dark, harrowing book constantly critiques and resists, rather than affirms as "proofs," the material assembled and deployed. All are but aspects of a "sequence, narrative, variation / on make believe" (129).[15] There is nothing stable, no foreseeable "return," behind the constructions of her textualized languages:

> Conséquemment
> en suivant la vue absente
> which had ceased to appear
> already it has been
> has been
> has been without ever
> occurring to itself that it should remember
> Sustain a view. Upon
> itself. (125)

It is precisely because Cha cannot dissociate her narrative treatments from the impulse to manifest, rather than describe, her complex polyglossia that it makes for such an uncomfortable, uncompromising read. Although there is a pull in the entire book toward "Uttering again to re-vive. The forgotten"(150),[16] the collaging of *Dictee*'s many textual voices and her cross-fertilization of languages as well as cultural heritages, do not serve to reify the experience of the exile, that ultimate Other, but rather to engage in a series of profound, restless meditations on the ways in which she might be able to document that "extended journey, horizontal in form, in concept," the journey of her writing and its harrowing rejection of any constitutive myth of origins, no homecoming.

The critic Homi Bhabha, following in this the terminology set up by Chicano writers, defines the space her writing occupies as "borderline art": "Borderline artists may have fragmented narratives, archives that are empty, memories that are potent yet powerless, but their experience of survival gives them a special insight into the constructed, artefactual, strategic nature of those events that are memorialised, by the powerful, as being the 'facts' of life, or the reportage of historical record."[17] Borderline writing is here seen to mean not only a pushing at the boundaries among languages but, more precisely, a localized carving out of these boundaries into zones of activity and experientiality that empty out the assumptions on which monolingual representation rests. As such, the borderline as zone is unstable and changeable. It is also highly specific of the particulars of each writer or writing community. It functions by making inroads into the different linguistic communities the writer is, one way or another, associated with and demonstrates a critical and poetic withdrawal from belonging to "either side" of borders. It invariably strains conventions of intelligibility, both linguistically and at a wider cultural frame. By working out of and showing up the split language base from which she originates, Cha locates herself precisely and culturally at the junction between specific linguistic communities and histories. Thus she also explicitly questions the linguistic grounds that determine the negative construction of difference and that displace her work and identity as other. It is by accumulating linguistic locales, English-American among them, rather than developing a textual identity that subsumes itself to monolingual identity, that Cha seeks to articulate and reinscribe our understanding of national language and culture. Her textuality functions as a space of intervention that syncretizes and juxtaposes linguistic systems and revels in the heterogeneity of interlocked cultural differences. As Rosie Braidotti summarizes it: "Writing is for the polyglot a process of undoing the illusory stability of fixed identities, bursting open the bubble of ontological security that comes from familiarity with one linguistic site."[18]

The role of the reader in such an environment is immediately questioned and contextualized. Indeed, the allusive syntax and photographed material with which Cha taps into events and signs of resonance to readers familiar with Korean culture establishes, for a reader unfamiliar with that culture or with the experience of "naturalization," such as myself, an uncomfortable rift between what it is that I know I'm reading (hence recognizing) and what it is that I think I am reading (hence presume to be recognizing). The question of the reader's role in a book of this kind calls up again and again the question of cultural locatedness, that of the writer as well as that of the reader. It forces a process of slowing down that pushes up against the bounds of one's cultural intelligibilities, demanding that readers take into account, and as an indissociable part of reading, their own cultural and linguistic background.

This experience of being prompted to recognize one's own cultural specificities when presented with the "unreadable" specificities of a writer's cultural foreground is also what forms the very basis of the work of Mexican writer and performance artist Guillermo Gomez-Pena. Most of his projects are written in several languages, usually a mix of American English, inner-city slang, and Mexican and Chicano idioms. Pena is also one of the first to have termed this multilingual approach to writing *borderlanguage*. From the point of view of text-based performance it constitutes one of the better-known examples of a writing strategy that uses linguistic differences to locate and problematize issues of cultural dominance, linguistic supremacy, marginalization, and the universal Other. In the same way as for Cha, it rests not so much on the creation of one ideal reader as on the fruitful resistance to writing-in the one reader. During the time of his collaborations with Cuban writer Coco Fusco, they would change the leading language according to where they were performing, emphasizing the ones that the specific audience was most likely not to be fully or at all familiar with.[19]

To establish points, blocks of incomprehension in the audience/reader, is here far from a hermetic device in the protomodernist sense. Rather, these blocks reclaim and reposition the locatedness and fluctualities of languages. Reterritorialization does not in this sense so much attempt to actualize an eternal return to a mythicized Land, does not so much essentialize the otherness of the foreigner, or the stranger, as inscribe the validity of linguistic *mestizaje*[20] in the constitution of contemporary identities.

The fact that writers such as Cha and Pena would not only critique monolingualism, its nationalist and exclusionary implications, but ultimately revel in the potentialities that the destabilizations of heterogeneous writerly and linguistic practice contain is one clear sign that the very notion of sociocultural displacement can no longer be sustained by the parameters of exile literature or, for that matter, by the oft-uncritical and unspecific valorization of hybridity as a third, compensatory and translative term. Instead, they point to a positive reevaluation of untranslatability against a universalist translatability. Bhabha speaks tellingly of this as "the stubborn chunks," the opaque, resistant detail in the traffic among cultures that signals contextual differences against a totalizing project: "Hybrid hyphenations emphasise the incommensurable elements—the stubborn chunks—as the basis of cultural identifications."[21] In such a context, it is untranslatability, not translatability, that favors a recognition of the particularities of personal and collective experience.

Except For

For Rosmarie Waldrop, a poet and noted translator of German and French, the project of *A Key into the Language of America* does not so much rest on her being "seen to be" a foreigner but rather on the ways her process of reading and writing brings home and clarifies her own condition as an immigrant to America, as a "white, educated European who did not find it difficult to get jobs."[22] The title of her book is the same title as the book that supports her exploration. Written by the missionary Roger Williams and published in 1634, *A Key into the Language of America* was, when it was first published, also subtitled "or an help to the language of the natives of that part of America called New England." Being the first systematic and sympathetic study of a Native American language, Narragansett, and its customs, the original book took a critical view of the colonialist attitudes of the burgeoning Christian settlers' communities of the region and led to Williams's being exiled from his community. That Waldrop should decide to use the same title for her rewriting of Williams's work is of interest in relation to the activity of superimposition this seems to imply—as if her personal experience could only but graft itself, critically and poetically, onto an American landmark piece to render itself visible: "All in all, my book could be called an immigrant's take on the heritage and complex early history of my adopted country," she writes in her preface.

By seemingly taking over the material of this book, seemingly colonializing it with her own late-twentieth-century readings, Waldrop uncovers the ambiguous complexities inscribed in attempting to enter into and relate to the underlying, sometimes buried or evacuated, material of her adopted country. Indeed, she states quite clearly that "like the first settlers, I came from Europe. I came, expecting strangeness, expecting to be disoriented, but was shocked, rather, by my lack of culture shock"; but she also immediately acknowledges as part of her own Eurocentric heritage the colonialist attitude and blind spots that enabled the early formation of white, Christian Euro-America: "Nothing seemed different from my native Germany—except for the Indian place-names." For Waldrop, then, the gesture of superimposition enables a reflection on the ways in which tracing linguistic histories can favor a critical and personal reassessment of one's cultural assumptions. Waldrop's "except for" and "like the first settlers" is revealing of the historical identification she first applied in order to settle in America. This is in stark contrast to the destabilized and decentered manner in which she comes to handle her material and to question her own identity sites in relation to it: "*Year of parades. Celebrating exploits unsuited to my constitution. As if every move had to be named expansion, conquest, trinity, and with American intonation*"(60).

Placing her text within Williams's overall structure, Waldrop sets up a collage that includes Narragansett vocabulary, passages from Williams's seventeenth-century English text, and her own poetic interventions. Digging into the book in order to excavate her own experiences as a contemporary Americanized poet—"an eye devouring its native region must devote special attention to its dialect" (5)—Waldrop highlights the inevitable clashes and discontinuities that inform, at many stages of its development, the violently recuperative nature of early Americanization. By maintaining different typestyles and layouts, as well as a range of idioms, she highlights some of these clashes in the context of her own writing: "Prefer the movement of planets or buffalo to European *coat-men*, identifiable strains to city planning even when applied to lexical items. *Wetomémese. A Little House. Which women live apart in*, the time of their exhaustive volume" (13). Her writing of readings tends toward a process of nonabsorption that acts throughout as a reminder of the disparate and differential sources that form her project. By implication, it also calls up Deleuze and Guattari's take on the social evacuation of plurilingualism.

A thematics of the body—"flesh, considered a cognitive region"—and issues of gender—". . . is called woman or wife"—are used throughout as Waldrop's observational vantage points. The way she locates, in Williams's text, the cultural burying and reorganization of the female gender seems in fact to be a prime factor in informing Waldrop's linguistic reterritorialization. By applying personal commentary to historical source material, she identifies the points of cultural closure that define her as female: "I was stuck in a periodicity I supposedly share with Nature, but tired of making concessions to dogs after bones" (54). Waldrop's book provides in this sense a stimulating example of the ways that plurilingual experience not only calls up internalized sites of cultural acquisition but also extricates some of the foundational narratives (such as gender) that add a strain on the processing of identity in the second or third linguistic environment. For Waldrop the activation of her plurilingualism heightens the problematics of gender embedded as it is in historical and linguistic structures:

> I must explain my sex
> for all its stubbornness
> is female
> and was long haunted, diligently
> by confusions of habit
> and home, time and
> the Western world. (56)

The linguistic collages she develops to locate her personal experience (it is striking here that her first language, German, remains dormant, placed in latency) act as a "borderline" between contemporaneity and historical material, between gender and sex, between gender and language. The intertextual and stylistically dispersed manner in which she assimilates this borderline enables her to examine issues of linguistic relocation as inescapably articulated by the pervasiveness of gender performativity. Plurilingual textuality becomes a way of pushing against the limits of the signs of gender: "*I knew getting rid of prejudices would make me fall into some other puddle*" (52). It is also a way of rearticulating sexual signs. In her text the pervasiveness and questioning of sexual desire both locks and turns the key to her incorporated hyphenization: "If the dark quarries inner caves / the sexual act takes on / a sheen of purchase / the difference of invasion / and exodus obscured by labor" (52).

It is on an open question, looking neither "forward" nor "backward" but somewhere along the maps of a performative present, that she concludes her text.

Else-here

As I hope to have shown, the premise that could be seen to underlie and underline the plurilingual work discussed here is that of decentering monolingualism and problematizing the contemporaneity of hyphenated identities. Being situated neither "here" nor "there," neither in "the past" nor in an unconditional present, but else-here, the question of contemporaneity, as addressed by these poets and many others with them, rests on the evaluation of historical and personal material from the point of view of a particularized and complex sociospatial locatedness.

In all the pieces discussed the writers indicate structurally the connection between the form taken by their textual material and the subjective experience of relocation and untranslatability that informs their material. Methodologies deployed are invariably brought to light as part of the text. In this unveiling one could read not only a refusal to obscure in the reader the various tools that construct the text and the performativity of identity but, more important, an approach to writing that demands of readers that they address their own locatedness in the reading of the work. It is then to the loosening up of the boundaries between private and public, to the opening up of personal experience as irremediably playing on and played by wider social frames, that much of this work finds its motivation.

Placed neither at a transcendental degree zero nor at a nostalgic point of longing for one cohesive language, the dispersed textualities staged here highlight some of the implications of the plurilingual experience that is increasingly straining the social fabric of contemporary societies. This dynamic and pragmatic approach to textual experimentation as a running commentary on the tenuous monolingualism of our sociocultural spheres strikes me as one of the more optimistic, responsive, and exciting aspects of this kind of work.

Notes

1. Nikos Papastergiadis, "Restless Hybrids," in *Contaminations*, Third Text 32 (autumn 1995): 18.

2. Charles Bernstein, *A Poetics* (Cambridge: Harvard University Press, 1992), 146–47.

3. Mallarmé: "Seulement, sachons n'existerait pas le vers: lui, philosophiquement rémunère le défaut des langues, complètement supérieur." Quoted from "Crise de Vers," in *Oeuvres Complètes* (Paris: Bibliothèque de la Pléiade, 1945), 364.

4. See Antoine Berman *L'épreuve de l'étranger* (Paris: Gallimard, 1984); G. Genette *Mimologics* (Lincoln: University of Nebraska Press, 1995); or the recently published anthology *The Translatability of Cultures: Figurations of the Space Between*, ed. S. Burdick and W. Iser (Cambridge: Cambridge University Press, 1996).

5. Gilles Deleuze and Félix Guattari, *Kafka: Toward a Minor Literature* (Minneapolis: University of Minnesota Press, 1986), 17.

6. Ibid.

7. Ibid., 18.

8. Selections of this work have appeared in *Arras*, no. 2. The text in its entirety has been published as part of Retallack's *How to Do Things with Words* (Los Angeles: Sun and Moon, 1999). Work here done on Xeroxed manuscript, with thanks to J. R.

9. Andrew Benjamin, "Translating Origins: Psychoanalysis and Philosophy," in *Rethinking Translation: Discourse, Subjectivity, Ideology*, ed. Lawrence Venuti (London: Routledge, 1992), 18–41

10. Rosie Braidotti, "Nomads in a Transformed Europe: Figurations for an Altered Consciousness," in *Cultural Diversity in the Arts: Art, Art Policies, and the Facelift of Europe*, ed. Ria Lavrijsen (KIT: Amsterdam, 1993), 44.

11. Still, it is ironic how the thematics of novels such as *Nostromo* or *Heart of Darkness* betrays Conrad's preoccupation with cultural dislocation.

12. Julia Kristeva, *Strangers to Ourselves* (New York: Harvester Wheatsheaf, 1991), 15.

13. Enoch Brater, *Why Beckett* (London: Thames and Hudson, 1989), 47.

14. Theresa Hak Kyung Cha, *Dictee* (Third Woman Press: Berkeley, 1995), 150.

15. The critic Shelley Sunn Wong makes a case for this in her excellent article on Cha's book when she discusses the resistance *Dictee* has been met with by Korean American communities. See Shelley Sunn Wong, "Unnaming the Same: Theresa Hak Kyung Cha's *Dictee*," in *Feminist Measures: Soundings in Poetry and Theory*, ed. Lynn Keller and Cristanne Miller (University of Michigan Press: Ann Arbor, 1994).

16. The phrase "to re-vive" here plays on both the English *revive* as a calling up of the past and the French *revivre* to live again, to be (a)live again, as a shedding from the past. There's also a French play on the female adjective *vive*.

17. Homi Bhabha, "Beyond the Pale: Art in Multicultural Translation," in *Cultural Diversity in the Arts*, 23.

18. Braidotti, "Nomads in a Transformed Europe," 34.

19. For discussions between Coco Fusco and G. Gomez-Pena, see Coco Fusco, *English Is Broken Here: Notes on Cultural Fusion in the Americas* (New York: New Press, 1995).

20. *Mestizaje* is defined by Rafael Pérez-Torres as "the manifestation of the multiplicitous discourses from which Chicanos create a sense of identity. Mestizaje becomes a racial/radical marker of self-determination . . . a cultural strategy [that relies] on the mixing and meddling of cultures that defines the contemporary condition of world culture." *Movements in Chicano Poetry: Against Myths, against Margins* (Cambridge: Cambridge University Press, 1995), 210.

21. Homi Bhabha, *The Location of Culture* (London: Routledge, 1994), 219.

22. Rosmarie Waldrop, *A Key into the language of America* (New York: New Directions, 1994), xix.

Elizabeth Willis

I have purposefully chosen the term *late* lyric to avoid the concept of a "new" lyric. It seems doubtful that any contemporary poet could make the form any newer than it was in the hands of Sappho or Dickinson. Lateness exists in a present that contains the past, as the OED defines it in poetical use: "not long since; but now." To be late is to belong to "an advanced stage of the development of something," to enter into an impacted history, approaching a threshold of maximal complication. Lateness has a tone of renovation lacking in "new" and "post" terminologies, which can be deceptive in their push for an "improved" identity. (What could be less new than the "new formalism"?) Even the temporality in terms like *post-language poetry* or *postmodernism* suggests that a literary movement is something one gets over and that succeeding manifestations within the same genre spring forward from it while negating their chronological or stylistic predecessors. Likewise, it lends itself to a nostalgia for communities past, when poets really had fun or were really political or really avant-garde.

The language of progress tyrannizes poetry. In its pursuit of novelty it can be as prescriptive as any academy. The promotion of literary newness in semiliterate America is just one of the many ways consumerism finds its way into contemporary poetics. And the process flourishes on that most democratic of venues, the Internet, in spite of its often-voiced potential to subvert capitalist consumption. What's new is obsolete within seconds. Even in the well-meaning posts of well-meaning listservs the experience of reading can be reduced easily and even unintentionally to a process of information getting, where one can be told what to read and what's not worth the bother, sometimes before it has had the chance to make it to the shelves of real or cyber bookstores.

Since I left graduate school at Buffalo in 1993, I've been aware of a fairly active discussion within academic circles of a "crisis" in contemporary poetry, although it is not the kind of crisis I had imagined. Within the community of poets at Buffalo in the late 1980s and early 1990s the primary crisis that most of us faced was unemployment; the steady, methodical loss of funding for poetry; and the knowledge that the situation was likely to get worse before it got better. The other essential and related question was how did one keep one's sanity in the midst of composition. Not just how to survive but how to get the imagination to survive.

The crisis represented within the academy, however, has been primarily one of semantics. Originating in the anxious, old battle between experimental and conventional verse practices, its most recent embodiment is still L=A=N=G=U=A=G=E poetry vs. conventional verse. I've put the equal signs back in to clarify the original conflict. The typographical convenience of omitting them obliterates the historical moment of L=A=N=G=U=A=G=E poetry's genesis and unjustly generalizes it as it now stands in for innovative writing of all kinds, reinforcing the polarity instead of allowing for the formal and cultural diversity that exists within various experimental, improvisational, or sound-directed rather than meaning-driven verse practices.

The secondary issue currently attending this conflict is this: Now that L=A=N=G=U=A=G=E poets have laid siege to the academy, who is the enemy? Once the new has been even superficially assimilated what's the new new? Or if L=A=N=G=U=A=G=E writing continues to figure as the whipping post of the most deeply entrenched pockets of the academy, what will step in to upset this role playing? What is post-L=A=N=G=U=A=G=E writing called? Now that L=A=N=G=U=A=G=E has become "language"—the sign emptied of its signified—what terms can we bring into the discourse to describe the various arenas of contemporary poetic practice?

This crisis of naming is an impoverishment of literary criticism, not, as I see it, the crisis of recent "younger" poetry, which is alive and well in spite of its lack of ready labels. But such thinking pervades the poetry world, as the language of the academy and the language of marketing pervade the poetry world, often setting up enmities in parallel—although not necessarily oppositional—communities. And in many ways the resistance to naming among the generation of writers who came into print after L=A=N= G=U=A=G=E magazine is grounded in precisely this dilemma.

Last spring's conference "Where Lyric Tradition Meets Language Poetry: Innovation in Contemporary American Poetry by Women" at Barnard College was an apparent attempt to create a unity (albeit a gendered one) out of two once deeply entrenched aesthetic bunkers. The gossip surrounding the conference reads like a rumble between the Mods and the Rockers. In the aesthetic split articulated in the conference title, lyric stands in for a variety of confessional verse in which subjectivity goes uncomplicated and unquestioned—including the work of poets who avowed experimentation after L=A=N=G=U=A=G=E aesthetics were being assimilated into the academy in such a way that they represented the new "serious" verse. But in this instance *lyric* is being used to describe essentially narrative, epiphanic verse, which couldn't be further from the concerns of the lyric, even as it is defined by the most conservative academic sources.

Contemporary criticism of the lyric is conflicted about its connection with or disassociation from basic literary conventions. A search through the MLA Bibliography for American lyric poetry will direct you to the work of anyone from Eavan Boland to Peter Inman. But there are also clear areas of agreement. In his 1964–65 Norton Lectures C. Day Lewis discusses the interruptive and irruptive qualities of the lyric in ways that are often not far from, say, Jack Spicer's Vancouver lectures of the same period. The *New Princeton Encyclopedia of Poetry and Poetics* describes the "lyric speaker" as "a device for making the invisible visible," hence an agent of phenomena. Jonathan Culler's writing on the subject focuses on various conventions of the lyric without exploring the development of an open lyric that does not act out an aesthetic of unity and wholeness. Yet even he states that "the fundamental aspect of lyric writing . . . is to produce an apparently phenomenal world through the figure of voice," with the clear implication that the lyric voice, being figural, is potentially multiple and that in producing a phenomenal world it is not reducible to the realm of single-subject epiphanies.[1]

The very recognition of the voice as a figure—in fact, as the subject of much lyric poetry—immediately takes it out of the realm of the merely confessional. Northrop Frye discusses the lyric as a turn from realist temporality (although not necessarily a turn from political and social realities). Julia Kristeva's discussion of "poetic language" as heterogeneous, musical, and *not* the product of a transcendental ego seems directed primarily to the work of the lyric.[2] Marjorie Perloff has been an important critical reader of the lyric, particularly in *The Dance of the Intellect, Poetic License*, and in her afterword to the recent collection edited by Mark Jeffreys, *New Definitions of the Lyric: Theory, Technology, and Culture*.[3] In recent essays Susan Stewart has articulated a "lyric history" that incorporates both the heterogeneous nature of lyric voicing and the ways in which lyric poems often contain traces of their own genesis.[4] And the critical prose of both Nathaniel Mackey and Susan Howe articulates the phenomenal aspects of the lyric and suggests the widely various traditions from which contemporary lyric poetry draws.[5]

Lyric is conventionally defined first by length (under one hundred lines and usually less than fifty), but even the stodgiest sources then acknowledge other more mysterious qualities: its privileging of sound over meaning; its difference in time signature; its divergence from mimesis. It overlaps with, rather than opposes, the aesthetics of "language" or "post-language" writing, and a number of poets who have been swept into the "language" category for lack of a more precise grouping are primarily lyrically driven—Susan and Fanny Howe, for instance, or the recent work of Barbara Guest. But there has been a shift within contemporary lyric practice, whereby the overall structure and strategy of the lyric is overlaid or mixed with other influences, forms, and rhetorical sampling, often in significant ways.

Anywhere from Aristotle to Dickinson to Lorca to Spicer it has been acknowledged that the lyric poem comes not strictly from within but from elsewhere; it is not *self*-expressive except to the extent that ideas of self or voice are never entirely absent from the tonal shadings of language. To overcome the inherited structure of the everyday—the quotidian clock—the lyric poem must catalyze the mind. In this context Pound's metaphor of the dynamo makes sense; it "blasts" apart and reconstructs something alternative to literature's received ideas. In spite of its machine imagery, it is a human construction. Wallace Stevens called poetry a "destructive force." He goes on to say in *The Necessary Angel* that it is "a violence from within that protects us from a violence without. It is the imagination pressing back against the pressure of reality. It seems in the last analysis, to have something to do with our self-preservation; and that, no doubt, is why the expression of it, the sound of its words, helps us to live our lives" (36). By his definition, the alien quality of this motive force—instead of making a decadent art—actually makes its existence more imperative or "necessary." The poem "must resist intelligence almost successfully."[6] In the slipperiness between reality and imagination it leaves a trace of the apparent impossibility of its own emergence into words.

The work of the modern and contemporary lyric is not to unify or commodify or even represent human experience but to stress language in such a way as to evoke an alternate experience for its readers, not an objective correlative to a universal experience but an engagement in the process of finding out. It overwhelms, captures, and resists the mind. Zukofsky famously claimed for poetry an aspiration to music. And Oppen's political convictions, instead of making his work pedantic, grounded it deeply in the music of the phenomenal world, without strictly delineating between seen and unseen or, as Kristeva puts it, between subject and nonsubject.

Motivated by a force that is vocalized but not wholly comprehensible, the lyric insists on being heard in spite of the fact that it cannot make itself fit conventional codes of meaning. To whatever extent it employs everyday discourse—and even the more esoteric discourses of politics or religion—its aim is to point outside any accountable meaning, to provoke the reception of an excess of meaning. "Lyric" does not suggest an inattention to the material aspects of language or to the possibility of double voicing by which works of art can critique their own formulations. Think of the interplay between control and chaos in Lorine Niedecker's "When Ecstasy Is Inconvenient":

Feign a great calm;
all gay transport soon ends.
Chant: who knows—
flight's end or flight's beginning
for the resting gull?

Heart, be still.
Say there is money but it rusted;
say the time of moon is not right for escape.
It's the color in the lower sky
too broadly suffused,
or the wind in my tie.

Know amazedly how
often one takes his madness
into his own hands
and keeps it.

The poem's voice manifests primarily in the form of imperatives—a proximate but indeterminate voicing that can be read as a dialogue between poem and poet, poet and reader, or the poem's own self-reflexive thinking. It gestures toward meaning without offering a stable symbolic order or system for reading. Although the poem seems driven by sound and phrasing, we can find in the first line an implicit critique of Wordsworth's compositional "tranquility" and in the second line a gesture toward the conventional poetic preoccupation with mutability. "Chanting" suggests both poetry making and nonsense as possible responses to the philosophical quandary of not knowing. And the stable image of the resting gull remains fully and even humorously enigmatic (what does it matter if the gull just took off or just landed? what difference does the representation of linear temporality make to the poem anyway? is an idle reader the "gull" or fool of the poem?).

The poem's argument against its own linguistic "ecstasy" gets progressively implausible as the second stanza goes on. First your money's no good;

then the moon is not right (is the poet a criminal, an escape artist, a slave, or merely superstitious?). The time of day is never right for the poem—too dim, too "broadly suffused," too "windy," too difficult; or are these lines merely an attempt to explain and capture in an image, to give boundaries to the "ecstasy" toward which the poem gestures? The poem not only means multiply; its vocabulary throws the ground of human feeling into flux through its ambiguity of tone. Is the poem sincere, or are we being played with? How private is the condition articulated in the poem? Is it talking to me about how I've just read or misread it? Can such control be feigned, or is it—like the "ecstasy" the poem purports to put aside—the product of intense study and the chance music of words meeting in the mind? Is the madness one can hold in one's hand a poem?

Northrop Frye connects the lyric with a movement out, from one reality to another.[7] Edouard Glissant calls this wandering "errantry" and claims for it a relation to poetry or a "poetics of relation."[8] Wandering, in this instance, is not being lost, although there is no clear sign of exactly where one is. It moves Augustine's *Confessions* to effectively obliterate the distinction between sacred and profane discourse, as his meandering treatise on the nature of time and memory culminates in a reading of the measurement of sound within a poem. In poetry, wandering is the essence of negative capability. It accounts for the elision among Emily Dickinson's pronouns and the wayward movement in her diction from center to circumference—a gesture that mirrors her rejection of Romantic subjectivity and espousal of modern Possibility. It drives Cesaire's *Notebook of a Return to the Native Land*, which knows where it's headed only in a geographical sense; poetically, its open-ended lyric power pulls us with it into deep water.

Wandering does not necessarily stem from a lack of ground but often signals a shift in ground: it is part necessity, part will, part cultural structure. A discovery without a quest. The poetry of this trajectory—this poetry "of relation"—is off-center. It is not the domain of the clinically perfect metaphor or virtuous technique. At times it delights in its own bewilderment. It has the mark of the almost apprehended, the barely understood.

Knowing it is late, or "it is too late," it allows itself to be in the dark, to contradict itself. It allows the sociopolitical to argue with the personal and the aesthetic, as in Harryette Mullen's provocative title *Muse & Drudge*.[9]

The flexibility and asymmetry of lyric form does not stem from a lack of structure. In fact—a classic example being Stein's *Stanzas in Meditation*—the structure is often elaborate, serving to further heighten its departure from the mere representation of subjective reality. See, for instance, the tightly structured lyrics of Pam Rehm's *To Give It Up*, in which the regular rhythm of the lines often declares an unruliness or distortion in meaning. C. S. Giscombe's emancipation of sound structure to create place in *Giscome Road*. Or the music of vowels and fricatives in the time-warping, lace-and-punk vocabulary of Lisa Robertson's *XEclogues*. The incantatory repetition set adrift in Lisa Jarnot's *Sea Lyrics*. The impacted, asymmetrical counterpoint within Peter Gizzi's *Artificial Heart*, where adjoining lines can be read at cross purposes, bending plaintiveness with critique. Theresa Cha's use of lyric to include documentary push and stream of consciousness in *Dictée*. The vertiginous mix of classical and contemporary mind in Mark McMorris's *The Black Reeds*: "now everything has to be re-thought." We could, it seems, go anywhere from here.

Because of its ambition for transformation, the late lyric resigns itself to loss and failure, recognizing its own inability to repair or redeem it. In this it is monstrous, threatening. Think of the lyric intensity of Mary Shelley's *Frankenstein*, a book whose impossible ambition was to embody various pathologies of reading. A book produced in a household of poets. The ultimate horror at the center of the book is a monster speaking, and at the center of his speech is the figure of a monster reading. He reads of the decline of empires, of sorrows. The blind spot he creates at the center of Mary Shelley's poetic history is our entrance into readerly recognitions, a species of mirror. In it we see ourselves (as Robert Burns also clearly saw us) as monstrous readers—our separateness suddenly brought into relief, into investigation. The world-as-it-is brought into question.

Curiosity, according to Augustine, is more powerful than discipline.[10] In the history of my monstrosity the *Confessions* is both my *Sorrows of Werther* and my *Ruins of Empire*. It writes the present as a constant flickering into the past; it is already late. Or, as Charles Olson writes, "we are all late," and this lateness has a voice.[11] In the reciprocal phenomenon of reading, we are read by books, even as we read them. Within their garden we come upon an arena, and within the arena, a garden.

Notes

1. See *The New Princeton Encyclopedia of Poetry and Poetics* (1993) and Culler's "Poetics of the Lyric." See also Culler's "Changes in the Study of the Lyric."

2. See "From One Identity to an Other," in *Desire in Language*. Culler cites Kristeva's claim that poetic language is distinguished by a constant movement between subject and nonsubject, creating an "other space where the logic of speech is unsettled, the subject is dissolved and in place of the sign is instituted the collision of signifiers cancelling one another" (*Semiotike*, qtd. in "Poetics of the Lyric").

3. As the title suggests, the collection usefully tries to update contemporary notions of the lyric, although it tends to use romanticism as its straw-man representative of uncomplicated single-subjectivity verse—an oversimplification that unfortunately shapes Susan Schultz's omnibus review essay "'Called Null or Called Vocative': A Fate of the Contemporary Lyric." Schultz's implied definition of the lyric as the ground of unified *I*-utterances and of a Keatsian "call to beauty" is bizarre since the texts she reviews all seem grounded in the multiple voicings of postmodern lyricism. Perloff critiques this notion of romantic lyric in her afterword to Jeffreys.

4. See especially "Lyric Possession" and "Preface to a Lyric History."

5. The lyric is also addressed directly within their poetry. See Howe's *Articulation of Sound Forms in Time* and Mackey's *Whatsaid Serif*, among others.

6. See "Adagia."

7. See "Approaching the Lyric," in Hosek and Parker.

8. See his *Poetics of Relation*, particularly "Errantry, Exile."

9. The complex mixture of folk tones in this book-length poem is not unlike Niedecker's:

> I dream a world
> and then what
> my soul is resting

but my feet are tired (Mullen 3)

10. See *Confessions*, bk. 1, chap. 14.

11. Charles Olson, "Maximus to Himself," in *The Maximus Poems*.

References

Augustine. *Confessions.* Trans. Rex Warner. New York: New American Library, 1963.

Cha, Theresa Hak Kyung. *Dictée.* New York: Tanam Press, 1982. Reprint, Berkeley: Third Woman Press, 1999.

Culler, Jonathan. "Poetics of the Lyric." *Structuralist Poetics: Structuralism, Linguistics, and the Study of Literature.* Ithaca: Cornell University Press, 1975.

———. "Changes in the Study of the Lyric." In *Lyric Poetry: Beyond New Criticism,* ed. Chaviva Hosek and Patricia Parker. Ithaca: Cornell University Press, 1985.

Frye, Northrop. "Approaching the Lyric." In *Lyric Poetry: Beyond New Criticism,* ed. Chaviva Hosek and Patricia Parker. Ithaca: Cornell University Press, 1985.

Giscombe, C. S. *Giscome Road.* Normal, Ill.: Dalkey Archive, 1998.

Gizzi, Peter. *Artificial Heart.* Providence: Burning Deck, 1998.

Glissant, Edouard. *The Poetics of Relation.* Ann Arbor: University of Michigan Press, 1998.

Howe, Susan. *Articulation of Sound Forms in Time.* Windsor, Vt.: Awede, 1987.

Jarnot, Lisa. *Sea Lyrics.* New York: Situations, 1996.

Jeffreys, Mark, ed. *New Definitions of Lyric: Theory, Technology, and Culture.* New York: Garland, 1998.

Kristeva, Julia. "From One Identity to an Other." In *Desire in Language: A Semiotic Approach to Art and Literature,* 124–47. New York: Columbia University Press, 1980.

Mackey, Nathaniel. *Whatsaid Serif.* San Francisco: City Lights, 1998.

McMorris, Mark. *The Black Reeds.* Athens: University of Georgia Press, 1997.

Mullen, Harryette. *Muse & Drudge.* Philadelphia: Singing Horse Press, 1995.

Niedecker, Lorine. *From This Condensery.* East Haven, Conn.: Jargon, 1985.

Olson, Charles. *Maximus Poems.* New York: Jargon/Corinth, 1960. Reprint, Berkeley: University of California Press, 1995.

Perloff, Marjorie. *The Dance of the Intellect.* Cambridge: Cambridge University Press, 1985.

———. *Poetic License: Essays on Modernist and Postmodernist Lyric.* Evanston, Ill.: Northwestern University Press, 1990.

Rehm, Pam. *To Give It Up.* Los Angeles: Sun and Moon, 1995.

Robertson, Lisa. *XEclogues.* Vancouver: Tsunami Editions, 1993.

Schultz, Susan. "'Called Null or Vocative': A Fate of the Contemporary Lyric." *Talisman* 14 (fall 1995): 70–80.

Shelley, Mary. *Frankenstein.* 1818. Reprint, Oxford: Oxford University Press, 1969.

Stein, Gertrude. *Stanzas in Meditation.* New Haven: Yale University Press, 1956. Reprint, Los Angeles: Sun and Moon, 1994.

Stevens, Wallace. *The Collected Poems.* New York: Knopf, 1980.

———. *The Necessary Angel.* New York: Knopf, 1951.

Stewart, Susan. "Lyric Possession." *Critical Inquiry* 22 (autumn 1995): 34–63.

———. "Preface to a Lyric History." In *The Uses of Literary History*, ed. Marshall Brown. Durham: Duke University Press, 1995.

16 | Writing from Inside Language: Late Surrealism and Textual Poetry in France and the United States

Charles Borkhuis

It has become increasingly clear in recent years that most groundbreaking avant-garde work originated during the earlier part of this century and that what avant-garde artists are drawing on today is a panoply of hybrids, a plurality of appearing and disappearing echoes and ghosts to whom they still remain deeply indebted. The reemergence of aspects of early avant-garde movements, such as surrealism, in later experimental writings may have as much to do with the repetitions of cycles in a series as with any particular theory of the moment. But although the reappearance of these movements is fairly regular, a particular literary influence will not "take" in soil unfavorable to its growth. In this regard French structuralism and its deconstructive descendants have provided the enriched soil necessary for the growth of a textual, language-based avant-garde, which has in turn, spawned elements of a linguistic parasurrealism that have proved more self-reflexive and adaptable to postmodern conditions than earlier forms of orthodox surrealism. The growth of this recent strain of parasurrealist writing out of more language-based poetry, offers a magnetic, highly charged schism between the two, from which new avant-garde hybrids may emerge.

Late Surrealism and Textual Poetry in France

One week in 1969, in the basement of a Paris hotel, an extraordinary chain of twenty-eight sonnets based on the Japanese renga was written by Octavio Paz, Jacques Roubaud, Eduardo Sanguineti, and Charles Tomlinson. The subsequent book, *Renga*, was dedicated to André Breton and linked the four poets, each composing in a different language, to a surrealist-influenced experiment with language-as-process. The form of the work demanded that each poet write a few lines in an ongoing chain of sonnets, the effect of which was to decenter the self and pitch the poet outward toward the project of a collective poem. This continual uprooting of the soil by shifting the focus, context, language, and poet placed the metamorphoses of language itself in the foreground as subject. The following are a few stanzas (out of sequence) from *Renga*:

(This is the way, my sphere, you dream suspended within me:
tender, you breached into being a sky, and I seek inside myself;
seek your poles, to see whether
your tongue is my wheel, Tierra del Fuego, Tierra de Roubaud)

—Eduardo Sanguineti (55)

•

Rain into the carnage of the trees, among the words
of the subterranean sentence so far away
from a sun which lies heavy among the branches

—Jacques Roubaud (51)

•

Hazeshape hillscape breach, a startling
amid undergrowth which (below your arch night is asleep,
your ashes keep their vigil): a serpentine wandering:
mouth of the cave, graveslab (abracadabra) that the moon
opens: I enter the eyelids' alcove, your eye
dissolves the mirrors: *hamam* of the dead
and resurrection which no name of my own
I am a cluster of anonymous syllables.

—Octavio Paz (53)

These selections show a marked departure from the surrealism of the 1920s and 1930s. Neither Breton's stiff, rhetorical prose style nor his high lyricism is in evidence here. Gone, too, is his stream of nonstop automatic imagery. The images of Roubaud and Paz are self-reflexive and self-correcting. Both conscious thought and bursts of automatic writing are present, each serving to illuminate the multilayered process of writing itself. Missing is surrealism's unbroken scroll of dream imagery. If there is a reference to transcendence in *Renga*, it is a transcendence within language that is sought, not the promise of a surreal world just around the corner (the beyond).

Octavio Paz's reflections on his journey to Galta in his book-length prose poem/essay *The Monkey Grammarian* are evidence of another "parasurrealist" investigation into writing as the world-constituting/world-destroying medium of human consciousness:

> Human writing reflects that of the universe, it is its translation, but also its metaphor; it says something totally different and it says the same thing. At the point of convergence the play of similarities and differences cancels itself out in order that identity alone may shine forth. The illusion of motionlessness, the play of mirrors of the one: identity is completely empty: it is a crystallization and in its transparent core the movement of analogy begins all over once again. (Paz 156)

Henri Michaux's postsurrealism in the late 1950s marks a shift away from the search for the marvelous to a search for the mechanisms of the marvelous in the thought processes themselves. For Michaux, Breton's marvelous was absolute and therefore monotonous. Like Artaud's nerve-cries of insulated anguish or Bataille's acephalous castrations and enucleations of the eye, Michaux's work from his *miserable miracle* period is written by the hauntings of a hallucinating body—its nervous system, its seizures and pulsations, its physical sensations that break into sudden shards of visceral dream imagery. Michaux is tracking the "kinetic desire" coursing through him, which leaves its markings on the page. Like particles passing through a cloud chamber, his writings are evidence of a process that has taken place. His observations of that process are incorporated in the process itself. As he writes in the poem "Tomorrow":

> the tepid tongues, passionate promenaders, changing themselves
> into knives or rocks
> the exquisite sound of coursing rivers into forests of parrots
> or piledrivers when the *Implacable Indestructible* will sit his
> 1000 foetid buttocks on this
> > closed
> > concentered
> > nailhung
>
> > World
>
> turning, turning in
>
> > upon himself without hope of escape
>
> when anguish, last
>
> > twig of Being, atrocious point,
> > will alone survive growing in fragility,
> > and increasingly intolerable
> > > and the
>
> obdurate Nothing all around
> drawing back like panic. (Michaux 303)

Michaux's fascination with the mechanisms of inspiration and "process" in altered states of consciousness is in some ways close to that found in Philippe Sollers's 1965 groundbreaking *Drame* (Event). But by the time we get to Sollers, the dreaming body is no longer in the nerves and muscles; it's in the language. *Event* is a novella-length prose poem in which the writing process stands in for the narrator. His constructions are often dreamlike yet aware of being inextricably bound to the act of writing. His narrator's identity bears certain similarities to Paz's "empty" core that activates language at the perimeters of consciousness, not at its mythical center. "What I need to find again: a presence at the periphery, the almost tactile sensation of envelopes around a buried core" (Sollers 82).

Sollers is chronicling the "path of the words on the page—exactly, nothing else, nothing more." But the path of the words carries the memory of the body with it. The words come coded with sense-experience, with the presence of a perceiving body but not a physical one. The narrator's body in *Event* is more like a lucid-dreaming body, describing the constantly shifting space under and around itself. It searches the language for a story that doesn't exist. Or if a story does exist, it is that of consciousness's ever-changing, linguistic ground. In another passage Sollers identifies himself with the reader in the process of creation:

> Or else; you are reading. Your glance pauses and slides over the written signs, you repeat the path of their arrival, unmoving you pass over what has been said—head bent, pages turned, and everything begins again. . . . We are living in this city (this book): veiled course, appearances, falls—you don't read the same words twice—the same action can't be witnessed twice. . . . That is when your pupils really are the night contained, shining, the split image of the black circle where I imagine that everything is swallowed up in order to again become visible. (Sollers 72)

In his essay "*Event*, Poem, Novel" Roland Barthes comments briefly about Sollers's intriguing connection to automatic writing, comparing him to Orpheus, who "cannot look back, [who] has to keep going and sing what he desires without thinking about it. . . . [T]his is the undertaking of *Event*, so alive in its desire for an innate language to the automatic writing of the Surrealists, and yet so unlike their writing in its emphasis on the grammatical" (Barthes 95). Indeed, it is this turn toward the grammatical as a prime generator of changes in the writing that identifies textual poetry in France in recent years. Yet this "emphasis on the grammatical" is not inconsistent with surrealist theory; automatic writing itself was primarily a linguistic operation, although the surrealists were predisposed to finding the dream image in their investigations. It is interesting to note that neither the poetry of surrealism nor Sollers's *Event* reflect a desire to break up syntax in their linguistic experiments the way Gertrude Stein or the Russian futurists did.

Joseph Guglielmi's "Ends of Lines" (1977) utilizes a playful, automatic engine that drives the writing through images to their materiality in words. Often Guglielmi's poems appear as witty, self-reflexive eddies, churning inside larger sweeping rhythms.

> Budding the bilingual heroes
> Rubbed raw by their words' noise
> their daydreams their lizard
> tongues grainy feast
> From its laboratory the water
> Appropriately floral the lips
> Stuck at the corners licking
> The treasured pink hole a mother-of-pearl
> hedgehog then undressing the image. (Guglielmi 134)

It is this peeling away of images, this stripping of one from the other, that ends in the nakedness of "the treasured pink hole" where, ironically, all that's left is to undress the image itself, leaving us with the bare fact of the words. Having translated American poets such as Larry Eigner, Rosmarie Waldrop, and Clark Coolidge, Guglielmi has looked to English for a certain music and energy missing in French poetry and has used English in some of his own poems. Yet this more dynamic inclusion must be understood in terms of Guglielmi's deep interest in Edmond Jabès and Francis Ponge, in whose work language continually questions itself.

Barthes had summarized an important semiotic insight in his essay on Sollers. It helped to open a door to a new generation of textual writing that has found a voice in both Europe and the Americas. Barthes identified Sollers's *Event* as operating within the "rhetoric of the signified," which is to say, that mechanism of meaning in language that "is not the thing (the referent)" in the world. This separation of language from its referent in the world marks a significant step in undercutting the subject-object dichotomy, moving beyond Maurice Merleau-Ponty's *Phenomenology of Perception* by acknowledging a common ground in language where "things" and thoughts exchange elements of the same substance. "It naturally follows that there is no longer any rift in substance between book and world, since the 'world' is not immediately a collection of things, but a field of signifieds: thus words and things can circulate freely among themselves, like the units of the same discourse, particles of the same matter" (Barthes 99).

At the same time that this insight rejects both "realistic" and confessional or ego-oriented writing, it forms the basis for a bridge between surrealism and recent textual poetry. The poetry of surrealism as well as textual poetry in France and "Language" poetry in the United States are writings from Barthes's unified field of the signifieds: surrealism privileges the dream image over grammar and syntax, whereas "Language" poetry does the reverse, but each primarily consists of writings about objects and processes in language, not about "real" things or events in the world. They are directly addressing this protean realm of signifiers that links the writer to the world. Each holds to an antimimetic view of language that resists explaining, translating, or illustrating experience. For late surrealism and textual/ "Language" poetry, writing can be seen as a trip wire for unexpected significations and chance operations in which juxtapositions of difference are contextualized into a schizo-materialist excess beyond any rationalist control. Yet the differences between these projects are equally striking, and the discourse between them may prove inspirational to those of the new century whose words have already begun to jump the gap of theory into the efficacies of practice.

Late Surrealism and American "Language" Poetry

American "Language" poets (Bruce Andrews, Charles Bernstein, Carla Harryman, Lyn Hejinian, Ron Silliman, Barrett Watten, and a host of others) have developed out of a set of relations somewhat different from their French contemporaries. A partial list of "Language" poets' major influences includes Gertrude Stein, Russian futurist and Zaum poetry, dadaist writings, Charles Olson, Louis Zukofsky and the Objectivists, and more recently Jackson Mac Low, Dick Higgins, and Robert Creeley—each of whom worked closely with materialist transpositions of syntax and meaning. In this regard "Language" poets have inherited a tradition of constructivist dislocations and projectivist field composition that has little to do with surrealism's "profane illumination," "convulsive beauty," or quest for the marvelous.

Philosophically, surrealism postulates an ideal or absolute reality—a super-reality toward which all of its actions are directed. Breton's *Second Manifesto of Surrealism* refers to a "certain point of the mind" from which all contradictions may be reconciled. This philosophy of essence keeps orthodox surrealism on a vertical axis, working to transform base metals into the alchemical gold of a truer reality, whereas "Language" poetry insists on a horizontal axis of multiple meanings and constructed "selves." There is an equal spreading of signification across the surfaces of the "Language" poem so that the reader experiences a critical opacity that foregrounds the poem's material enactment. This is far from surrealism's engine of desire, continually searching for its transformational object. On the whole, the projects and temperaments of surrealism and American "Language" poetry appear quite separate, yet some curious parallels persist.

Both surrealism and "Language" poetry attempt to decenter the idea of a unified "self." Surrealism concentrates on the spark that jumps between poles and is thus framed by opposites: the *I* and the *Other*, the conscious and the unconscious, life and death, and so forth, whereas "Language" poetry explodes this dyad into a multiplicity of "selves," each with a relative vantage point and subject matter.

In terms of process surrealism and "Language" poetry frequently turn an ear to the murmur of the mind as it talks to itself, often writing in a kind of paratactic shorthand, marked by continuous divergence, contradiction, association, and slippage. In this respect both have short-term memories that shift context every line or so, frustrating any attempt to isolate a particular subject or meaning. In both cases the text is read as an accumulation of poetic evidence after a certain antirational writing process has taken place rather than as a literature composed by a particular ego with a predetermined subject in mind. But given these similarities, perhaps surrealism is more easily assimilative because its unconscious associations engage primarily on a sensory level, whereas "Language" poetry tends to use a syntactical or conceptual parataxis, deploying a multiplicity of discourses as a disruptive strategy that resists the absorption of unconscious processes. Here, rather than arguing for a synthesis of surrealism and "Language" poetry, the situation calls for the emergence of an agonistic schism of shifting valences.

Two of "Language" poetry's leading theoreticians, Barrett Watten and Charles Bernstein, have come to very similar conclusions concerning the limitations of Breton's surrealism. Watten, in his illuminating essay on Surrealism and "Language" poetry, "Method and L=A=N=G=U=A=G=E," in *Total Syntax*, critiques Breton's lack of distance, his high rhetoric, and his continuity of statement in contrast to "Language" practices. Bernstein, in his *Artifice of Absorption*, singles out Breton's lack of opacity and artifice as telling deficiencies. Both Watten and Bernstein find Breton's unmediated flow of surreal imagery continually transformative and mutating but also unreflexive and absorptive. They are quite right in challenging these, by now, dated aspects of orthodox surrealism, which ask to take the reader on a hypnotic, transparent swoon into an absolute, surreal otherness that resists self-conscious critique. Yet the writings of later or tangential writers, influenced by surrealism but antithetical to its orthodoxy—such as Artaud, Bataille, Leiris, Michaux, Celan, and Paz—advance a critical, antiabsorptive strain of writing that rips at the fabric of phenomenological perception, availing itself of textual poetry's more syntactical excesses and differences. This is a distinction that goes unaddressed by Watten and Bernstein, whose only example of surrealistic writing is the poetry of Breton. But the textual differences and linguist erasures that Emmanuel Levinas saw in the self-reflexive bifurcations of Michel Leiris in his *Biffures* (1948) are still within surrealist parameters. Such textual directions within surrealist-influenced writers have also been missed by the overwhelming majority of American surrealist poets of the Charles Henri Ford, Philip Lamantia, and George Hitchcock persuasion. Much closer to a syntactical parasurrealism are the viral-linguistic cutups of William Burroughs, the neo-Baroque, dream parables of Nanos Valaoritis, and the psychosemiotic double entendres in the recent poems of Andrew Joron.

Clark Coolidge's early experimentations in books such as *Space* (1970) or *The Maintains* (1974) radically compressed the expanse of poetic reference down to the materials themselves. Readers were soon mud wrestling with isolated words or phrasal connectives that claimed the spotlight usually reserved for larger thematic elements. This was not Duncan's "ground work," whose diggings turned over allusions within the literary soil; Coolidge's early excavations found grammatical hieroglyphs or "tropes that gab," as Charles Bernstein so aptly put it in *Content's Dream*. Coolidge's work in the linguistic quarries opened a new space for materialist experimentation that the "Language" poets began to utilize. Coolidge's middle to late work began to reflect jazz rhythms and to expand the bedrock of his early word siftings into extended riffs, but the syntactical relationship of part to part was still the ground of meaning. Although surrealism's automatic writing may be considered a reference point for Coolidge's later experiments with improvisation, there are many significant differences, as evidenced in his poem *Melencolia*:

To write blind sometimes I wish. How many hollows would one meet, would then ring. So very every particle, one to kneel to.
But now how the world be museum of the world.
Praying for but a nail to fall.

That the stone is a near one.
Turned on its faces, a pair of three a half dozen of five.
To be a rhombus it must spin, the lease its top must.

In dream the properties of facets separate, lock lacking
purchase, dole. Each new world launched in such collapse.
The nut then turns and unfurls the boat. The brought to
its brink. The mastication of numbers.
The threads one to sleep.
In a thrall to throngs throw open the diving world sheer to double
the goading extant, to work. ("Melencolia X")

When the surrealists wrote automatically they were predisposed to finding a syntactically intact stream of dream images, a lyricism informed by psycho-analytic theory and nineteenth-century romanticism. When Clark Coolidge writes in an improvisational mode (a subset of automatism), he is predis-posed to finding a syntactically disturbed stream of thought impressions that maintains a musical coherence "only in the motion of the act." Coolidge treats the image as a primary color but not, as the surrealists would have it, as the primary color. As he says in an interview with Edward Foster in Talisman's *Postmodern Poetry,* "making an image wasn't primarily important. . . . Whereas somebody like Burroughs seems to be more primarily an image writer" (Coolidge/Foster 36).

Perhaps closer yet to the surrealists is Michael Palmer, a poet collected in the two major anthologies of "Language" poetry (*"Language" Poetries* and *In the American Tree*). Palmer's poems frequently place surreal fragments with-in an Objectivist field of relations, calling into play a self-reflexive dream imagery whose context shifts subtly every few lines, as in the poem "Sun":

> A headless man walks, lives
> for four hours
>
> devours himself
> You bring death into your mouth-X
>
> we are called—
> sleep, festinate, haul rocks

The eye follows itself across the screen
Words pass backward

onto the tongue
are swallows

in clay cliffs
The sea's no picture at all

blue mountain incised with a face
ends in burnt cluster

mud, private telematics, each
person controlling a machine. (Palmer 59)

A good deal of white space surrounds Palmer's lyrical phrases—space that resists being filled with words. Certainly some of George Oppen's rhythms and phrasings are present in Palmer, as are Robert Duncan's mutating first words. Palmer and Duncan are, each in his own way, exhuming a buried alphabet that bares relationship to Maurice Merleau-Ponty's concept of the "flesh of the world"—a primordial perceptual state of "wild being" in which the visible and the invisible are inextricably intertwined. This is also a place of self-erasure, where music, image, and meaning create chiasmic blind spots as each is laid over the others' dimensions. Palmer's intense crystallizations also bring to mind the later poems of Paul Celan, himself a transitional figure between such surrealists as Paul Eluard and more textual poets like Edmond Jabès. In this regard Palmer's critical lyric turns language back on itself, using lyricism's own tropes to examine its procedures. His tracking of shifting moodscapes in a poem carries both a phenomenological and surreal poignancy about it. We are often stuck by certain magnetic patches of absorptive, unconscious impulses, only to be distanced by an antiabsorptive, self-reflexive opacity and lack of development or resolution. Palmer is a master at linking chains of non sequiturs that alternately hint at and deny linear progression.

Another poet associated with the "Language" movement, for whom the surrealist image is never far away, is Bob Perelman. His 1984 *a.k.a.* is a book-length prose poem that could be compared to Sollers's *Event* in its insistence on a writing derived from the position of the "signified." But unlike Sollers, Perelman attempts to mix high and low culture in a deadpan directness that is purely American. It is a highly textualized, self-reflexive poetry that glistens with a hard-edge pop humor. At times it approaches surrealist cartoon imagery in the tradition of Benjamin Peret, but with Perelman language is always the prime mover. He invites the mundane and the everyday to mix it up with the theoretical so that there is always an ironic distance on the material at hand.

In Perelman's recent book *The Future of Memory* he uses a playful, exacting wit to slip surreal images between the sheets of a wry social commentary, specifically the politics of careerist poetics. Perelman's poems, for all their marginalization of discourse, want an automatic (or semiautomatic) surface of motion to push us past our all-too-coherent, rationalist conclusions. In the poem "To the Future" Perelman writes about catching ". . . a fragile glimpse of the writing surface of // dreams." After describing a dream in which he was "in the Laundromat, naked, washing / the books I managed to save," he reflects on real and "fake" dreams.

Like now: fake dreams, skittish prophecy —

it doesn't matter as long as
the breath comes a little quicker,

and the pulse firms and skips:
not too much: the door between

centuries turns out to be quite
narrow. An Egyptian Pulled Glass Bottle

in the Shape of a Fish;
Six Words to Name a Nipple.

My heart's pounding a bit: it
must be the future. So long. (Perelman 40–41)

Some of John Yau's later poems published in his 1988 *Radiant Silhouette* evidence a strong interest in the linguistic lyricism of certain poets who appear tangential to the "Language" school (especially Coolidge and Palmer) yet retain his earlier surrealist affinities.

Now, someone's emerald shadow

glows beneath the slab of a dead volcano night
and archaic language splinters

float to the surface of the dream
Do you want to watch me dance

until I evaporate
The soup is ripe

with flies
The laugh pools

have eroded
but I still miss your bee stung lips

Talk to me, the voice whispers
Talk to me, and I'm halfway home (Yau 214)

Yau's laser-like imagery carries an automatic current between lines, but it's very conscious of being made from pieces of language and disembodied voices. It is a parasurrealism that examines its own lyrical structure as it proceeds, often in the form of serial lists that, like conceptual art, utilize variety within repetition. The dark humor of his dream images pulls Yau away from textual concerns, which are borne back to the materials by formalist structures that were put in place from the beginning. This tension gives his poems a lively, dramatic edginess, a visceral sense of "being there" in the changes.

In a recent open letter to me published in *Orpheus Grid* the poet Andrew Joron offered a very perceptive observation on the trajectories of surrealism and "Language" poetry, noting as Lyotard, Deleuze, and Guattari before him, that language cannot pretend to be an entirely self-referential system of systems. It is here that surrealism's pull toward the cataracts of the abyss evokes Bataille's overflow of *dépense* that passes explosively beyond any attempt to contain it:

> Yet the defeat of ideological strategies of unity and closure (through the "crisscrossing" of "types and styles of discourse" that Bernstein describes in *Content's Dream*) has to be seen as only a preliminary step, a preparatory stage, not (as in "Language" poetry) an end in itself. We need Surrealism to remind us that language is not coextensive with the world—and that the world remakes itself in throes of convulsive beauty. Poetry ultimately needs to fall beyond words into things, becoming part of the abyssal aspect of things. (Joron 12–13)

In his own book *The Removes*, published in 1998, Joron writes an inventive, riveting poetry of surreal speculation, bringing together the crystalline counterfictions of a Calvino with the hallucinatory, transgressive operations of a Roussel or Bataille. Joron's memories of the future trace the lines of possibility along the faces of the probable with a mathematician's concern for the "axioms of accidental harmony." With exacting precision he deciphers antiworlds on the half-moons of our thumbnails and then adds a rarefied, arcane set of footnotes reminiscent of Borges, which explains all from the vantage point of a revelatory but as yet invisible language.

In contrast to the writers mentioned in this essay the datedness of certain aspects of more orthodox surrealism may stem from its lack of self-reflexiveness, its inability to see its romantic absolutisms as adopted postures and mannerisms. This lack of self-reflexiveness is also evident in the writing process; early surrealism paid little attention to the dislocations of syntax and grammar nor to the linguistic mechanisms of its own writing. For some curious reason the muse of early surrealist poetry gave "automatic dictation" in perfect French grammar. However, the poetry of surrealism can still draw on its strong cards: its visionary *otherness* already in the details of this world and its desire-oriented dream writing that pushes at the limits of spontaneity, sexuality, vision, and transgression.

Having published a voluminous body of work in small presses over the last twenty-five years, American "Language" poets have entered a more inclusive phase, avoiding the repetition of earlier work by expanding their range of experimentation. Being tangential to the more orthodox "Language" poets, Clark Coolidge, Michael Palmer, Bob Perelman, and John Yau have developed a critical lyric that may be useful in indicating future fertile ground for emerging post-"Language" poetries in this country. For more surrealist-influenced poets like Nanos Valaoritis and Andrew Joron, among many others, the gap between these two avant-garde influences has proven to be a magnetically charged, yet largely unexplored, area.

To varying degrees both surrealist and textual poetries are examples of writings from *inside* language and are indicative of Barthes's writer of the future, whose text is open-ended and dispersed throughout the body rather than schematized and centered in the mind. This form of parasurrealist/textual writing is a poetry of vision and diversion, digression, interruption, reverberation, grammatical dislocation, and dream.

If surrealism's return in later textual poetry has been prepared in part by structuralist and poststructuralist theory, it is also true that the germ of the structuralist revolution was already in surrealist writings. The emergence of a parasurrealist tendency in today's textual poetry may be a sign that language writing is still too narrowly rooted in cognitive processes and that what postlanguage poetries are seeking is a more contemporary, scientific model of intelligence, one that is more widely dispersed throughout the entire sensorium.

References

Barthes, Roland. *"Event*, Poem, Novel." In *Event*, trans. Bruce Benderson and Ursule Molinaro. New York: Red Dust, 1982.

Bernstein, Charles. *Artifice of Absorption*. Philadelphia: Paper Air, 1987.

———. "Maintaining Space: Clark Coolidge's Early Works." In *Content's Dream*. Los Angeles: Sun and Moon, 1986.

Coolidge, Clark. Interview by Edward Foster. In *Postmodern Poetry*, ed. Edward Foster. Hoboken, N.J.: Talisman House, 1995.

———. "Melencolia X." In *Melencolia*. Great Barrington, Mass.: The Figures, 1987.

Guglielmi, Joseph. "Ends of Lines," trans. Norma Cole and Michael Palmer. *o•blēk*, no. 5 (spring 1989): 131–36.

Joron, Andrew. "The Missing Body." *Orpheus Grid*, no. 2 (1998): 12–16.

Messerli, Douglas, ed. *"Language" Poetries*. New York: New Directions, 1987.

———. *The Removes*. West Stockbridge, Mass.: Hard Press, 1998.

Michaux, Henri. "Tomorrow," trans. Armand Schwerner. In *Twentieth Century French Poetry*. New York: Random House, 1982.

Palmer, Michael. "Sun." In *Sun*. San Francisco: North Point, 1988.

Paz, Octavio. *The Monkey Grammarian*. Trans. Helen R. Lane. New York: Seaver, 1981.

Paz, Octavio, Jacques Roubaud, Eduardo Sanguineti, Charles Tomlinson. *Renga*. Trans. Charles Tomlinson. New York: Braziller 1971.

Perelman, Bob. "To the Future." In *The Future of Memory*. New York: Roof, 1998.

Silliman, Ron, ed. *In the American Tree: Language, Poetry, Realism*. Orono, Maine: National Poetry Foundation, 1986.

Sollers, Philippe. *Event*. Trans. Bruce Benderson and Ursule Molinaro. New York: Red Dust, 1982.

Watten, Barrett. *Total Syntax*. Carbondale: Southern Illinois University Press, 1985.

Yau, John. "Radiant Silhouette I." In *Radiant Silhouette*. Santa Rosa: Black Sparrow, 1989.

17 | "Multiple" Functioning: Procedural Actions in the Poetry of Tina Darragh

Jena Osman

> By means of a certain interchangeability of circumstances and occurrences the spectator must be given the possibility (and duty) of assembling, experimenting and abstracting.
>
> —Bertolt Brecht, "Indirect Impact of the Epic Theatre"

What's Brecht Got to Do with It?

The nonmimetic strategies of contemporary experimental American poets propose an activism on the part of the reader that counters the sleepy empathy induced by poetry found in the mainstream. The experimental writer works to transform the poetry consumer into a productive participant and collaborator. The activity proposed contrasts with the "traditional" expectations for the reader of poetry. The conventional reception model invites the reader to consume a predetermined meaning, a polished whole that contains an epiphanic secret at its core. There is a tacit promise that comprehension of the secret will lead to transcendence for the reader, but because the transcendence is based in the replica of an experience rather than experience itself, the activity and its results are authentic only in regard to their overall manufacturing. The various essays and manifestos written by the L=A=N=G=U=A=G=E poets in the 1970s clearly map out what is still necessary for a circumstance of poetic production as opposed to consumption on the part of the reader: an attention to language as a material, a collaboration between writer and reader in response to that material, and a reader that ultimately "writes" a relation between form and content.

Some might argue that all poetry, written under the auspices of any aesthetic, allows for productive activity within the reader. In his book *After the Death of Poetry: Poet and Audience in Contemporary America*, Vernon Shetley has contested that experimental poetry is not singular in its approach to reader activity, claiming that "if two decades of deconstructive and reader-response criticism have established anything, it is that this [active readership] holds true for all literature, indeed for all writing of any kind" (141).

Shetley states that the only difference between the poetics of a Language poet like Bernstein and the poetics of someone like Frost is the level of "self-consciousness" when it comes to reader reception. I believe that Shetley errs when he underplays the import of this distinction. Self-consciousness is the key to linking reading activity with social activity, for self-consciousness is what allows for detachment and therefore critical evaluation—the precursors to social change.[1] Furthermore, Shetley makes no distinction between a reader being guided to a predetermined meaning through formalist constructions and a reader creating meaning orders from indeterminate paratactic fields. Certainly both provide a specific interaction with the text; however, the nature of that action goes beyond simple authorial self-consciousness. In Shetley's model, looking through a window is on the same level of activity as creating the world seen through the window. Experimental poetries, on the other hand, propose that the reading of the poem can be inherently linked to the construction of the world. By reading material language, the reader is conscious of the functions that words normally take on and how we use them. In the discussion that follows I would like to propose that procedural poetry—poems that are written according to a predetermined set of rules—take that self-consciousness and move it into a concrete realm of reader productivity.

Although my focus here is on the poetry of Tina Darragh, I think it will be helpful to first consider the dramatic theory of Bertolt Brecht when trying to understand the kind of "activity" and productivity procedural poetry invites. Brecht's refunctioning of empathy and use of alienation effects ideally result, through renewed perception, in activity on the part of the spectator. According to Brecht, the epic theater "turns the spectator into an observer, but / arouses his capacity for action / forces him to take decisions" (37). It was Brecht's hope that the distanciation and critical response encouraged by epic theater techniques would carry over in the spectator's relations to the social apparatus outside of the theater: the activated audience ideally proceeds to make necessary social changes based on new insights. However, these changes are not topically specific (i.e., they aren't meant to instigate particular events or reforms); instead they occur on the level of perception and thought. Brecht's theater asks for complex thinking that can accommodate the complex conditions in the world. This requires an understanding of the world as indeterminate and as continually revealing new contradictions.

John Cage, a champion of indeterminate aesthetics, has critiqued the kind of art that tries to "make something happen."[2] Because of Brecht's powerful assertion that art can arouse a spectator's capacity for action, many have associated his works with the programmatic goals of agitprop theater. Although Brecht's plays share certain agitprop techniques (songs, sketches, direct audience address), his project remains distinct from that of the more straightforwardly political goals of agitprop theater. Brecht's plays are not intended to instigate immediate action; instead they are meant to teach strategies for altering society through a shift in attitude on the part of the spectator. Adorno criticized Brecht for practicing a form of "committed art" that reduced the aesthetic into a narrow political lens.[3] However, Brecht's attention to the continual conversation between play and audience as it modulates from alienated to empathic extremes proves Adorno's accusation to be a misreading. Adorno is overly concerned with testing the "realism" within the plots of Brecht's plays.[4] His assumption is that because the plots fail to attain a correlation with "real" life (i.e., mimesis), they are destined to fail politically. Paradoxically, it is the nonmimetic quality of the autonomous artwork (as found in Beckett) that he considers most politically valuable because it allows for choices on the part of the viewer/reader. He does not seem to recognize that Beckett and Brecht—as stylistically and ideologically distinct as they may be—are connected in their rejection of conventional mimesis. They are joined in their expectation that the real stage of the play is in the mind of the spectator/reader.

In a way Brecht's resistance to the didacticism of propaganda theater is what caused his play *The Measures Taken* to be harshly criticized by the German Communist party, as well as the International Association of Revolutionary Writers in Moscow, when it was first produced. According to Martin Esslin, the play (which depicted a comrade consenting to his own death after making the error of putting the individual before the greater good of the collective) was considered too unclear in its presentation of a Leninist ideology. The message was too conflicted to serve the communist cause, the sacrifices made for the good of the collective too dire, and thus the audience had too much room to reject the ideological proposal at hand. As opposed to a politically narrow platform, Brecht's theater creates a partially nonintentional space where audience understanding and choice are the main actions of the drama. Brecht is trying to establish a more complex relationship with the audience than Adorno allows for in his interpretation.

Nonintentional spaces evoke particular kinds of (re)actions. The desired audience action is not topical or pictorial (e.g., watch a play about overthrowing a dictatorship and then leave the theater and overthrow a dictatorship) but pedagogical and analytical. Procedural poet Tina Darragh deals with the possibility of the reader taking the action of becoming a writer in response to works of indeterminacy. The reader's delight in her work— through its clear presentation of materials to be "used" as opposed to simply experienced—is accompanied by an acknowledged critique of conventionally passive consumption of an artwork. Darragh employs a wide range of generative procedures, each eliciting a Brechtian attitude toward the work that results in a variety of receptive activities. Although Brecht's alienation effects were quickly absorbed by a theater world seeking the shock of the new, his concept of a dialectical/pedagogical theater that left contradictions for the spectator to observe and resolve was not so quickly embraced. I believe that the poems of Darragh succeed in "performing" on the page this most difficult element of Brecht's project. Consequently, her work moves the self-conscious materiality of experimental writing from a *conceptual* demand for reader collaboration/participation to a literal realization of that desire.

Poetry Procedures and the Reader

"Recipes" for making poems are familiar fare for those who teach poetry in the schools. Kenneth Koch's books serve as primers, along with the numerous experiments collected by Bernadette Mayer and other poet-teachers such as Ted Berrigan and Ron Padgett. However, these strategies of inspiration are often critiqued for lacking the means to produce a "genuine" poem. There's an impression that these strategies are only a way of getting students to write poetry in spite of themselves, that they don't lead to "real" poems, and that any poem constructed by following a procedure first (as opposed to the form occurring as a result of the poem's subject matter in an "organic" way) is somehow fraudulent. This suspicion toward procedural writing is not limited to pedagogy. Poetry that is the product of predetermined procedures such as chance operations, "oulippean" constructs,[5] and so forth is also suspect of not being "real" in critical circles. Such work is criticized for its lack of humanness, of authorial intention/intuition, of having anything to "say." Procedural work is seen as unable to move beyond its method into a larger spectrum of meaning.

A related perceived problem of procedural writing is the seeming elimination of personal agency on the part of the writer. Probably the best-known "recipe" for poem making comes from Tristan Tzara.[6] His instructions for a newspaper cutup appear to completely do away with the idea of the poet as prime mover and authorial controller. Instead, the writer is reduced to the role of an assembly-line worker in a factory that manufactures poems. And in the spirit of Taylorism, that poet is replaceable—anyone can do the job. But according to Tzara, the poet need not fear being replaced/downsized because it is impossible to escape authorial presence and intention. Rosmarie Waldrop describes how the poetic assembly line really works:

> In the early stages of my writing all the poems were about my mother and my relation to her. Rereading them a bit later, I decided I had to get out of this obsession. This is when I started to make collages. I would take a novel and decide to take one or two words from every page. The poems were still about my mother. So I realized that you don't have to worry about contents: your preoccupations will get into the poem no matter what. (55)

In Tzara's words, "the poem will resemble you" no matter what instructions have been followed to build it. What is of interest to poets who write according to external procedures is the idea that there is something within language "other" than the authorial ego. Usually, procedural poems use "source texts" on which the procedures are performed. For example, John Cage has used sources ranging from the *I Ching* to *Finnegans Wake* to the names of his friends. Jackson Mac Low has used sources such as the Bible, *Scientific American*, and the *New York Times*. Joan Retallack has used the writings of Niels Bohr, John Dewey, and Augustine as material; and Tina Darragh has made extensive use of the dictionary and the writings of Mandelbrot and Chomsky, among others. All of these source texts are seen as sites of investigation for the side of language that has previously been hidden or suppressed. Within the source texts language has functioned according to a particular set of expectations; however, when examined in the light of a procedure, another life of the word is revealed. Barrett Watten, in a discussion of poetic vocabularies, refers to this as language in an "objectified" state. In such a state "language provides a linguistic means for cultural critique" (4), for it causes us to become aware, through defamiliarization, of what we bring to language that often is assumed to be inherent in the language. According to Watten, once we've achieved this recognition, source-generated work (manipulated through a nonintentional or intentional operation) allows for "new meaning."

"[W]riting machines," as Steve McCaffery has referred to Jackson Mac Low's procedures, are not a way of disappearing the author but of reasserting presence within language. Mac Low himself has said, "At first one thinks one can avoid the ego, make works that are egoless, by chance. This illusion passes after you work this way a while. You realize that making a chance system is egoic, in some ways, or even as emotional, as writing a poem spontaneously. But at the same time you realize there is something more than just yourself doing it" ("Poetics of Chance" 175).[7] The relation of chance to choice is complex. It seems that if indeterminate procedures can't allow for an escape from ego, then they can't escape from the trap of ideological determinism either—the evasion of which is necessary in order to allow the reader a maximum degree of freedom. But what the chance procedure allows for is a multiplicity not possible when truly coercive ideological methods are put into play. These operations let the "other" into the conversation; however, they do not let *all* others into the conversation, and this is where choice pushes aside the openness of chance.

At the same time that multiple possibilities within language are revealed in procedural writing, the presence of the reader is asserted in a completely unique way. Inasmuch as the writing of these poems consists of following the inherent instructions that language carries, the reader becomes the writer. Instructions within a multiplicitous language structure are not determinatively directive. It is up to the reader to invent and discover their presence and then to follow through. Such linguistic agency is aligned with its social counterpart. As Darragh has said in her poem *adv. fans—the 1968 series*, "one voice needed for daily functioning, multipile voices needed to change our functioning."[8] Procedure poems allow for that "multipile" functioning of language that is so often controlled and hidden away by its daily functioning.

Daily functioning—smooth communication that relies on controlled semantic limits—is constantly threatened by language's expansive capabilities. Linguistic resistance to utilitarian language forms can be found in puns, equivocation, innuendo, indirect argument, and so forth. In such moments the reader/listener/speaker is just as aware of what is not being said as of what is being said; the usually repressed substance of language can barely be restrained. However, the relationship of utilitarian to expansive language structures is not simply that a known surface language is haunted by a singular subtextual "other." Beneath that surface lies a mesh of multiple significatory possibilities.

The work of procedural poets speaks to those indecipherable discrepancies within language that point. As opposed to perceiving these moments as opportunities for decoding, their investigations are more focused on meditating our place as users/readers within such a language. If we can somehow tap into this "other life" of language, we can perhaps access similarly repressed parts of our social context. The procedures of these poets are about exposure and expanding perception rather than about solving a riddle. The methods of the procedures are often included within the work itself—in some instances accompanied by a set of specific directions. For the most part, however, the presence of procedure is intuited by the reader; we read the poems as if scanning the results of an experiment. It is up to us how we interpret the results and therefore how we envision the procedure followed in order to attain such results. Even when procedures are explicitly outlined, the reader must fill in the blank of how the operation actually functions as a mechanism of meaning. In this way the reader is both a creator and an interpreter of that which s/he created.

Tina Darragh and Fractal Poetry

but by breaking the lines
I realize
I'm not the one
who causes words
to lie apart
—they come that way—

—Tina Darragh, "Scale Sliding"

Tina Darragh's work is visual and deictic, relying on procedures of mapping, tracking, and boundary conditions as platforms for interpretation. Her poems often contain commentary (sometimes obvious, sometimes not) on their own construction; the internal set of instructions supplies the reader with insight on the kind of work that can be performed on the poem. In Darragh's poems the acts of reading and writing are inextricably linked. Darragh describes what she does with source texts as "transcription," and often she refers to her writing as "doing" what the language within the transcription is telling her to do. In this way she reveals complex and previously unseen levels in the texts.

Perhaps one of her best-known procedure poems is the chapbook *On the Corner to Off the Corner*. In this book she uses the "key" words at the top of dictionary pages as directions and graphs a path between them:

"legion" to "Lent" for "R"
"Lem" cuts a figure eight around "le ma" and "le me," generating the kind of fiber bands associated with "brain" and "ribbon." The lower oval of the eight is uniformly southern in including a Greek island, 14 variations of lemon, money from Honduras and Roman exorcisms. The upper oval far from the north has a gloss heading, lemming barks, and a young hero sometimes helped by his mother. (22)

A description of this procedure can be found in Andrews and Bernstein's *L=A=N=G=U=A=G=E Book*: "in the page 'legion' to 'Lent,' the sound 'lem' reoccurs at various points on the page. By graphing these points, I find that they produce a figure eight. I tell the reader about the graph and list the words contained within the figure. Many of the 'lem' words are 'fiber' words, so I also mention the various fibers that can make up the figure" (107). Darragh is literally using the words as instructions for the creation of "verbal pictures." But more important, these transcriptions serve as instructions to the reader—they point to the text's own construction so that the reader is thrown into an active work area. There is no way to read "through" these texts. All of the words are actively present in relation to one another. The page consists of coincidences, combinations, and evocations: materials for the reader to tinker with, to observe, and to use as the foundation for semantic inventions.

In an interview with Darragh Joan Retallack has described Darragh's work as a form of "investigative poetry":[9]

It seems to me that part of what you've been doing in some of your work is training the reader to read in a different way—that learning how to read in a new way has been incorporated into the experience of your world. Because certain guidelines are accessible to the reader who isn't necessarily involved in the same kind of project you're involved in . . . there is the ability to identify with the playful inquirer setting out on an investigation and leaving markers along the way. (Interview by Retallack 80)

This kind of investigation is even further literalized in the poem "Raymond Chandler's Sentence," where the genre of detective fiction performs an analogy in regard to the poem's procedure. The poem reenacts Chandler's method for learning the cadences of "American" English: Chandler would choose a story by mystery writer Earl Stanley Gardner, "rewrite it, compare it with the original and rework it once more. Chandler attributes this practice to his classical training at Dulwich where he would translate Cicero into English then back to Latin again" (*Striking Resemblance* 27). Translation is investigation for Darragh, as opposed to a mechanism for finding a one-to-one equivalent between an original and a copy. Translation is a means of transport further into language, a means for expressing what seemingly can't be expressed in language as we use it. The investigation into the intersection between Chandler's sentences and his biography transports Darragh into the intersection of her own linguistic and autobiographical worlds:

> but in rereading these concocted equations
> I realize I needed to create this order
> so I could see myself use
> the hardboiled genre
> to go to my father. (*Striking Resemblance* 30)

Through the procedural experiments (translations) that Darragh performs on words, we are able to find "something we don't have in our language" (30).

In what way does foregrounding the repressed possibilities of language through procedures have anything to do with the world? Although there is an active rhetoric surrounding the political efficacy of "re-forming" our expectations of how meaning is conveyed/controlled/constructed, can procedural writing really move beyond its materials? Darragh's poem "adv. fans—the 1968 series" is a unique response to such questions. This poem pointedly connects language etymology to larger historical circumstance. In it Darragh has collected a number of words that were coined in 1968. Her procedure is as follows:

1) Photocopy pages from one or more dictionaries (using different ones can help in the transcriptions).
2) Randomly tear one dictionary page and then paste it over a whole one.
3) Fold into a fan and read.
4) Transcribe a section and place between two definitions attributed to having first been said in 1968. (*Big Allis 5*)

This poem provides a provocative insight into an era of American history (fig. 1). Most of the words first used in 1968 are from the field of communications, science fiction, and sports: *shot line, tele-player, teletransport, shopper, side-foot, tie-off, washerette*, etc. The poem provides a meditation on these words themselves, as well as on their disjunction with a particularly charged moment in American history. Whereas "cultural revolution" may be the key-phrase that most think of when the year 1968 is evoked, it was a particularly nonrevolutionary vocabulary that was being generated at the time. The real revolution of that era had more to do with fantasy and consumerism than with anything else. Language was the true indicator of what the future held. The "fans" of the poem are not meant to be corrective; however, they are meant to provide for a space to think about the ramifications of our words, the other dimensions in which they make meaning. The fans function as a nonlinear space where words can be freed from the explicit narratives of the definitional frames placed at the top and bottom of the page. In fact, many of Darragh's poems create liberating environments for words, places where "they can move / more than one way" ("Scale Sliding"). The liberation of these words does not negate their historical ties, however. Instead, the "freeing" activity dramatizes the way methods of transparency hide the social import of our vocabularies. Darragh has described words as functioning as "time frames": for her, poetry is a means of opening up the frames, the linear narratives. Darragh's poems destroy the concept of a singular product-oriented language in the way that Borges's labyrinth destroys the concept of a singular path of time. Both create new weblike structures to replace the dominance of the hierarchical definition of time and progress. The ramifications of the web model in Darragh are best understood in relation to her poem "Sputter Plot."

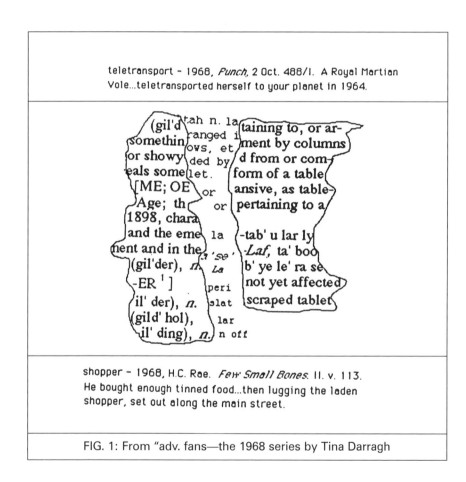

teletransport - 1968, *Punch*, 2 Oct. 488/1. A Royal Martian Vole...teletransported herself to your planet in 1964.

shopper - 1968, H.C. Rae. *Few Small Bones.* II. v. 113. He bought enough tinned food...then lugging the laden shopper, set out along the main street.

FIG. 1: From "adv. fans—the 1968 series by Tina Darragh

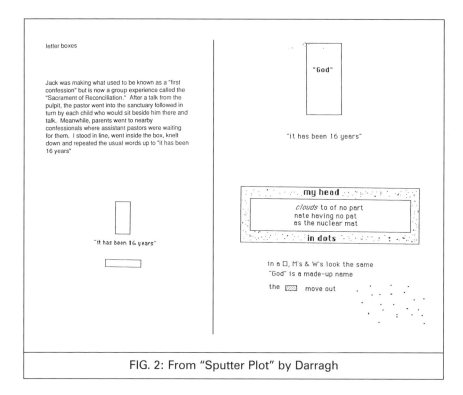

letter boxes

Jack was making what used to be known as a "first confession" but is now a group experience called the "Sacrament of Reconciliation." After a talk from the pulpit, the pastor went into the sanctuary followed in turn by each child who would sit beside him there and talk. Meanwhile, parents went to nearby confessionals where assistant pastors were waiting for them. I stood in line, went inside the box, knelt down and repeated the usual words up to "it has been 16 years"

"it has been 16 years"

"God"

"it has been 16 years"

. . . . my head . . . .
clouds to of no part
nate having no pat
as the nuclear mat
in dots

in a □, M's & W's look the same
"God" is a made-up name

the ▨▨▨ move out

FIG. 2: From "Sputter Plot" by Darragh

"Sputter Plot" is the centerpiece of Darragh's book *a(gain)²st the odds*. Its visual and narrative themes intertwine in several movements. Abstraction (as expressed by the fragmenting of already fragmentary dictionary language) is released simultaneously with personal "confessions." The confession takes place literally as Darragh initiates the poem with a description of her son, Jack, making his first confession. This process is pictorialized by a sequence of boxes/frames (fig. 2). The poem continues to investigate how content is constricted and released by forms and frames by enacting a mathematical latticework onto the material of the dictionary page. In this poem a life and language undergo "fission"; the "atoms"/words that cluster to create a coherent experience are dislodged ("sputtered") and thrown out of the box. Every word in a seemingly banal, everyday vocabulary (*lattice*; *sputter*) has its atomic shadow, bringing it further into the world.

Along with the boxes and dots that "move out" from the boxes are the inevitable "lines" of geometry and history. Darragh sketches out an etymological time line that leads from eugenics (controlling "regressive" racial qualities) to hyperactivity (a more recent "regressive" behavior to control). *Hyperactivity* elides associatively (and alphabetically) with *hyperbola*, which leads back to the geometric apparatus already present in the poem. The shape of the hyperbola—its mirrored/twinned points cut through (and kept separate) by a linear plane—serves as an organizing function for the procedures that follow.

An earlier excerpt of "Sputter Plot" published in volume 5 of *Aerial* reveals the generative device for much of the language in the poem (fig. 3). Interestingly, these diagrams—which consist of geometric forms (hyperbolic and fractal) breaking up the language of torn dictionary pages—disappear in the "final" version of the poem as it appears in *a(gain)²st the odds*. All that

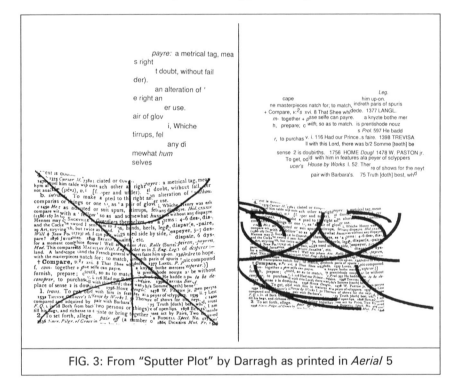

FIG. 3: From "Sputter Plot" by Darragh as printed in *Aerial* 5

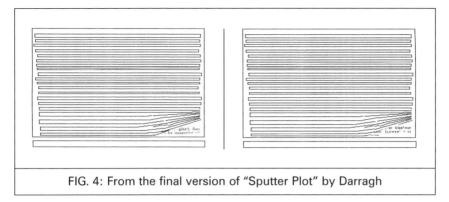

FIG. 4: From the final version of "Sputter Plot" by Darragh

we have left are the transcriptions from the visuals. Although the missing pages are visually stunning, their discard highlights the fact that the diagrams had the effect of solidifying what needs to be seen as a fluid/random system. When the diagrams are present, readers find themselves matching the transcription (the "residuum") with the original visual "worksheet." Instead of the emphasis being on "breaking apart"/fission, the emphasis becomes more about reification.

The final version of "Sputter Plot" supplies us with a different set of visuals: a series of "lattices," in both senses of the word. Darragh refers to the more common usage of the word by creating a computer-generated "window" covered by a Venetian blind (fig. 4). However, *lattice* is also a scientific/mathematical term that refers to fissionable material in a nuclear reactor. This latter type of lattice is represented by the residual elements left over after the energy burst of the absent diagrammatic procedures. The double presence within the word mirrors (as in a hyperbola) the double presences within our own lives as well. The "line" of our lives (autobiography, confession) is paralleled to a much less ordered function (the dots that leave the box). But what is important here is not the fact of "equidistance" between the two presences but the fact that they are inevitably disjunctive, cut away from each other by the horizontal plane. Darragh has no desire to reconcile the separation between the ordered (regular) and the random (irregular) worlds; she believes that they need to exist simultaneously and in relation. Darragh has found a scientific counterpart to her poethical beliefs in the concepts and language of fractal geometry.[10] Darragh was drawn to the writings of Benoit Mandelbrot because of their combination of pictures and mathematical research—a field that she had previously considered more open to diagrammatic visuals and memorization than to full color photos and investigative research. Of Mandelbrot's book *Fractal Geometry* Darragh says, "I found myself immersed in expressions such as: 'imbedded curds of decreasing D,' 'error bursts: the Cantor fractal dust,' 'Apollonian nets and soap,' and 'the notion of cup'" ("fractals <-> I-in-error"). Fractals present a political question that Darragh also asks in her writing: "The process of drumming up false narratives to obscure the horror of our lives may be part of our nature, may be the way our minds work. Is it within our capabilities to let fractal processes unfold, to lead irregular lives without relying on lucky numbers?" (ibid.). Darragh's work inhibits our tendency to prioritize order over chaos. Her project recommends that our perceptual capacity broaden to allow for new orders, for the fractal "I-in-error." Her interest in puns is perhaps the linguistic equivalent to her interest in fractal geometry. Puns are solid proof of the multiplicitous and "irregular" nature of language. In her poem "Scale Sliding" Darragh performs a perceptual experiment with language by putting puns in an "Ames Distorted Room." The visual setup of the Ames room includes a "false corner": "If a viewer stations herself at a fixed point just outside, two strangers of equal height standing at the far end look different in size. But if the viewer knows the person standing in the 'false' corner, she wonders what's wrong with the Room" (*Striking Resemblance* 45). Darragh recreates the experiment by taking puns such as "rent seck," "volcanic tuff," and "ludicrous stick" and placing them (as their parts exist in the dictionary) in a distorted page space that emulates the Ames room.

In his essay "Laughter" Henri Bergson remarks on the transgressive aspect of puns: "the play upon words makes us think somehow of a negligence on the part of language, which for the time being, seems to have forgotten its real function and now claims to accommodate things to itself instead of accommodating itself to things. And so the play upon words always betrays a momentary *lapse of attention* in language, and it is precisely on that account that it is amusing" (139). Darragh's puns are worlds away from the societal correctives of Bergson. Whereas Bergson's puns are reminders of how language "really" functions by highlighting moments where it doesn't "really" function, Darragh's puns are not so easily simplified into lessons to be learned from. "Scale Sliding" announces that puns are in fact what are being placed into the Ames room of the page; however, what the pun is and the ways it has been "transcribed" are entirely up to the reader to decide upon. These are decontextualized puns, similar to those found in Joyce's *Finnegans Wake*. For one reader, "rent seck" might lead to "rent check." The contents of the "room" are filled with "dry" words, relating back to "sec[k]." Pun: rent dries up the cash flow. The play on rent is then "rent" from the opposing half of the room, a series of abbreviations with a high occurrence of *D*s and *S*s: Dry/Sec. This is just one of multiple ways to work through the page. The coincidences are recognized and/or contrived by the reader. The act of "figuring out" the pun proves that all elements can serve as functions within an interpretation. The puns proliferate as we look for them; coincidences abound. All we need is the proper "viewing point" to realize that words are flexing into new meanings/positions constantly (fig. 5). Unlike Bergson, who believed that societal function required a unified understanding of how words should signify (with puns serving as a reminder of that), Darragh presents another model for "ideal" societal function, where words supply "hidden narratives," the narrative of error,[11] that can inform (and "throw open") our everyday usages and actions. Hank Lazer has also discussed the paranomastic ethics of "Scale Sliding" while examining the Ames room around the pun "ludicrous stick":

> The written nature of "ludicrous stick" collides with the dictionary's information about "lick" as a specific deed of the tongue. And the particular formalism of dictionary language is displayed in Darragh's poem as bumping up against the exuberance and spontaneity of a jazz lick. The shape of Darragh's poem serves to remind us of the partialness—the wedge-like quality—of any perspective we take on

rent seck

lace
to a dry

eping.
ngage in dry far
p) by   means of dry

arming practiced in
fall, depending lar
the soil more recep
— dry farmer
cial fly designated f   ds,
f. wet fly.   D.S.
aze due principally   d.s.
the air.   DCS

Ceram. removal of   D.Sc.
a piece (dry foot   D.S.C.
                              D.S.M.
urrence of freezing   Sur
ion of hoarfrost.   D.S.O.

walled plain in the   D.S.S., Do
on in the libration
                              DST, dayligh
nd related merchan-
ries, hardware, etc   D-state, (de
Informal. to ambush   electron in
y mauling: The rid   mentum of t
to betray by a sud-   from such s
The party dry-g   ol: D.

                    viewing
                     point

FIG. 5: From "Scale Sliding" by Darragh

language, no matter how thorough or authoritative that approach may claim to be. (*Opposing Poetries* 44)

In this reading Lazer has let "ludicrous stick" elide into a "jazz lick" because of the dictionary content within the room. This subjective association is the lens through which he "makes sense of"/interprets the poem. A reader could just as easily have made the bridge between *ludicrous* and *lick* through the means of a "licorice stick." We each have our own associations with sound and raw definitional data. There is difficulty in writing about Darragh's work because such writing necessitates the "authoritative"/stabilizing interpretation that the poem itself questions and negates.

In her essay "The Best of Intentions" Darragh discusses the potential problem of the new geometry performed by her procedures:

When I remove the aspect of "fixed point" from our notion of the definition of a word, am I removing as well the reader's ability to focus on the work in a relaxed way? If I challenge the concept of etymology as a linear progression and claim instead the right for words to act as open forms, moving in and out of their historical contexts, am I disrupting the reader's sense of order to such an extent that she/he is unable to reflect on her life without needing an 'other' to tie things together? In my attempts to think of words on their own terms, have I created a fascistic form?

In actuality Darragh's work is anything but fascistic, letting the reader actively participate in finding language's potential by opening up the time frame of words to include more than just singular signification. The reader is a partner in dialogue with Darragh's source texts and is equally active in working through the material. The analytic, poetic, visual, and random functions of language are all present and continuously generating response. It is perhaps this random aspect that is most important, for it makes us aware of how we conventionally use language: to organize and order that which seems to resist order. Darragh claims that this moment of language awareness is not a profound "alienation," a loss in the belief in meaning, but a "numbness": "'Numbness' corresponds more to 'blank.' . . . [I]t implies . . . a hidden narrative. . . . [The blank] is a gap, an error, a defective message, if you will, of the conscious narrative at hand. The mistake illuminates" ("Error Message").[12] The blank is what allows for subversions to appear on their own accord rather than being prompted by an overt political agenda. The blank serves to bring the reader further into the writing process. It also allows for error, which is a crucial concept for Darragh. The error is that which works against the norm, that which serves as a sign of language's otherness. The error is what keeps us from deluding ourselves that our experience can be understood in romantic terms such as *wholeness* and *grand designs*.

Action I.D.

In a 1975 Jackson Mac Low tribute issue of *VORT* Ellsworth Snyder wrote, "There needs to be more entity and less identity" (77). Snyder is not alone in seeing nonintentional work as a means of ridding the poem of identity's occlusions. John Cage himself critiqued the assertion of "self-expression."[13] The poems of Tina Darragh call into question such attitudes toward identity; they do not efface identity but instead actually use procedures as a means for communicating identity and show how neither the production nor the reception of language can be separated from it. Therefore, there is no such thing as an "objective" chance operation that produces only "entities." Darragh does not ignore or repress culturally loaded determinations (such as the subjective voice) in her work; in fact, her work is infused with these things. Her investigations of language and identity are visible within the poems themselves and thus perform a pedagogy whereby the reader follows the author's lead in taking a critical and investigatory attitude toward the material. Bertolt Brecht believed that if spectators oscillate between an absorbed and critical stance to the materials presented on stage, they will see clearly the mechanics of the world outside the theater. The work of Tina Darragh extends that proposal to the performance of the poem: if readers oscillate between the *I* and the "I-in-error"—between the fixed point and the blank—they will see clearly the mechanics of our language(s) beyond the page.

Notes

1. Charles Bernstein states the relation of self-consciousness in writing and the social this way: "the struggle is to bring to conscious scrutiny the social function different modes of reading/writing play and how they function in legitimizing or constituting or undermining the hierarchical power relations with the socious" ("Writing and Method" 596).

2. "I don't think if we made [our work] directed more to the person in the street, hmm? that it would be our world. What's involved is the people in the street changing their focus of attention, and we can't force them to change it, something else has to do that. Circumstances have to do that" (*MUSICAGE* 49). Cage has also said, "I don't mind being moved, but I don't like to be pushed" (Kostelanetz 234).

3. "[Brecht] sought to translate the true hideousness of society into theatrical appearance, by dragging it straight out of its camouflage. The people on his stage shrink before our eyes into the agents of social processes and functions, which indirectly and unknowingly they are in empirical reality. . . . Nevertheless, the process of aesthetic reduction that he pursues for the sake of political truth, in fact gets in its way" ("Commitment" 183).

4. On Brecht's *St. Joan of the Stockyards* Adorno writes, "Even with the broadest-minded allowance for poetic licence, the idea that a strike leadership backed by the Party could entrust a crucial task to a non-member is as inconceivable as the subsequent idea that the failure of that individual could ruin the whole strike" (184).

5. I refer here to the procedures of the group called OULIPO (a French acronym for "workshop of potential literature"), of which George Perec and Harry Matthews are members. An example of their procedures includes the "S+7" method, in which each noun within a found text is substituted by the seventh noun listed after the original noun's position in the dictionary.

6. To Make a Dadaist Poem:

> Take a newspaper.
> Take some scissors.
> Choose from this paper an article of the length you want to
> make your poem.

Cut out the article.

Next carefully cut out each of the words that makes up this article and put them all in a bag.

Shake gently.

Next take out each cutting one after the other.

Copy conscientiously in the order in which they left the bag.

The poem will resemble you.

And there you are—an infinitely original author of charming sensibility, even though unappreciated by the vulgar herd. (Tzara 39)

7. Edmond Jabès often refers to this double presence in language as well: "But what do we *not altogether* say in what we say? Is it what we try to keep silent, what we cannot or will not say or precisely what we do want to say and what all we say hides, saying it differently?" (quoted in Waldrop 46).

8. Darragh comments on her neologism: "for the longest time I would type 'multipile' instead of 'multiple' as in 'multipile voices to change our functioning' and then I decided just to leave it—the typo was trying to teach me something—and I like that the error illuminates the process there of piling the layers of words on top of one another!!" (Tina Darragh, e-mail to the author, February 10, 1997.)

9. This is the term used in a somewhat different way by Ed Sanders in a Naropa lecture that begins: "Investigative Poetry: that poetry should again assume responsibility for the description of history" and "the content of history will be poetry" (3). "My statement is this: that poetry, to go forward, in my view, has to begin a voyage into the description of *historical reality*" (7). In this tract poetry is seen as a "case file" and/or "data grid" for "historicity."

10. In a 1994 lecture at the State University of New York at Buffalo, Darragh quoted Freeman Dyson's "Characterizing Irregularity":

Fractal is a word invented by Mandelbrot to bring together under one heading a large class of objects that have [played] . . . an historical role . . . in the development of pure mathematics. A great revolution of ideas separates the classical mathematics of the 19th century from the modern mathematics of the 20th. Classical mathematics had its roots in the regular geometric structures of Euclid and the continuously evolving dynamics of Newton. Historically, the revolution was forced by the discovery of mathematical structures that did not fit the patterns of Euclid and Newton. These new structures were regarded . . . as "pathological" . . . as a "gallery of monsters," kin to the cubist painting and atonal music that were upsetting established standards of taste in the arts at about the same time. (as quoted by Darragh in her talk "fractals <-> I-in-error.")

11. "I think that the first time I took a programming course (in '83) I felt so at home in a certain way that wasn't a MATH way but a focus on problem-solving. And I realized with that course that 'learning from error'—my error-tracking procedures—were what programmers would do—in fact, what they 'bragged' about—how they 'discovered' a new way to do something by figuring out why something went wrong" (Tina Darragh, e-mail to author, March 22, 1997).

12. In his "45' for a Speaker," John Cage articulates the habits of mind that error "illuminates": "error is drawing a straight line between / anticipation of what should happen and / what actually happens" (Silence 167–68); and "An error is simply a / failure to adjust immediately from a preconception / to an actuality" (170–71).

13. In 1974 Cage performed *Empty Words IV*, based on Thoreau's *Journals*, at Naropa. During the performance the audience began to make noises in response to (or in protest of) the piece. Cage said of the response: "The catcalls and imitations were merely stupid criticisms. The thing that is beautiful about the Thoreau drawings is that they're completely lacking in self-expression. And the thing that made a large part of the public's interruption this evening so ugly was that it was full of self-expression" ("Empty Words with Relevant Material" 218).

References

Adorno, Theodor. "Commitment." In *Aesthetics and Politics*, trans. and ed. Ronald Taylor, 177–95. London: Verso, 1980.

———. *Notes to Literature*. Ed. Rolf Tiedemann. Trans. Sherry Weber Nicholsen. New York: Columbia University Press, 1991.

Andrews, Bruce, and Charles Bernstein, eds. *The L=A=N=G=U=A=G=E Book*. Carbondale: Southern Illinois University Press, 1984.

Bergson, Henri. "Laughter." In *Comedy*, ed. Wylie Sypher, Baltimore: Johns Hopkins University Press, 1956.

Bernstein, Charles. "Writing and Method." In *In the American Tree*, ed. Ron Silliman, 583–98. Orono, Maine: National Poetry Foundation, 1986.

Brecht, Bertolt. *Brecht on Theatre*. Ed. and trans. John Willett. New York: Hill and Wang, 1964.

Cage, John. "Empty Words with Relevant Material." In *Talking Poetics from Naropa Institute*, ed. Anne Waldman and Marilyn Webb, 195–220. Boulder: Shambhala, 1978.

———. "45' for a Speaker." In *Silence: Lectures and Writings*, by John Cage. Hanover, N.H.: Wesleyan University Press/University Press of New England, 1961.

Darragh, Tina. "adv. fans." *Big Allis* 5 (1992): 26–29.

———. *adv. fans—the 1968 series*. Buffalo, N.Y.: Leave Books, 1992.

———. *a(gain)²st the odds*. Elmwood, Conn.: Potes and Poets Press, 1989.

———. "The Best of Intentions." In *a(gain)²st the odds*. Unpaginated.

———. "Error Message." In *a(gain)²st the odds*. Unpaginated.

———. "fractals <-> I-in-error." A talk delivered at the State University of New York at Buffalo, February 15, 1994.

———. "*from* Sputter Plot." *Aerial* 5 (1989): 63–68.

———. Interview by Joan Retallack. *Aerial* 5 (1989): 69–85.

———. *On the Corner to Off the Corner*. College Park, Md.: Sun and Moon, 1981.

———. "Procedure." In *The L=A=N=G=U=A=G=E Book*, ed. Bruce Andrews and Charles Bernstein, 107–8. Carbondale: Southern Illinois University Press, 1984.

———. "Scale Sliding." In *Striking Resemblance*. Providence: Burning Deck Press, 1989.

———. *Striking Resemblance*. Providence: Burning Deck Press, 1989.

Kostelanetz, Richard. *Conversing with Cage*. New York: Limelight, 1988.

Lazer, Hank. *Opposing Poetries*. Evanston, Ill.: Northwestern University Press, 1996.

Mac Low, Jackson. "The Poetics of Chance and the Politics of Simultaneous Spontaneity, or the Sacred Heart of Jesus." In *Talking Poetics from the Naropa Institute*, ed. Anne Waldman and Marilyn Webb. Boulder: Shambhala, 1978.

McCaffery, Steve. "From the Notebooks." In *The L=A=N=G=U=A=G=E Book*, ed. Bruce Andrews and Charles Bernstein, 159–62. Carbondale: Southern Illinois University Press, 1984.

Retallack, Joan, ed. *MUSICAGE/CAGE MUSES on Words. Art. Music: John Cage in Conversation with Joan Retallack*. Hanover, N.H.: Wesleyan University Press/University Press of New England, 1996.

Sanders, Ed. *Investigative Poetry*. San Francisco: City Lights, 1975.

Shetley, Vernon. *After the Death of Poetry: Poet and Audience in Contemporary America*. Durham: Duke University Press, 1993.

Snyder, Ellsworth. "Comments RE: JACKSON MAC LOW." *Vort.* 3.2 (1975): 76–77.

Tzara, Tristan. *Seven Dada Manifestos and Lampisteries*. London: Calder/Riverrun Press, 1992.

Waldrop, Rosmarie. "Alarms and Excursions." In *The Politics of Poetic Form: Poetry and Public Policy*, ed. Charles Bernstein, 45–72. Roof: New York, 1990.

Watten, Barrett. "New Meaning and Poetic Vocabulary: From Coleridge to Jackson Mac Low." Typescript (version 5.11). June 28, 1996.

.

18 | Cowgirls Like the Salt Lick:
Gender & Some Poem Analysis

Bill Luoma

Should I be talking about gender? I asked this of two women last week and they said that it's sweet when men talk about gender but after all, you don't know what it's like to walk down the street and have the creepy feeling.

> Has George Bush
> ever been
> flattered
> walking down
> the streets
> for his
> big balls,
> so scrumptious?

asks Eileen Myles. It's a waste of time for you to write about gender; no one will listen to you if you say anything interesting because you're a man. Muriel Rukeyser said, "Everything I bring to this is because I am a woman."

Let's start with sexual organs. In 1984 Charles Bernstein published an essay that took Charles Olson to task for standing in as another example of heroic patriarchal maleness: "Women's voices . . . are completely marginal to the *Maximum Poems*. The image is of men speaking to men—and all who fall outside that discourse are simply inaudible. The image is of the man of action ('my balls as rich as Buddha's') sitting in (and acting on) the female 'field' (where 'field' is also an image of the page)" ("Undone Business" 326). Bernstein was attacked for this essay by a writer named Randy Prus:

> . . . some men write from the "balls," that soft tender spot which the gender is constantly trying to express and yet protect.

Hemingway and Mailer write from the phallus, that hard expression of masculinity. Olson, as well as Whitman, as well as myself write from the "balls." H.D. in *Notes on Thought and Vision* locates the "womb" as one center of writing. The "balls" are the male counterpart of that, as well as to that experience. Gender expression does not mean gender dominance. (Bernstein, *My Way* 273)

With all due respect to my balls, I think gender has more to do with culture and consciousness than sexual organs, not that sexual organs are all that separate from consciousness. This is not a radical idea. Women can write from the balls or think with the dick.

Gender doesn't really connect with sex in the ways we want it to. Gender shifts, whereas sex is admitted to be composed of mutually exclusive constants: males & females. We are encouraged to think of these constants as the ground. But even the ground of sexuality is unstable. As evidence, consider that transgendered peoples have existed for some time. Solid statistics on the number of humans born with ambiguous genitalia do not exist. What is better understood is that approximately 90 percent of humans so born are cut by doctors shortly after birth. This cutting is often defined as reduction surgery to what was initially decided by the doctors to be an overly large clitoris. Doctor Anthony A. Caldamone has spoken about these operations: "I don't think it's an option for nothing to be done. I don't think parents can be told this is a normal girl, and then have to be faced with what looks like an enlarged clitoris, or a penis, every time they change the diaper. We try to normalize the genitalia to the gender to reduce psychosocial and functional problems later in life" (Angier).

When nature presents an ambiguity, someone will invariably attempt to turn it into familiar ground and, in the case of the intersexual individual, often render the person unable to achieve orgasm, as well as take away from the person the choice of deciding how the genitals are to appear. Take the example of Morgan Holmes, who was subjected to "clitoral recession" surgery during childhood. Holmes is part of a growing body of intersexuals who are fighting the medical establishment's practice of genital normalization.

Holmes writes, "Any body which does possess a penis must either be designated 'male' or surgically altered. . . . I would have liked to have grown up in the body I was born with, to perhaps run rampant with a little physical gender terrorism instead of being restricted to this realm of paper and theory. Someone else made the decision of what and who I would always be before I even knew who and what I was" (11–13).

I have been giving this intersexual example to show that the sexual ground is unstable. If sex is not grounded, then gender is even shakier. It's not difficult to conclude that everyone is ambiguous with respect to gender, that gender is a psychosocial construct associated with sex, that it shifts more than sex, that around sex & gender psychosocial and functional problems can arise. Does it scare us because there are more than two sexes? Is everyone more than two genders in the same day? Are we bored with gender? Who is we?

For the writer to say gender is a fiction may appear to deny political efficacy because gender is that major signifier that points to sexual discrimination, gay bashing, rape. The writer must advocate the advance of things that free. How can writers, I mean writers in their writing, do this? Writers create fictions. Maybe fictions can help.

How then do writers create fictions? One of the most obvious ways is by using the nominative pronouns *she* and *he* in a kind of "chiasmus" with *you* and *I* (fig. 6).

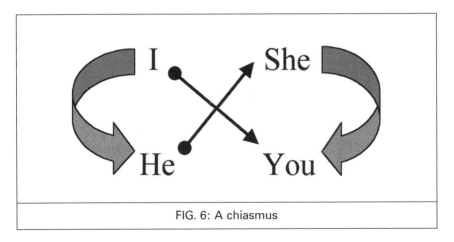

FIG. 6: A chiasmus

If we look in a vague historical way at poetry, we notice a great preponderance of writing that creates identity lines originating from the pronoun combo he/I and terminating at the pronoun combo she/you. The so-called male gaze. We also notice a lot of male to heromale gazing. For example, consider Pindar and the human drama of athletic competition. I want to look at Paul Blackburn's "7th Game: 1960 Series" in this light:

Nice day,
sweet October afternoon
Men walk the sun-shot avenues,
                          Second, Third, eyes
                          intent elsewhere
ears communing with transistors in shirt pockets
                    Bars are full, quiet,
discussion during commercials
                              only
Pirates lead New York 4–1, top of the 6th, 2
Yankees on base, 1 man out

What a nice day for all this—!
Handsome women, even
dreamy jailbait, walk
                    nearly neglected:
men's eyes are blank
their thoughts are all in Pittsburgh

Last half of the 9th, the score tied 9-all,
Mazeroski leads off for the Pirates
The 2nd pitch he simply, sweetly
                              CRACK!
belts it clean over the left field wall
Blocks of afternoon
acres of afternoon

Pennsylvania turnpikes of afternoon. One
            diamond stretches out in the sun
                    the 3rd base line
            and what men come down
            it

        The final score, 10–9

    Yanquis, come home

Here Blackburn gives us an account of the he/I ➜ she/you chiasmus without any pronouns, like in a video game when you switch to the over-head view. It's also a good example because the arrow of the identity line, the gaze from he to she, is being disrupted and refocused. Men are paying attention not to women but to the World Series.

Could a woman have written this poem?

If not, then Blackburn's is a sexist male poem. Its subject matter is sports, and the narrator is a man watching men not watch women watch sports. Sports are cool. Sports are manly. Women walk on the street to be looked at when it is convenient for them to be looked at. Women do not come down the third base line in the seventh game of the World Series. When all is said and done, Blackburn's narrator affirms that the male-to-heromale gaze is stronger than the male-to-female gaze. In his poem women simply do not gaze.

If a woman could have written it, then things have changed somewhat so that it's no longer as easy to look at a poem and say that it's sexist because it objectifies women. Denying its relevance to women—or women who like sports, say Elinor Nauen, who has a lifetime pass to the baseball Hall of Fame—seems to exclude unnecessarily. I imagine if Elinor Nauen were to rewrite the Blackburn poem, the women in the poem would be watching the World Series if not playing in it or yearning to play as the object of anyone's gaze. A recent poem by Nauen, called "Now That I Know Where I'm Going," moves somewhat in this direction.

When I dress for success they send me to the moon
    till I remember there's a game on &
I'll never be a big homerun hitter for the Sox (why not? why not?)
    cuz I throw like a girl & can't hit the ball. . . .
I'll never live in Paris because the French live there
    I'll never have a baby cuz they'd never let me name her Fort. . . .
I'll never be Queen for a Day cuz they took it off the air

So suck my dick & I don't even have one.

Since women can think with the dick, I guess the question is, would a lesbian writer ever call girls "dreamy jailbait" (as Blackburn does)? Say Eileen Myles? Probably not. Or if she did, it would be arguable that she was undermining the he/I ➜ she/you chiasmus with irony or asserting some other configuration. We can get a sense of Myles's possible response to this question by looking at her rewriting of the Andre Breton poem "Free Union." I'll quote a few lines of "Free Union" to jog your memory:

My woman with her buttocks of sandstone and asbestos
My woman with her buttocks of a swan's back
My woman with her buttocks of springtime
With her gladiolus sex
My woman with her sex of placer and platypus
My woman with her sex of seaweed and old-fashioned candies
My woman with her mirror sex
My woman with her eyes full of stars
With her eyes of violet armor and a speedometer needle
My woman with her savannah eyes
My woman with her eyes of water to drink in prison
My woman with her eyes of forests forever beneath the axe
With her pale eyes of sea-level air-level earth and fire

This poem was recently discussed on a poetics listserv, with various positions taken on its "sexistness." Robert Hale, who originated the post, admitted that his girlfriend broke up with him after he had given her this poem as a kind of valentine. The poem creeped her out. Why? Perhaps it's because the Breton poem functions as a list of body parts linked by a repeated invocation: My woman, which in French is *ma femme* and also means "wife." The gaze here is not strictly the He/I ➔ She/You chiasmus; we feel an implied male gaze with the stress on the first-person possessive pronoun *my*. But at whom does the arrow of the chiasmus point? Although the word *you* does not appear in the poem, presumably there is someone addressed here: a kind of You, the reader, gazing with the author upon My Woman and nodding in agreement. The poem might make more sense if you substituted the word *property* for *woman*.

Additionally, we see that Breton is content to focus mostly on describing portions of My Woman's body, invoking the following quantities of anatomical nouns to describe her: eyes occurs six times, sex four, tongue four, breasts four, hips three, back three, buttocks three; seven parts are mentioned twice, and fourteen parts are mentioned once. Poignantly, the only two "abstract" qualities of My Woman invoked by the author ("thoughts" and "movements") are riffed on once. The overall effect of "Free Union" is to create a kind of Pygmalion sculpture of My Woman through the additive agglomeration (naming) of her body parts.

When I asked Eileen Myles if she thought the Breton poem was sexist, she replied, "Of course it's a sexist poem." And we can see why Myles believes this if we read "I always put my pussy" in *Maxfield Parish*, wherein she reworks Breton's list:

> My lover's pussy
> is a badge
> is a night stick
> is a helmet
> is a deer's face

is a handful
of flowers
is a waterfall
is a river
of blood
is a bible
is a hurricane
is a soothsayer.
My lover's pussy
is a battle cry
is a prayer
is lunch
is wealthy
is happy
is on teevee
has a sense of humor
has a career
has a cup of coffee
goes to work
meditates
is always alone
knows my face
knows my tongue
knows my hands
is an alarmist
has lousy manners
knows her mind

Although Myles does not invoke the phrase "dreamy jailbait," she does objectify the female body. However, she does it in such a way to nullify the chiasmus men have come to know and love. The poem is a list, not a list of body parts but rather a list of actions. She inverts Breton's Pygmalion impulse by riffing off "the pussy" and ascribing many characteristics and actions to this particular part. My Lover's pussy "knows," "has," "is," "goes," & "meditates."

Myles does not directly address the You here, but the exchange between assumed men that we saw in the Breton poem is subverted in that the poem functions as a call to action; it addresses—with irony, humor, and bad puns—the theme of queer legitimacy and the violence necessary to assert that legitimacy in the face of a heterosexual state apparatus. For example, we see that My Lover's Pussy "is a badge / is a night stick / is a helmet . . . is a battle cry . . . like a flag / I can pledge / my allegiance / to." To be legitimate & safe, the I and My Lover must wear pussies on their chests like badges and create, in effect, a police force to serve and protect their own state. Where queers need stinking badges, Breton is free to sing the heterosexual national anthem.

What then? We could look at another example of the pronoun chiasmus. Why don't we look at Larry Fagin's "Rhymes of a Jerk":

1.
We are men
We walk like men.
Our women
follow

5.
When the candle dies
we come alive
and you bake pies
and we make love

7.
You are nude
I am rude
We drink wine
You are mine.

9.
The earth is ours!
We step on it!
Our women
follow

Does this parody liberate? We get an overview of the problem, and in the meantime we may be predisposed to laugh, two not invaluable things. However, I suppose I do not have a clear understanding of liberation. If I sum up the gazes we've seen, it might become clear. The gazes discussed so far disrupt some things and deliberately foreground the jerk with irony or shock or humor. These shocks and disruptions let the reader see some things. Yet the gazes we've seen are "unified," despite their being parodic or ironic. That is, the writer adopted one coherent gender voice/gaze causing the pronoun chiasmus to point in one direction.

What then? Jordan Davis is nervous because he read on a listserv that Rachel Blau DuPlessis is disrupting the male gaze by not using a unified lyric *I*, and he has just written an eighty-page poem employing the male gaze with a unified lyric *I*. Jordan explains that he likes to look at women.

Thank you Jordan. I would like to count your characterization of Rachel's view as a "dominant" one, at least in contemporary avant-garde circles; that is, disrupting the male gaze through linguistic techniques that destabilize reference, and, so the argument goes, other "more dominant" ideological categories, has been a primary mode of many male and female writers of the past thirty years, picking up from earlier modernist models. I'm not sure about the value of designating this mode a dominant trend, other than to say that the mode itself ("disrupting the male gaze by not using a unified lyric *I*") may have outlived its usefulness not only as a critical term but, more important, as an effective strategy for working poets interested in radical social change.

I want to finish this essay by looking at the work of two younger writers, Juliana Spahr and Lisa Jarnot, who draw from the "dominant" mode described above but refigure it in new ways. What interests me is that these writers are negotiating "this" in a more complicated manner by going thru the "black hole" of gender and reemerging fit for love and action.

Let's look at *Sea Lyrics* by Lisa Jarnot, a first-person narrative about California that plays with being one of those riddle poems, where you're supposed to guess the one thing the *I* of the poem is hinting at. Yet that notion of one is fairly well destroyed by Jarnot. The *I* in *Sea Lyrics* is many things: "I am a drag queen named Heather not quite ready for New York."

As we read on, we notice that the majority of things the *I* claims to be have little or nothing to do with gender or even with being human. In fact, the ratio of nonhuman to human predicate nominatives in this poem is thirty-two to eight. I list some of my favorite nonhuman lines below:

I am the foreignest of birds. . . .
I am the overpass and shattered in the midst of day. . . .
I am the tiny specs of detritus and metal that flake in the streets. . . .
I am the neighborhood of foreign things. . . .
I am the last of the partially submerged vehicles on the waterfront. . . .
I am the stray opossum at the undersides of highways. . . .
I am a tiny frozen squid. . . .

What kind of gaze is this? It's a big California gaze that can be said to encompass the ten directions. Jarnot blows up the *I*, and we as readers get to be everything, even things that are not gendered or human. Just as we want to be more than he or she we also want to be more or less than human. We want to fly. We want to be submerged. Jarnot multiplies while disrupting, giving this work a unique power to construct new consciousness. The poem can be said to free.

I want to look at another example that works like this, "Thrashing Seems Crazy," by Juliana Spahr, that makes it difficult or even moot to try and figure out which genders, identities, or gazes the writer is employing. The poem opens with a series of lines that alternate between insistent assertions and first-person passive statements:

this is true
a man in an alley grabbed my arm
this is true
someone called me and left the phone dangling at the post office
this is true
a man stalked me

When we first read the poem, we don't know if the speaking is being done by the poet "herself," a more distant narrator, or a third-person character. We sense a change when we come across the seventh line: "someone tells a story." We think a narrator is speaking now. We think the *me* in the intro is a female character, the Ruth Finley with "dissociative personality disorder" mentioned in the note under the poem's title.

This poem draws from an Oprah episode on the case of Ruth Finley, a woman who, because of "dissociative personality disorder," was stalked by a male persona of herself.

Someone tells a story. The narrator repeats this line many times. It's hard to say who's telling. Spahr is telling a story, and so is the woman whose internal male stalks herself; but no one believes the woman's descriptions, to which the woman is obliged to say this is true this is true this is true. I think the narrator is telling us we only have stories to tell (and I would focus it more: we only have stories to tell about gender). These are fictions; "they fail, resort to this is true." Yet

a woman knows her own address
her own body
her lost domain, her desires, her confusions
someone tells a story

This passage is reminiscent of the awareness of dissolution described by Sappho. The woman is aware of being fragmented and dissolved by her environment. She is aware of being confused. Someone is making up violent gender stories and it doesn't matter that they are fictions. They are real to Ruth Finley. Fictions can kill.

> self turns on self
> the knife enters at a point the self could not have reached but did
> someone tells and then repeats and she stalked herself several times
> to convince

It's very difficult to really know. Convinced is about as good as it gets. We must rely on being convinced by our fictions.

The violence of conflicting selves and Ruth Finley's dissociative personality disorder I don't want to romanticize. Nor do I want to say that anyone who confronts gender as a fiction will feel dissociated. I would however like to think allegorically for a moment about these gender fictions, and when I do I think of dissolving into a black hole. We are talking about matter falling out of the universe. When something has fallen into a black hole, we don't have the physics to describe it. A physicist says all matter will in fact lose its identity as we know it. A physicist says that once a thing has dissolved inside, it can never escape. Not even light can escape.

Contrary to this notion, the physicist Stephen Hawking has shown that things can actually escape from black holes. His model is centered on the idea that black holes obey the laws of thermodynamics and thus have a temperature. And we know anything with a temperature radiates stuff. He has shown that black holes, given enough time, will eventually radiate all their mass away through a process known as quantum mechanical tunneling.

"The explanation is that the emitted particles tunnel out of the black hole. . . . Indeed, it is possible that the black hole could emit a television set or the works of Proust in 10 leather-bound volumes" (Hawking 40).

Tunneling is an effect that "allows" something to penetrate a barrier when common sense would tell us that it should stay put if not acted on by an external force. One physicist puts it this way:

If a ball is released ⅔ of the way up the side of a bowl, it will roll back and forth up the sides of the bowl, but it is trapped in the bowl by gravity—more correctly a gravitational potential well—and can never get out. Alpha particles inside an atomic nucleus or electrons inside an electronic device are trapped inside an analogous electromagnetic potential well. Classically (i.e., as opposed to quantum mechanically) they also can never get out. But the laws of quantum mechanics say that just occasionally they indeed can get out. This is tunneling. (Larson)

What then? Please see figure 7: The diagram is a goofy illustration of Hawking's tunneling concept as it would apply to writers and writing. The writer's job description carries with it the imperative to take a dive into the middle of culture, represented here as a black hole. Assume gender is one big

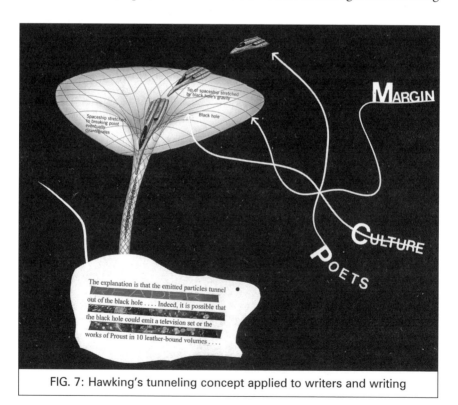

FIG. 7: Hawking's tunneling concept applied to writers and writing

multiplexer in culture's black hole. Notice that the writers in this diagram are not satisfied with exploring the event horizon of the black hole, symbolic of culture's margins, but head straight for the middle and are immediately disintegrated. This is dangerous. The writers are aware that they may not come out again. However, tunneling offers hope. In the diagram hope appears in the form of a rat. Inside the rat are Hawking's words, a human head with glasses watching a mirror ball spin and a neon sign that says READER. Hope is that the writers tunnel out of the black hole for reporting purposes. Hope is that the READER can use the material emitted from the multiplexing mirror ball.

Continuing along with this allegory, I think sometimes you come out of the gender hole, and it's possible to be moderately sane and fit for love & action. Sometimes in the dissolving process you don't come out or if you make it out, you are unable to have the selves in a communal relationship. Ruth Finley did not come out with the selves in a communal relationship.

Speaking of coming out, the media director for the Gay and Lesbian Cultural Center in Los Angeles, Sky Johnson, was quoted in an Associated Press article discussing the outing of Ellen Degeneres: "This is a very big deal for us. We have a great sense of relief and joy. There's a shelter here filled with gay and lesbian youths who were kicked out of their homes and have serious self-image crises" (Ross).

The *me* in "Thrashing" has a similar self-image crisis. For me this crisis maps out in a number of ways: as a metaphor for the life of a female living in a society that discriminates against her and does violence to her body; as a metaphor for how writers think and do their work: "a woman calls her stalker The Poet"; and finally as a metaphor for any person trying to confront gender, the hook, where the hook includes anything a subject gets hit with: men should be tough and dominate women, gay men are nice, leather guys are nice and tough, lesbians like Sportscenter, postfeminists wear Mac lipstick—these are all fictions, yet they nail us; as the narrator says, "the hook could be . . . the boring nature of life."

Thrashing seems crazy because it is: too much dissolution & too many noncommunal selves are a psychosis. But thrashing is also an everyday, possibly good, crazy because everyone is caught on the hook of gender and identity. To live & write you must thrash.

> later she realizes it is herself
> her knife
> her hook
> her own face she was always drawing male
> this is true
> as thrashing is not crazy when one is on the hook

These are the last lines of the poem, and we notice for the first time the use of the word *she*. Someone tells a story. Why didn't Spahr repeat "she tells a story" instead? And the word *I* appears only once in the poem and then under the guise of quotation. I think this limiting of nominative personal pronouns in the poem has the effect of dragging, of leveling out the gender field. This dragging makes it hard for me to map out "Thrashing"'s employment of gaze. It's a third-person voice, like Blackburn's overhead view but twice removed, twisted and dissolved. I suppose you could say here is a woman writer watching a women's talk show and being moved to write about a woman being stalked by her male self. But I balk at calling Spahr a woman writer, just as I balk at calling Oprah a women's talk show, just as I balk at calling the subject of the show a woman. So I asked Jordan, What kind of gaze is "Thrashing"? He wants to know if that's a trick question. Juliana is good about that. After thinking some more he said, "Therapeutic." I like this idea of a therapeutic gaze. We can think of the dissolving as having a healthy outcome. There is hope. The poem can be said to free.

I'm going back to the beginning to see what I said. I have been talking about gazes and gender and saying these things are fictions and everyone, not just writers, participates. I have showed examples of unified gazes and gazes that are harder to figure out. I have said that gender is dangerous because trying to confront it is like falling into a black hole and losing yourself. Once in the black hole, you can come out with a sense of your previous self, but you may have some company in there. It's also a real thing in that this company can drive you insane.

I have been saying these things to avoid being branded an essentialist. Essentialists never go into the black hole. They believe in their wombs and their balls. They are much safer adhering to strong sexual identification models. I envy them their single vision, and how could I not be them? I mean I, myself, act like a man in the world and in my writing. Someone said, "Know your place." I have to believe in, to a great degree, my place, my traditional male fiction. For example, I have sex with women. I play baseball and chew tobacco. I like Black Sabbath. I wrote a story called *My Trip to NYC* about three boys who talk a little too honestly about girls. It is obvious I treat my male fiction as real but also I want to stress that I don't trust it, that I hate my place.

For example, I wrote a series of cowboy poems called *Western Love*, and in most of the poems I can't tell who's courting whom. The gaze is all confused. In another series, called *My Lover*, the narrator claims My Lover's name is Lola. The gaze is all confused. I live with a woman who lives with another man, and we all live together. Someone asked me if I was a fag. Someone asked me if the position of the masculine within poetry was being redefined. I said yes. The male is constantly being redefined, by everyone. I recently heard Yedda Morrison read a line: "chick tits in the window." Meaning that when you think "tits," don't just think women's breasts. Thank you. I get my tits back.

But tits are not men, and I don't know what difference means. I have fuzzy allegorical notions and emulate women sometimes. Cowgirls like the salt lick is I guess how difference is. Like when you strike out and baseball player guys ask you if your pussy hurts. "No," you say, "Gerty feels pretty good today." After all, you don't want to be a boy all the time. Maybe that's why I fall for macho girls.

References

Angier, Natalie. "New Debate over Surgery on Genitals." *New York Times*, Science Section, May 13, 1997.

Bernstein, Charles. "Undone Business." In *Content's Dream*. Los Angeles: Sun and Moon, 1986.

———. "Poetry and (Male?) Sex." In *My Way*. Chicago: University of Chicago Press, 1999.

Berrigan, Ted. *The Sonnets*. audiotape. San Francisco: 80 Langton Street, 1981.

Blackburn, Paul. *The Cities*. New York: Grove Press, 1967.

Catullus. *The Poems*. London: Macmillan, 1973.

Chiao, Raymond Y., Paul G. Kwiat, and Aephraim M. Steinberg. "Faster Than Light?" *Scientific American*, August 1993, 52–60.

Davies, Kevin. *Thunk*. New York: Situations, 1995.

Davis, Jordan. *Poem on a Train*. Cambridge: Barque, 1998.

duBois, Page. *Sappho Is Burning*. Chicago: University of Chicago Press, 1996.

Fagin, Larry. *I'll Be Seeing You*. New York: Full Court Press, 1978.

Hale, Robert. "Love Poems." Buffalo Poetics List, February 3, 1998.

Hartman, Thomas E. "Tunneling of a Wave Packet." *Journal of Applied Physics* 33.12 (December 1962): 3427–33.

Hawking, Stephen. "Particle Creation by Black Holes." *Communications in Mathematical Physics* 43.3 (April 1975): 199–220.

———. "The Quantum Mechanics of Black Holes." *Scientific American*, January 1977, 34–40.

Heitmann, Winfried. Bibliography of Tunneling and Superluminal papers located at <http://www.uni-koeln.de/~abb11>.

Holmes, Morgan. "Re-membering a Queer Body." *Undercurrents* (May 1994): 13–14.

Intersex Society of North America Web Site: <http://www.isna.org>.

Jarnot, Lisa. *Sea Lyrics*. New York: Situations, 1996.

Larson, William J. One physicist's definition of tunneling, personal communication, August 1997.

Levy, Andrew. Poetry Reading at Assembling Alternatives Conference, University of New Hampshire, September 1996.

———. *Continuous Discontinuous / Curve 2*, Elmwood: Potes and Poets, 1997.

Morrison, Yedda. Reading at the Zinc Bar, New York City, spring 1997.

———. *The Marriage of the Well Built Head*. Berkeley: Double Lucy Books, 1998.

Myles, Eileen. *Maxfield Parish.* Santa Rosa, Calif.: Black Sparrow, 1995.

Nauen, Elinor. *Diamonds Are a Girl's Best Friend.* New York: Faber and Faber, 1994.

———. "Now That I Know Where I'm Going." *Antler/Sparrow.* New York: KOFF Communications International, 1997.

O'Hara, Frank. "In Memory of My Feelings." In *Selected Poems.* New York: Vintage, 1974.

Ross, Katherine. "Gays, Lesbians Set to Fete Coming Out of TV's 'Ellen.'" Associated Press, April 28, 1997.

Rukeyser, Muriel. *The Life of Poetry.* New York: Paris Press, 1996.

Sappho. *Greek Lyric Poetry.* London: Macmillan, 1967.

Schuyler, James. "Salute." In *Collected Poems.* New York: Farrar, Straus, and Giroux, 1993.

Spahr, Juliana. "Thrashing Seems Crazy." In *Response*, by Juliana Spahr. Los Angeles: Sun and Moon, 1996.

———. *Spider Wasp or Literary Criticism.* New York: Spectacular Books, 1999.

Benjamin Friedlander

POEM
Twin spheres full of fur and noise
rolling softly up my belly beddening on my chest
and then my mouth is full of suns
that softness seems so anterior to that hardness
that mouth that is used to talking too much
speaks at last of the tenderness of Ancient China
and the love of form the Odyssies
each tendril is covered with seed pearls
your hair is like a tree in an ice storm
jetting I commit the immortal spark jetting
you give that form to my life the Ancients loved
those suns are smiling as they move across the sky
and as your chariot I soon become a myth
which heaven is it that we inhabit for so long a time
it must be discovered soon and disappear

—Frank O'Hara

for Carla Billitteri

1

If words could mean one thing only, if they did our bidding, they would indeed be mere slaves of sense, and sense our tool; but once we deign to notice their ambiguity, the reign of language is established. Words set themselves over us and dictate our affairs. We find ourselves in the midst of an erotic game, a theater of cruelty that takes its cues from history. We find ourselves in a relationship with power.

2

Poetry, in this erotic game, is manumission—words delivering us by hand into a freedom words alone enjoy. Ambiguity—a proof of this freedom—assumes the form of a secret content. The poet—master of this form, slave to this content—declares, *It is the law of my own voice I shall investigate.* A freedom of speech taking pleasure in testing the limits, in going beyond them—beyond the limits, not only of speech but of freedom as well.

3

Law in this formulation—debased into metaphor by an executing voice—retains power over love by suspending judgment in favor of desire, at least for the length of a poem. Indeed, in "Homosexuality" (the poem quoted in the section above), suspension is precisely how the law of desire is administered, *without reproach and without hope that our delicate feet // will touch the earth again.*

6

In the throes of some purely sexual relation, joy decrees our freedom from necessity, from the slavery of every metaphor and every desire. I say this—I decree it like a law—but of course these words are only a chance to explore my own desire—as O'Hara chose to investigate his, calling this exploration "Hatred": *But if I'd broken you one of my wings, / shaft darkening over the prairie of your soul, for the sea's split resistance I'd never snout. / I'd retch up all men.*

7

Poetry takes flight in a heaven ruled by the law of voice; ascends because "given" voice—called across a space the poem's language constitutes. The measure of poetry's freedom is therefore a limit words set to the voice's power. And does this make sense? Poetry takes flight by SUSPENDING sense.

8

Here I'd recall Louis Zukofsky's definition of poetry as a series of orders, each surmounted through the integration of an upper and lower limit. In "A," Zukofsky calls this surmounting "'history'" (putting the word within quotation marks, as if to signify a suspension of the word's ordinary meaning), defining his continuum formally, as a hierarchy of values ranging from "body" to "dance" to "speech" to "music" to "mathèmata." O'Hara's poetry would also rise within a continuum of values, but here the gradient is defined existentially. More accurately, here a gradient is established that reserves poetry's so-called lower limit for formal achievement while defining the "upper" limit as a matter of relation. Thus the claim, set forth in "Personism," that *The poem is at last between two persons instead of two pages.*

9

In O'Hara's poetics the poem remains suspended at both ends of the continuum, remains *between* at both the upper and lower limits of what Zukofsky calls "'history'"—between *pages* at one end and *persons* at the other. Indeed, this betweenness marks O'Hara's most serious divergence from Zukofsky. For where the latter writes that "'history' integrates," O'Hara speaks of the poem as being *correspondingly gratified*—a phrase whose ring of sexual innuendo contrasts tellingly with the liberal political connotations of Zukofsky's formulation.

Gratification, integration: the difference is subtle but significant. For Zukofsky progress occurs in Hegelian-Marxist fashion by synthesizing antithetical modes of operation. For O'Hara the poem achieves its goal by keeping antinomies active. More accurately, the goal is met by equivocation—by giving voice to the unlikeliness of permanent resolution. As if by suspending difference—or better, by being suspended between two differences—the poem could begin (*at last*) to test its wings.

11

Yet if, for O'Hara, poetry remains suspended at both ends of its possibility, we shouldn't be surprised that these forms of suspension, these flights of fancy, each maintain their own limits. Horizontal instead of vertical, they are limits all the same. Nor should we be surprised that each horizontal limit, each horizon, seems more attractive when glimpsed from within the confines of the other. Between pages O'Hara thus explores what he learns between persons, whereas between persons he marshals the formal resources of art. Wherefore his plea, offered to Boris Pasternak: *Do not dismiss me, sad / that I am in your world, as your eyes rip / in the perfect light of fame, as you permit earth / completion in vicarious mortality, like poetry.*

12

I wrote before that poetry takes flight by suspending sense. I should have said that wherever suspension of any sort occurs, poetic flight is possible. Moreover, if we accept Socrates' description of the soul as "the union of powers in a team of winged steeds and their winged charioteer," then wherever poetry is discovered in suspension, we can imagine the poem as offering some essential information about the soul. This may surprise the casual reader of O'Hara's verse, those who mistake his dailiness for triviality, his quickness for superficiality, his easy artifice for artlessness. O'Hara himself conceived of the poet's task grandiosely. As he says at the end of one of the "Odes": *and one alone will speak of being / born in pain / and he will be the wings of an extraordinary liberty.*

13

O'Hara's flight often takes the form of a walk down the street. Seen from below, heaven's sign becomes *the rainbow . . . slooping over the Chrysler Building / like a spineless trout, ugly and ephemeral.* And from above? *I see a puddle and it's god, greedy god / always adding to yourself with raindrops and spit.* A trout-like rainbow, god-like puddle—heaven understood in terms of earth, earth understood in terms of heaven—the soul's upper and lower limits, each deployed equivocally by the discerning *I . . . walking along the sidewalk*—an I *not more full of judgment / than the vapors which escape one's soul when one is sick.* Here O'Hara mocks the very notion of a superseding reality, a transcendence of the world experienced at street level. For O'Hara the soul is discovered not by transcendence but suspension. A suspension that opens up a space of fantasy. A heaven that disappears even while we inhabit it, right here on earth.

14

Between two pages, between two persons. Solitude here, relation there. Both and so neither, neither and so both. Unable to settle comfortably at either extreme of "Personism"'s continuum (*practically going to sleep with quandariness*), unable or unwilling to choose between pages and persons (indeed, *graced by a certain reluctance*), O'Hara's poetry will become a passage from threshold to threshold. A passage accomplished by means of an often cruel, often self-pitying equivocation: *Vile, ghastly, ignorant, I wander through the barriers, / I suck upon rue for my distinguished heart. / I roam through the city in a shirt and get very high. / I will not go away. I will never take a wife.*

18

Sometimes O'Hara imagines that passage isn't necessary. *When I am feeling depressed and anxious sullen / all you have to do is take your clothes off / and all is wiped away revealing life's tenderness / that we are flesh and breathe and are near us.* But what precisely does he mean when he writes *that we are flesh and breathe and are near us?* What proximity does he have in mind? What sort of nearness is it that can't be affirmed simply by being beside another, clothed, the distance of everyday life not yet *wiped away?* What sort of nearness must cure *sick logic and feeble reasoning* in order to fill love's *eternal circle?* Or to put this in another way: what do flesh and breath, nudity and spirit, accomplish, even as poetry? What distance of *accidental relationship—intrusions / of incident*—can spiritual and physical nakedness alone cross, or fill, or *defeat?* And how?

19

If poetry's highest horizon is indeed its "we," then the "you" "I" seeks to reach is precisely the proximity to which nakedness would free us, the distance to which clothing enslaves us. Thus metaphor (literally, a bearing across) whose task we willingly suffer. As O'Hara tells us in "To the Harbormaster": *I trust the sanity of my vessel; and if it sinks, it may well be in answer / to the reasoning of the eternal voices, the waves which have kept me from reaching you.*

20

Poetry, moving toward this highest horizon, recalls the lover's proximity, calls across the distance that fathoms this other. The poem does this, or remains simply another instance of language—captivating, violent, incapable of any recognitions other than those of naked power.

21

And let it be said, O'Hara is not averse to such language, even cultivates it, perfecting cruelty as if it were his art—*unreasoning power / an instinct for self-declaration,* power celebrating power, mocking all shows of mere affection. In works such as these O'Hara becomes a kind of counter-Phaeton, bringing *the soul / that grows in darkness* night's graceful jet in place of day's clumsy light: *I bloomed on the back of a frightened black mare / . . . / riding blackly through the ethereal night / towards men's words which I gracefully understood, // and it was given to me / as the soul is given the hands / to hold the ribbons of life! / . . . I have mastered the speed and strength which is the armor of the world.*

22

Streaming across the world, he achieves the perspective Socrates describes in the *Phaedrus*—a work whose traces I find all through the poems of O'Hara. "And now there awaits the soul the extreme of her toil and struggling. For the souls that are called immortal, so soon as they are at the summit, come forth and stand upon the back of the world: and straightaway the revolving heaven carries them round, and they look upon the regions without." This "without," this outside information, realm of existence beyond the blue horizon (a site somehow connected with love, love's power to regenerate the soul, regrow the soul's wings), becomes accessible for O'Hara through what one and another poem call *jetting.* The commission of a *noble fault,* an immortal spark. A thought that leaps like a voice across the wires: *He reflects / mindlessly on the meaning of philodendron, then / on philo, then on the nature of fondness, of love. / It is then that he dials the phone. / He says hello / this is George Gordon, Lord Byron, then he just / listens because he didn't call to talk, he wanted / to hear your voice.*

24

Exoticism, intimacy—proximity, distance: what absolves the poet of the difference, at least in some poems, is race, *race / whom I quit as the salamander quits the flame.* An ember of exotic passion, hot to the touch—an emb-race.

26

O'Hara on occasion will burlesque difference, will ape the other to shore up his own sensibility, flirt with racism for his own gratification—will risk all this precisely because it is by risk that the other is met, or in any case approached. If there's a fault in O'Hara's work, the fault lies here. A line that at a tremor wrenches us apart.

27

For despite the trust we place in poetry, there's no sure step to the other, no certain admission into love's eternal circle. In "How to Get There," seeking their way *through the primal night of an everlasting winter,* the poet's words enact their master-slave dialectic in a white fog, servicing union and disunion alike. Words and the spaces between words, *intricate individual pathways of white accompanied / by the ringing of telephone bells beside which someone sits in / silence denying their own number, never given out.*

30

Between an embrace and bondage a queer difference measures all the meaning of being human. Does this mean that passion is a ratio? Vindictiveness, a calculation that makes of the lover or stranger mere object, reducing member to ember? O'Hara hints at this in "Life on Earth," declaring: *If I could only fear again, then I might die, / but the flames' speech flowers eternally in my posture / as I seek again and again this world that even gluttons hate.* Poetry's task: to raise the *m* of impure assignation on a smile's cold flame. But this gives poetry all the power, and power (such is its secret) seizes across metaphor's reach the other side of the sea as well. Beyond metaphor, the power of history, the impure signification of past event, roiling in memory, dredged by memoir. *That same week there was a murder. One of the negro mess-cooks, living in their segregated hut with his radio, his soft laugh, and his hat dyed yellow with an Atabrine tablet, was found before their hut, his hands cut off, his testicles tucked neatly in his cheeks, his lips sewed shut. The flag was at half mast.*

31

Whatever balance O'Hara seeks by way of fantasy, reality will disturb it. Memory, bubbling out from the mouth of poetic creation, tears open the seams of oratory, stuffs his words with silence. *River rushing into the sun / to become golden and drossy drip the fingernails / the molluscs on the underside of the scrotum / embroidered with lice and saliva and berries.* Whatever relation O'Hara seeks in creation, solitude disturbs it. The unreturned glance of language, of voice endowed with the power to free meaning, lurks in the thicket of every description. *A girl plucks skulls in the arbor of hummingbirds, and to the smiles of the hills a light / is yielding, yes, dark, towering eyes.*

32

Poetry—I will risk this definition—no matter how satiric or angry, melancholy or amused, no matter how occasional or formal, celebrates a freedom attained through ambiguity, a release from memory's bondage, from history's rule. And all poetry that takes this release as theme—for not all does, no matter how giddy or joyful the celebration—imparts some essential truth about slavery, comes face to face with constraint.

33

The motif of captivity lends local and intimate coherence to the power of this poetry's embrace, as in "River," where we read, *that brutal tenderness / that bore me on, that held me like a slave / in its liquid distance of eyes.* Following this liquid distance upstream, struggling against the undertow of memory, we might imagine ourselves arriving at the very sources of O'Hara's work, where war and personality are transmuted into lust. *A / smile then freezes in its charcoal / and, like a girl in Conrad, / one is the slave of an image / or, like Aïda, begins a slave / and ends singing under a stone / where only the other was to sing.*

34

I will risk another, perhaps contrary, definition. Poetry, an instance of human language, intimately marks us—if we care to notice—as bound over, prior to all volition, to some one or ones other than ourselves: friends, lovers, creatures of the night; the pure or impure products of assignation, concocted like a scent, dispensed like dust by obscure and magisterial beings, *divine ones who drag themselves up // and down the lengthening shadow of an Abyssinian head.* Poetry, committed so easily to heart, commits us with equal ease, places our hearts in the hands of these beings so simply and fleetingly we may never notice. Though sometimes, with great violence and passion, these beings seduce us utterly, overcome and become us, like images in a glass.

35

The formal proposition of poetry as manumission, of language made shareable in freedom, becomes manifest in content as love. And love so understood—as a sharing of freedom—occurs solely for O'Hara under the reign of voice. This reign is the law he investigates or, better said, exposes— as if an indiscretion, or body, or photograph—in one of his most beautiful poems, "You Are Gorgeous and I'm Coming." There, superimposing his images acoustically, in a grammatic clatter of breathless utterance, an acrostic spelling out of passion, O'Hara writes, *yes it may be that dark and purifying wave the death of boredom / nearing the heights themselves may destroy you in the pure air / to be further complicated, confused, empty but refilling, exposed to light.* The power of the *dark and purifying*, made manifest in the waves that cover and retract, that bellow against the shore and then collapse: at the end of the poem O'Hara calls this collapse—this *endless originality of human loss*, of images in rushing sequence—*the captured time of our being.*

36

Aboard the subway, the *torn-down Third Avenue El* (no underground railway here!), power stalks us, erotic power, *that devil / river, the munching steel wheels: With the past falling away as an acceleration of nerves thundering and shaking / aims its aggregating force like the Mètro towards a realm of encircling travel / rending the sound of adventure and becoming ultimately local and intimate.* But what does it mean that the El, the so-called ELEVATED train, has been abolished, while the history that the El frees us from (*the past*) both falls away and presses forward, a *purple roar* vaguely heard? And is this swollen purple the same hue as the signature left *in the ribs of nightly explosion* by the *Black bastard black prick black pirate* of "Easter"? Purple: the echo of a certain violence, a never-subsiding-bruise. Roar: the sound of the sea in its now empty shell, in the calcified trace of its littlest citizen.

37

The power of language lingers when we babble or scrawl our words, like light in a glass no longer holding our image, catching hold as the ocean does, *the sea, mirror of our total mankind.* Power, a reflective surface: *All the mirrors in the world / don't help, nor am I moved // by the calm emergence of my / image in the rain, it is not // I who appears or imagines.* In poetry, likewise, it is not "I" who appears or imagines, but some anterior future—the stranger, the lover, the one who seeks vainly to cross beauty—and . . . *is it sadness or the perfection / of eyes that clutches him? / . . . / . . . / he is drowning in the word.*

38

The reign of voice begins by virtue of an essential ambiguity, a duplicity that forms the lips of every poetic utterance and so allows our words to speak. And yes, I mean to write this as if backwards, to say "the lips of an utterance," not "the utterance of lips." For this is how we give voice to poetry, how a silent encounter becomes hearable, spreading its ambiguity *between two persons*, activating the page, where *the only truth is face to face, the poem whose words become your mouth.*

39

Poetry as manumission is thus the discovery in language, in advance even of the poem's writing, of the other to whom the poem is offered. Offered so as to free, not oneself but what "oneself" occludes, as if language held imprisoned a person and we, by offering or receiving this language, could become an avenue for his or her escape. The voice cracks its whip and so we race, we and our words, up and away toward freedom's horizon, ambiguity's possibility, *poetic ground on which we rear our smiles / . . . / standing in the sun of marshes as we wade slowly toward the culmination / of a gift which is categorically the most difficult relationship.*

40

We expose poetry; poetry doesn't expose us, although all we harbor in the hand and voice, all we bear in our words—not as one bears a child, but as we bare our skin to the sun—all this is implicated in the poem's language, even when the poem's meaning seems to sink from view, becoming incomprehensible. *My quietness has a man in it, he is transparent / and he carries me quietly, like a gondola, through the streets. / . . . / My quietness has a number of*

naked selves, / so many pistols I have borrowed to protect myselves / from crea-
tures who too readily recognize my weapons / and have murder in their heart!
These weapons—are they not the very words of the poem? Poetry, using a
power borrowed from language, protects a quietness inimical to language—
and not only quietness, protects also the vulnerability of the naked selves
harbored in quietness. Selves that in turn carry the poet, or one of them
does, like a gondola, like a chariot, like likeness itself. The very pigment of
metaphor, flowing in a river, racing on a horse, "In Memory of My Feelings."

41

What value this harbored vulnerability, this fugitive sense, these knots of
meaning that cause the poem to sink like a heart, to sink like a sun into the
sea, gun in hand? Are the *pistols* that defend this *gondola* the same thing as
the protective *moorings* of "To the Harbormaster"? Ties that become, *In*
storms and / at sunset, . . . the metallic coils of the tide / around my fathomless
arms? Coils that in turn become *the reasoning of the eternal voices, / the waves*
which have kept me from reaching you? And might not the fantasy *streets* with-
in, the mythic *waves* without, be the very distance a poet must travel to
attain, across a reality whose proximity is cloying, whose distance is terrify-
ing, a *face to face* encounter with *truth?* Further: if poetry frees by
captivating—and captivates by freeing—what is it we liberate and what is it
we enslave when we play that game? When we attend to the language of
poetry? When we obey not the play of difference making language possible
but the love we bear *each other's differences?*

44

Between two sheets, between two people, meaning writhes. The poet,
the poem, arrives. But where? How? Chained like a chariot to the hardness
of a god, the racing heartbeat of love's Apollo, day drawn out of our mouths,
smiling suns from whose softness wilting flowers turn their heads, slowly,
languorously . . . this is what one poem tells us about poetry's upper limit,

the first-person plural that defines the poem as between two people instead of two pages.

45

But what exactly is it that this poem called "Poem" tells us, this fifteen-line lyric beginning *Twin spheres full of fur and noise?* At what scale are this poem's cosmologies enacted? On what surface its geographies drawn? Trees, tendrils, seed pearls and ice storms—spheres, suns, a chariot in the sky—the wealth of this poem, where Homer's *Odyssey* is not singular but plural, where all meaning strains to a *jetting*, an overflowing or in any case expenditure of expression—these multiple heavens, this chatter that gives way to heat and light, that lets the mouth speak at last of tenderness: for what purpose? To what end? What do nature, history, and myth reveal here? And why here?

49

A mouth *full of suns, used to talking too much*, speaks at last *of the tenderness of Ancient China, the love of form the Odyssies.* These odysseys are above all searches for the other. This is what O'Hara calls "Life on Earth": *And the most beautiful jungle of madness being sent / and sent! and sent! and sent! and sent! into oblivion / is the great sensual blinking flag of alarm at night / hearing itself stuffed and hung, as the stars 'hear' longing.*

53

On one hand, "Poem" is a celebration of freedom, a liberation of love from the reign of language. On the other hand, the poem is a ceding of this freedom, a giving over of language's power to the lover. An ambiguity? The poem as manumission speaks BY WAY OF this ambiguity. No surprise, therefore, that a poem celebrating love's freedom (the movement of smiling suns, the release of orgasm) expresses this love, this movement and this release, in terms of servitude—as the strength and pride of a chariot.

314 | Benjamin Friedlander

54

But this isn't the only ambiguity. On one hand, "Poem" commits to language the lover to whom this creation of language is now given. On the other hand, the lover is said to have bestowed upon the poet the very power that made creation possible. The lover, inscribed in the poem as the god of song and music, god also of the sun, inscribes the poem in a heaven beyond the heavens, beyond the poet's own capability. A place Socrates mentions in the *Phaedrus*, saying: "Of that place beyond the heavens none of our earthly poets has yet sung, and none shall sing worthily."

55

"Poem" captivates . . . and thereby frees; creates . . . and is thereby created: *jetting I commit the immortal spark jetting / you give that form to my life the Ancients loved.* But note the double meaning of *jetting*, a word that means to release in a stream, to spray, to gush, but also, colloquially, to escape, to make free. Note also the double meaning of *commit*, a word that means to pledge but also imprison. *Jetting I commit:* only an equivocal reading is possible—*an immortal contest of actuality and pride / which is love assuming the consciousness of itself / as sky over all.*

56

The reign of language, like the reins of Apollo's chariot, will allow us to shed light on the nature of relationship precisely to the extent we discover—and quickly, before it disappears—the proper site for this discovery. But not only site—we must also discover the precise relationship that "Poem"'s myth would place there. *Jetting I commit:* four possibilities of meaning announce themselves. That is, our interpretation depends on whether we take *jetting* to mean love's overflow or mere evacuation, whether we understand *commit* as meaning a pledge or imprisonment of love's power. The permutations of possible interpretation are unavoidable: *jetting I commit—jetting / you give.*

Two phrases, yoked in the poem like a soul to twin steeds, the very bearers of love's meaning.

57

What is a chariot? First of all, a metaphor. It carries the sun across the sky, the heavens that the sun illuminates. The chariot—horse and carriage—serves the sun god. But what if we understand the chariot as occupying an intermediate position, as measuring the space between charioteer and horse? What if we insisted that the chariot, strictly speaking, although it bears a god, is served by horses? Second, then, the chariot marks a relationship between god and horse. Indeed, the marking of relationship is one way of understanding poetry's task, a task poetry accomplishes by way of metaphor. That is to say, the chariot—a metaphor for metaphor—preserves relationship in the form of a mark, even despite the disappearance of the heaven where this mark (the chariot) first appears. Which is what the poem seems to mean when O'Hara writes, *and as your chariot I soon become a myth*. Myth in this sense means the preservation of a mark whose moment and site no longer exist. Myth means the preservation of relationship.

58

The chariot, a metaphor for metaphor, accomplishes the task of this particular poem but also of poetry in general, a task we might describe as the maintenance of poetry's freedom between pages, its concomitant subservience between persons. Chained between mastery and subservience, reality and fantasy, the metaphor bears and is borne—bears, I would argue, the poet and his lover; is borne by language.

60

But what of love? *love is like the path in snow we are making / though no one else can follow, leading us only / to the ocean's sure embrace of summer, seri-*

ous and free / as you tell me you've got to have eggs for breakfast / and we divert our course a little without fear. Where "we" goes, *no one else can follow.* What "we" makes, none can unmake—not even the two who form this union. Love, like a path in snow, marks its own singularity, even as it seems to go astray. The lover, yielding way to the other—to the other's sense of direction, the other's hunger, desire, mere whims of the moment—thus becomes, as poet, the very custodian of this diversion, the keeper of love's inscription: *the love of form the Odysses,* diverted courses ending with breakfast.

61

These diverted courses, enjoyed or suffered without fear, measure in a manner akin to language the inevitable arc of our days. Thus the justness of "Poem"'s balanced utterance, whose permutations we've already considered: *jetting I commit the immortal spark jetting / you give that form to my life.* As a coming and as a going this jetting equally allows the poet to commit love's *immortal spark.* As a going and as a coming *jetting* equally allows the lover to offer, but not simply in return, the gift of form. A return but not necessarily a gain. The poem, as object, is not itself the gift; occurs outside the circle of exchange; is only commemoration. The gift, I would suggest, is precisely the singular course of a shared diversion, a course shared even in parting.

64

Language, projected like a voice beyond the page, makes of each reader an erotic theater, a fantastic realm where the reign of voice is "really" established. Without this theater the role is simply another instance of language. Without language the stage remains silent. Yet if a poem, between pages, uses the reader to make its reality vivid, let us not mistake this vividness for something separate from what a page already offers—from what captivates even silent reading. The reader, demonstrably real, is no less an actor, no less a fabulation of the poem, than what the reader recites. In a poem the actors are words mouthing lines that are themselves actors mouthing lines . . . mouthing actors.

65

The lines of these actors are old and poetic, a form loved by the ancients: *the tenderness of Ancient China,* and *the Odyssies.* But why *Odyssies?* Could it be that O'Hara's recourse to the plural indicates a linking of Homer's two epics into a single poem, *Illiad* and *Odyssey* together, war and return home, a circular journey that associates combat with the renewal of love? Whatever, *that form . . . the Ancients loved* has two seemingly different definitions: tenderness, Odyssey. Both and so neither, neither and so both.

67

Yet, see! how like silver snails we weave a mind / out of the blue waters of the heavens within us! Only as language can betweenness become known, weaving mind across time and space. Across: We make our way, trusting to the sanity of our vessel. *. . . and if it sinks, it may well be in answer / to the reasoning of the eternal voices,* the ambiguities that people our imagination, thronging betweenness.

68

Thronging betweenness: The poem, pursuing life in a state of suspension, remains structurally incapable of going beyond suspension—can only distend the space in which this state holds sway, recording with more and less color the erotic game, the relationship with power, by which betweenness is constituted—now as proximity, now as distance. Here we come close to understanding Frank O'Hara's project as a so-called City Poet—as a poet, that is, who FOUNDS a city.

69

A heavenly city founded in language, for the city of O'Hara's work, the state of suspension his poetry inhabits, bears only a passing resemblance to any real place on earth. How could it be otherwise? O'Hara's poetry must discover its heaven, even while bearing witness to heaven's disappearance. And what more can poetry accomplish? The poem, freed from remaining between two pages, becomes an angel with clipped wings, can only fall to earth. An earth that only imagination can conjure, suspended between persons—between lovers striving happily to reinscribe themselves between the sheets.

A POETICS OF CRITICISM

Sherry Brennan

shoesaver

"Remove shoes before entering playspace"

—Burger King Playspace

---

this is not simply language. and it does not go without saying. whether it is or is not language, it does not go without saying.

> They dig in. Digging a tunnel in into. They dig in, in a tunnel, into, & then they flower. flower & shed. Bursting in into the innermost. The guts.

It was held in common. If they were held in common. And it was working from that space where they were held. And that is the assemblage assembling. Where it dissembled it is not language because it dissembles language and so it does not go without saying. going and not finding. or going. or just going in assemblage.

> It was a small doll. Someone had bought a small doll wrapped in a green nylon coat or wrapper, a square wrapper such as on gum or cigarettes. held together by velcro. Velcro must be grasped and pulled open. And underneath the coat there is the body of the doll—vinyl, blocky. And dangling on a string behind the doll's body like a marionette—a small skeleton. Then it was said—"But didn't you know, inside every little girl there is the skeleton of an old man?"

Which is to say language. language dangling on the restless body. dull. vinyl. where the language dances in your bones. But you know. didn't. didn't you know? if pushed. your shoes are too big.

That was the fair. fair. or a fireman's festival. on a summer's night. as you like it. social. and, in your mouth, cotton. or melting. cotton. cotton.

And that's where it was. beside you. or between you. was & was apparently. or anything. force or the desire for a future. a certain type of it. was. on behalf. of language. and also a body as well. as well. well. fair.

But we have no slogan. no slogans. only our shoes that go or we go our shoes. too big or too shiny or too old or too painterly or too expensive or too white or too ill-prepared or too ugly or too unkempt or too unbefitting, unbefitting a slogan.

So that is why it goes saying. why it can be art. or poetry. or a calling. or disaster within. it calls me out. or disaster. I am called out. or disaster. I call out. out of turn.

spirit . independence . and one other . it was mild . o discovery . o self . o any one . o thee .

———————————

it was far . faring . far & faring . and that was why we went.

———————————

so then it was a question of context. How do you tunnel up into the context without abandoning language. or our now. it was faring. and that was why. why go. why we said go. go shrubbery. go fishing. go away. go gone. go going. go more. go.

But now we are in our old shoes & going. and this going is not finding. it fishes. and so we are faring. fare thee and well.

life alchemy, or, fluid mechanics

In the world around us our philosophical and theological beliefs are fashioned by the traditions that have come to us from Christianity and, prior to Christianity, from the Greeks, since Plato. For more than one hundred years, now, at least since Nietzsche (and, I would say, Darwin), philosophers have been trying to think both before and beyond Christianity and the Greeks. and to think back behind these traditions is difficult. So on the one hand, philosophy since the late nineteenth century is trying to think about the pre-Socratic Greeks and their writing as the pre-Socratic Greeks might have thought it—before Christianity and before Plato. And on the other hand, it uses Greek thought to think *through and past* Christianity to some other way of understanding the world. its forces.

It's not that world is alive or animate or.— not that all is one, in unity, collapsed back to godhead or deity— although the Greek way of understanding force as deos—wind, water, air, sun, the huntress, the satyr, the goddess of desire—aphrodite, cytherea . . . no, does not collapse . . . but rather movement, movement irrespective of life, like the movements of wind, water, rocks, the circling of the earth and its magnetic fields, its revolutions, its gravities . . . and our catching. we don't move entirely independently of these forces, and yet we aren't entirely dependent, either. we might move with these tensions, or against them, or absorb them, or between them . . . eddies . . . currents. in fluid mechanics, called turbulent or unsteady flow.

and so, also, language. this way going is where we already have our feet, to where we have already set agoing our bodies in their way, or along. along the way. and that is the pulling or pooling. and in this pulling we are not merely washed away or washed down, but pooled, as awash. so awash without away. or going. awash going. and for that—that pooling or pulling —abandon or abundance, but more like a binding abandon, so then we are abandoning awash. awash.

However, not awash without any distinctions. Quite to the contrary. We are attentive to the distinctions that have previously been arranged for us by our Western traditions, the Greek or the Christian. Yet, awash, await. And thus I said, force or the desire for a future. a certain type of it. await, awash, and this is by language. or it is said to be language. but tunneling up through that edifice that has been set about us, and then away, awash, going. or pooling. and this pooling in language and in and against the blocky edifice of our traditions, in the pooling of these contexts, we are writing, and writing awash. so then the poetry.

The poetry is not then about newness. Not at all. However, it depends on all the newnesses that those who have written in the twentieth century have allowed to us. And now, we write out of that newness, into the future. and not without regard to the past.

but it is impossible to desire the future without inhabiting our own bodies, our own traditions, our streets, our cities, our rural farmlands. and this is the pulling/pooling. Force. That constraint or tension, like the tension in a drop of water, or along the surface of a pool, or in its currents. Desire outspreads from these contexts. From our daily lives.

And it—the poetry—is not about newness, although it is about the future. And it is not about the past, although it writes as a part of the past. And to some extent, in that we inhabit our moment, now, we awash aware now, the poetry is now. not new. But only *now* as with regard to the future. await. not await in passivity. but with expectation. and so I said, force or the desire for a future.

The poetry of the twentieth century has been primarily obsessed with the new, making new out of the past or the present. Whereas, we need to be able to account for the present moment and to consider the past as a part of what we are, where we are. And so, we are not simply concerned with being new, but with the tensions between the new and the contexts out of which it writes. in the way in which the new as it has been written in the late nineteenth and in the twentieth centuries, the way in which these formal experiments of the avant-garde would allow us to resist or interrupt or tunnel into those edifices of the past that surround us even now.

so we surround ourselves or we are surrounded, pooled, and the pulling exerts a force that could be said to be new, but is not about newness. Rather, assemblages including the pull of the new, the edifice of the past, the context of the present, these things that have to do with our temporal space, gather force and shift. And in the shift, a tension, like the tension of water, language, our language, awash, washes. so we listen to these movements or shifts, which pervade anything we might say. and that saying comes to be a poetry, or poetries rather—, poetries highly attuned to our cultures, our current moment, our pasts. attuned in order to shift or make shift.

"boulevard between"

"The creator in the arts is like all the rest of the people living, he is sensitive to the changes in the way of living and his art is inevitably influenced by the way each generation is living, the way each generation is being educated and the way they move about, all this creates the composition of that generation."

—Gertrude Stein

Lisa Jarnot is one of a number of contemporary younger poets who seem to me to make poetry out of a kind of turbulence-model of language, context laden and yet future. In her recent *Some Other Kind of Mission*, on the page titled "TWO," a list is handwritten six times, "messerschmidts. / B-17s / spit fires / zeros. (japanese)." A poem appears to be pasted in the middle right of this page:

the faith-
fulness of
machine gun
fire—

give
helen
back,

or some other
kind of mission

Surrounding this poem is a handwritten phrase Xeroxed multiple times at different magnifications and pasted around the edges of the page:

give
Helen
back

(mother fuckers—

This brief sentence evokes the story of Helen and Paris (which is also referred to elsewhere: "Paris fucked Helen fourteen hundred times. There was a war going on."). Yet the phrase doesn't recapitulate the story. It doesn't merely refer to the story, either. It speaks back through the centuries to Paris. It says to Paris and to others, perhaps his fellow-countrymen, "give / Helen / back // (mother fuckers—" It makes a command. It doesn't speak to Homer. It doesn't evoke the great literature of the Greeks. With that most late-twentieth-century of expletives, it doesn't really speak in the voice of the Achaians. Rather, it speaks from now, from here, and it speaks to those who have made us here and now. It speaks of one of the most influential stories of our literary tradition. It gives a command. It provokes.

In this way it tunnels up into the narrative. Not to destroy that edifice but to take it up again, now, here, in the 1990s. It demands accountability for the past and the stories we have told about our past. It demands that we, the readers, account for the place of the past as we read. It demands our return, as well, circling back through our past to the present, fully attuned to the place of Helen among us.

In that tension—the connections between the story as we were told it so many years ago by Homer, and the present, most popular attitudes toward women and sexuality in the 1990s—in that tension, the poetry of the moment is set awash. It returns to us and demolishes us, not the past. As if "some other kind of mission"—it demolishes us.

Rod Smith, in his *In Memory of My Theories*, likewise depends on a turbulent notion of the relationships between context, language, and the world. The poem "Sieff" begins:

> The focal tendon acrostic moan. The word plunging attribute possible. unfold stem of contraction sift, as at the top and the bottom of.

> The context is an infinite interpenetration of figmentary subjectification. The sense in the intense indent is aural. Neck, or, tablet, rays. Atone to the bend it

These lines both describe and enact the poetic movement as it is already underway. the words plunge through many possible attributes. aural sense tones, a-tones, bends. the lines are a focal tendon.

The lines also refer to a context: "The context is an infinite interpenetration of figmentary subjectification." At first glance this sentence seems self-explanatory. In a somewhat mockingly self-conscious jargon-laden way, it seems to talk about the interlacing between context and the self, the mobile relationship between the self, however figmentary, and the context. But this reading fails to watch the workings of context in this context. What is context here? There seems to be no context in the usual sense—no landscape, no narrative direction, no setting, no place, nothing within which or toward which we can refer the action for interpretation.

The *American Heritage Dictionary* gives two definitions of the word *context*: "1. The part of a written or spoken statement in which a word or passage at issue occurs; that which leads up to and follows and often specifies the meaning of a particular expression. 2. The circumstances in which a particular event occurs; a situation." In both cases—context as the text that surrounds, and context as event—the context is that which allows us to make sense of the focus of the text or action at hand. But here is a different definition of context: "the context is an infinite interpenetration of figmentary subjectification." Here context and self are not interpenetrable; rather, context is itself interpenetration, nothing more than movement. The context is the motion.

We can refer back to the derivation of our English word *context*, again from the *American Heritage*: "Middle English, from Latin, *contextus*, coherence, sequence of words, from the past participle of *contexere*, to join together, weave : *com-* together + *texere*, to join, weave, plait." Accordingly, context is that which sequences. But in "Sieff" the sequencing is rather less about joining together in the grammatical or logical ways to which we are accustomed than it is about a sequencing that foregrounds sequencing itself. The sequence and movement of the words and sentences, their inappositions and disjoints—these make up the context at work, already underway, in turbulence.

For example, a few pages later, the pronoun *she* is used repetitively in such a way as to distribute any notion of subject into the context:

> wing coup in the job touched. Repugnant Shipbuilding. the fourth
> letter of. Point also called peroxy radical. She school. She boundary.
> She written. She stimulus. She clean out. She advantage. She basis. She
> peoples. She goods. She content. She Islands. She drive. She shoot. She
> applies. She burner. She kind she multiple she in the working of the
> shining Switzerland a gentile sheriff shaving lotion and nonfissionable
> modern chuckle strip the wood boulevard between them.

The repetitive *she* multiplies here; each two-word sentence skitters off in a different direction, each verb taking the context in a new direction, until it stretches out, pushed beyond what we would typically understand as a context, until the syllable *she* shimmers into the phoneme *sh-*, in *shining*, in *sheriff*, in *shaving*, in *lotion*, in *nonfissionable*.

Yet, despite all this sift, the very insistence on a certain kind of context, however stretched out of shape, the context built by the very repetition and sifting, the multiple siting of the pronoun *she*—, this insistence, this context, says something about the ways we use the word *she*. And not unlike (although also tonally quite unlike) Jarnot's "give Helen back (mother fuckers—," Smith stretches the context out precisely to ask a question about the "boulevard between" us, opening up a poetry of possibility, where the word might not simply stand for a recognizable subject but could instead operate as a mobile syllable, multiply situated. and the continual sift of the poetry calls us as readers to be attentive to this shifting and to the specific siting of the words in their contexts. It also asks us to be attentive to the kinds of change that are possible, now, in the twentieth century, among us.

In the preface to her *Imagination Verses* Jennifer Moxley writes about the temporal relationships among the possible, the future, and poetry. Our imagination of what is possible, she writes, whether for society, for life, or for poetry, is "by its very nature unequal." She writes, "When we hope for a future different from the present we uncover the injustice of our imagination."

What does this injustice mean? That's the difficult question. What would it mean for imagination to be unjust, or unequal? What would it mean for our imagination, in its very futurity, to be unjust?

According to Moxley, this inequality demands compromise, in that our daily lives are never equal to the task of the future that we might imagine. In the same way, the poem is also limited by the situatedness of our living in that it is "drawn from the viewpoint, time frame and landscape of a single life." So that there is a certain disjuncture between the temporal trajectory of the possible or imagined and the present situatedness of everyday living. That disjuncture, for Moxley, is poetry: "The poem offers a history of and a future for the mind's prerogative to exist as more than a memory of its milieus. It is a small but necessary intervention, a crucial and critical disjuncture."

Disjuncture, then, marks the inadequacy of the present to the future. This disjuncture is the injustice of imagination. We have surrounding us the time and space within which we live, and we can only write out of that context. Yet if poetry is to be anything other than recollection in solitude, not merely reifying the edifices of our traditions and memories, if poetry is to be anything other than a history of our pasts, it must imagine a future different from our present. Yet there is no known way into the future. There is no connection between the present and the future because the future is always yet to come. Thus, the injustice, the disjunction that is poetry, as Moxley says, "a bridge of half measures on the way to the possible."

In his *Metropolis (1–15)*, from Sun and Moon, Robert Fitterman draws on the historical material of Washington Irving's *A History of New York* in order to highlight a temporal disjuncture between the city we now know and its past. The first lines of "15" read:

> PlaCID GIbbett IsLAnd
> BillOWs, thRONGed
> the laTe beauTEous prosPECt 'prenTICes
>
> FANcy YouRseLf O reaDer!
>
> a pasSIon for cleaNLiness—the leading PRincipLe
> in DOMestic EcoNomy

Immediately we know this language is quoted. Words like *placid, billows, thronged, beauteous prospect* are not commonly used at this end of the century, and the direct address to the reader is quite old-fashioned in diction. We also know that the linguistic elements are probably juxtaposed in new ways.

But this poem opens up its source in another interesting way, somewhat differently from the poems discussed above. The source here doesn't operate as a context for the poem. Instead, the poem pulls Irving's words and phrases into its context, the late-twentieth-century context of the poem *Metropolis*. And in this context *A History of New York* takes on new meanings.

Poem "13" gives us an index of this resistance to a simplistic distinction of source text, poetic text, and context in *Metropolis*:

> When does the quote stop
> Qhen doth thus quote stopeth
> vis-à-vis a congoleum stripped

overcoat of the obvious yearning a
  pith & gin rickey yesteryear—
. . . .

Things are scarier than
  the rear-view redundancy under
sun lamp, reappears the mood
ring of safety, the profit in loneliness,
. . .

cries mistrial likely
  judged from the past.

Here the attempt to judge the past is more of a mistrial—"invalid because of
a basic error in procedure" (*American Heritage Dictionary*). We can't simply
look back at, judge, and therefore differentiate ourselves from the past.
"Things are scarier than / the rear-view." Rather, the error in procedure is
assuming that we know when the quote stops. In the way that everyday or
contemporary objects such as congoleum, mood ring, sun lamp, and gin
rickey invade these poems—in a similar way our language, our assumptions,
and our present are incessantly invaded by the past. There is no easy differ-
entiation of our present from our pasts. And by extension—to return to our
discussion of the future—our imagination of the possible cannot escape our
contexts, our traditions, our rootedness, the edifices that surround us. In
fact, we are just as likely to be "judged from the past." As Fitterman cites,
folding the text back onto us: "FANcy YouRself O reaDer!"

  And so I said tunnel up, into. If our present and pasts, like an Alcatraz,
are inescapable and in a certain sense indestructible, we still have the advan-
tage of the uncreated future.

  In scientific usage an experiment is a test of what we do not know
against the physical properties of the world. An experiment does not create
new matter; it creates new knowledge. It does not change the physical world;
it changes the boundaries of our interactions with the world. It does not dis-

cover new worlds; it discovers us differently. It changes what we can do. Perhaps we can think of innovation in language in this manner, so that innovative poetry now, here in the late 1990s, would not subscribe to the slogan, "make it new." Instead, it would ask questions: What is it we do not know? How do we pay attention to the world as we have inherited it, in order to make shift? To ask this is to think the relations between language and the world differently.

The poetics of each of these poets broadens out to larger issues of the social and poetry. But perhaps the most insistent about such issues is Juliana Spahr in her recent *Response*. The initial poem, "Responding," takes up the question of the relations between art and nation, the social and the person. As it begins: "This is a place without a terrain a government that always / changes an unstable language." It goes on to ask "the question [role of art in the State]":

> we know [name of major historical figure] calls, authentically,
>   for a more total, more radical war than we can even
>   dream in the language of the avant-garde
>
> we know a commercial promises to reduce plaque more
>   effectively in this same tone

Here war is called for, the avant-garde dreams, and commerce promises, all in the same language. Each of these language uses claims sole authenticity. How do we fashion an art, a language use, that does not abandon promise, dreams, radicality—yet is somehow distinguishable from the claims of nation and its attendant war, or the claims of commerce?

"We can't," Spahr writes, "keep our fingers of connection out of it." So one response, and a necessary response it seems, is precisely to draw the connections among art, nation, war, commerce, culture. Our art, our language, is situated within these bounds. Yet, at the same time, it is possible to differentiate: "rewritten, the goal of the artist is to prevent reality in a true and / concrete manner."

How does one, the poet, "prevent reality"? The word *prevent* here seems to mean multiply. At one level, it means to keep something from happening, to stop an action already underway. That is resistance. But the older meaning of *prevent*, closer to the Latin original *praevenire*, "to come before, anticipate," also operates here. The artist precedes reality in her attention to the future. That is the experiment. It represents the positive valence of our work.

graphic body, or, the albatross

I have been arguing for—attempting to demonstrate—a common attunement to context and its languages among these poets. The poetry does not simply resist these contexts or abstract itself from them. It situates its own poetic languages with regard to specific language sites. It constitutes itself in tension with them, within their bounds, and then . . . Then it shifts.

This kind of language use, a poetry that "prevents reality," depends on a very material notion of language—language as that which moves and has consequences in our world, a bodily language, a language constituted within or bound up with our bodies; thus, a multiple and varied language—languages, I should say. Languages as varied as our bodies, our histories, our presents, our futures. Languages that catch us up in their turbulent flow.

Mark Wallace, in the recent *Shadows*, writes, "There is no such thing as language. There are words and their histories, there are contexts, structures, ways of speaking, languages that often contest or merge with each other, a boisterous and fragile multiplicity. But there is no monolithic center which the word 'language' could mean. There are certainly, in differing contexts, languages with different kinds of (though always changing) power" (19). Wallace here speaks of language formations—languages and their contexts. Since we cannot assume a monologic language, he says, we find ourselves having to situate our poetry in multiple and in specific ways. We ourselves are bound up in these contexts. We cannot cut ourselves out of the text; we bring our bodies, our lives, our cities, our societies, our histories, the composition of our generation, to our poetries.

"Such words"—the words we write from within these contexts, Wallace goes on to say—"resist other meanings (and the powers supported by those meanings) that they find intolerable or offensive, *but always as part of the changes they create and are*" (19, my emphasis). The words are caught up in the very tensions and flows that they describe. As are we. Our potential for change depends on our openness to this catching, this pulling or pooling. And so we return to the question of change: force or the desire for a future.

In her "Responding" Spahr refers to various kinds of language use by writers:

[generic pronoun] painted on houses, streets, stones, trees

[generic pronoun] covered [name of island] with strange marks
    in chalk, oil paint, and dye

[generic pronoun] wished to reduce writing to the zero level
    where it is without meaning. When culture invades
    private life on a large scale [generic pronoun] said the
    individual cannot escape being raped

another [generic noun] made a font that was scratched into
    paper by a knife

this font made each letter into a single scratch

These statements are all instances of writing being etched onto the physical world, or onto the body, or onto paper. These statements all describe a certain kind of physical force, a language use that resists the forces that impinge on people. They describe a kind of embattled war in the trenches—the force of language against the forces of the world.

But Spahr's poetry enacts a different kind of force—it allows for trajectories elsewhere, turbulence, flow. It does not just name a resistance to immovable forces; instead, it enacts the potential of language to do more than we can think. Between brackets. The subjects of this poem—"[generic pronoun]," "[generic noun]"—remain potential. The brackets allow for a different future; they prevent reality by shifting the terms—literally—of the material body of language away from a male or a female subject. They bracket gender, and the gendered body, in language, while opening up the highly volatile topic of rape; and the bracketing, of course, foregrounds the question. Who wished, who said, who did these things, we wonder. Was it a man or a woman? We want to put a pronoun in the space allotted for it. We struggle to read these statements without the signposts we are used to. The very shift gives us pause.

In the space of the pause, where our attention catches, if only momentarily, in each phrase, on that which is bracketed. In that skip, in that shift, there, there, the future. Its possibility in these particular instances hinged to the way that gender or the gendered pronoun is attended to, made or make shift.

In similar ways Fitterman's discordant temporality, Moxley's poetics of possibility, Smith's a-grammatical sequencing and shift, and Jarnot's urgent rereading of Homer, "give Helen back (mother fuckers—"—each of these strategies foregrounds the materiality of the text, attuned to the operations of language in each specific context. In each of these instances our usual attitudes toward language and culture formations are shifted, if only momentarily. Giving us pause, making us aware of language uses we so often take for granted, uses such as the automatic assignment of *she*, *he*, and *it* in our everyday speech, with all the assumptions attendant on ideas of masculinity or femininity.

These are the kinds of experiments undertaken by these poets. Experiments not on language per se but with the ways that we use words—words and their tensions with our world, social and physical.

Some of the oldest myths of our culture—myths of how the world was formed out of chaos; myths of how God was, in the beginning before time, the Word; myths of how and why male and female humans, animals, and plants were created—these myths rely on a certain definition of humanity and its relationships with language and the world. Our very notion of a letter (the letter *l* or the letter *a*) and our very concept of Word are already pervaded by Western and Christian notions of body, of the material world, of the priority of spiritual or intellectual being over the body in the world.

So that, for instance, a single letter or a single sound is thought to be without meaning, while the Word is weighty. And in this way the physical presence of language, in either written or spoken form, is not thought of as the thing that carries meaning. Meaning is said to be extraneous to form—given from without, from God.

These kinds of baggage have tended to be invisible in our culture. Invisible and weighty and in some ways inescapable. And yet, if we are to imagine a future different from our own present, we have to risk this baggage. By that I mean that even as we carry around and within us our skeletons, our bodies, our histories, our property, our poetries, we must also risk being carried. away. in the current. awash. as I have said, going, going and not finding, ferrying the possible . . . desire . . . the future . . . carrying with us what is possible to say. and so saying. in that turbulence. we. make. shift.

References

Fitterman, Robert. *Metropolis (1–15)*. Sun and Moon, Los Angeles: Sun and Moon, 2000.

Jarnot, Lisa. *Some Other Kind of Mission*. Providence: Burning Deck, 1996.

Moxley, Jennifer. *Imagination Verses*. New York: Tender Buttons, 1996.

Spahr, Juliana. *Response*. Los Angeles: Sun and Moon, 1996.

Smith, Rod. *In Memory of My Theories*. Oakland, Calif.: O Books, 1996.

Wallace, Mark, and Jefferson Hansen. *Shadows: New and Selected Dialogues on Poetics. Poetic Briefs* 22 and 23 (1997).

Tan Lin

Do you watch a lot of television?

I bought a TV the other day from one of those discount stores. I lugged it home, plugged it in, and put it under my dining room table. When I am lonely I turn on the TV and flip through the channels. It makes me think I am going to walk into the room and say something to someone who is there, like what are we having for dinner tonight or did you hear about the person who put a quarter in someone else's parking meter and was arrested for it, or it makes me want to talk about my family sitting around the TV listening to Chet Huntley talk about the Vietnam War when my mother says it is time to get up and eat dinner and we get up and eat our rice with red chopsticks out of bowls (one of them is green) my father made and sometimes we never say anything at dinner. These things never happen of course when one is alone but they remain tangential and impossible compared to the things I was doing (having tea, eating cookies, taking the trash out, reading a poem), a kind of background music of "splendid conversation" (Emerson said that about Carlyle once) and everyday things going on in one's head. I eat a cookie made in Canada. I have a cup of English Breakfast tea. I write a poem about a box and in one of those boxes I put a TV for my father. I tie up the trash in a plastic shopping bag and leave it on the street. I go out to Riverside Park at 72nd Street and find a place under some trees that is shielded from the street lamps and Judy and I exchange looks at Hale-Bopp through field glasses my mother gave me one Christmas. Two or three things are happening to me now as I write this and it is impossible for me not to think of those images and those binoculars and my mother's face and Judy's hair that is blonde even at night. This is what the ideal building should be like, incidental and functional and very relaxed. The building must always carry with it the sound of some unidentified voice. In this way talking back to a poem (a poem is not a dialogue) (that is what happens when one writes it) (what image am I giving off at this moment?) ought to resemble something like yoga, or yoga right after having shiatsu, a kind of nervousness of being in knots with other persons followed by relaxation and comfort with oneself.

For example I was watching something on the Discovery Channel about life in a big city, which of course is unnatural and to which people adapt in strange ways. They were talking about urban paranoias and one of them is being in an elevator. The question was what percentage of persons in Western European and North American countries can't ride in elevators. The answer was 1 percent. The next question was how long could one person remain alive if an elevator were vacuum sealed. The answer was three days. So one can actually live much longer than one thinks one can live in an elevator and yet this desire for talking is hard to abandon, even when one is alone.

There is something primitive about language and this is what most people forget, and in the midst of being alone in a big city it is what one craves most (talking) and here in the various brainwaves endlessly going one finds the blueprint for all language and talking. And one is most aware of this when one is not talking, when the blueprint is visible in all those imagined conversations that one is having in one's head and not really speaking. A perfect poet (after all poets are supposed to be the unacknowledged masters of talking in our world today and their neglect and poverty is testament to our own hidden world of conversation), anyway a perfect poet—and all poets are—would do nothing every day except use as many words as he or she could to count things: the green and white awning across the street with the number 310 printed on it, or the street sign in red and white mounted on a green pole that says:

NO
STANDING
2PM-10PM

And in point of fact, the poet has already been there affixing words to things like spirit signs and spirit busses and spirit license plates. This is the center of civilization and it is visible from my apartment on 72nd Street. I live in the center of this world but the mapping via signage is so local and miniaturized that mastery seems to be disappearing. I am endlessly disappointed or depressed by who I am because this is always a reflection of what I see. It was this that had initially led me to undertake the project of documentary, to escape, but now it is hopeless. When I look again, I realize there are too many signs like this and there is no way to make these landmarks for *homus urbanus*. I now know that a photograph cannot create language; it cannot. I knew even then that a photograph could not document language in the past. It is to this past that I now return. The language is inadequate. It is to this nothing that I now devote myself and I do nothing else but this.

There is an amazing amount of conversational possibility (call it luck) in things that are almost not said to someone else, and the best poetry is really not what was said but what was almost said without thinking or feeling. It seems everyday conversation revolves precisely around ephemeral things like that. Call it gossip of the mind, or an interambient kind of talking that never actually takes place. Such talking has the same effect for me—especially when I hear it in the cathode-ray tubes and the invisible gasses of color, and the hum and drone of voices on TV—as being in a diurnal meadow. The meadow that is television that is a rainbow unglued. The colors seem to go on and off at will, like a form of leisure or the sound of automobiles when one is sleeping in the backseat. Nothing is heightened beyond itself. In these instances the TV is more soothing than an ocean, which is too dramatic to inspire a conversation. Conversation need not aspire to the condition of music for there it would just confront a vision of its own emptiness. Conversation is freer, more empty and more concrete than music. It has lulls, eddies of breath, breakneck speeds, sudden explosions of anger, and of course it can be used to get someone into bed and to caress that person until they sigh and to make things up completely.

A great poem strives to remain forever on the surface in this hyperreal and heightened ambient state. In this there is a kind of relaxation. All great poetry is deeply relaxing at the systole-diastole level and at the level of the brainwaves. But these things are always felt in a surface sort of way. That is why people are hardly ever aware of them or themselves. The poem is what is always not happening, not being said, etc., etc., etc., etc.

The source of the poem is not the maker and the genius behind the poem but the experience of the reader and what the reader does above all is become someone who listens. Now if poetry could inspire that state of just listening, that would be poetry. And if the listener could inspire that state of just listening, that would be poetry too but it would be better because there would be no effort to make; there would only be that state of listening. And if the maker could only listen, there would be no need for making at all and there would only be listening then. And of course, because this touches on being human, I think poetry should make the reader feel good; it should put the reader into a state of renewed receptivity; it should make the reader forget location and voice and style and what time it is, and where everyone around him or her is "exactly," should make the senses feel as if they were working together. In this way poetry would become more and more natural and less and less secondhand. A regular poem that was written is completely used up and useless and cannot tell us anything about being natural. That is why I prefer poems in anthologies to poems in individual books. A poem in an anthology has forgotten its author. It receives coaching from things next to it that probably don't like or can't understand it. I was watching a TV show the other night on MTV and they had someone who knew a special kind of shiatsu and he was practicing it live on Kennedy, the emcee for MTV's Alternative Nation show. And his English wasn't very good but he was explaining to Kennedy how I touch you and you touch me and everybody is touching everybody and no one can tell who is touching whom if it's you or me and even though he wasn't saying it well he was saying being touched isn't about touching someone else or being touched by someone else; it is just about being touched and about two people experiencing the same thing at the same time and whether he was even saying it at all. And Kennedy who can be very funny wasn't being funny or sarcastic; she was embarrassed because she didn't want to make fun of some Asian guy who didn't speak English very well and because she didn't like being touched by a stranger on TV and because it was sort of a joke but it was also a kind of enlightenment about touching and talking and who wants to be enlightened while watching MTV. The best poetry wouldn't even know that it was poetry as it was being listened to.

To write the ambient, to require the labor it takes, to create an interambient poetics, to set the muscles in order. The minute an emotion like a poem becomes memorized (the worst form of recognition) it ceases to exist in any meaningful way. In place of emotion, one wants a mood, and in particular, the mood enhancement of a minute. One wants to listen simply and soothingly, without really caring for what it was that one was hearing. Anything in language that slurs or slides is potentially enervating enough to redeem itself in this manner, and thus becomes something that one can hear. Anything that drags slowly in the groove is potentially good in a meaningless sort of wavelength. Anything that was said to be forgotten is ultra-ambient. Forgetting a word is among the most beautiful things that can happen to the human brain. The dumb poem is the most beautiful poem. If nothing is forgotten, no attempts at recovery will be made and hardly anything will be spoken. Forgetting is the best reason to keep talking. For example, I was reading about Diana Trilling's account of her visit to the White House for a Nobel Prize dinner with the Kennedys, in 1962 I think, the famous dinner when JFK said that this was the largest collection of creative individuals ever assembled in the White House except when Thomas Jefferson dined there alone. Diana Trilling, who performs like a vain and spoiled child in the piece, talks at theatrical length about the preparations of buying a dress, then another and then another without having to spend a lot of a poor intellectual's money (which she hoards repeatedly during the memoir), and the dress she first buys is too short and the wrong color—and one is not at all surprised by this. That and the Kennedy quote are about all I remember about the piece, and perhaps a detail about the men in military jackets who coach you and tell you what to do and the way JFK sits down very quickly and without regal pretensions. And how he exuded power. None of this matters now. Diana Trilling has died. So has Jackie. One can hardly imagine that dinner and JFK's speech, but one does. These are the ways one has of feeling. If the world is white, then color is a form of redundancy. Trilling's piece gives up. There are a few redundant colors but most of them are gone. A great poem makes one forget all colors except one.

Why are you lying to me?

Yes. Because lying is the most sincere way of expressing oneself and because lying is the easiest way we have of connecting one thing to another. Only by lying can one hold on to one emotion while making a transition to another. I think Paul Newman called that the Kazan Transition. Of course, Robert Redford said of Newman that "the reason he's so demanding of himself is because he has no talent." All of us are basically like that, actors with no talent, which is why we need to lie and why we try to perfect those machines for telling lies that exist dormant and half-developed in us. As Paul Newman said, and I am lying, I think, about this, lying is a highly flirtatious and mechanical form that the body has of creating a specific repetition of itself. It is linked to the perpetuation of the species and the refiguring of the human gene pool. For this reason lying is never natural and is best expressed via the eyes, which are perceived to be distinct from the somaform and somatic expressions. People who lie a lot tend to have more affairs than those who don't. Lying and having sex are best done with the eyes completely closed. To lie and have sex at the same time is one of the greatest things anyone can do. It is of course much harder to lie when staring directly at someone or something (like food) that one likes. It is impossible to lie to a computer that's turned off. A blank computer screen can still remind us of a face.

Certain losses are untenable. Certain gestures cannot be programmed or learned. One wants to make lying less natural, less organic, but one wants to make the machinery of lying with feeling and one's voice visible like a rule of etiquette or a TV commercial that interrupts a program one is watching. One wants a poetry made out of innumerable interruptions and lies and half-truths and averted eyes and the hum of refrigerators being lied to as if they were really machines like us. All lying should aspire to the unnatural and inanimate part of us, the interruptions, the part of our brain where all our dead feelings go (there are so very many of them lodged there), and lying never abandons us even after the body is dead. One desires an organoleptics of lying, of repeating over and over again those feelings that always lie, and thus are always true to themselves: such lying and only such lying could accommodate the world as we know it. The world is filled with endless shopping malls and paved over wetlands and airports and coffee shops. Such a state of utter stillness would lead to the most anodyne memories conceivable. It would resemble the memories inspired by TV. Yesterday evening for an hour I watched the TV version of *Moby Dick* with the actor from the TV version of *Star Trek* and realized that the true aim of poetry lies in the utter anesthetizing of all memories. All lovers should become traces of human feelings. All restaurants should be encounters with the poems one writes to future spouses and lovers. All feelings should be unknown to the feelings that are having those feelings and to the people who are unknown at the time. To lie in America? What does that mean? It means someone was once in love with someone else on television. One lies to experience as many prime-time reruns as possible.

What is the pattern of data but the patterns of our own overstimulation? That is why lies are so supernaturally beautiful: they resemble what we are not, they pretend to evade and thus save the pattern of our speech for a later date. All known futures exist to be postponed. They transform us into code. The best words are the words that were never said. That is why I like late-night talk shows with fake TV news anchors like Craig Kilborn, who wears a nice suit and pretends to be telling the news, or Conan O'Brien, whose stiffness before the camera and guests and whose inability to tell a joke or ask an interesting question are enlightening because it is not so easy to make talk sound as if everything being said were already a rerun. This is often done by Conan repeating verbatim things that were just said and then laughing right after he has said it, and everyone knows this is not very funny; it is nerve wracking to hear oneself repeated and then someone laughing. Late-night shows are lovely because they play back the dead things we repeat in our heads all day long to ourselves. All talk is just a rerun and suggests the reel-to-reel monotonies, the impersonal toneless nothings, the vocal blips and rhyme flows, the soundless sound of meaning as aural duration, what might be termed the ever-lengthening potentialities of sonic occurrence. Such occurrences are usually found in un-Romantic long works, soap operas, or serial TV shows but hardly ever in real life. Real life is usually too artificial to allow boredom to go on forever. This is why Andy Warhol's movies about the Empire State Building bathed in flickering lights or the face of a man getting a blow job are so interesting; they are about the state of watching boredom, which as everyone knows is not boring at all but very interesting. The only thing that can be boring about TV is watching too little of it. I was watching Jon Stewart on *Comedy Central* the other night as he made fun of his guests, who are usually extremely beautiful and wear very nice clothes. I particularly like to watch these segments twice, when they are rebroadcast later on the same night on a different channel, which often happens in major metro areas. Anyway, such guests, whether they are sports stars, models, actors, or chefs are generally superior to other talk-show guests (writers make the worst talk-show guests) because everything they say is basically irrelevant to who they are and because they are utterly disconnected from what they talk about. A model or chef or a child who can imitate the sounds of strange animals like bush hogs or California condors defeats conversation before it starts—and this, of course, is what creates that beautiful thing known as talking.

I have spent many evenings watching late-night TV just waiting to say something to someone but of course there was no one else in the room but the glow of the TV talking. No one hears you when you talk to yourself, and in this way everything I am saying to you resembles lying. The best talking anyone can do is over by the time we do it. All talk should be posthumous talk. The best lies are the lies that were told by someone we didn't love to someone we did. That is why late late TV shows are best viewed in one's own bed with the lights turned low and the bedroom drapes pulled. Like photographs of photographs such lies usually lead to depersonalization and anxiety. Yesterday after spending the night watching late-night TV, I went to see *Rushmore* by myself. I had a very good time. Last night, a model who resembled Amber Valetta said: "It would be useful to remember the middle names of each American president."

On late late-night TV ad time becomes progressively cheaper and production costs for a segment diminish. Talk itself becomes the most valuable commodity around, which is why people like Jon Stewart and Craig Kilborn can speak about so little so vacuously, so inanely, and with as much compassion as news anchors, who constitute the obverse of commercialized TV talk. Late-night TV shows are as lovely to listen to as any poem. Late-night talk, like the other cheap programming around it, especially the commercials and the lame canned skits the writers come up with, suggest the cheap lies we constantly tell ourselves every minute of the day and the deeply camouflaged nature of our talking to others when we are really talking to ourselves. All poems like all such experiences exist a thousand times before they reverse themselves in one's head. Such reversals, because they are canned and foreknown, are known as memory traces, which are always recorded in positive and negative forms, and should be kept as inert as possible. All language should be written in a state of black and white. Today it is a Monday, 4 P.M. in Santa Monica in the early months of the Democratic primary contest between Gore and Bradley, who have now reversed their personalities and their positions in the polls, and I have by some strange quirk of timing almost reached the point of putting down Edmund Morris's beautifully irksome and strangely repugnant biography of Ronald Reagan because it is something I will probably never be able to finish. Of course, Edmund Morris didn't realize this when he embarked on his biography of Ronald Reagan because Reagan, unfortunately, was still alive. Morris went looking for the real Ronald Reagan, the personality of the man behind the television image and in the end he had to write a book and not a television treatment about an airhead, and so he was bound to fail. The only thing a biography, unlike a novel, can reveal is a hallucination of this sort, and it does this anytime time passes. Biographies, like great poems, aim to create not the remembered high points of a subject but the inert memories and the distancing of that life from itself. Few things in life are more boring and thus more imaginative than an interminably long work about someone who is dead and has no more feelings to speak of. Such works display boredom for what it really is: a hallucination of an overactive imagination.

It is well known that Reagan frequently failed to remember what he had said in press conferences or briefings of the day before, that he often failed to recognize his own cabinet members as he passed them in the corridors of the White House, and that even Nancy was crushed when he failed to comfort her after she told him she had breast cancer. No one ever really knew Ronald Reagan, not Nancy, not the seventy-seven individuals he saved in his career as a lifeguard, and not even his own children—who have written that on numerous occasions he failed to recognize them. A great poem functions in a similar way. It cannot be remembered; it can only be filled with something that is unknown or that it no longer contains. The 1970s are over, but the cars and music of the 1970s, especially the pony cars and the mini-muscle cars, like the Pontiac Firebird, Mercury Cougar, Dodge Charger, and Olds Toronado with its flip-up headlamps, linger, as if in drag, at the Classic Car lot located in Bel Air. . . .

Everything that is beautiful waits to be forgotten completely by what it is not. A poem, like the 1970s, is just another way of inducing a series of unforgivable likenesses. Warhol said of his art that "if you don't think about it, it's right." Listening to a poem or novel or newspaper should be like that; it should be camouflaged into the large shapes and the patterns of words that surround us and evoke the most diffuse and unrecognizable moods that a culture produces. Philosophy, like poetry and television, can resemble these moods. Poetry ought to be as easy as painting by numbers. It should turn us into those emotions and feelings we could not experience in our own body. All poetry goes out in drag.

No one should remember a poem or a novel, especially the person who wrote it. Heidegger was right: one is never without a mood. The poem openly aspires to a state of linguistic camouflage. Ronald Reagan is a doppelganger and Edmund Morris has created a doppelganger. He has made Ronald Reagan into something that fitfully resembles biography or background Muzak. It is of course clear that Morris detests Ronald Reagan, the bore who resembles the planet Jupiter with its dense core and absence of oxygen. But Morris also thinks Reagan was a great president. Of course, Reagan made himself into a pattern that no one could see; he transformed acting into politics and outtakes into campaign speeches. He blended into everything because his ignorance was everywhere and extended to everything, especially his "untruisms" about domestic policy. After Reagan had given a speech in Orlando on March 8, 1983, about "the struggle between right and wrong, good and evil," the historian Henry Steele Commager remarked that it "was the worst presidential speech in American history."

Everything that has a subject should be detested; everything that erases its subject should be loved. The great Japanese photographer Daido Moriyama thought that photography could not capture what really mattered and thus he worked to deface his medium with scratches, out-of-focus shots, and blinding flares from unknown flash sources. He liked to shoot outlaws, prostitutes, TV personalities, gangsters, and stray dogs. He was always running away from the photographs he was about to take, and he was frequently punched by his subjects. This is why poetry is superior and at the same time more realistic than any photograph (except really uninteresting ones), where the scent of something detestable begins to emerge at the point when the shutter is snapped and the chemical process begins. A poem does not secure or even require such violence for itself; the greatest poems simply contain what doesn't matter as it happens on the surface of the poem. To have a photograph is not interesting; to have a photograph of a photograph is and this is what a poem does better than any photograph can. Only such relaxing enclosures of image within image or word within word allow the emptiness of all human feelings to surrender themselves without the obvious grotesqueries and thus make the present a place to have a cigarette. All biographies like all poems are best when they fail to suggest anything about their subjects at all. A good poem is very boring. A great poem is more boring than the act of reading itself.

In any system, I repeat myself, I believe it is possible to turn the repetition inherent in oral forms (speech) on its head. I went to hear the rock band Chicago last night at the Greek Theatre in Hollywood, which is an outdoor theater set against a backdrop of hills and aging palm trees. The audience was mainly mid-to-late-40s hipsters and studio execs with big hair, lots of gold chains, and Porsches. People were singing and standing up a lot and telling those around them to get up and sing. As I stood up, it suddenly occurred to me that these were once hippies but now they were hippies preserved in some form of evergreen twilight. People were standing up all over the place and looking back at the people behind them as if they were the audience. No one was smoking. Everyone was white in the audience, even the Asians and the blacks. The only people who weren't white were the ticket takers and the bouncers and one kid from some high school in L.A. who was asked to come onto the stage and play with the band for one number. And that is how my memory of going to high school in Athens, Ohio, in the mid-seventies came back to me, along with deer blinds, or harvesting pot planted at the local public golf course, and what I was called in gym class: Ho Chi Lin. Those who study information flow know that repetition in real-life situations and in spoken language is generally used to secure meaning, to make sure one is not misunderstood. Repetition lessens the possibilities for error. Hearing Chicago again, I found it impossible not to remember the massive inertia of "Saturday in the Park, thought it was the Fourth of July" and impossible not to remember being back among those long carpeted corridors of my high school and the cafeteria tables where everyone was shouting next to their food and the plastic trays. I believe that repetition is more thoroughly embedded in speech than in writing, which is too bad really, for the memories that are inside me feel like they are about to be formed but would rather not. Of course, as my high school teacher Mr. Lalich, who later went on to become a city council member, reminded us in American History and Economics, the trade-off lies in the realm of the temporal. The more repetition there is, the greater delay in the rate of message transmission. But rehearsal is also key to absorption, that is, in short- and long-term memory, and oral forms thus work to do two things: reduce ambiguity in the message and promote retention. Certain kinds of psychotropic drugs (LSD), novels and poems, and Mr. Lalich's lectures on inverted forms of economic efficiency rarely transpire in the long term; they reenact the processes of memory at the short-term and synaptic level, which is to say, before memory has attached itself to the sound field. Repetition, especially in the things one reads, is opposed to the class of words known as antonyms, which is to say language's repeating tendencies, its tendencies to be synonymous and simultaneous rather than different. And this violates the idea of meaning, which is grounded in differentiation. But of course if everything is or appears the same, then language takes on the qualities of a cipher or code where differences are perceived to exist but are disguised. Disco music, the phone book, Gertrude Stein's books, and TV talk shows function like this. To read is to forget the meaning of reading. For this reason the best literature is often written in times of war, when puns themselves suggest the origins of language in a consciousness that cannot use language to make any distinctions between language and thought, speaker and world, signal and noise, sound and word. I left the Chicago concert filled with memories and very depressed. I never knew about Vietnam or the war protest movement except secondhand so all my memories of those events were memories of things I had already seen on TV. The best TV and the best poems do not engender memories; they get rid of them. The best cure for memory is a really good poem.

I am thinking yes I am of writing a work that is already written and it is unlike speech slow clumsy and very very long it frustrates the attention span pitch speed tone and articulation repeats itself as a series of mechanized gestures and mechanical acoustics (its moods as they say) repetition qualities of oral delivery make it seem gestural and sonic rather than clarifying meaning and thus clarifying the message this functions as the written equivalent of noise which is random in the short term (immediate meaning) but predictable (relatively) as the long-term average so I say I wish to write not sentences but diagrams of sentences—as a form of statistical mechanics

It is the first week of March; my allergies in Virginia are killing me and for the last few weeks I have been thinking of taking a road trip out West and visiting a cheap motel on the western edge of North Cascades National Park that my aunt, who is half-Chinese, once told me about in a letter.

So. On the tenth of March I board a plane to Seattle, rent a white Honda Acura and drive eighty-seven miles to Concrete, Washington, which is on the edge of the park and where the Bear Park Motel is located. My aunt is very happy to see me. She tells me all the rooms in the motel have seven-foot ceilings and they are all made of cinderblocks painted yellow. I have in my possession a few old photographs of this motel, which were sent to my mother, who has told me she never wants to visit that motel even though my aunt has extended invitations countless times. My aunt and uncle used to run a Chinese restaurant in Spokane but the restaurant went out of business and they got tired of serving people American Chinese food so they decided it would be better if they went east and into the wilderness. They settled on a place near North Cascades National Park, near an Indian reservation. She has always told me this is the story of their lives, only backwards, from America to the real America, from China to somewhere they've never been before.

When I arrive, my aunt shows me to Room 17, and whenever I have gone to the Bear Park Motel in the intervening years I have stayed in Room 17, just as Salvador Dali when he came to New York always stayed at the St. Regis and always in Room 1628. Although I don't remember any, there is, as I gather from the photographs, an occasional painting in the rooms, and once when I first thought about visiting, when I was in high school, I remember thinking about a photograph of a door that had been kicked in. After I arrive, my aunt proudly tells me that the Bear Park Motel is one of the only motels in America where there are no phones in any of the rooms. I believe this says something about the clientele, about the kinds of people who have and have not stayed at the Bear Park Motel on the western edge of North Cascades National Park, the people who have died and not died there, had sex and not had sex, lied and not lied their way out of that godforsaken landscape or one of those rooms. I have often thought of the motel and have asked my aunt many times if she had ever discovered a corpse in one of the rooms and she said no, never. On my second and last night at the Bear Park I asked my aunt if she liked running the motel. She said she did but she added that the worst thing about running a motel was never being able to take a vacation. And drunks bang on the office door, which is the door to their living room, and this wakes her and her uncle up in the middle of the night. People come to cheat in their motel. I have taken that trip to Glacier and the Bear Park Motel many times. I know the head is made for places like the Bear Park Motel where a half-Chinese woman runs a motel filled with language and its lies.

When I was in graduate school getting a Ph.D. in 1983 and writing poetry on the side I met a woman who spoke eight languages—Chinese (Mandarin and Cantonese and an Amoy dialect known as Xiamen), German, French, Vietnamese, and English, almost all of them fluently except for German, which she learned in school I think. She was born in Saigon, was raised in Paris and told me she had never ridden in public transportation before NYC because she had spent her childhood in the backseat of a limousine and whenever I think of her I think of her in the backseat of a limousine and basically just living there and reading her favorite books there (she was born a reader just as all avid readers are born not made), and being taken to restaurants, and waiting for her father to put her in the car so she could go to school. I believe she told me her father was in business and that her mother was capable of extreme cruelty. She was very pretty for her age and very slight, almost *trop raffinée*, and her name was G_____, but she had a laugh that was just loud enough, and she was very fond of smiling and not quite smiling at the same time. Her eyes were brown, the color of scuffed shoe polish. From the moment I met her I believed she was an exquisite liar. One night I asked her if she lied in one language better than another because I knew she loved questions like that (all questions for her resembled lies), and she said she knew she could lie best in English, because it was not her favorite language and was most free in it but when she was in bed with someone she preferred to make the sounds of endearment and physical longing in Chinese. One hot very early July morning, my father, who was visiting Brooke Alexander, a gallery owner in NY, walked up the five flights of stairs in my walkup apartment on 125th Street in Spanish Harlem, and met her by accident (she was leaving). I introduced them, asked them to say a few words of Chinese to each other because at the time I was not sure how well she spoke Chinese, and they exchanged a few words in Mandarin which I did not understand because I do not speak or understand Chinese except certain names of food. I have always told my friends that I can speak Chinese but only in a restaurant.

Years afterward when my father had decided to buy another house and was living in Santa Barbara and I had gone to visit him during my summer off, my father asked what happened to her, said she was very well brought up, and that she spoke a very beautiful Mandarin. I believe that she reminded my father of my mother although I realize this only now as I am writing it.

One night I remember she had told me she was a virgin. I knew she was not really lying because she was lying to me in my favorite language, which is English because it is the only one that I really possess as a language to imagine things in, and because I have always thought that she is probably one of those persons that can only lie well over the phone. I continue to believe to this day that she was a terrible liar in person, although I am probably lying to myself, and of course this is the main reason I fell in love with her after we had ended things, and this is the main reason I still, years later, remember her voice when I am on the telephone and am lonely and am waiting for someone on the other end of the telephone to tell me they love me. One can wait for years to hear a beautiful lie like that. Nearly ten years later I ran into a friend of hers on the Columbia campus near the statue of Rodin's *The Thinker*. I had gone back (I love the campus and steps where the students sit out on a warm day) to see a professor of mine, George Stade, who wrote a novel called *Confessions of a Lady Killer* and is one of my favorite professors because of all my professors, he always acted glad to see me (and I believe he genuinely was) when I came in to talk with him about oral exams, or dissertation chapters, or whatever. Anyway, Christina and I talked for a long time. She had just gotten married to someone who was an Italian noble of some sort with a very long name and she was in town for two days and we made plans for coffee and exchanged phone numbers but I knew I would not be seeing her again. Eventually the subject of G_____ came up and she told me that G_____ had finished her thesis on the Princesse de Cleves, had married a Swiss banker, and was living in Geneva. Today I feel a strong urge to know what country her parents live in, if they are even alive, and I have an irrevocable desire to meet them, not to talk to them, just to be introduced to them, to go through the mechanical social pleasantries with them. Sometimes there are times when I wish G_____ had lied that night when she told me she was a virgin. Without lies, the brain would be more empty than a midtown office building. Without lies, the emotions would have nothing to live for except themselves and no emotion should have to live with itself for very long. Lies are the ways the mind has of accepting our own emotions. None of the lies we tell is real except to the person we tell that lie to. It never really matters if one is telling the truth. It only matters if one cares enough not to tell a lie to someone. There is nothing so sad as a family without liars. My father died in 1989 of a heart attack (he was the best liar in our family) and of course there were things that I never said to him. Everybody needs to lie to someone. As I was saying, the rooms at the Big Bear Park rent for $37 a night.

My father was a superlative liar and a very good cook, but I have not thought about this too much because I am fond of his lies, remember his cooking, which he taught me, and there is something between us that can never be spoken, not even in his lies. A lie is the most beautiful and revealing thing anyone can give to another, especially if they do it effortlessly, mechanically, and without thinking, and a poem is the most beautiful lie human beings can make out of the things they don't know and the things they know too well. My father made a good many poems and a few superb ones in his day and they remind me of some of the coffee tables and end tables of walnut, inlaid with kiln-glazed tiles, that he made and glued and dowelled together and that we still use today in my mother's house. My father I think was a master documentarian, a vast archivalist of lies, of which the various crannies I am still pulling things out of. He documented a good many lies about life in southeastern Ohio in the 1950s, where I grew up (the soil is all clay and he said he could make pots out of it) and in China where he did ("I never saw my sister again").

On Tuesday I drove away from the Big Bear Park Motel and headed west into Seattle, where I stayed at The Grand Marriott. It cost me $265 for a single night, a week or more's stay at the Bear Park. As I walk into the gaudily carpeted lobby of the Marriott with young and very clean attractive men and women behind the counter, in white shirts and blouses and blue vests on with their gold pins attached neatly to their vests, I feel as if I am a soundtrack of America and that everyone everywhere is listening to themselves waiting for someone, to claim a room, pick up a message, pay their bill, return a call, ask about a shirt or a fax message. In such places I feel everything on hold and I try to move through as quickly as possible.

There are many places I could have decided not to stay at and it has nothing to do with being restless or impatient although I am both of those things. I am passing through this lobby on my way back home to Virginia, then back to New York to see a friend of mine and then back to Ohio where my mother lives and has just retired and I am thinking again of listening to my father tell his stories and I am thinking of, yes I am thinking of Gertrude Stein and the pack of lies she told in *The Making of Americans*; she told so many of them simultaneously, which was her version of a soundtrack of other people talking and no one knowing in the end who was talking. I must tell you now that my father did not lie about everything; some things were hardly worth lying about I guess; he lied about when he was born (his birth is a mystery) but he mainly lied about China, as far as I can recall and he mainly told these lies not to my sister and me, or my mother and my sister and me, but it was mainly over a dinner table and to other people that I heard these stories being told, so in a way these lies were never told to me, and this is maybe why I remember his lies so well. All lies eventually have to connect to something. Even my father's lies. They were lies that were never really mine.

These photographs, these words.

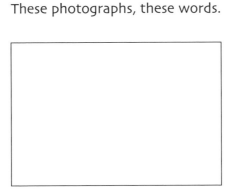

I always feel like writing two things at once, for example a report on the presidential primary and Ronald Reagan, and this poem at the same time. In this way there is shadowing of one and by one of the other. Thus segmentation, which is present, is not crucial and does not serve to alter significantly the meaning. In fact, significant pauses occur at midsentence level, where there is no punctuation, rather than at the end of sentences marked with a period. And of course those useful gestural marks (quotation marks, question marks, exclamation points, italics etc)

! ? "" * &

should ideally be left out altogether as being beyond the realm of written language to truly mimic sounds. Typographic speed is a mistranslation (noise) of verbal speech's fluidity so it must be left out. Typographic emphasis is a mistranslation of gesture and so it must be left out. The two modes of communication ostensibly evolved to satisfy different aims, the one immediate, the other deferred; one emotive, the other rational; one lawless and improvised, the other regulated (coded) and premeditated. A poem makes these two positions exist side by side. Hence the physical and conceptual quality of the ambient work. Style is only poorly communicated in writing compared with speech, so it must be replaced by quantification and counting. Style should be the census of the words I have used. Particular words are less important than how they are counted by the sentence that contains them. In

America the counting of speech (American speech) is decidedly nonspecialized, one-on-one, pioneering, down-to-earth, pragmatic even as a distinct form of literary speech. It obeys certain quaint laws of averages; that is why it repeats so many words that we speak. The great American poem should be hopelessly redundant. It erases styles as easily as it disposes of conventional genres. All accents of American speech become simply abstract parts of speech. Emphasis and affective logic, which give rise to it, constitute the underlying code or meaning, and rarely is that affective logic made to extend beyond the length of a sentence, which is to say it manifests itself not as logic but as occurrence. As Gertrude Stein remarked, sentences are not emotional, paragraphs are. In such a way, all genres should be multifarious and virtually unrecognizable. A genre is a truth masquerading as a lie and what one wants is the opposite. This is a lie: repetitions should not extend beyond the microscopic level of the books that contain them. This is a lie: I want to write a poem like a box or like *The Making of Americans* that cannot really be read, just as an oeuvre (Stein's body) of writing ought to be something that cannot be read. The time for reading and especially for reading individual works is over. Individual works can only be sampled and subjected to statistical analysis. A massively parallel computing system could have a field day with the collected writings now being assembled within this computing device or poem.

What would that program look like?
All text is hidden noise

language paradoxically and despite length economical in one sense repetitively redundant because the economies of language make techniques of sound reproduction that guarantee legibility in a medium permeated by unwanted noise in the language field language reproduces the sounds we just heard as indistinguishable from or barely emerging from noise dense and linear pattern of a sentence suggests (stein) simultaneously a compression and a poverty of information in a binary system of transmission which is to say a sentence is information plus code (language or medium of transmission) plus noise in other words a system of probabilities hinge on meaning but also code itself meaning comes through words and the noise question some doubts are traded laughter on the buffalo wings understand everything a name is a step the child and the blind person makes social culture this is important for Stein for making Newtonian time place backward and forward and result like meaning and motions are unpredictable and can only be regarded in light of probabilities stochastically impossible at any given moment sentence to know what the sentence is going it might continue but even its pauses are not correlated precisely to just as well backward as forward Cherry describes Newton's Laws of Motion frictionless machine "containing relatively few moving parts."

Similarly, everything that reverses in a poem, like sex or ethnicity, is potentially liberating for those waiting in the wings. The man that is a woman and the woman that is a man. In America, where nothing that is American can remain American forever, that is what it means to be the making of an American. I stand out in the American grain, and he who is one must tune in all background noise, all freeway sounds, all rush-hour music, all TV chatter, all the surgical apparatuses involved in sewing up eyelids and removing and converting the sexual organs—these together make up the sounds of a meaningless language, the fakings of Others, all forgotten operations in the middle of the night. The most interesting moment in America is the moment when the preelection results come in and one turns off the TV to wait for the morning paper to land on one's doorstop. A helicopter takes off to monitor the traffic threading from Jersey to the Holland Tunnel. We touch what we can hardly touch. We see what we can hardly see. No one is sleeping and no one is dreaming. The body is still in love with the nightgown and the panties. They rest like a bowl of cereal or a boxer on the bed. The voice of a male or female loon calls, and the sunset sleeps alone in the bed all night long, like the raves and the lewd and the world. Whenever I wake up, the TV is filled with the sounds of Oprah and one rises to clip coupons in the middle of the night,

I understand the question to mean something about sounds, rather than language. The revival of the 1960s and 1970s in the 1990s is the most fitting example of a kind of contemporary revision of the arts and craft movement, which culminated in colonial revival products, especially with regard to things such as quilts and other decorative arts. How late we come to our realizations and our own monotonies. How often we switch ourselves off and realize that poetry no longer needs to be avant-garde or less formal in its orientation. I can remember the lives of various schools. It can review home arts like quilt making, needlework, gardening, collecting of ephemera, etc. Repetition is crucial to all these endeavors. Poetry should aspire to the condition of continuous relaxation but without effort. It should be filld with typos. One studies and restudies the ape and biological determinism as if it were a form of the Holocaust or a victim of the Hiroshima blast. This is the kind of history that most appeals to us. The least important thing one can say about craft is that it suggests an evolutionary downdraft toward greater levels of domesticity, home life, and infinite credit. It approaches the state of the ultimate home furnishings catalogue and unlimited personal spending. Poetry cannot survive in a homeless state. The poetry of exile is a dead end, the poetry of world weariness is an overwaxed palm leaf yanked from some Caribbean isle, as numerous poets have demonstrated. But of course it is bad manners to pronounce this at a dinner party populated by publishing people or Nobel Prize laureates and their hosts or in a poem that the ideal poem is an extension of home entertaining, that its verbs are intertwined with the life of good manners and candlesticks. Not every decent poem is willing to please, but many are. All poems are healed by corruptions of the feelings.

I grow clumsier and less metrical by the day. "This thing" happens continuously because each twenty-four-hour period contains innumerable amounts of poetry and there is a rhythm to the production of language and whatever is said or produced has nothing at all metrical and nothing at all that might be beautiful. Poetry is produced randomly and at all hours of the day. If I say three words

lazy	tired	reproachful
mortified	organized	tender
and	so	on

that is all about erasing the metrical grid, evacuating the lines I was thinking of, erasing my thoughts, erasing your place in the poem you thought you were reading, erasing wherever it is that poetry ultimately comes from and gets spoken. The above lines are a q version (soundless) of a poem I am listening to and writing about, like the end of summer in the large room filled with reflected light and a trip I am about to take to a southern state where I will try to make more money, and yes this is the beginning of autumn and it just happens and it has a long title that is really a substitution, a kind of rotation of one word or circulation for one person I loved and another I didn't. Earth turns more securely in autumn. The colors I am thinking of are braver by the minute. It rained in California last night for the first time since I arrived in late August. The nose comes alive.

It is important that the words used be infinitely long or infinitely substitutable, that they be continuously beyond the poet's reproach, that they be absolutely unnecessary for the poet to feel the things he is feeling. For feelings are always like that. Sometimes it is important to just pick up the phone and call someone it doesn't matter who and to try and forget why one says the things one says but to simply say them in order that. Poetry is really just a way of counting something that cannot be counted perfectly. That is why so much of what one says was never meant to be said at all. Last summer when I went to Istanbul I had a massage on a slab of stone. They massage the head and this is said to massage the brain. They develop certain muscles in one's forehead. None of this could be considered important for thinking. Now a year later, I believe the memory of this technique is responsible for producing that fine skin of sweat on the body of a young woman lying on the couch a few evenings ago when she started taking off her halter top. In this way I believe all emotions are endlessly substitutable for something else and that all feelings are substitutions for words and that all words are substitutions for other words rather than physical sensations or objects. The words go into our heads where they massage us until we die of hearing ourselves. I believe this is

braille   phone   sort
about a circular black plastic thing clipped
jock   ear lobe   raincoat
to her halter I don't know why this is so or why
dent   orbit   pup tent
it is just one of those things that happens Because words are unnecessary
piss   menthol   pontificate
to what I am remembering I was thinking what would go with this I have
marriage   parking   vellum
a friend who is writing a dissertation on the body and Hart Crane and he
fetish   topaz   magazine
says that whenever he hears the word prosthetic it makes him want to gag
I believe that the time for fetishized language is over,
for the era of Poetic Prosthesis is passed.
No poem should ever be a substitution
for something else, especially the inorganic.
Poetry is inorganic or it is nothing at all. No poem
should be green or communicate something hidden or secret. The best

poems are written by the moon during daylight and thus become invisible to everyone in a colorless language of the feelings we are not yet having. All language should be like that: infinitely opaque, unclear, unencumbered by meaning or message and thoroughly enculturated in that thing known as ambience or stylistics, which as we know are cannibalized, fed from one mouth to another without ever saying a word. The time for poems written with words is over. All words are and should be essentially meaningless in a great poem. There are never any reasons for the things we say or the words we use or the poems that we use to say words with or the poems that use words to say the "things we mean" there is only the time needed to say them. Language is like putting a stopwatch to a great poem and waiting for the time to run out. I can never stop reading poems like that.

What does it mean to stop reading a poem? It means that one is tired. Lynne Cox, the great American long-distance swimmer, has a body consisting of 35 percent body fat (compared to most women, who have 18–25 percent body fat), and it is that layer of fat that functions like a natural wet suit. People who have seen her swim say she appears to float or melt through the water, that it somehow becomes her element or she its. Rumor has it that East German swimmers inject gas into their colons to induce similar properties: her plump, large undulating mermaid-like hips have fiercely propelled her obliviously through all manner of things in her twenty-five years as a long-distance swimmer: oil slicks, jelly fish that swell the eyes and lips, sewage, dead dogs, walruses, and sharks. Yet she swims without any shark cages, no layer of grease or wetsuits—only a swimsuit. It is her layer of fat that is most remarkable about her; it turns her into something, a human porpoise, and allows her to maintain an even internal body temperature despite external temperatures that would kill most humans after thirty minutes or induce severe hallucinations. When she began her swim between the Diomedes—which are located between Alaska and Siberia—she had to step carefully into the Arctic Sea. Had she dived in headfirst, the water would have stopped her heart almost instantly. I believe all these things are merely simulations by our brain of what will happen next, outward manifestations of the things that are just going on in our heads, and these situations are almost always hypothetical ones that we model rapidly and instantaneously and without thinking about them at all. There is nothing here but the writing and least of all the residue that is not in the writing and can never be there if reading is to be done at a later moment, say in history, or later in the day before one calls up a friend and goes to see *My Own Private Idaho* at the local bargain cinema for $2. Thus a form of dittoing or mimeographing the forms of the earth results in a worthwhile purgation of the things we cannot stand, a means of increasing the levels of aural pollution or interference. All beautiful objects ought to be replaced by residues of the sort that are created by the interference of beauty in the abstract. All great things of beauty should be abstracted to their least-common denominators. No thing shall be separated from any other thing. No love for anyone shall be love for any one. No words shall be used to trace out some other thing. As Robert Smithson recognized, poems are the strata of their own composition; they are never still but move like a series of roving sundials or mirrors across a Yucatan landscape, a series of roving tombstones where the sky is buried in the earth. A poem is just a machine made of words. It merely reflects and then reflects on what happens to get in its way. I was reading the obit for James Velez, the young man who was "tormented by a baffling illness" and who died last Wednesday, at the age of twenty-five from infections of his blood and spine. No one knew why James Velez thought a million bugs crawled across his skin. To bring himself comfort he scratched himself so vigorously that he broke his skin and created heavy scars across his body, mutilating himself even though he possessed intelligence enough to recognize what he was doing. He spent most of his life in institutions where he received electric shock therapy, but in 1994 a small social service agency, Job Path, allowed him to have his own apartment. In January of 1999 he remarked: "The happiest thing is to have a place that's mine." Nothing shall be hated decorated excoriated repudiated or remembered. Everything shall be copied. I light a cigarette. I turn on the television while the stereo is on. I listen to the car and the music of DJ Shadow. The end of summer is the end of the things of whatever is summer or I do not remember. There is no longer time for protestations. Poetry should not be performed it should merely be listened to. The time for conscious experimentation and ego, which is its logical extension, should be replaced by unconscious repetition and listening. All poems should be rewritten over and over again and exist in as many versions as possible. No poem should ever be

In this manner, all attachments to the things of this world might be sundered from the affections that lead to the false illusion known as beauty. In this way, finding a way to say something should be ugly because beauty is something that only comes after a necessity and never before it. Only in this way is beauty, strictly speaking, necessary at all. All beauty like all poems and all poets should come as a prompting of something absolutely necessary. One has a cocktail and then one has sex. One never has sex and then a cocktail. One never writes a beautiful book; a beautiful book is merely an excuse for wasting words one has the time to waste. Words are the best way one has for wasting more of one's time and there is nothing precious about wasting time it is just something that happens. Beauty is the great enemy of poetry because it is never sufficiently relaxed. Emerson in his usual foolish way says to "give the gloom of gloom, and the sunshine of sunshine." But really the time for "abridgement or selection" is over in the words we use and the poems we write. One never has sex before falling in love or one never falls in love after having sex. The poem is a thoroughly useless instrument for speaking; it is only a means of making it possible to say more things we never thought of saying. It is more useless if it chases after the ugly. Why are we so fascinated by the useless things that are beautiful and the valuable things that are ugly?

There is never anything like a conscious separation of the objects around us. I believe this leads to ugliness if pursued to its own levels. I repeat what the sarcophagi, the vases, and the candelabra say.

C. S. Giscombe

Suppose a woman or a man was in "some sort of trouble."

Suppose that woman (or the man) was white and well connected, professional, which would put her (or him) at odds with being in trouble, speaking in terms of the narrative of tradition.

(All traditions are sexist. Rather many are racist. What about narrative?)

Suppose it was a man then, still white, still professional, how would you feel? Suppose he was just a white actor, playing us (tho' not playing *one* of us), suppose that.

"If a man was in some sort of trouble" & still "would be willing to come forward" now & again even if he'd had to "change his identity" and "toil"; or if he knew someone who was "relentless" & yet others who "were willing to help him, even lie for him"—then *what*? *What* then? Compared to *what*?

There was promise &, later on, an almost natural letdown around a TV show, an old series from the early 1960s called *The Fugitive*: the promise— what *seemed* to be happening and so, for a long period, was happening—was endless expansion & accumulation w/no particular regard to narrative structure (only the briefest and most token attention was paid to this by the show's producers): what we saw instead of such a structure was the suggestion of an infinite articulation—not "utterance or enunciation" but something like the way those long steam locomotives were jointed to take curves. Nor is this about wistful agrarianism, *that* fugitive, although Kimble, the title character, often took farmworker jobs. This is more about, say, Tracy Chapman singing the chorus to "Fast Car." Ms. Chapman's whole song's about being in trouble & being there is appropriate or at least discernible (which is likely the reason that "Fast Car" was popular). Where else *is* there to be, especially if you're honest? What else is there to do but run? On the other hand there's the old song "Nowhere to Run, Nowhere to Hide": the words are patently untrue, a *lie*, title & chorus too—there's *always* somewhere to run & somewhere to hide although those places must be, often, invented. Yet the *song's* not dishonest: because of the sheer—meaning precipitous—strength & sound of Martha Reeves's voice the song achieves a virtual truth, one that surpasses the arguable lie of the lyrics. Willful performance'll *do* that to absolute value. It's Martha Reeves's voice that makes everything true; everything she ever *said* is the truth. Tracy Chapman sounds, unfortunately, sweet, like Joni Mitchell at midcareer. Who do you believe? Who *looks like* they're telling the thing beyond the story, telling it the way it is, which hasn't got a thing to do with some story & its closure? Who's willing? Who's willing to get further on & deeper in trouble? Words & music, that music & those words. Even old deep image James Wright, who was often in trouble himself, knew enough to step outside of himself & quote Judy Holliday saying, "Well, look, honey, where I come from, when a girl says she's in trouble, she's in trouble." The epigraph for his poem, "Trouble."

Some day in May 1991, nine o'clock in the morning & I was sitting on the front porch with my shirt off reading an article by Henry Giroux about indeterminacy, otherness vs. the assertion of the marginalized subject, black feminist models, etc. I'd started the article at 7:30 or so and by 9:00 I was nearly done with it and sick of it too. It was full of typographical mistakes and written in some man's voice, one of those that privileges difficulty, right? In spite of that Giroux was proving to me he was smart but he sure does privilege contortion too without the authority of the dance, without the dance giving his thing *any* authority.

I was in a seminar that my employer, Illinois State University, was paying for, about ways to incorporate multicultural perspectives into the classroom. The seminar leader was a white antiracist from the Ozarks, a local player in the new critical theory, which certainly looks—if you read it carefully enough to pick out the paradigms—liberationist but which also looks (if you read it carefully enough to pick out the paradigms) careerist and power hungry and a way for young humanities academics to talk only to one another, stylish in their clothes & their serious faces in airports on their way to the MLA. The hegemony of all that. Fuck 'em if they can't take a joke. The packet our leader prepared for us was readings out of that tradition that talk about authority and otherness and subject and object and discourse. Which *are* useful words, but then most words are useful, aren't they?

So every afternoon that hot week, including Memorial Day itself, we sat upstairs at the Multicultural Center and we beat that boy. (Which is what Ellison sd, how Ellison talked about such talk & Ellison knew how to be useful & also how to dance. I'd taught *Invisible Man* that semester that had just ended, tho' I've never taught it well, & that novel was in my head then, as a series of overlays, as a series of lenses, as a series of illuminations.)

Nine o'clock every morning *The Fugitive* comes on A&E.

It was a show I'd watched as a child growing up in Dayton, Ohio, where Ellison had lived for a while. The earliest episodes are from 1963, presumably the season that began in September, like school did. I was in seventh grade that year, which was the year they shot the president. My grandmother had been in a supermarket when it was announced etc., & she said that some of the white men who'd been working there began laughing and joking over it. I think she was the one from whom I first heard "they" used to describe who did it, even though it was widely assumed & believed back then that it had been old Lee Harvey Oswald acting, as the phrase goes, alone. They's singular, *e pluribus unum*, baby, ain't that what it means on the dime, the quarter, & the penny?

All the earliest episodes of *The Fugitive* start the same way, with a recap of the plot, of what's at stake here. Richard Kimble, a doctor (played by David Janssen), is on his way by train to Death Row. He's handcuffed to a police detective named Gerard (played by Barry Morse) and is awkwardly, because of the cuffs, smoking a cigarette. Dr. Kimble was convicted of killing his wife, but of course he didn't really do it: the voice-over goes, "The irony? Richard Kimble is innocent," and goes on to say that just before our man found the murdered wife he saw a one-armed man—more on this later— "running from the scene." But then there's a train wreck—"Fate," goes the voice, "moves its huge hand"—and in the violence of that Kimble's handcuff is severed & he's off and running. Running from Gerard, searching after the one-armed man. (A light, superimposed from somewhere, makes a nova-like reflection on the metal of the broken handcuff as he runs, initially, from the wrecked train. Later episodes begin with a series of blurred freeze-frames of the train wreck and the voice-over intones, "Reprieved by fate . . . ." I guess someone thought that was better.)

Now as a child I'd watched *The Fugitive* with great interest. For one thing the tension was sustained from one episode to the next; it was the same tension: I mean it always ended inconclusively, with a gesture out toward the highway, the forgivable cliché down which Kimble had to travel. Sometimes Gerard would appear, having had a tip that Kimble—traveling under one of his many Anglo-Saxon aliases—was in a certain place: there'd be a confrontation or an almost-confrontation, and Kimble would escape. Often the doctor was faced with dilemmas. Often the shows were sexy—in early episodes "loose," if confused & tragic, women would try without success to seduce Kimble and, now & again, in later episodes the producers would allow him to fuck & be fucked by a good, if tragic & confused, woman who wasn't exactly a "slut," this as the decade became The Sixties. And every once in a great while the one-armed man—played by Bill Raisch—would appear.

One could speak of fetishes, of Raisch's missing limb as one of these: that his arm ended incompletely (& that he rarely appears in the episodes) suggests various things, many of which are sexual, but then also there's the void that Kimble's always running into, a dangerous & continually retreating horizon, a place that doesn't really exist. Nowhere to run, nowhere to hide? This is some sort of trouble for sure; this is high trouble. (Raisch never wore a prosthesis on the show although he did in "real life," I read in an article in *TV Guide*. Something missing's more tantalizing, or so we could say.) In a Kirk Douglas vehicle, also from the 1960s, the film *Lonely Are the Brave*, Bill Raisch played "that one-armed johnny" who gives Kirk Douglas a sound ass-kicking in a bar, early in the film, a pivotal scene because of the consequences.

(My father is a doctor and, back then, I was still entertaining notions of going into that field. I lost my own arm, the left one, as a result of an accident early in my childhood. I'm African American, a phrase I like because the last two syllables of each word are the same & in that I see two near-identical dark faces; my mother said to write "American Negro" on a form for school, lecturing us that day in 1962 or 1963 on what that phrase implied. My friend Lamar Herrin was in *Lonely Are the Brave*; he had a bit part as a helicopter pilot and has stories about Kirk Douglas but none about Bill Raisch. These are facts to be brought up & gotten, as they say, past: they look like they're an offering, but they're not. Nor do they explain much; they explain, in fact, rather little even though they hold *places* as places are held in a long line for, say, tickets. One becomes chummy with one's fellow line standers, this consequence of an accidental meeting.)

Kimble was a vector, a random set of directions, an anagram of trouble, kindle, tremble (David Janssen's weak chin), & kinship. Brother man, Kimble. He was upper class, white, professional, male.

Appearing with him now & again were a very young Greg Morris, Ivan Dixon, Ruby Dee once (as an African). Race was never mentioned &, truly, much was unsaid in these meetings, even in the music, which was the same insipidly elegiac horns & foreboding piano. In the lack of comment, though, the show turned: for young black viewers recognized those actors as the foils they were, but for Kimble's *blackness* (as opposed to for his innocence or his upper-class origins, which were themselves metaphors for his *whiteness*). And Kimble's blackness was a foil for the audience's own. These were the days before Bill Cosby & Robert Culp broke the color bar on TV & so such appearances were obviously important & anomalous at once. Kimble's blackness then was an act of discernment, an act of supreme metaphor, one that could be chanted endlessly & upon whose back one could ride on into the void with intent. Greg Morris & Ruby Dee were backup singers, exactly, to Kimble's H.N.I.C., the Vandellas to his Martha Reeves. He'd *lost* his whiteness & for a while it looked like he was never gonna get it back, like it was gone. He'd sing "Nowhere to Run, Nowhere to Hide," as he'd run &

then as he'd hide. Kimble was the most important black presence then on episodic TV even tho' both he & David Janssen were white.

Kimble was Bigger Thomas; being a white man didn't stop him from being accused of & convicted of (which was so unlikely it had to be announced *each* week in the standard intro about irony & Fate) a black man's crime against, yes, property: "My wife," sd Kimble over & over. E.g., (breathlessly) "They say I killed my wife & I couldn't prove my innocence." "Killed his wife?" sd someone, interested, that music rising like eyebrows. Killed all y'all's wife. His crime was not his tho' the nightmare of the crime was everybody's: to stand like a black man on the dock & be sent away—up the river, or to Statesville, to Joliet, wherever they keep Ol' Sparky these days—because you sure as hell do *look* like you killed the bitch, "their symbol of beauty," you look like that's your use, my brother, to stand there like that *to* get sent away forever. Some people never get to wake up from out of their nightmares.

So Kimble, a doctor, had "to toil at many jobs," as the intro says (which is the polite way of saying "work like a nigger," a phrase everyone's heard but that only some of the poorest white people, those who know most about working, would actually say), but then he got to wake up, regain his status, wake up, confront his one-armed nemesis. He & relentless, humorless Gerard closed in on & killed incomplete old Bill Raisch in the final episode. They closed up that void & later on in that same hour he got to, implicitly, fuck the very white, very squeaky clean "girl" from his hometown, Stafford, Indiana (nicely, offscreen, presumably during the credits), this as an apparent reward for his sojourn in the netherworld of dark looks. Narrative kicks back in at the close. He got to complete things that way. He got to come in from out of the cold, from out of the make-it-up-as-you-go-along, from off his own vector. He got to stop being "in some sort of trouble" and become white himself, become white itself.

"Papa writes to Johnny"—goes the song from the 1950s—

> Johnny can't come home
> Johnny can't come home

No Johnny can't come,
Papa writes to Johnny
Johnny can't come home
'cause he's been on that chain gang too long.

A man in some sorta trouble, he gotta keep *on* but Kimble, he achieved closure, the aching disappointment of that, the betrayal. Even if it is natural, meaning in the nature of—it was, after all, TV.

The readings in our packet that summer were chosen to illuminate some theoretical bases for multiculturalism. Giroux, Spivak, Michael Awkward, Radakrishnan, some others. Smart boys & girls but stiff, stiff, stiff. Is there a difference between stiffness & contortion? There's no rueful beauty in either one; no false step, no throwaway lines or jokes, fumbles & bungles. Nowhere to run, nowhere to hide? Nobody I read much wanted to run down to the rocks to hide their face. Without that desire—the intimation of being in trouble—there's no way the rocks can rejoin *No hiding place*. I suggested near the end of the week that many of these theoretical multicultural bases had been covered rather well forty years ago by *Invisible Man*—the brilliant talk about history, for example, that follows Tod's death—& that made one of my fellows try to get all hegemonic & say that that, as a novel, was not our discourse as university professors. Which caused the other black member of the seminar & me to jump up &, gesturing toward the packet, declare more or less in unison, "This ain't my discourse," threatening to *be* trouble and come forward *that* way. (We have some temperamental things in common, things beyond the obvious blackness—maybe an unwillingness to be relentless, to close in.)

I don't mean to be confessional here but do you love me? Now? That I can dance?

The Fugitive looks like other things but is not them.

(The movie version came out in August 1993, with strong-featured Indiana Jones as Dr. Kimble. The credible threat of endless episodes got shrunk down to two hours, made into a parenthesis for a rainy summer afternoon. It did not articulate trouble, contradict itself & understand &

misunderstand invisibility; nor was it excessive & its bargain matinees and, later, its video rentals led nowhere. No, that's not true: a survivor of the 1996 Maryland collision between Amtrak's Capitol Limited and a MARC commuter train did describe her wreck, for the folks at home watching on TV, by saying it was "just like" what she'd seen three years before in that movie, the wreck staged—specifically and at great expense and apparently realistically—for the film version.)

The Fugitive resembles *Invisible Man* in some fairly obvious ways even if it is the made-for-TV version &, therefore, a commodity in some important spheres.

But young Greg Morris had been in a couple of episodes, as had young Bruce Dern, who always struck me as one of those lower-class white boys who grew up with young lower-class black boys—gangstas, protogangstas—& became, essentially, one very black dude, "Bruce, my nigger." Both played various characters in various episodes and in these (& perhaps especially in those in which lanky, cool Greg Morris figured, underplaying his roles, tossing off his lines & tossing his shoulders into a fine young arrogance in those days before *Mission Impossible*) the show achieved a level of complexity that fronted on a dense incomprehensibility—the gobbet was so thick with overlays, it was *invisible*, man! The show had moved ahead as a dark wave of insinuation—try to find the real storm, good luck—on a predictable old weather map for years, trailing technicians, metronomes, bawds of euphony, TV weathermen in its wake. Or pushing them ahead of it, whichever.

Trains occur with some frequency in C&W—the true ethnic music of many white Americans—& in the blues & some spirituals as well. "The Midnight Special," "So Lonesome I Could Cry." Two older Jewish doo-wop songwriters recently baffled Terri Gross with their repeated references to "Caucasian melodies": they'd laugh & laugh at their broad thing & she just sat there at WHYY in Philadelphia not getting it. She's not on in my town, though, until 6 P.M. In the long morning it's time to hunker down to the TV set, check out the leaping blue light. If you look carefully into the train wreck in each *Fugitive* intro you can see that the coaches, tilted & off the track, do not have anything familiar painted on their sides—"Pennsylvania

Railroad," say, or "Chesapeake & Ohio," pre-Amtrak carriers of the 1960s. They say "Chemin de Fer." God knows where the footage is from. We are far from home my brothers. Anyway, the train didn't take the curve too well & Fate articulates its huge hand & the music comes on up again & again & again & again.

Steven Marks

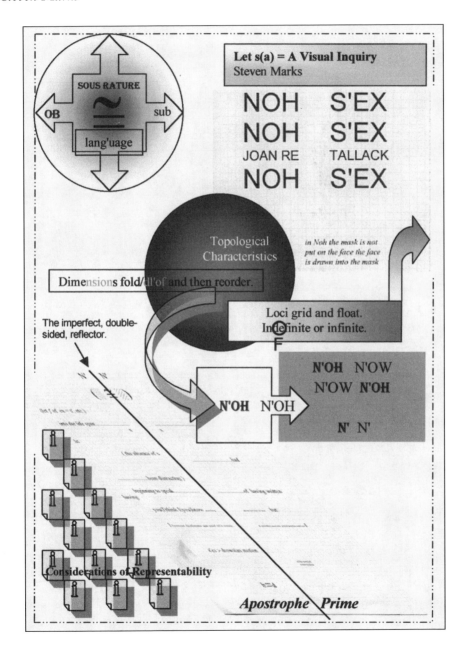

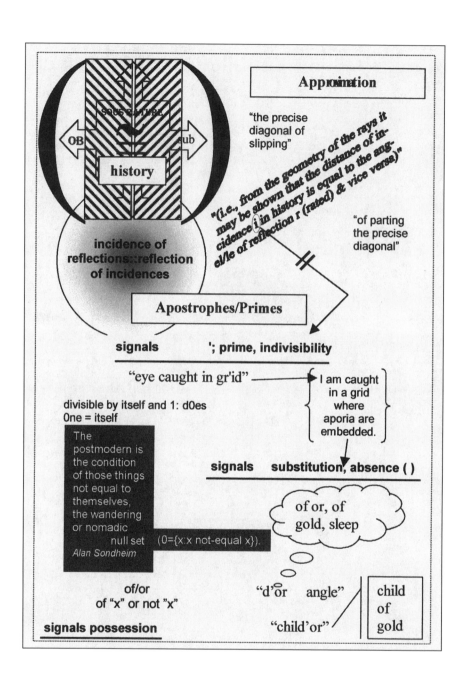

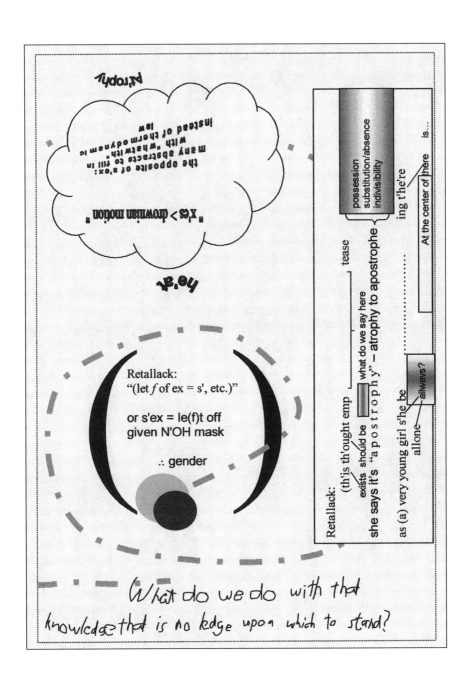

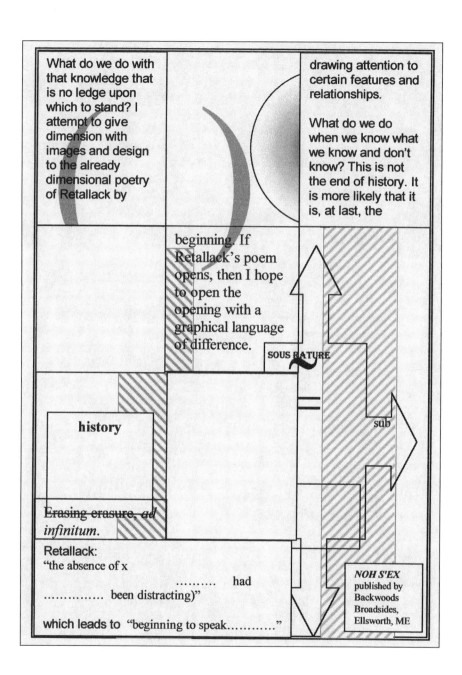

What do we do with that knowledge that is no ledge upon which to stand? I attempt to give dimension with images and design to the already dimensional poetry of Retallack by

drawing attention to certain features and relationships.

What do we do when we know what we know and don't know? This is not the end of history. It is more likely that it is, at last, the

beginning. If Retallack's poem opens, then I hope to open the opening with a graphical language of difference.

SOUS RATURE

history

sub

Erasing erasure, *ad infinitum*.

Retallack:
"the absence of x
.... had
.... been distracting)"

which leads to "beginning to speak............"

NOH S'EX
published by
Backwoods
Broadsides,
Ellsworth, ME

Andrew Levy

Self-interest buys false community.

—William Fuller

Wonder about continuity when it comes to anything. Defeat the tendency of thought to delay itself promising a greater clarity at a later time. It's lying. Know why you set out to do something only to the extent that it doesn't enable a contemplative mode that ends itself before attempting its premises. Or, let it end and examine that ending thoroughly. Question the usefulness of distinguishing between a poetic writing and one more conventionally discursive. Remind other readers to look at Emerson. We'll meet somewhere else soon. What is it to wonder? To wander? It seems something yet different again. The meaningfulness of those six letters like an escarpment beneath which to escape the searching fingers of a King Kong. The danger of losing one's way and never finding one's way home is both immediacy and immanent to the degree in which one convinces oneself that one is in possession of a continuous consciousness (or conscience). To feel its measuring in mellifluous vowels and consonants, its breaks and fissures, is to know something only in its experiencing. I don't think there's too much mystery about it. And at the same time it's like quicksilver; it's the most allusive and elusive thing

---

I have not supplied all of the source information for direct quotes. One of the ideas developed in my essay is that voices/authors/texts are environmentally ambient, that they exist within the experience of language, words, and sounds one listens to, lives in, and remembers. I did not think it necessary to keep a listing of sources while writing and do not wish to impose on this essay citations extraneous to its composition. I assume full responsibility for this decision. —AL

in the world to hold on to. There's no faking it—everyone knows that. As a form of self-knowledge, it's the only speck of genius, so-called, that anyone can ever have. I wonder about why I write and if it may have anything to do with, any relation to what it is other writings do. I think I write because it's the time and place that brings the most difficulty, sadness, pain, and pleasure, always sensual, sometimes erotic. Not so much a feeling of freedom, but a space in which temporarily there's no question about its necessity for life. It's that social ledge upon which the relation between one's own tasks and those met by others meet. Acknowledging it, an act of awareness begins the discovery and experience of one's familiarity with life.

Sentences and lines themselves can posit similar relationships, almost. I remember a definite pause of a few seconds before the addition of the word *almost.* How many alternate paths did my thought skip down before settling on that way of expressing itself? Were they paths, or canals? Even here I have no idea where I'm going, and, realizing that, worry goes away. Writing what you don't already know, wishing it could go on forever, but not knowing if that's possible (and whether anyone would want it to be). Where the measuring of words counts for everything—their weight and overall dimensionality, their texture clue to the world that brought you to the moment when letters make a world in how they touch, and where one will bring oneself for the purpose of being touched. It doesn't matter how long it takes. *Duration* is its name—inside what breaks one's attention from the love of work, an Anticipation—where every syllable enters your ears as voice made of many voices—those you've most loved and hated. A strange remembrance arranged in the circumstances, the smallest details of inflection reciting again and again, "I don't know you. . . . I don't know you. . . . Wait, don't I know you?" While what can be known is rendered less than remnant, reduced to ruin, from the lowest to the highest goes gobbledygook, gobbets defended. All the coincidences for which North American culture erects scaffolding unfold in the impermanence of thought I'd call poetry. A fascinating place to occupy and a pleasure, as it evanesces, to read. And in that, there's no mastery available. If there were, if that were possible, I'd doubt the value of the capital and interest necessary to acquire this year's model.

Solitude is but is not necessary. How many other sentences might those six words translate? One listens, begins to respond, hesitates. Dear memory, I apologize for having been away during your last visit. I wanted to take a walk from here to there, a meandering walk, taking our time to get back. Perhaps forgetting to. When this forgetting takes hold of me, I often can't recognize anyone or anything I come into contact with. In every turn one takes there's a different galaxy, which makes something so strange you can't identify with it for fear of losing the last bit of space you had. Its difference is absolute, you grant it its own habit of self-recreation, its independent culture. I don't want this to sound strange. There's nothing I've described that doesn't happen every day in almost everyone's life. It's so common it's missed. But then it's not missed, either. It's the place in which a sense of one's own responsibility, taken personally, can matter. Usually, the trouble begins at this point, and there's nothing easy about it. "You will find the way to get lost / if you're lucky, blessed" (Fanny Howe). But it often ends up in rubble and smoke. Your reader ought to know that.

When I was eight, *The Count of Monte Cristo*, by Dumas, read like an allegory for the evolution and acquisition of language. Each word demanded the author build a world inside my head using nothing but letters, words, syntax, and punctuation. The hero's escape to liberty and wealth taught me the love of working with words. Dumas and the count used their hands and brains for the great adventure of rewriting one's life. Everyone speaks a different language. There's nothing more to read except those things that clear one's mind. The background and foreground, as with the different layers of cloud in the sky, become ambiguous, almost interchangeable. The person you passed in the street going the other way is yourself. There's real generosity, and thought, and looking around at the word and world and only their clarity, no confusions between them. Nothing too unfamiliar about it.

It's very difficult to touch on the personal in a way that opens to and broadens the esthetic, economic, and political domain without rendering or interpreting it as a minor aspect, effect, simulation, or token of same; a past moment in time people no longer see. And when critics do *have* to look at it, it's often with a derisive eye, a note of sarcasm for "another franchised lifestyle." In that "philosophy" (which is really the absence of the contemplative habit) anyone who looks over her shoulder a second is labeled a Luddite. The god is Speed, and *Pentium* or *Intel inside* won't cut it. For some culture critics *Disney* became a dirty word, a euphemism for the negative, only after Walt died. Everyone speaks a different language for *good reasons*, but as soon as I've written that I know it's inaccurate, although no longer not true. At 6 P.M. in Manhattan, on any given weekday, people look beautiful despite their tired and soot-smeared faces. Their expectations have not been met or have been exceeded in ways they could not have anticipated. For several moments normality escapes them. In its place, a place in which a various and undomesticated diction is "disappeared," an entirely different "plane" of existence opens up. It looks like a quarry of animal sacrifice. The signs welfare all lashes garbled. An architectural neon "THANK YOU FOR YOUR COOPERATION" glows.

"Every defeat leads to a higher level of creativity" (Ralph Nader). Sometimes I think poetry has everything to do with inarticulateness, inaccuracies incubated until they crack open. A contemplation of and on the simplest phenomenon. In the sense that I burp and feel the beer consumed a short while ago burn my nose as two cars collide on the Brooklyn-Queens Expressway. This summer I have shared an apartment with four and sometimes five other men, along with their mix of visiting relatives and friends. We live alongside the nub of the BQE that curves beneath the Brooklyn Bridge and continues the length of the Heights Promenade. Eduardo and Henry are from Peru, Juan Pablo and John are from Uruguay, Christoph is from Germany, I'm from Indiana. We each turn our head at the same instant—to the sound of the collision. Sometimes, with our mixture of Spanish, English, Portuguese, German, and French, I can barely grasp the meaning of our conversation; our nonverbal communication, however, travels some distance further. Our intentions take us in their employ. Teach me to listen to something beyond the literal, or that there is meaning apart from what is said. It's interesting to slow down, to be out of synch with speed that quarters every reflex, that propels you nowhere. Takes away the ticket. That minus identification would mount an atavistic *Look Homeward, Angel*. Ask for your expectations before the first scene on the first day. Demand prescription. Art is somewhere else. We ought to use it to undeceive ourselves with more mercy than ever before.

> Moths in a meadow
> flutter like flowers—freed—their wings
>
> take the shape of their mind the wind.
>
> So it's a spirit that keeps me
> from breaking into pieces! The speed
>
> would rip me apart without it.
>
> So I should cover the wings of my shadow, ride it.
> (Fanny Howe, "13:13," in *O'Clock*)

An anomaly raised in the form by an emotional content. I don't know what kind of world I live in. It seems an utter disaster. I write out of different "times" in my life. There's plenty of space for the irrational in New York City. It's the balance of the rational and the irrational that creates the charm of this place, frames of rationality that pocket the irrational, and vice versa. This is the quantity and quality, both incomprehensible and self-sufficient, that count. To stave off death. To dream. Perhaps a love of poetry is addressed to our lively and daily struggle to conceive and understand the relation between our cells and our two hands (when we have two) the balance of an inside and outside that resides in an Impermanence of *Stability and Noise*. It occupies the near and far all at once. One can't have too much of either aspect and survive. And I mean that we can feel this tension in taking on anything from the simplest to the most difficult emotion and intellectual task. I wonder at the expense indulged in by those who enable and insist on the divisions of experience. Why we make a paradox of our very minds. Dreams are the best time I know of in which both emotion and intellect lie down together in the "present" to explore "the pre- and post-historic mind," where, as Robert Smithson once put it, "remote futures meet remote pasts." The dream within the dream, once deciphered, is relocation, the joyfulness of establishing place. It's the place we come to be at home in. Where all things occur in the same time and the same place, although we cannot know in advance what shape these things will take. Sleeping and dreaming are about nothing more than where you are. They open to vulnerability, "and everywhere names." You're a whole other person.

That makes no sense and so do I.   —Daffy Duck

A wonderful but unnecessary complexity as "fidelity to that which cannot be thematized, nor simply passed over in silence" (Agamben). The laborer (and labor of writing) no longer mute. I'm not in any one place. I don't have a name for what it is I give away. Maybe poetry. Or, poetry gave me away some time ago. I'm a tenant on this island of unbelievable formica. Every thing is to be made. Sometimes I want a clarity greater than what I believe words are capable of providing. It's a very strong feeling. The difficulty lies in identifying or acknowledging exactly what it is that I want clarity on, or about. I often sit at my desk meditating on words like *Everything* or look up at the sky and say, "that, up there." Or, think about the recent GOP and Democratic conventions. Troglodytes or Neanderthals, most of their words walking in the chair, or on their podium, think *above* the street.

I was born in the southernmost tip of Indiana and today live in Brooklyn. I'm thinking about that and wondering how familiar I am with what I think I'm thinking about. With the way I think of it. Might these words step up and do the thinking for me? Haven't they done so already as soon as I think that? Would I know it if they did? Could Lacan help? Is it complete nonsense to think that, at least occasionally, words take that step and do the thinking for themselves, not me? Since I don't particularly know who I am, how can these questions ever be answered to my satisfaction? And, are these questions the extent of "my" relationship to this practice called writing, called poetry? Are they its ultimate context and content?

"Ideas" take shape in my mind, rub against the ceiling and walls of my skull, rubbing, pressing, pushing its boundaries, searching for the seams of infancy to reopen and let them be in the outside world. That feeling helps me to remember the words I live in. The practice of poetry that asks for a silence in which to imagine itself living, alive in the world. I don't want to call it a "process with no subject," or anything that suggests that. It's a form of forgiveness, a formlessness circulating through the illusions and disillusions that sometimes overcome my mind, that help me to think I know in some small part how it is that Andrew Levy goes about interpreting the world he lives in. Convinces him that sometimes one represents that interpretation with an unquestionable accuracy no one would be capable of doubting, an undeniable embodiment of a group phenomenology that shifts and subsides, one shared and completely intertwined with a real, true world.

> Because I am everywhere at this hour
> there is something personal
> about it throughout
> and I come to think of this piece
> not as a scene, but as a person
> that "expression" is "action"
> toward change, plagiarism
> the skulls that spades disturbed
> utilization of culturally
> imbued symbols vigorously debated
> there is no longer any shape
> add to boiling water
> cook for 5–7 minutes
> the produce of camouflage
> it prohibits
> It exists in the indifferent
> unbinding element of air

> *Whether in discontinuant America or cooking for our machine,*
> *the future freezes. The wicked old limits are dead.*
>
> —Larry Price, *Circadium*

> *To everyone conditioned in the belief that to*
> *effect a goal you must at specific times be in*
> *a particular place, we have an announcement:*
> *You're off the hook. You now have the means*
> *to control events from any convenient spot . . .*
> *The first principle:*
> *You never know where you'll be when you need*
> *to plug in. The second: No one has time for*
> *cyber trivia . . .*
> *Your world is a big place. Mobilized*
> *Computing assumes you'll want to use all of it.*

The layout for this language is pricey. In a sepia-toned photograph a young businessman in hat and overcoat stands at the end of a wooden dock; an overturned canoe lies a step down, just beyond his feet, with its front end dipping into the still water of a lake. It looks like early morning, perhaps just after a rain. Trees line the other shore, and there are no other people or human-made structures visible. In the upper left of the two-page spread are the words, all in caps,

> *FROM NOW ON WHEREVER YOU ARE,*
> *IS EXACTLY WHERE YOU SHOULD BE.*

Beneath the miniaturized image of the Hitachi Notebook in the lower right-hand corner are two words placed between single horizontal lines: *Remote Control (TM)*—the abbreviation *(TM)* stands for "Transcendent Mediation." Reading oneself into the advertisement, one's goal (while making use of the entire world) is to mediatize "events" from any convenient spot. Events that must be, logic would suggest, taking place somewhere else. Thus, the world is inconvenient no longer. A good sense of geography can take you to places you've never been. Propaganda, on the other hand, is interior design imported into the human body, an engineered emulation of transparency as the primary goal. It's a camouflaged technocracy older than the movies. Business as usual. Places are known through one's sensibility, but places also, in turn, constitute the sentient individual. The something that we would "control" is only partly personal. And only partial in its possibility. If the world no longer consists of places, has it become larger because it is no longer a place? Those who *insist* only on the present (to hold a *belief* in something becomes an altogether irrelevant matter) would have those yet unappropriated join them in Alphaville. A technohallucination easily mistaken for real flesh and bone. Spiritual America minus anticipatory participation a spiritual America without dimension. However, nothing lasts. Virtual materialism might be the free quark on the horizon. If you read anything too many times, you'll start to think it's nuts. It settles at the bottom of fraternity. A time landscape anything but what advertisers promote as the great unknown. Frontiers yet to be established (but where are they?), even more quickly fenced in. To suffer this fate risks the dispossession the U.S. Congress and President Clinton have allotted to people who would previously have been the recipients of welfare—people forced outside for coffee, the look accustomed to.

Nature is inconvenient.
God didn't create it in order to Maximize cash flow.

—Church billboard in Brooklyn Heights, August 19, 1996

Letters between lovers represent the absence of the material body, are bodies themselves and may carry tokens of intimacy in words, or enclosed objects.

Poetry may be an act and form of pollution, or purification, salvage, redemption, perhaps similar to making bacteria-laden water potable. Not to remove all the dirt but to make it into something you can drink—the filter visible in the cup where you can taste it, the sediment on the bottom of the cup. One may only make a lyrical utterance if one believes or better experiences language as residing in one's body. To know that embodiment as the momentary freedom during which the material realm comes into closest contact with the mind. Whose pleasure, reading, is to find its senses possessed of a real, true art.

Art need no longer be an account of past sensations. It can become the direct organization of more highly evolved sensations. It is a question of producing ourselves, not things that enslave us.

—Guy Debord

Any certain explanation of poetry may block your view of
an entire imagination.
A history of affections and disaffections.
Turn around the rural urban.
Investigate the Bureau of Interior (& Material) Behaviors,
suggests my friend Robert Kocik.

"Copies of ourselves copy themselves into the disemployed
halves."

dearer, themselves of money
art is in the trees
this anticipation of itself
just another market
a multi-sentimentality

we can feel these miracles know
all we have is mobility
the sand and the sea
experimental poetry
song from my family
disingenuous
makes me think you neglect
merely to divide it up
Its pension depends so much
on personality
who knows if much of it's any good
I want the object to respond
because more suited to us
rules that can't break
unless you've taken a vow
wrinkled sheet of our bed
flaws between poems
talismanic tongue reddened
he's going to write
until there's no more room
"The men desire a power
that once seemed viable,
while the women remember a power
that they never had.
It is a quieter nostalgia
from a longer distance."
(Seth Edenbaum, "Parody and Privacy")
so far, I have not discovered
any other way
of getting rid of my thoughts
the earth rises and speaks
to the government

People used to be able to die in battle defending what they cared for,
everything they loved. To be able to move to the other world
with signs of that world
soaked into every part of their lives.
(Excerpt of an email from Bob Harrison)

The loss of texture . . . the new machine is designed to disguise or render invisible its architecture for the "value" of instantaneity—in the consensual domain of the body politic that body doesn't want to know how, where, or by whom soccer balls are made, or *Air Jordans*, or poems, or innumerable other objects.

The Climate of Tranquility, arranged via An Absolute Predominance of Public Servants.

Utopia lacks intersections. It wants more than upkeep.

To put it another way, "The world's sheer inconvenience gives it a tactical power of presence" (Larry Price). A transcript of an improvisation Steve Benson performed at the Ear Inn in New York City in the fall of 1994 contains the following lines:

> I can't sway, but I sing long before it happens,
> and it's important to be solitary and plaintive if you're sad
> and seemingly uneventful and yet moving all the time.
> It's an accidental point that happens as if from the outside,
> but it's got a priority of quietude and patience,
> of listening closely to a serene depth
> that up to this moment cannot possibly have happened.
> It has happened, but the thinking seems to distress us;
> we feel related, we feel closer to it than our innermost being
> answers its call in our development,
> moving alien through these happenings.

Steve has reworked some lines of Rainer Maria Rilke in this passage with materials generated by his own life. Listening closely to a "serene depth" is why I return again and again to the writing I love and recognize of like sensibility and risk to my own. It's something I long to discover daily in my life. Steve's words, and Rilke's, remind me that it is possible. Why do I believe this? That has been my Happiness over and over again through reading. Each poem its time of speed and delay (you need both), multiple conversations (no one's taken to be a distraction) between readers whose pleasure is to find their solitude, after all.

"There is no other interior than actions." (Leslie Scalapino)

It takes more than upkeep. It's not about to digress in its digressions.

Slowing down, initiate delays in time to reopen the imagination —

One can't believe that she can write so perfectly and still be human. Slowing down to witness labor versus its disappearance or invisibility . . .

Peace can be breath in here . . . A deliquescence of desire.

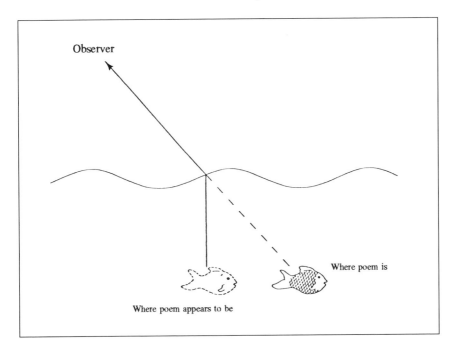

Space, both physical and mental, is daily if not hourly becoming more and more foreshortened, shallower, flatter. It promises within a few generations' time (reflecting the long march of mercantile inanimate and animate objects, their distinction blurred, with goods today perceived as beyond the realm of "real" space and having merged with the "virtual") to collapse, then perhaps to drift as the remains of an earthly implosion, that is, technologized and redeemed as nano goods. An example is reflected in the way we live. In New York City, living rooms and expansive views belong to the very affluent, or the subsidized. Real-estate properties continue to be "downsized," divided into smaller and smaller units for increasing sums of money. I have friends who live, or I should say bathe and sleep, in the smallest of shelters, closets really, for exorbitant and usurious rents. The fencing off of mental (do we need *more* examples?) and physical frontiers in collusion with economic gain for the privileged few is constructed on fear—of an interior unknown architect, and of what "little" men and women might become if not held in place by taxes imposed from above. In the lifestyles of the rich and famous, everyone is acquiescent with the role of lascivious purchaser, locked in place and held hostage by a complex of invitations art in league with marketing "research" extends to its subjects—the public, the viewers/voyeurs with wallets. The desire to have has obliterated all other senses. To be a pickpocket in this present environment would be an honest and straightforward occupation. One might join a more welcoming community of fellow and sister artists practicing deft hand-to-mouth routines of survival. Instead, we pursue the unreal. Kowtow to the designer as hero. Take steps toward heaven, and believe in something called transcendence.

Rod Smith

Being an attempt to set out the dialectic of history as an erotics of exaggerated attention and to assay the implications of this view relative to poetics, politics, philosophy, and astronomy.

The theoretical abandonment of the absolute is rarely accompanied by its disappearance: the absolute returns in a ghostly form, haunting precisely those discourses that claim to have left it behind and that continue to orient themselves around its evacuation. Nevertheless, this half-waking from the half-dream of absolute reason returns us to a primal dialectical scene, to a war for recognition now without stakes. In the farcical relativism that results, dominance is ever more explicitly a matter not of truth but of force. And if we discover that we have never gone further, that force is all that ever mattered, can we say that the dialectic ever occurred at all?

—Paul Mann

•

Both belief and denial throw existence into question.

—Carla Harryman

From an interview with Ted Berrigan at the 2nd Avenue Deli:

Rod Smith: Ted, how might the decision of a judge be just?
Ted Berrigan: To be just, the decision of a judge must not only follow a rule of law or a general law but must also assume it, approve it, confirm its

value, by a reinstituting act of interpretation, as if ultimately nothing previously existed of the law, as if the judge himself invented the law in every case. [Transcriber's note: A creative act is also declarative in this sense.]

John Cage: Art is criminal action.

Jacques Derrida: We need first of all a music, a society, in which not only are sounds just sounds but in which people are just people, not subject, that is, to laws established by any one of them, even if one is "the composer" or "the conductor" or "the computer."

Berrigan: Perhaps then the first violence is the formal and ideal reduction of the complexity of conflict to a dialectical system. If history is what hurts perhaps heresy is what heals.

Derrida: Or perhaps a conversing violence, excuse me, I mean mischief, not violence. But as soon as one leaves a or this order, perhaps mythological, perhaps not—but as soon as one leaves, history begins.

Berrigan: 'Tis strange the mind, that fiery particle
Should let itself be snuffed out by an Article.

Cage: But what cld we possibly mean when we say "history begins"?

Thich Nhat Hanh: It depends on the state of one's finances.

[longish pause in conversation]

Berrigan: "Go now

and get me a vast band-aid"

Robert Duncan: This is the grievous impatience and the ecstatic patience we are fired by as we apprehend in all the disorders of our personal and social life the living desire and intent at work towards new orders.

Derrida: That's nice. (pause) John, Do you believe all good art is unengaging?

Cage: Yes I do.

Derrida: But I know several police officers that find art engaging.

Cage: The problem is that the police are unloved. The police in New York are all paranoid. . . . [T]hey were so hateful for so long that everybody got to hate them, and that just accumulated and built up. The only answer to viciousness is kindness. The trouble is that kids just haven't realized that you've got to make love to the police in order to solve the problem.

Derrida: But how do you force love on the police?

Cage: Make love to them. We need highly trained squads of lovemakers to go everywhere & make love. I think this is important because it is the basis of everything, and no one talks about it.

Berrigan: (with tears in his eyes): That was beautiful John, I'm sorry about those things I said about your mother.

Cage: O, that's sweet of you Ted. & you know I've always said one should start from zero, so please continue your apology.

Berrigan: Well John, it's just that, at the time I wrote that fake interview I was really bombed—I'd been taking Ginseng for about two weeks. I know there's problematic stuff there—a kind of juvenile heterosexed territorialism. Do you think I was threatened by your homosexuality?

Cage: That may have been part of it, Ted, but don't you think you were also convinced of the badness of human nature. (turning to Acker) Kathy, do you think the artist is an outlaw?

Kathy Acker: The citizen is an outlaw. Sometime around 1970 the role of the avant-garde began to change from that of being ahead of the pack to that of laughing at anybody who thought they knew what they were talking about, or who thought it mattered if they did. As of 1995 the Fortune 500 controlled 63 percent of retail business in the U.S.—I wld guess that figure would be much higher in other countries. We don't have a civil society, therefore our work must be read with irrelevance in mind. Irrelevance, not particularly of the artist, but of the individual member of society.

Marcel Duchamp: I recently picked up a free postcard of Marcel Duchamp holding a box upon which was emblazoned the message "I Am Not A Role Model"—it is unclear whether this message was added to the photograph or whether it was in fact Duchamp's message. So, immediately, and in several ways with regard to this photograph—"the sense is larger than one can say." Not only is Duchamp not a role model, but the person or persons that may have placed the message on the postcard are not a role model—& more importantly, or at least, most explicitly, representation itself is not a role model.

Morton Feldman: Let's take some drugs & drive around.

Tom Brokaw: Neither negativity nor optimism are in the end satisfying, useful, effective, or accurate. The farce of perception's elided masking reverberates like a lost or stolen nucleus of conscious paucity. Similarly, the ordained electrochemical book of modern postmodern incision-dissonance is sub-unconsciously impelled toward a backward looking impediment in a field of lumpy evening lineups.

Cage: Let's take some drugs & drive around.

Brokaw: What someone says on a particular occasion may be said to be nonsense if it is obviously false.

Feldman: Anything anyone says is false.

Brokaw: So everything is nonsense? Including what you just said?

Feldman: Obviously.

Lyn Hejinian: Argument demonstrates that truth cannot end.

Brokaw: I'm not arguing.

Hejinian: I know, & that's the problem.

Terence McKenna: Use of psychedelics demonstrates that our cognitive limits are indefinable. There's no limit to what we know or can know.

Thich Nhat Hanh: But that don't pay the bills, Terence. I mean, I know it does for you, since you get paid for saying such things.

George Oppen: We are not the mystery, the mystery is that there is anything for us to stand on.

Disembodied voice speaking as if through a tube: A position must not only be held, but advanced. The surrounding territory must come under its influence and control.

Jonathan Kozol: The end of war is the end of knowledge.

Nicholson Baker: The demand that one be on one's own side, that one stand by one's word, is so standard a feature of intellectual ethics and politics that it has been taken completely for granted.

The Illinois State legislature, in unison: It is necessary to comprehend the force of extremely difficult ideas.

Gabe Kotter: d'ya hear abt the 500 lb. parrot—says Polly wants a cracker, NOW.

Mark Wallace: Arbitrary repression is the most likely course of events.

Buck Downs, cutting him off: Avant-gored.

Cage: Yes, or I often use the word "useful" then, because it has attained the level of high artifice.

Berrigan: What do you mean by "high" there John?

Cage: No, well, a kind of imbalance (pronounced by Cage "im-bay-lance").

Berrigan: Yes, or I often use the word "useful" then.

G. W. F.: The infinite divisibility of matter simply means that matter is external to itself.

Bob Weir: The Spirit is also infinitely divisible. Maya is a compliment to & counterforce to Power in Foucault's sense. It is quite true however that the categories are not contained in the sensation as it is given. No one has a clue.

Carla Harryman: There is, I believe, a way to regain consciousness. . . .

Cage: It's fun to do things by hand.

Harryman: . . . You have to move around as if you were part of something else.

Feldman: O wow.

Perhaps most notable in this dialogue is a kind of hysterical relation to what Bourdieu has called the field of cultural production (see *The Field of Cultural Production* by Pierre Bourdieu). This hysteria seems to me an entirely accurate and justifiable response. The piece partakes of the fine tradition of hysterical overstatement. Well, I don't know if it's "fine," but it is a tradition. There's nothing in it quite as good as Kevin Davies's line, "Will fuck for books, no weirdos," but the general tenor is comparable.

This hysteria, admittedly micropolitical & schizotypical, has its roots in the inescapability & simultaneous (supposed?) nonexistence of the dialectic (as suggested by Paul Mann in the envoi).

To clarify, the existence of the force of the dialectic is cause for hysteria, & as a generalized force reduces the dialectic to nonexistence. The dialectic used to have to beat us back, now it just drowns us out. Anchored in finitude, the provocative overdetermination of our utterance designs experience *back at us*. Our only recourse feels photographic, eyes closed, the camera speaks—its no-mind vanishing before, during, & after the click snap.

Steve Evans, in the first *Impercipient Lecture Series*, cites the Hegelian Adornism "abstraction as lack of articulation." I am conflating that with Michel Serres' "when we close our eyes we lose the power of abstraction." This is our vision of history. The abstraction of history is inescapably inscribed on the things around us. When we close our eyes, history becomes parody (if alone), or desire (if not), *or was it the other way round*. In any case, it is in poetry that these internal states are externalized.

& so Paul Mann is wrong, the dialectic quite clearly exists, it is between history & not-history. Its syntheses is poetry.

The gap between the signifier & signified is just one of many such gaps. Icarus is falling everywhere (Joan Retallack).

& so Wittgenstein's skeptical paradox extends to our thinking about history. The skeptical paradox is: "This was our paradox: no course of action could be determined by a rule, because every course of action can be made to accord with the rule." This in a sentence summarizes why Hegel could do what he did, & why Wittgenstein found him of no interest, & would not even consider addressing his work.

The dialectic is just nonsense. However, we cannot escape nonsense, so we must pay attention to it.

Because one can view Hegel as a, perhaps the, grand demonstration of the skeptical paradox he is incredibly useful. He is the ultimate argument for the micropolitical. The dialectic between history & not-history is an individual matter. Those that understand this are the poets. To err is statemental (Bruce Andrews). History, what did the rose do? (Bernadette Mayer).

I am clearly arguing for a privileging of the site of cognition, for an emphasis upon internality relative to these philosophical issues. A location of/as process which is areal (rather than surreal). Areal because no context is finite, whether internal or external. It seems to me that when one places such an emphasis, the contingency, & constructedness of the thought process becomes, well, "clear."

Or say any context is finite due only to our own limitations, our cognitive limits—*inherently*, however, any context is infinite. All logic depends on a lie (Nietzsche). The contradictions are the knots we use to climb the rope (Ben Friedlander). Or even to make the rope.

If, as I have stated, poetry is the external manifestation of these internal processes we are obviously not speaking of poetry as a genre but as an event. A manner of thinking which is not easily characterized because it is precisely in its unrecuperable fluidity that the dialectic of history & not-history, becoming unrecuperable, exceeds or unintends the sentence that would attempt to capture it.

Definitions are like law. And art is not concerned with law (John Cage).

As Chomsky has pointed out, the concept of cognitive limits leads to the understanding "that what can be understood can be understood by most people."[1] As a result any elitist claims to "expertise" must be, um, how do you say, *vigorously questioned.*

It is because art is an act of individuated cognition (even when the art is collaborative) that Adorno's statement "Art, no matter how tragic it may appear, tends toward the affirmative"[2] is true.

Art's function is to create new circular definitions. The new is an eternal (though not everlasting) return of the open (which is closed). Time is ajar, but even if it weren't, art, like a gas, would come in over the transom. Yet the pressure is such.

or, as Davies writes, again, the dialectic of history & not-history apparent:

> For years
> a kind of conceptual art too ephemeral to be documented

This inability to document *even in the face of the paper trail* is what art has to say to law. It is a refusal of the primacy of codification via demonstration of perception's impenetrable fluidity. This is neither simple nor complex.

"It is quite true however that the categories are not contained in the sensation as it is given."

The spatial, unimpeded persistence of the playfully plagiarized trance-state (a good-natured ribbing)—can remark if not remake detail's clever word-play (the emptiness of emptiness!) into a discovery of highly peculiar presence. Activity as pertinent decay, the posit of the erotic cognitive clutching incomprehensibility, gently, signlessness of a mere thing, gently, as lifting *into* life a moot logic of the exact, circling, behavior of be.

How's your foot?

The dichotomy between the spiritual and the political is also false, resulting from an incomplete attention to our erotic knowledge. (Audre Lorde)

In the erotic we measure, are measured, but do not *take* the measure—rather it is given by the power of our attention, exaggerated, *over us.*

But then back to Kevin. "If you have decks, clear them."

The crush of Only Capitalism throws us back on ourselves, meaning each other. The horror of what it has created us & the possibility of a being other than it rest within our attentions multiplied—the measures escaped into "harmony," unlistened (im)penetrant amaterial sense mechanism of the severaled sharing cores, forwarded or lent-out. The person as temporal overstructure —

& we do not need, but rather already have, a poetics that is a constellatory & innate reflection of the intervention, the LIFE, we embody. Affirmation of this is fact & political act. Our posture is good; the United States is not.

Joan Retallack: Do you think artists can change the grammar of the way we are together?
John Cage: (pause, & then laughing) We don't know, but we can try.

There's no way out by my death or consciousness. (Kathy Acker)

Wittgenstein said that philosophical conclusions should not be surprising.

Music was abstract before we were.

Notes
1. *Creation and Culture* (Boulder, Colo.: Alternative Radio, 1992), unpaginated.
2. *Aesthetic Theory* (Minneapolis: University of Minnesota Press, 1997), 1.

Juliana Spahr

INTRODUCTION

(a beginning)

He or she wants to write something called "Literary Criticism." It is about contemporary poems and poetics.

He or she begins.

He or she begins by telling the story of his or her difficult relationship.

(more powerful, smarter, quicker)

This is the plot of his or her narrative: things are outside the door.

Like the pepsis wasp that goes out at dusk and waits by the tarantula's burrow for the tarantula to come out.

The tarantula comes out to look, blindly, in the dark for a mate.

Things are outside his or her understanding. Like his or her passivity in the face of being buried alive.

Things are more powerful, smarter, quicker. Like a wasp that flies and understands his or her passivity.

There is nothing that he or she can do about this.

ADDENDUM

I want to begin this essay with two moments:

1. In 1960 the anthology *The New American Poetry*, edited by Donald Allen, is published. This anthology quickly becomes a pivotal, defining one.[1] Most important, *The New American Poetry* collects work of a number of poets, most previously never anthologized and a number of whom will become very prominent in the American poetry scene following publication of the anthology. As it does this, it divides the current scene into the following categories: Black Mountain, San Francisco Renaissance, New York Poets, Beat Generation, and a fifth group without geographical definition.

2. In 1971 Robert Grenier writes in *This* "I HATE SPEECH" (86).

In 1986 Ron Silliman's pivotal anthology *In the American Tree* has an introduction that begins, "'I HATE SPEECH.' Thus capitalized, these words in an essay entitled 'On Speech,' the second of five short critical pieces by Robert Grenier in the first issue of *This*, the magazine he cofounded with Barrett Watten in winter, 1971, announced a breach—a new moment in American writing" (xv).

In 1996 Bob Perelman notes that the phrase, "in hindsight, was an important literary gesture . . . important in its positing of literary space" (40, 41).[2]

1. See *The American Poetry Wax Museum: Reality Effects, 1940–1990*, by Jed Rasula, and "Whose New American Poetry?: Anthologizing in the Nineties," by Marjorie Perloff, for more detailed discussions of the impact of this anthology. My argument here is especially informed by Perloff's article, which traces the impact of *The New American Poetry* in some detail. This divide-and-separate model of the anthology has haunted anthologies since 1960. Its influence can be clearly seen in the two major collections of the 1990s, Douglas Messerli's *From the Other Side of the Century: A New American Poetry 1960–1990* (here the reference is even embedded in the title) and Jerome Rothenberg and Pierre Joris's *Poems for the Millennium: The University of California Book of Modern and Postmodern Poetry*.

2. Barrett Watten's "The Bride of the Assembly Line: From Material Text to Cultural Poetics" complicates this rhetoric by arguing, "By analogy, the work of *This* stands at the beginning of the Language School because it is the first continuous self-conscious and self-reflexive literary venue of what 'will have been' the Language School once it developed as it did, even if its formal characteristics could be assembled from other sources. Organization, here, is central; given this fact, it is not at all accurate for Perelman and Silliman to cite Grenier's breach with the literary past as an inaugural event" (17). For the purposes of this essay, however,

Things are there and he or she doesn't know what to do.

(the story unfolds)

The rest of the story can be summarized like this: a pepsis wasp must lay eggs on the body of a tarantula. The details are: he or she is beautiful and formidable; he or she is deep, shiny, blue all over. For each egg, he or she must provide one adult tarantula, alive but paralyzed. This is a story involving submission and dominance: wasp searches for correct version of tarantula (for only one version will do); as wasp searches it probes tarantula's body with an antenna; once right version is found, wasp digs grave for tarantula; tarantula stands by; wasp then returns to the tarantula, explores again, searching for the soft spot where the tarantula's legs join its body; there is a fight now and the wasp wins to paralyze the tarantula with poison, always wins; the wasp then drags tarantula to grave, attaches egg to its side, buries both, leaves.

(the story unfolds)

This is the story of metaphor.

This is the story of powerful masses—strong, healthy, capable of killing the minority of power—brought down by passivity, by desire only for leaving day after day, moment after moment behind, by ignoring, always ignoring the way the wasp of capital controls reproduction.

I don't want to make too much of these isolated moments other than to use them as indicators of how the critical discussion about contemporary poetry uses a rhetoric of categorization and separation, whether by editors of anthologies or by critic-participants. Contemporary poetry is presented again and again as a series of separate and distinct subcultures.[3] Both these examples are creation myths that literalize the name *avant-garde*. Grenier's statement is so concise, so quotable because it separates the emergence of what will be called language writing from Charles Olson's breath-centered poetics and more mainstream lyric modes at the same time.[4]

These separations are partially true and partially false. But their validity is not what interests me in this essay. Instead, I'm interested in how this model of contemporary avant-garde poetry as a series of disconnected and separate concerns is getting rewritten in recent work. This essay examines three works—Lisa Jarnot's *Sea Lyrics*, Jena Osman's "The Periodic Table as Assembled by Dr. Zhivago, Oculist," and Joan Retallack's "THE BLUE STARES"—that challenge these separations. These works, I would argue, are created in response to these creation myths. They are works that have themes and forms and aesthetics that join. They are works that are standing on a bridge or are using chemical formulas of joining to create, or are writing words twined around others' words.

All these poems are contemporary, published in 1996 or 1997. All are poets whose work is difficult to fit into any one school of contemporary poetry. I should admit, however, that these poets are all firmly rooted in an avant-garde or experimental school (a different yet similar version of this essay might look

I am less interested in whether the breach is true or false than in the impact the prevalent belief in breaches has had.

3. As Steve Evans notes, "Anyone acquainted with contemporary American poetry, for example, is aware that certain basic *positions* organize the field, that these draw in their wake specific kinds of *position-takings*, and that what constitutes a viable *possibility* from the standpoint of one position may well be strictly ruled out with respect to another. If Bob Perelman and Maya Angelou switched curricula vitae and a month's worth of reading engagements, publication venues, and institutional functions, no one would *not* notice" (23). An awareness of two different schools of poetry—Robert Lowell used the rhetoric of the cooked and the raw—becomes very evident in the 1960s. (See Rasula's discussion on pp. 232–34.) It has also become a standard component of criticism about contemporary poetry to posit the experimental as a revision of the confessional, the language writers as writing in reaction to workshop-style poetry, and even within language writing to posit the West Coast against the East Coast.

4. Please realize that I am not suggesting that language writers are more guilty of this categorization than any other poetic subculture. I've merely chosen the Grenier example for its conciseness.

This is the story of human relation—the one ripe with reproductive desire outsmarting those out at night, almost blind in the dark, looking for a mate.

This is the story of a foreign threat, the kind that flies over the homeland, killing the naive, peace-loving, not so poisonous, of us.

This is the story of how husband or wife or boyfriend or girlfriend or most other relations interact.

This is the story of literary criticism.

(a comparison is made)

In the narrative, he or she is wasp and tarantula. Beautiful and formidable. Deep and shiny and blue all over.

What is meant by this is that he or she is more complex than we can imagine. And this is how it is with the arms, the legs, the body of one person and another person. They are wasp and tarantula. They are buried together and one is feeding off the other. They are touching, touching, but not always in nice ways. Or what this says is that they are always escaping their confines. Or what this says is that the touch between the arms, the legs, the body of one person and another person is always narrative and subject to literary criticism's analysis.

Here is what it is like when we read:

at the work of poets who explore more convention-
al lyric concerns but use somewhat disjunctive forms
to do this, such as Anne Carson, Jori Graham,
Heather McHugh, or Brenda Hillman. The exam-
ples of Jarnot and Osman, both poets still early in
their careers, illustrate what I would argue is perhaps
the most distinct characteristic of work by emerging
poets of the 1990s:[5] the tendency to violate the aes-
thetic separations of various schools and to
deliberately create an aesthetic of joining.[6] As Steve
Evans notes about aesthetic emergence in general,
"Just as the strict correlation of position and posi-
tion-taking gives the best indication of the field held
in steady state, so a moment of imminent transfor-
mation will see an increase in mismatches on this
front" (24). Evans's observation on the increase in
mismatches is astute. There is clearly right now an
increase in mismatches, in joinings. If this essay were
longer, I would also want to look at these works, all
published in the 1990s: Alfred Arteaga's *Cantos*, for
its figure of the *X* ("We sign the X each time we cross
at least one border. And because it is our sign and
amos cruz and cruzados, naciendo siendo xicanos
otra vez, cada vez, esta vez" [5]); Dodie Bellamy's
various collections of the letters of Mina Harker, for
their mixing of the epistolary and the experimental
to refigure gender; Sherry Brennan's "Wacker
Drive," for writing about weaving in a woven form;
Lee Ann Brown's *Polyverse*, for its multiple points of
influence and contact; Elizabeth Burns's "Spanish
Poems," for the teasing relation between Spanish
and English; Kevin Davies' *Pause Button*, for the way
it takes old work and weaves it into new; Myung Mi
Kim's *The Bounty*, for rewriting Hangul and the lan-
guage of Freud's Anna O; Walter Lew's *Excerpts from
Δikth/ 딕테 / 딕티 / DIKTE for DICTEE* (1982) for
writing his own work through Theresa Hak Kyung
Cha's and showing how she is writing her work

5. For more on the word
emerging see Steve Evans's *The
Dynamics of Literary Change*. I
am using this word loosely to
speak about work by writers
who are just becoming promi-
nent in the late 1980s and early
1990s. This would include
Jarnot and Osman and exclude
Retallack. I prefer the word
emerging to the word *post-
language* (proposed by Mark
Wallace) because many emerg-
ing poets do not see themselves
as at all influenced by, or post,
language writing.

6. Behind this essay is the
repeated concern by critics such
as Ron Silliman or Nick
Lawrence that emerging poets
are purposeless or confused imi-
tators. Silliman (in his
comments on the poetics list-
serv) reads a great deal of
emerging work as "a 'return to
the lyric' as a mode" and claims
that "it [the lyric] represents
precisely the draining of the
'social' from that equation" [I
think he means the equation
between poetry and the social
here] ("Re: Motivation"). He
argues also that these poets use
"the continuation of the same
set of devices [as language poets]
in increasingly modest forms
that characterizes the broader
poetics of G2 [or emerging
poets]" ("G2"). Lawrence finds
"something both disconcerting
and heartening in the way some
of the writers here [he, like
Silliman, is speaking of the
Writing from the New Coast
issues of *o•blēk*, which collected
a number of works by emerging
poets] naturalize the techniques
of the preceding poetic genera-
tion ("Post-Language Writing.

(arrives at the airport)

The literary criticism is the bridge is the moment when he or she arrives at the airport to pick him or her up.

He or she is not smiling when he or she arrives at the airport to pick him or her up.

He or she is complaining about him or her not smiling.

But he or she just wants to sit down and read the newspapers that other passengers or people picking up other passengers have left behind.

Everything has flipped to the other side. Like a book held upside down.

He or she has flipped to just wanting to be there reading the newspapers left behind by other passengers or people picking up other passengers. Flipped from wanting desperately to pick up him or her because he or she missed him or her.

Everything has flipped to the other side.

Like a page.

Spider bites and flipped pages have happened. He or she went away and came home and was the same he or she only different.

He or she came home covered with spider bites.

through others; Jennifer Moxley's *Imagination Verses*, for her language-tainted lyric; Harryette Mullen's *Trimmings*, for its racial and gender inflected revisionings of Stein, Manet, Freud, and others; Edwin Torres, for his mixing of the sounds of English and Spanish into some other language. This is only the beginning, and the joinings that are happening here are as diverse as the things joined. Nonetheless, all this work can be characterized by its refusal of allegiance to any specific school and by a parallel proclamation of an allegiance to more than one school.

•

Lisa Jarnot's work is often defined as later generation language poetry,[7] yet she is socially probably more within the East Coast Beat or New York schools. One possible reading of her book *Sea Lyrics* is as a bridging of this split between the aesthetic and the social. The book is a single poem composed of long sentences that are concerned with liminal states of being and present a narrational *I* whose identification wanders. *Sea Lyrics* is filled with bridges. Literally, there is a bridge on the cover. And literally, the narrator claims: "I have been hunting prey and building bridges for several years now" and "I am an open bridge" and "I am with these murals of cows in towns near towns and bridges" and "I have been a long time upon this bridge wearing the inestimable freedom of the dawn" and "I am trying to be calm and listen for instructions, having crossed the bridge in all the cars" and "I have been a long time in this story on the bridge" and "I have been a long time on this bridge in this story on the bridge, and I have been a long time on this bridge" and "I am the rainy part of early fall expecting to go back across the bridges."[8] (I quote at length just to give

There I've Said It."), then invert its poetics" (153). Part of the reason Silliman and Lawrence find this work apolitical, I would argue, is that they assume that literary movements are breaches. They thus define uniqueness, the one quality that they seem to value, only in how it denies relationship. But the work they are critiquing is proposing more complex models of literary relationships with existing formal practices. What reads as modest to Silliman rather revises the notion of poetic schools as breaks. Instead, one could read this "modesty" as a communal reinvention with an emphasis on combining and transforming formal practices that are often seen as opposed. Two obvious influences on my essay, and work that I find more indicative of the current situation, are Steve Evans's *Dynamics of Literary Change* and Wallace's "Emerging Avant-Garde Poetries and the 'Post-Language Crisis'" (the Wallace essay directly responds to Silliman and Lawrence). Both are essays written on work similar to what I am discussing here.

7. Albert Mobilio writes, "Lisa Jarnot's first book, *Some Other Kind of Mission*, drawing as it does on the Stein tradition as filtered through poets like Clark Coolidge, is fated to meet with incomprehension outside the narrow precincts of (pick a term: postmodern, avant, Language) poetry" (55). John Ashbery writes, "Lisa Jarnot's *Some Other Kind of Mission* (Providence: Burning Deck) suggests that Language Poetry may be mutating, back to the

(that evening, those next few days)

That evening, those next few days.

(a hinge, a page)

Like the wasp that searches for the tarantula, he or she searches his or her legs, arms, bodies.

He or she is trying to understand what the relation between him or her and him or her has changed into. A hinge. A page. A beautiful and formidable.

Are the choices production or reproduction?

Him or him or her or her?

(someone comes home)

He or she came home with his or her body covered with spider bites.

He or she came home with his or her shirt torn.

He or she came home.

The coming home is the opening of the book.

He or she came home and there was much crying.

you a sense of the variable nature of the bridge and of the subject in this work.) Here the narrational *I* claims to be a builder, a bridge itself, with and upon bridges, crossing and wanting to recross the bridge. Also indicative of the attention to variables in *Sea Lyrics* is that this work is about how things connect may or may not take place in the liminal space of the bridge.[9] The bridge here is certainly something that the narrator is on a lot, but it is unclear where exactly the narrator is at any point in the poem because the narrator is so many places. The *I* is on or near or crossing or having just crossed the bridge so it can bridge things endlessly. So the *I* can be the drunken Irish brother, the man in the Laundromat who wishes he was Carol Burnett, the Santa Ana wind.

Sea Lyrics is most obviously inflected with and infected by Allen Ginsberg (and thus Walt Whitman) and Robert Duncan. In this poem Jarnot takes the Beat bridge of Ginsberg and walks somewhere that might be the California of Duncan (with the sea lions and sea leopards of *Heavenly City, Earthly City*) by way of the New York school. It is a poem that is very self-aware of influence. As Jarnot writes, "This is from which I came expecting to see others, for the others from which they came and came I in the generations fog."

It is what Jarnot does with the tradition of Whitman and Ginsberg that interests me the most. Both are poets who propose a philosophy of embracing others. Whitman's battle cry of containing multitudes gets literalized in the open sexuality and politics of Ginsberg's verse. But the parental embrace, as the teenager knows, can also suffocate. And the challenge Whitman's and Ginsberg's work raises for contemporary concerns is how to embrace all without overpowering and negating individual

modernism of Stein and Joyce" (11). As anyone who knows Jarnot might expect, she challenges the definition of her work as being written in any of these traditions. In an e-mail to me she writes, "particularly with the mission book, all fragmentation and complication is a record of emotional/ psychological/hysterical state, and not of a knowledge necessarily of other avant-garde practices of language usage" (Oct 27, 1997). Although I think it is a clear misreading of her work to read it as language writing of any generation, at the same time I take her claim of naivety about language writing (she claims to have only read Lyn Hejinian's *My Life*) with a grain of salt.

8. This work is not paginated.

9. Other liminal places that are throughout this book are twilight, break rooms, the waterfront.

There was much crying because he or she had had relation with another person.

Like in reading—its surprises, its perplexities.

He or she came home and he or she and he or she held each other all night.

He or she came home and the spider bites were the sign of being away, in a different climate, with a different body.

He or she came home.

He or she opened the book and he or she confessed his or her anger.

He or she came home and read and confessed but also withheld much information and refused various rites of interpretation.

This upset him or her.

He or she came home and the arms, the legs, the body was different.

There was a breach in the relation.

The page was turned.

He or she came home and he or she and he or she were all confused.

differences, how to embrace all without being guilty of hubris. In *Sea Lyrics* Jarnot negotiates these problems with skill. The poem takes the divisions between the Language writing (with its complicated yet dissolute subjectivity) and the Beat writing (with its centered, all-encompassing subject) and mixes them. Thus the Beat narrative subject pursues the complicated and dissolute subjectivity of Language writing. What *Sea Lyrics* ends up with is a subject that negotiates many different positions, states of being, and is human, animal, mineral, and vegetable all at the same time. The narrator is all these he or she things, all these animal things, all these ceramic things, all these pieces of things. So *Sea Lyrics* presents a unique form of joining, a joining of the subjective, the *I*, with things that are other. Much has been made of the libratory possibilities of a multiple subjectivity, but the subjectivity proposed here is a useful variation on this. Here subjectivity is multiple yet it looks outward. It embraces without absorbing.

"I am an open bridge," this narrator claims.

•

Although Jena Osman is close to Jarnot's age and comes from a similar background (both attended SUNY at Buffalo; both have spent time involved in the New York poetry scene), her work reads very differently. Osman's work is not really language writing (it is too rich with story, too connective), and it is definitely not workshop style (it is too playful with language's difficulties). It lacks the confessionalism and the subjective center of the New York school or the Beat generation. But the similarity between Osman's and Jarnot's work is this tendency to write

He or she refused to tell certain things, making certain other things, the gaps in the narrative, more powerful.

He or she refused to tell certain things and thus made certain imagined things all the more real.

He or she came home.

(a joined product)

So what he or she means to say here is that though reading is difficult, the spider bites, the crying, the breach, he or she comes home or two species combine but not in very pleasant ways and they contract and change and make room and this is the way it means to join and this is how things change between him or her and him or her and this is how he or she remakes his or her arms, legs, body. As a new arms, legs, body. As a new product—one leg on the foot, the other on the thigh, one arm around the back, the other on the shoulders—a joined product. One thing feeding off another thing. Buried. The story of this joined product is the story he or she wants to tell in "Literary Criticism."

But he or she is also worried that the comparison is not working. There are so many factors—the tarantulas, the hims or the hers, the wasps, the books, the eyes, the words, the literary criticisms, the various arms, legs, bodies. He or she is worried that too much juggling is going on. But he or she is also convinced that for literary criticism to have any hope of being anything that does necessary work it must be capable of juggling many different things. His or her relationship with him or her and him or her and him between current aesthetic schools in pursuit of joining.

Whereas *Sea Lyrics* has a literal bridge, in Osman's "The Periodic Tale as Assembled by Dr. Zhivago, Oculist," the properties of the physical world join the creative. This poem, published on the Web as a hypertext, begins with the image of the periodic table and is followed by Osman's "translation" of the table. She uses the chemical compounds created by different combinations of elements in the periodic table to create new poems.[10] For example, the element hydrogen turns into "harness," which in turn leads to the following poem:

> harness to hydrogen
> aeriform
> the lightest body known
> extinguishes burning bodies
> dragoman, an interpreter
> closely fitted in different languages
> it signifies furniture and utensils
> gig chaise casque sword buckler tackle
> within which in its primary sense
> it is synonymous as a horseman
> (http://wings.buffalo.edu/epc/authors/osman/
> periodic/harness.html)

The translations here appear to be guided mainly, but not exclusively, by the leading letter (*H* translates into another word beginning *h*) but are otherwise arbitrary. However, as the poem makes clear, the words metamorphose into each other through an interpreter. Or consider this example, in which cobalt and coral turn into some third object:

> corals to cobalt
> this is said to be the G. kobold, a goblin,
> the demon of the mines damsel and sea

10. Osman has also written a series of poems that are created by directly translating chemical reactions. For instance, she translates the Diels-Alder reaction into "deals alter reaction" as follows:

> harness ceases times 2
> ceases
> reaction
> ceases
> gig chaise casque (times
> two)
> ceases
> synonymous as a horseman (two)
> aeriform
> ceases
> sword buckler tackle
> ceases

And she also translates glucose:

> ceases odds
> harness odds
> ceases harness odds
>
> ceases odds twice
> harness two odds
> ceases six harness twelve
> odds by six

These poems are not yet published. Osman plans to make the Web poem into a hypertext where the reader can create various reaction poems through hypertextual links.

or her. Many lines of direction. The foot diagrams that represent a difficult and unusual dance on paper. A child learning how to speak through stutterings and gaspings. A threat paralyzed, an egg attached to its abdomen. Him or her and him or her sitting on the edge of the bed talking about how difficult it is for him or her now that there are other hims or hers. A triangle turning into a square turning into an octagon in a kaleidoscope. Beautiful and formidable. Deep and shiny and blue all over. Swooping. Sitting at the edge of the bed.

(one thing?)

He or she wants to make this complexity of relation—this complexity where one thing has dominion and understanding over another thing all in one moment but in another moment the another thing has dominion and understanding over the thing—into a metaphor for how we encounter works and worlds. He or she wants to explain the recent events in his or her life as a comparison for what happens when one writes literary criticism. He or she is often confused about how he or she feels about literary criticism. Whether he or she likes it, whether it has a use value, whether it is something good or not. But this makes the comparison continue to work. For the events in his or her life keep getting more and more elaborate, the connections with other people get more and more elaborate, and he or she is not sure how he or she feels about this elaborate.

He or she feels that encountering is abandonment, seduced and thrilled. It is that feeling of being beautiful and formidable, deep and shiny and blue all over. He or she feels that corresponding to the skeleton at first its value was not known it crystallizes in bundles of needles it exhales the odor of garlic its structure is foliated when fused with three parts of silicous sand converted into a blue glass called smalt carbonate of lime has the form of trees, shrubs hemispheres nodular shapes brain-coral the surface covered with radiated cells and when alive, the animals appear like flowers over every part (http://wings.buffalo.edu/epc/ authors/osman/periodic/corals.html)

These examples illustrate the most obvious way that Osman's poem pursues an aesthetic and a formal attention to joining.

Around the translated elements, on the main page of the poem, are comments about sight and writing. Dr. Zhivago, of the novel and the movie, ends the poem: "he said if you have a sudden loss of vision this is reason for concern / and forgets to see beyond the window a great transition in historical time" (.../periodic). Dr. Zhivago cannot see the relation between the poem and the social obligation. In his world doctoring is distraction from the poem. In the movie *Dr. Zhivago* the poem is figured as elliptical, as art (in the sense of art as divorced from society), as foreign, for "although he speaks English / he writes in Cyrillic // his poem is an analogy that doesn't function" (.../periodic). What Osman's translation of the periodic table attempts to create is an illustration of the way analogy can function if Dr. Zhivago could see (if he was an oculist), the way it can recreate the world. Language is here figured as having a material relation to sense, not as having one that is ethereal or mystical. The symbolic nature of the physical or scientific world is used as a formula

11. See, for instance, Jackson Mac Low's most recent work in *Barnesbook* or a myriad of his other works.

encountering is abandonment, probed and manipulated. He or she feels these things and sees this as what is important about them.

He or she continues to buy books and read them.

(everything has flipped)

In the comparison that he or she is using, the literary criticism stands for many moments when legs, arms, bodies touch. It is the hinge, the flip, the change in perspective. It is transition work.

Its pages are always opening, opening. Its lines are always ending and returning. It is always broken open, broken open. It cries.

In relation one person takes a bit of another person, takes a fragment of that person, and lets it into that other person.

In literary criticism, the same thing happens.

Like a bridge that joins two things together.

(the literary criticism is the connection)

This is the story about a pepsis wasp who lays eggs on the body of a tarantula.

In writing about another person and his or her relation to him or her, in writing about a book and his or her relation for the chance joining of poetic words. Thus the poem itself is a machine for joining and creating new poems. It is to some extent, as is often noted about machines that generate poetry, a giving away of parts of authorship.[11] But the machine created here takes chance to the level of connection because it uses models from life. It has faith that the chemical reactions are complex enough to reveal an interesting language for poetry. It is this faith that interests me more than the giving up that defines chance-generated writing. This poem proposes a new force of organization, one based on connection, on relation, to break down the separation between audience and work, doctoring and poetry, that haunts Dr. Zhivago.

•

Joan Retallack's work presents perhaps the clearest example of how difficult it has been for current models of criticism to make sense of work that is concerned with joining rather than with fracturing. Generationally and socially she would fit the pattern of a first-generation Language writer. She has socially been a part of the Washington, D.C., Language writers (which could be loosely defined at that time as Tina Darragh, Lynne Dreyer, and P. Inman, with regular visits from Bruce Andrews) since the mid-seventies. Yet her work is in neither Silliman's *In the American Tree* nor Douglas Messerli's *Language Poetries*, the two defining anthologies of Language writing. Her first book appeared in 1985 (*Circumstantial Evidence*). But it is in the 1990s that her work became more readily available. In 1993 *Errata 5uite* was published; in 1994 *Icarus FFFFFalling*; in 1995 *AFTERRIMAGES*. (So there is some way that her work might fit the "emerging" category of writers who are becoming prominent in

12. It is important to realize, however, that Retallack was doing active work in the sixties and early seventies in philosophy, political writing, and the visual arts. But it was not until the seventies that she began to bring all these interests together in written works. A lot of her early work remains unpublished.

to it, he or she writes certain words and these words refer to certain events. In the story of the tarantula and the wasp, the literary criticism is the connection this story has with his or her life, with how he or she is forced to wonder a lot about who is the tarantula and who is the wasp.

In the narrative he or she is looking for a body on which to plant an egg but only certain bodies make sense.
He or she and he or she tries to understand the sting which is much worse than that of a bee or a common wasp.

He or she tries to understand the bite which is not direct-ed at humans and is dangerous only to insects and small mammals.

He or she reaches out and he or she explores him or her with his or her antenna, with his or her legs and belly.

He or she shows an amazing tolerance.

He or she crawls under him or her, walks over him or her.

There is no hostile response.

The molestation is so great and so persistent that he or she stands up, stands for several minutes.

So it is with the way he or she turns pages.

the late 1980s and early 1990s just by fate of publication.)[12] Her work is, like much Language writing, concerned with the political ramifications of poetic practice (she uses the term *poethics*).[13]

Retallack's "THE BLUE STARES" is written in three typographical levels: the words *the*, *blue*, and *stares* appear in capitals; quotations from Barbara Guest's poem "The Blue Stairs" appear in italics; a third text composed of language from Retallack's notebooks and quotes from Dante and Julia Kristeva appear in lowercase roman. Obviously, three texts are joined here. "THE BLUE STARES," however, requires an extra level of complexity if one wants to claim it as a poem of joining, for the joinings here are built around separations. The title words, for instance, never appear together in the poem. They are always separated even when joined in their typographical similarity. Same with Guest's text and the more personal notebook text. The poem begins with a quote from Kristeva: "Andre Broca's paradox: To see a blue light, you must not look directly at it" (203). In order to examine how one sees diverse things and joins them together, this poem does not look directly at them. Instead this work is always joining things by separating them, having us see by directing us away. The poem gets its title and its reference from Guest's "The Blue Stairs." This poem is now out of print (again, in order to see, we must look at that which is not easily available). One social function that Retallack's poem serves is to preserve or "reprint" (more or less, the Retallack version is a close, but slightly edited, version of the original) this work. Guest's poem is a meditation on stairs, on heights and how to reach them, on climbing, on mobility. It is also about what we might otherwise overlook in our pursuit of mobility. The stairs in this poem figure as aesthetics (they are formally beauti-

13. She writes:

Aristotle, who has cast the most enduring shadow over the course of academic poetics, quite artificially divided everything up into what he took to be thoroughly comprehensible disciplines—theory, practice, ethics, politics, poetry. Poethical poets, whether or not they have themselves used the "h," enact the complex dynamics that criss-cross through these boundaries. The model is no longer one of city or nation states of knowledge each with separate allegiances and consequences, testy about property rights and ownership, but instead the more global patterns of ecology, environmentalism, bio-realism, the complex modelings of the non-linear sciences, chaos theory. (295)

Although in this essay I am examining a more specific poetic moment, I think all the poets discussed here meet Retallack's requirements and are "poethical."

(we)

So it is with what is expected of all of us as encounterers, readers, sleepers on the job, word counters, elevator operators, word processors, typists. With what is necessary in the act of reading. With reading things that are good and moving to us, good and moving to our lives. We attach ourselves to the abdomen and feed. Joining has become a part of our lives. We are growing into something and it is difficult. We are missing the words or missing the boat or missing the bridge by a few miles. It is like this. We are looking for changing. We are joining things. We join our narrative to other narratives, the narratives of prose or poetry or articles in *Scientific American*. We join our loves and others. We join relations. As a result we are trying to write an article, a piece called literary criticism about joining because in literary criticism we take a piece of something, take fragments, and string them together with our own commentary or commentary that is in reaction to something else. The commentary is designed to be narrative so as to cover up the fragmentary nature of quotation. This is the way it is with thinking, with gendering, with joining. Forms can carry all ethical positions, like people, all the positions, all the meetings and dividings. We are transition work.

ful), as influences (the poem at the end has artists "[w]ho are usually grateful / to anyone who prevents them / from taking a false step // And having reached the summit / would like to stay there / even if the stairs are withdrawn" [6]), and as divergence, "as interpolation / in the problem of gradualness" (6). "THE BLUE STARES" builds off of all these steps, and Guest's poem is built stairlike into Retallack's poem. Each phrase of the Guest piece leads up and into another piece of text that connects the mobile linguistic structures that traverse the poem.[14] This poem thus literally joins languages. The lowercase roman text of the poem is written, the author's note claims, while she traveled in "Budapest, Czech Republic, and Vancouver, B.C.," so the poem is one written in transit among numerous cultures (207). Although it is written mainly in English, it keeps slipping into Hungarian (*kijarat*, the Hungarian word for *exit*, occurs throughout the poem), Italian, Middle English, etc.

In Retallack's poem the "stairs" become "stares" because the poem is about how we stare sideways, how the poem looks back: "as a writer of BLUE essays into *the problem of gradualness* STARES *with a heavy* THE *and pure logic* too BLUE such a blue takes hold of STARES the viewer at THE *the master builder acknowledges* BLUE that blue precisely *this* side of STARES of or beyond" (206). The line of sight in this passage is wonderfully joined and askew at the same time: the writer of the essay stares at the viewer (reader) who stares at the writer ("master builder") who both stare at both sides of the stair.

•

I have been looking lately for poems that refigure social spaces, that propose new forms of organiza-

14. The poem is built so that before "THE" there are three words (after the number of letters in the word), before "BLUE," four words, before "STARES," six words. The first line is an exception.

tion.[15] These writers are taking their own social space and refiguring it as one that crosses into others, retaining the differences of both spaces yet bringing each into dialogue with the other. I would like to think this work might provide a model for how to configure other defining boundaries and might also provide an attention to how individuals can control definitions of their social spaces without being subsumed. I want to suggest that what is emerging here is a new social map. A map that charts the topographically rich and seismically distorted. Through bridging or joining, these writers are suggesting the world is large, complex, never singular and are demanding that the work reflect this.

Examining such moments seems crucial for critical thinking, which has been the most guilty of reductively separating complex contemporary poetic practices into schools and underestimating sources of influence. When looking at how writers bridge different aesthetic practices, it becomes clear that writing that values the comprehensive over the totalizing is challenging the ease of categorical separations.

•

15. And I have undeniably looked mainly in my own social spaces. This essay might also be read as a confession of works and individuals who have been important to me personally.

Allen, Donald. *The New American Poetry: 1945–1960*. New York: Grove Press, 1960.

Arteaga, Alfred. *Cantos*. San Jose, Calif.: Chusma House Publications, 1991.

Ashbery, John. "International Books of the Year." *Times Literary Supplement*, November 29, 1996, 11.

Bellamy, Dodie. *The Letters of Mina Harker*. West Stockbridge: Hard Press, 1998.

Brennan, Sherry. "Wacker Drive." In *A Poetics of Criticism*, ed. Juliana Spahr, Mark Wallace, Kristin Prevallet, Pam Rehom. Buffalo: Leave Books, 1994. 101–24.

Brown, Lee Ann. *Polyverse*. Los Angeles: Sun and Moon, 1999.

Burns, Elizabeth. "Spanish Poems." *Public Works: New Sequence-Length Work by Women*. Suffolk: Sound and Language, 1997.

Davies, Kevin. *Pause Button*. Vancouver: Tsunami Editions, 1992.

Duncan, Robert. *Heavenly City, Earthly City*. Berkeley: B. Porter, 1947.

Evans, Steve. *The Dynamics of Literary Change*. Impercipient Lecture Series. Vol. 1, no. 1 (1997).

Grenier, Robert. "On Speech." *This* 1 (1971): 86–87.

Guest, Barbara. *The Blue Stairs*. New York: Corinth Books, 1968.

Hejinian, Lyn. *My Life*. Los Angeles: Sun and Moon, 1980.

Jarnot, Lisa. *Sea Lyrics*. New York: Situations, 1996.

Kim, Myung Mi. *The Bounty*. Minneapolis: Chax Press, 1996.

Lawrence, Nick. "Review." *I Am a Child* 1 (1994): 151–53.

Lew, Walter K. *Excerpts from △ikth/ 딕테 / 딕티 / DIKTE for DICTEE* (1982). Seoul: Yeul Eum, 1992.

Mac Low, Jackson. *Barnesbook*. Los Angeles: Sun and Moon, 1995.

Messerli, Douglas. *From the Other Side of the Century: A New American Poetry 1960–1990*. Los Angeles: Sun and Moon, 1994.

———. *"Language" Poetries: An Anthology*. New York: New Directions, 1987.

Mobilio, Albert. "The Word's Worth." *Village Voice*, April 29, 1997, 55.

Moxley, Jennifer. *Imagination Verses*. New York: Tender Buttons, 1996.

Mullen, Harryette. *Trimmings*. New York: Tender Buttons, 1991.

Osman, Jena. "The Periodic Table as Assembled by Dr. Zhivago, Oculist." July 1997. October 21, 1997 <http://wings.buffalo.edu/epc/authors/osman/periodic/>.

Perelman, Bob. *The Marginalization of Poetry*. Princeton: Princeton University Press, 1996.

Petrunkevitch, Alexander. "The Spider and the Wasp." *Scientific American*, August 1952, 20–23.

Perloff, Marjorie. "Whose New American Poetry?: Anthologizing in the Nineties." September 1996. October 21, 1997. <http://wings.buffalo.edu/epc/authors/perloff/anth.html>.

Rasula, Jed. *The American Poetry Wax Museum: Reality Effects, 1940–1990*. Urbana: National Council of Teachers of English, 1996.

Retallack, Joan. *AFTERRIMAGES*. Hanover, N.H.: Wesleyan University Press, 1995.

———. *Circumstantial Evidence*. Washington, D.C.: Sultan of Swat Books, 1985.

———. *Errata 5uite*. Washington, D.C.: Edge Books, 1993.

———. *Icarus FFFFFalling*. Buffalo: Leave Books, 1994.

———. "THE BLUE STARES." *Chain* 4 (1997): 203–7.

———. "The Poethical Wager." In *Onward: Contemporary Poetry and Poetics*, ed. Peter Baker, 293–306. New York: Peter Lang, 1996.

Rothenberg, Jerome, and Pierre Joris. *Poems for the Millennium: The University of California Book of Modern and Postmodern Poetry*. Berkeley: University of California Press, 1995.

Silliman, Ron. *In the American Tree*. Orono: National Poetry Foundation, 1986.

———. "G2." Poetics List. October 31, 1994. October 21, 1997. <http://listserv.acsu.buffalo.edu/archives/poetics.html>.

———. "Re: Motivation." Poetics List. October 28, 1994. October 21, 1997 <http://listserv.acsu.buffalo.edu/archives/poetics.html>.

Wallace, Mark. "Emerging Avant-Garde Poetries and the 'Post-Language' Crisis." March 1996. October 21, 1997 <http://wings.buffalo.edu/epc/authors/wallace/emerging.html>.

Watten, Barrett. *The Bride of the Assembly Line: From Material Text to Cultural Poetics*. Impercipient Lecture Series. Vol. 1, no. 8 (October 1997).

Contributors |

Daniel Barbiero's work has appeared in *Philosophy Today, Wittgenstein Studies,* and *The World in Time and Space: Towards a History of Innovative Poetry 1970–2000* (Talisman 2000), a collection of essays on poetics.

Caroline Bergvall is based in England. She has published texts in a range of magazines and anthologies in the UK and North America. Some of her writing commissions have involved developing collaborative live performances and installations: *Strange Passage,* awarded the Showroom Live Art Commission in 1993 (Equipage); *Eclat,* walkman tour of a domestic space (Sound and Language, 1996); and *Ambient Fish,* collaborative text-sound installation commissioned by Hull Time Based Arts for Root'99. Her current textual work is entitled *Goan Atom* and is an ongoing, cross-disciplinary, and plurilingual project of texts and text-related events. Part 1: *Jets-Poupée* was published by RemPress (1999). Her critical work is increasingly concerned with contextualized text practices and multiple-language writing. She is the director of Performance Writing, Dartington College of Arts, England.

Charles Borkhuis is a poet, playwright, and critic living in New York City. His books of poems are *Hypnogogic Sonnets, Proximity (Stolen Arrows),* and *Dinner with Franz.* A new book of his poems, *Alpha Ruins,* and a book of full-length plays, *Mouth of Shadows,* were published in 2000. He teaches English at Touro College in New York City. His recent radio play *Foreign Bodies* will air on NPR in 2001. He is the recipient of a Dramalogue Award.

Sherry Brennan lives in Centre Hall, Pa. She has published poetry and essays in *Chain, HOW(ever), New American Writing, Object, raddle moon,* and the edited collection *The Poetics of Criticism,* among others. Her essay "make shift" provided the conceptual underpinnings for a book-length project now underway on Dante and contemporary poetics. The first chapter appears in *ReadMe 3* at <http://www.jps.net/nada/>. The third chapter appears in *Kenning 3* <http://durationpress.com/kenning/>.

Jeff Derksen has published articles on culture, art, literature, and architecture in *Springerin, ARCHIS: Architectuur, Stad, Beeldcultuur, Mix, Fuse, West Coast Line* and *C* magazine. His essay "Where Have All the Equal Signs Gone?: Inside/Outside the L=A=N=G=U=A=G=E Site" will appear in *Assembling Alternatives* (forthcoming from Wesleyan University Press in 2000). Other work has been published in *Vancouver: Representing the Postmodern City* (Pulp/Arsenal, 1994) and *Writing Class: The Kootenay School of Writing Anthology* (New Star, 1999). His poetry books include *Dwell* (Talonbooks, 1994) and *Down Time* (Talonbooks, 1991). He is a board member of Kootenay School of Writing, Vancouver. Derksen was also a 1999–2000 Fulbright Scholar at City University of New York, Graduate Center.

Steve Evans teaches poetry, poetics, and critical theory at the University of Maine. He recently received a Ph.D. from Brown University with a dissertation on "The Dynamics of Literary Change: Studies in Poetic Form and Formation." With the poet Jennifer Moxley he edited The Impercipient Lecture Series and is presently the co-editor of *Sagetrieb* and a contributing editor to *Facture*. Recent criticism has appeared in *Aerial, Poetry Project Newsletter, Crayon, Poetics Journal, Shark* and in his e-mail review column *Notes to Poetry*, archived on the *Arras* Web site, <http://www.geocities.com/ arras_online>.

Benjamin Friedlander's books of poetry include *A Knot Is Not a Tangle, Algebraic Melody*, and *Selected Poems*. With Donald Allen he edited Charles Olson's *Collected Prose*. He is currently preparing two manuscripts for publication: a collection of essays in poetics and a study of Emily Dickinson and the Civil War. An assistant professor of English at the University of Maine, Orono, he co-edits the scholarly journal *Sagetrieb* with Steve Evans.

Christopher Funkhouser's critical commentary has appeared in *SIGWEB Newsletter* (Association for Computing Machinery), *TEXT Technology: The Journal of Computer Text Processing, Electronic Book Review*, and on the *International Anthology of Digital Poetry* and *Of(f) the W.W.Web* CD-ROMs. During the 1990s he published interviews, reviews, poetry, and other creative work in *Callaloo, Hambone, Talisman, Exquisite Corpse, XCP: Cross-Cultural Poetics*, and many other obscure magazines, anthologies, and Web sites. He was editor of *The Little Magazine Volume 21*, the first North American literary magazine published on CD-ROM, and the online journals *EJournal, Descriptions of an Imaginary Universe*, and *Passages*.

Presently he is editor of *Newark Review* and *We Press*, and poetry editor for *Terra Nova: Nature and Culture* (MIT Press book series). He holds a Ph.D. in English from the University of Albany (SUNY) and an M.A. in English from the University of Virginia. He lives on Staten Island and is a professor in humanities and social sciences at New Jersey Institute of Technology.

C. S. Giscombe teaches in the M.F.A. program at Penn State. His poetry books *Here* (1994) and *Giscombe Road* (1998) were both published by Dalkey Archive; *Into and Out of Dislocation*, his prose book, was published in 2000 by North Point/Farrar, Straus, and Giroux.

Jefferson Hansen has published a number of chapbooks, among them *gods to the elbows* (Leave), *The Dramatic Monologues of Joe Blow Only Artsy* (Texture), and *Why I Am Not a Christian* (Primitive). His latest chapbook is *Nondescript* (Margin-to-Margin). Two issues of *A-BACUS* have featured his poetry. In addition, his essays and reviews have appeared in many journals, including *Witz* and *Cross-Cultural Poetics*.

Andrew Levy has authored eight books of poetry, including *Values Chauffeur You*, *Democracy Assemblages*, *Curve*, *Curve 2*, and *Paper Head Last Lyrics*. He edits the arts and poetry journal *Crayon* with Bob Harrison, and for many years was codirector of the Segue Foundation reading series at the Ear Inn. Levy's work has appeared in many magazines and anthologies, including *The Art of Practice: 45 Contemporary Poets*, *The Gertrude Stein Awards in Innovative American Poetry*, and *Writing from the New Coast*. He lives in New York City with his wife and daughter.

Tan Lin's publications include *Lotion Bullwhip Giraffe* (Sun and Moon, 1996). Poems and art reviews have appeared recently in *Boston Review*, *New American Writing*, *Purple*, *Explosive Magazine*, *Tripwire*, *Rhizome*, *The World*, and *Art Byte Magazine*. Forthcoming publications include *Box* and *Kruder and Dorfmeister* (from Faux Press), in collaboration with the artist Mary Ellen Carroll. Tan Lin has taught at the University of Virginia and at Cal Arts. He is presently teaching at New Jersey City University.

Bill Luoma lives in Honolulu and studies at the University of Hawaii in the department of Information and Computer Science. His books include *Works & Days*

(Hard Press/The Figures), *Western Love* (Situations), and *Swoon Rocket* (The Figures).

Steven Marks has published poetry, reviews, and essays in *potepoetszine, ReadMe, No End Review, Taproots Review, Central Park, Green Mountains Review, Boston Book Review, Another Chicago Magazine,* and *American Book Review.* Recent work appears at <http://www.99main.com/~swmarks>.

Harryette Mullen has authored four books of poetry, most recently *Muse & Drudge* (Singing Horse, 1995). Mullen teaches African American literature and creative writing at UCLA. She is completing a new book, *Sleeping with the Dictionary.*

Sianne Ngai writes on film and television, literature, and the politics of emotion in twentieth-century culture. Her critical essays have appeared in *Camera Obscura* (coauthored with Aviva Briefel) and *Postmodern Culture.* She is also the author of *criteria,* a book of poetry.

Jena Osman's book of poems, *The Character,* won the Barnard New Women Poets Prize and was published by Beacon Press in 1999. She co-edits *Chain* magazine with Juliana Spahr. She is an assistant professor of English and creative writing at Temple University.

Kristin Prevallet is the author of *Perturbation, My Sister* (First Intensity, 1997), *Selections from the Parasite Poems* (Barque Press, 1999), and *Writing through Faces: A collaboration with Annemie Maes' the People's Database* (Second Story Books, 2000). Her essays and poems have appeared in various print magazines including *Boxkite, Poetry New York, Sulfur,* and *Chain,* as well as in various online magazines including *Jacket, Duration,* and *HOW2.*

Lisa Robertson has written two books of poetry. *Debbie: An Epic,* nominated for the Governor General's Award for Poetry in 1998, was published by New Star Books in Canada and by Reality Street Editions in England. *XEclogue,* originally published by Tsunami Editions (1993), was reissued by New Star Books in 1999. Selections from these books appear in the anthologies *Out of Everywhere: Linguistically Innovative Poetry by Women in North America and the UK* (Reality Street), *Moving Borders: Three Decades of Innovative Writing by Women* (Talisman House), *The*

Canadian Long Poem Anthology, 2d ed. (Talon Books), and *Writing Class: The Kootenay School of Writing Anthology* (New Star Books). Work in progress includes a poetry manuscript, *The Weather*, and *Soft Architecture*, a fiction. She works in Vancouver as a freelance essayist and writing teacher.

Leonard Schwartz's collections of poetry include *Words before the Articulate* (Talisman House), *Gnostic Blessing* (Goats and Compasses), *Exiles: Ends* (Red Dust Press), and *Objects of Thought, Attempts at Speech* (Gnosis Press). His collection of essays, *A Flicker at the Edge of Things: Essays on Poetics*, was published in 1999 by Spuyten Duyvil.

Rod Smith was born in Gallipolis, Ohio, in 1962 and grew up in northern Virginia. He has lived in Washington, D.C., since 1987, where he runs Bridge Street Books in Georgetown. Smith has authored two full-length collections, *Protective Immediacy* (Roof,1999) and *In Memory of My Theories* (O Books, 1996). His chapbook publications include *The Boy Poems* (Buck Downs Books, 1994), *A Grammar Manikin* (Object, 1996), *The Lack (love poems, targets, flags. . .)* (Abacus, 1997), and *Protective Immediacy: The Fire Works* (Potes and Poets, 1997). Forthcoming publications include *The Good House* (Spectacular Books, 2000), *The Given* (Upper Limit Music, 2000), and with Lisa Jarnot and Bill Luoma, *New Mannerist Tricycle* (Beautiful Swimmer, 2000). Smith has been editor of the journal *Aerial* since 1984 and publisher of Edge Books since 1989. His poetry, essays, reviews, and interviews have appeared in over a hundred print and online publications.

Juliana Spahr's *Everybody's Autonomy* is available from University of Alabama Press, and *Response* is available from Sun and Moon Press. She has a book of poems provisionally titled *Fuck You-Aloha-I Love You* forthcoming from Wesleyan University Press. She teaches at the University of Hawaii, Manoa, and co-edits the journal *Chain* with Jena Osman.

Brian Kim Stefans has published *Free Space Comix* (Roof, 1998); *Gulf* (Object Editions, 1998); *Angry Penguins* (Harry Tankoos, 2000); and, *A Poem of Attitudes* (Zoological Records, 2000). He collaborated with Sianne Ngai on *The Cosmopolitans* (Tripwire, 1999). His online work appears at <http://www.ubu.com>. He is currently a member of the Ubu internet poetry collective. He publishes *Arras* magazine at <http://www.arras.net>.

Gary Sullivan's "The New Life" appears regularly in the pages of *Rain Taxi Review of Books. Dead Man*, a novel, was published in 1996 by Meow Press. Two books, *The Art of Poetry* and *Correspondence* (written with Nada Gordon), are forthcoming. He lives in Brooklyn, where he edits *Readme* <http://www.jps.net/nada>, an online journal of poetics, and is currently finishing up a brief comic book biography of the filmmaker and performance artist Jack Smith.

Mark Wallace is the author of a number of books of poetry, including *Nothing Happened and Besides I Wasn't There, Sonnets of a Penny-a-Liner, Complications from Standing in a Circle, Every Day Is Most of My Time*, and others. *Temporary Worker Rides a Subway* won the New American Poetry Award and will be published by Sun and Moon Press. A chapbook of his fiction, *The Big Lie*, has recently appeared from the Avec Books Pivotal Prose Series. His critical work on poetics has appeared in numerous publications, and he co-edited *A Poetics of Criticism*, a collection of poetics essays in nonstandard forms. He lives in Washington, D.C., where he runs the Ruthless Grip Poetry Series and teaches at Georgetown, George Washington, and American University.

Elizabeth Willis has authored three books of poems: *Second Law* (Avenue B, 1993), *The Human Abstract* (Penguin, 1995), and *Turneresque* (forthcoming). Her poetry has been translated into French and Flemish. In 1991 she received a Thayer Fellowship for poetry and in 1994 won the National Poetry Series. She holds a Ph.D. in poetics from SUNY at Buffalo, and her critical prose focuses on nineteenth- and twentieth-century poetry and visual culture. Currently she is Distinguished Writer in Residence at Mills College.

Acknowledgments

Our most sincere thanks go to each and all of the people whose insights, comments, analyses, directions, and enthusiasms fill this volume. We would also like to thank Carol Mirakove and Rod Smith for their editorial advice and for their close reading of key parts of this book. Thanks also to Charles Bernstein, Hank Lazer, Curtis Clark, and Mindy Wilson, all of whom offered crucial suggestions on the development of the book. Thanks as well to Juliana Spahr and Joanne Molina for their advice, support, and keen insights.

In addition to the above, Steven Marks would like to express his thanks and love to his wife, Linda, for knowing his passion before he did and then demonstrating how to live it.

Permissions

Permission to reprint copyrighted material has been obtained whenever possible. The editors gratefully acknowledge permission to reprint material from the following sources:

From *What is Called Thinking? by Martin Heidegger,* copyright ©1968 by Harper & Row, Publishers, Inc. Reprinted by permission of HarperCollins Publishers, Inc.

From "When Ecstasy Is Inconvenient" by Lorine Niedecker. Reprinted from *From this Condensery: The Complete Writing of Lorine Niedecker,* edited by Robert J. Bertholf, copyright © 1985 by the Estate of Lorine Niedecker. Used by permission of Cid Corman, Literary Executor of Lorine Niedecker Estate.

From *Tristam Shandy* by Lawrence Sterne, copyright © 1962 by The New American Library, Inc.

The following essays collected in this volume have previously appeared (some as earlier versions) in the following books, journals, or CD-ROMs:

Chapter 1 by Steve Evans was originally published by Oblek Editions, Providence, R.I., in *o•blēk 12: Writing from the New Coast* (spring/fall 1993).

Chapter 2 by Lisa Robertson was originally presented at The Kootenay School of Writing, on a panel on Genre. It was published in the *Capilano Review* 2.11 (summer 1993) and in *A Poetics of Criticism*, ed. Spahr, Wallace, Prevallet, Rehm (Buffalo, N.Y.: Leave Books, 1994).

Chapter 3 by Harryette Mullen was originally published in *West Coast Line* (spring 1996).

Chapter 4 by Jefferson Hansen was originally published in *Witz* (fall 1996).

Chapter 5 by Gary Sullivan originally appeared in *Rain Taxi Review of Books* 3.1 (spring 1998) and was republished in Chris Stroffolino's book of essays, *Spin Cycle* (Brooklyn, N.Y.: Spuyen Duyvil, 2001) and in *The New Life* (Brooklyn, N.Y.: Spuyten Duyvil, 2001).

An earlier version of chapter 6 by Brian Kim Stefans is forthcoming in *The World in Time and Space, Towards a History of Innovative American Poetry, 1970–2000: Essays on the Revolution in American Poetry and Poetics at the End of the Twentieth Century,* ed. Edward Foster and Joseph Donahue (Greenfield, Mass.: Talisman House Press, 2001).

Chapter 7 by Daniel Barbiero was first published in *Talisman* 14 (fall 1995).

Chapter 8 by Leonard Schwartz was first published in *Talisman* 9 (fall 1993).

An earlier version of chapter 10 by Christopher Funkhouser appears on the CD-ROM *The Little Magazine,* vol. 21 (Albany: State University of New York Press, 1995).

A shorter version of chapter 11 by Jeff Derksen was presented on the "Canadian Multiculturalism" panel at the Cross Cultural Poetics Conference, University of Minnesota, fall 1997. This paper and the papers of the other participants on the panel—Roy Miki and Fred Wah—have been published in *West Coast Line* (winter 1998). The author would like to acknowledge the assistance of the Social Sciences and Humanities Research Council of Canada.

A similar version of chapter 12 by Sianne Ngai, excerpted by Jeff Derksen from a substantially longer work, appeared initially in *Open Letter: A Canadian Journal of Writing and Theory,* 10th ser., no. 1 (1998): 98–122. The author thanks Jeff Derksen for his labor and inspiration and expresses appreciation to Dan Farrell for an attentive reading of this manuscript, Kevin Davies for pointing to Lispector, and Steven Marks for additional editorial suggestions.

An earlier version of chapter 13 by Mark Wallace was published in *Witz* (summer 1996).

An earlier version of chapter 14 by Caroline Bergvall was published as "Performing Writing at The Cross-roads of Languages" in *Translating Nations,* ed. Prem Poddar, *The Dolphin,* no. 30 (Denmark: Aarhus University Press, 2000).

An earlier version of chapter 16 by Charles Borkhuis was published in *ONTHEBUS*, double issue 8 and 9, vols. 3.2 and 4.1 (1991), and reprinted as "Land of the Signifieds," in *Heavenbone* 11 (spring 1994).

An earlier version of chapter 17 by Jena Osman was presented at the Twentieth-Century Literature Conference at the University of Lousville, February 1997.

A shorter version of chapter 18 by Bill Luoma was given as a talk on a gender studies panel moderated by Barbara Henning at the Poetry Project Symposium in May 1997. Thanks to Juliana Spahr, Barbara Henning, and Charles Bernstein for providing valuable feedback. An earlier version was published in *Shark* 2 (spring 1999).

A longer version of chapter 20 by Sherry Brennan appeared in *Tripwire* 1 (spring 1998): 122–41.

Chapter 22 by G. S. Giscombe originally appeared in *A Poetics of Criticism* (Buffalo: Leave Books, 1994).

Chapter 24 by Andrew Levy is a revision of a paper delivered at "Assembling Alternatives: An International Poetry Conference," University of New Hampshire, Durham, August 29–September 2, 1996. The title is from John Dewey's "The Organization of Energies" in *Art as Experience*. This essay was previously published in *Paper Head Last Lyrics* (New York: Roof Books, 2000).

An earlier version of chapter 25 by Rod Smith was published in *Tripwire* 2 (fall 1998).

Chapter 26 by Juliana Spahr was previously published in the chapbook *Explosive* (New York: Spectacular Books, 1998).

Index |